The Tain of the Mirror

The Tain
of the Mirror

*Derrida and the Philosophy
of Reflection*

Rodolphe Gasché

Harvard University Press
Cambridge, Massachusetts
and London, England
1986

This book is printed on acid-free paper, and its binding materials
have been chosen for strength and durability.

Library of Congress Cataloging-in-Publication Data

Gasché, Rodolphe.
The tain of the mirror.

Bibliography: p.
Includes index.
1. Derrida, Jacques.   I. Title.
B2430.D484G37   1986   194   86-4673
ISBN 0-674-86700-9 (alk. paper)

Acknowledgments

I am grateful to David B. Allison, Alan Bass, Barbara Johnson, John P. Leavy, Gayatri C. Spivak, and others who have translated Derrida's work into English. Thanks to their expert translations, I was able to complete my own work without cluttering the text with numerous references to Derrida's French. Grateful acknowledgment is made to the Johns Hopkins University Press for permission to quote from Jacques Derrida, *Of Grammatology,* trans. Gayatri C. Spivak, as well as to the Northwestern University Press for permission to use Jacques Derrida, *Speech and Phenomenon,* trans. David B. Allison. Acknowledgment is also made to the University of Chicago Press for lines quoted from the following works of Jacques Derrida: *Dissemination,* trans. Barbara Johnson, copyright © 1981 by the University of Chicago; *Margins of Philosophy,* trans. Alan Bass, copyright © 1982 by The University of Chicago; *Positions,* trans. Alan Bass, copyright © 1981 by The University of Chicago; and *Writing and Difference,* trans. Alan Bass, copyright © 1978 by The University of Chicago. I am grateful to Jacques Derrida's English publishers for permission to quote from his works as follows: The Harvester Press, *Margins of Philosophy,* trans. Alan Bass; Routledge and Kegan Paul, *Writing and Difference;* and The Athlone Press, *Positions* and *Dissemination.* I would also like to thank the State University of New York Press for permission to quote from the two following works by Georg Wilhelm Friedrich Hegel: *The Difference between Fichte's and Schelling's System of Philosophy,* trans. W. Cerf and H. S. Harris, translation copyright © 1977 by State University of New York; and *Faith and Knowledge,* trans. W. Cerf and H. S. Harris, translation copyright © 1977 by State University of New York.

A first draft of the first two parts of this book was written in 1981–82, while I held an American Council of Learned Societies fellowship. Without the assistance and support of the State University of New York at Buffalo, it would not have been easy to complete this project. Several sections of the book have been published independently. A first version of Chapter 6 has appeared in Italian under the title "Eterologia e decostruzione," trans. Stefano Rosso, in *Rivista di Estetica*, 25, no. 17 (1984). A section of Chapter 9 entitled "Infrastructures and Systematicity" has been published in *Deconstruction and Philosophy*, ed. John Sallis (Chicago: University of Chicago Press, 1986). Part of Chapter 11 has been printed under the title "Quasi-Metaphoricity and the Question of Being," in *Hermeneutics and Deconstruction*, ed. Hugh J. Silverman and Don Ihde (Albany: State University of New York Press, 1985).

Very special thanks are due to two people—Cheryl Lester and Philip Barnard—for the meticulous care and continual generosity with time and advice with which they prepared the manuscript for publication. Many improvements in style and substance are the result of their discerning eye. Finally, I am deeply indebted to Bronislawa Karst for the patience with which she awaited this book, and for so much more.

Contents

The Tain of the Mirror

Tain (tēin), sb. [a.F. *tain* tinfoil, altered from
F. *étain*, tin . . .].

Oxford English Dictionary

The breakthrough toward radical otherness (with
respect to the philosophical concept—of the
concept) always takes *within philosophy,* the
form of an aposteriority or an empiricism. But
this is an effect of the specular nature of philosophical reflection, philosophy being incapable of inscribing (comprehending) what is outside
it otherwise than through the appropriating
assimilation of a negative image of it, and dissemination is written on the back—the *tain*—
of that mirror.

Jacques Derrida, *Dissemination*

ABBREVIATIONS OF WORKS BY JACQUES DERRIDA

The abbreviations that appear in the text, followed by page citations, refer to the following works by Jacques Derrida:

AF   *The Archeology of the Frivolous,* trans. J. P. Leavy (Pittsburgh: Duquesne, 1980)

D   *Dissemination,* trans. B. Johnson (Chicago: University of Chicago Press, 1981)

LI   "Limited Inc.," in *Glyph 2,* trans. S. Weber (Baltimore: Johns Hopkins University Press, 1977), pp. 162–254

M   *Margins of Philosophy,* trans. A. Bass (Chicago: University of Chicago Press, 1982)

O   *Edmund Husserl's Origin of Geometry: An Introduction,* trans. J. P. Leavy (Stony Brook, N.Y.: Nicholas Hays, 1978)

OG   *Of Grammatology,* trans. G. C. Spivak (Baltimore: Johns Hopkins University Press, 1976)

P.   *Positions,* trans. A. Bass (Chicago: University of Chicago Press, 1971)

S   *Spurs: Nietzsche's Styles,* trans. B. Harlow (Chicago: University of Chicago Press, 1979)

SP   *Speech and Phenomena,* trans. D. B. Allison (Evanston, Ill.: Northwestern University Press, 1973)

VP   *La Vérité en peinture* (Paris: Flammarion, 1978)

WD   *Writing and Difference,* trans. A. Bass (Chicago: University of Chicago Press, 1978)

Introduction

❧

Any attempt to interpret Jacques Derrida's writings in the perspective of philosophy as a discipline is bound to stir controversy. Indeed, many philosophers and literary critics alike agree that Derrida's work is literary in essence. For the philosophers in question, however, such an assertion is one of uncompromising reproof, for it is based on what they perceive as an incompatibility with philosophical sobriety, a lack of philosophical problematics and argumentation. For the literary critics, by contrast, the epithet *literary* is a mark of distinction, based on the fact that Derrida has written extensively on literary works and has also thematized a number of concepts crucial to the literary-critical enterprise. Above all, the qualification *literary* refers to what is viewed as Derrida's playful style and fine sensibility to the very matter of literature: that is, language. Yet to judge Derrida's writings as literary—to exclude them from the sphere of "serious," that is, philosophical discussion, or to recuperate them for literary criticism—is a feeble attempt to master his work, one that cannot do justice to the complexity of the Derridean enterprise. To reject such a characterization of Derrida's work does not, however, imply that it must therefore be philosophical. If philosophy is understood as constituted by a horizon of problematization exclusively determined by the traditional desiderata of a canon of issues, and if, in particular, such problematization is identified with one special technique of argumentation, then Derrida's writings are certainly not philosophical. If philosophy is understood in this manner, the purpose of this book cannot be simply to reappropriate Derrida for philosophy.

Yet my exposition of Derrida's writings is manifestly philosophical, for at least two reasons. First, what Derrida has to say is mediated by the canon of the traditional problems and methods of philosophical problem solving, as well as by the history of these problems and methods, even if his work cannot be fully situated within the confines of that canon and history. My interpretation is philosophical insofar as it focuses on Derrida's relation to the philosophical tradition, and emphasizes the manner in which his writings address not only particular philosophical problems and their traditional formulations, but, more important, the philosophical itself. Second, my study is philosophical because it tries to prove that the specific displacements of traditional philosophical issues by deconstruction amount not to an abandonment of philosophical thought as such, but rather to an attempt at positively recasting philosophy's necessity and possibility in view of its inevitable inconsistencies. Indeed, Derrida's inquiry into the limits of philosophy is an investigation into the conditions of possibility and impossibility of a type of discourse and questioning that he recognizes as absolutely indispensable. The philosophical meaning of such an intellectual enterprise is certainly not easy to grasp. Its difficulty stems not simply from philosophy's notorious transgression of commonplace representation, but from an attempt, made in full respect of all the classical requirements of philosophical argumentation and development, to question the laws of possibility of that transgression itself, without, however, aiming to do away with it. Therefore, reading Derrida requires not only the traditional surmounting or bracketing of the natural attitude, ordinary consciousness, or habitual modes of thought that all approaches to a philosophical work require, but above all an additional retreat or abstraction, whereby the philosophical gesture and mode of perception themselves become thematic. In short, my exposition of Derrida's work is philosophical to the extent that we understand his debate with the condition of philosophical generality to be "philosophical" in intent.

Apart from the fact that I believe that Derrida's thought can be adequately understood only if approached philosophically—that is, shown to be engaged in a constant debate with the major philosophical themes from a primarily philosophical perspective—it must also be admitted that some of my emphasis on the philosophical dimensions of Derrida's work is clearly a function of his reception in this country, particularly, by the proponents of what has come to be known as deconstructive criticism. Undoubtedly deconstructive criticism has greatly profited from Derrida's thought, both thematically and methodologically. But to quarry from Derrida's writings is not automatically to become deconstructive in the eminent sense. Indeed, many deconstructionist critics have chosen simply to ignore the profoundly philosophical thrust of Derridean thought, and have consequently misconstrued what deconstruction consists of and what it seeks to achieve. From the perspective of what I establish here as to the nature of deconstruction, hardly any deconstructionist critic could lay claim to that title. Yet my sometimes harsh judgment of that sort of criticism is not meant to be a wholesale rejection. Undoubtedly deconstructionist criticism has brought fresh air and imagination into the otherwise stuffy atmosphere of the critical establishment. It has led to exciting and highly valuable readings of literary texts. But deconstructionist criticism also has a specificity of its own; it obeys laws and follows intentions that are not at all those that underlie Derrida's philosophical enterprise. Indeed no one was more aware of this discrepancy between ventures than Paul de Man, as I have tried to demonstrate elsewhere.[1] Moreover, deconstructionist criticism is the offspring of a heritage that has little in common with that of Derrida's thought. Deconstructionist criticism must be understood as originating in New Criticism; it is a continuation of this American-bred literary scholarship. It is against this criticism's appropriation of a philosophically purged notion of deconstruction, but also against many philosophers' misreadings of Derrida as literary humbug, that some of my emphasis is directed.

Yet since this book is concerned neither with the history of deconstructionist criticism and its miscomprehension of deconstruction in a strict sense, nor with establishing the distinctive specificity proper to this type of criticism, I have avoided all detailed debate with deconstructive criticism. In order to undertake such a debate at least two things would be required, neither of which this book could hope to achieve: a determination of the autonomy of this type of criticism, and a definition of a criticism that would yield to deconstruction as developed herein. Rather this book confines itself to an analysis of the philophical background and implications of deconstruction, and to a discussion of some of the premises of a criticism based on it. In short, anyone will undoubtedly be deceived who expects me to establish what a "true" deconstructionist criticism would be, beyond what Barbara Johnson has diagnosed, in an elegant phrase, as the double infidelity of deconstructionist criticism, which, through its incursion into the exotic—the seductive foreignness of Derrida's thought—comes to remember what it was that had appealed to it in what it was being unfaithful to: that is, New Criticism.[2] But all these tasks are dependent precisely on a prior elucidation of that which deconstructionist criticism is unfaithful to in Derrida's writing, and that is all I want to establish here.

Some may argue that my attempt to present Derrida's thought in a perspective of disciplinary philosophy, although perhaps feasible in the case of his earlier work, which is obviously philosophical and conceptual in a technical sense, could be successful with the later work only if this portion of Derrida's writings were viewed somewhat selectively. As a matter of fact, this book is based on almost the entirety of Derrida's writings up to *La Vérité en peinture* (1979)— with the exception of *Glas*—as well as on a host of essays. Putting aside the delicate question of what is to be counted as more philosophical or more literarily playful, not to mention earlier or later, I have admittedly given greater prominence to the more philosophically discursive texts. It has not been my intention to cover the totality of Derrida's oeuvre up to this point, or to speak for what he may publish in the future. This book certainly does not claim to be exhaustive. The question, then, is whether the analysis of the supposedly earlier and more philosophical texts has any bearing on Derrida's later writings. But has not Derrida insisted time and again on the continuity of his intellectual enterprise? For instance, in "The Time of a Thesis: Punctuations" (1982), he remarks that "all of the problems worked on in the Introduction to *The Origin of Geometry* have continued to organize the work I have subsequently attempted in connection with philosophical, literary and even non-discursive corpora, most notably that of pictorial work."[3] Indeed I believe firmly that all the motifs of the earlier texts continue to inform and direct Derrida's more "playful" texts. The difference between the more "philosophical" and the more "literary" approach consists, primarily, in making philosophical arguments in a nondiscursive manner, on the level of the signifier, syntax, and textual organization. As is well known from the Platonic dialogues, such a procedure is itself thoroughly philosophical, and thus shows these texts to be concerned with problems similar to those discussed in a technically conceptual manner in the explicitly philosophical works.

To affirm such continuity, however, is not to deny difference and evolution. An extensive evolution is evident as one passes from the earlier to the later work, insofar as Derrida comes to speak on subjects he had not taken up before. But more important is the intensive evolution rooted in Derrida's deconstruction of the constitutive rhetorical and literary devices of philosophical argumentation. Indeed, if the making of arguments in a literary or poetic manner is itself eminently philosophical, Derrida's mimicry of these devices nonetheless outdoes philosophy's mastery of the signifier. His earlier work is very much concerned with the inevitable problems of concept formation and argumentation; the later work adds to this the dimension of the problems that follow from philosophy's involvement in the materiality, spatiality, and temporality of its texts. In his so-called literary texts, Derrida pursues the same problems on yet another level, a level that adds both a quantitative and a qualitative aspect to his later work. Yet this complication itself becomes intelligible only if we first elucidate the thrust of Derrida's philosophical debates. Neglecting to do so leads to the unfortunate designation of the later protean texts as literary, regardless of whether "literary" is understood as *merely* literary. Although in some degree I indicate an approach to these texts, for the most part I have limited myself to expounding the more argumentative side of Derrida's writings. This explication is necessary if one wishes to come to grips with what amounts to a deconstruction of the philosophical rules for staging an argument in texts.

To expose the essential traits and the philosophical thrust of Derridean thought, I have chosen a triple approach. First, I situate and interpret Derrida's philosophy with respect to one particular philosophical problem and its history: namely, the criticism of the notion of reflexivity. Second, while choosing that form of presentation, developed since Aristotle, that proceeds by logical dependency, I also link together a multitude of motifs in Derrida's oeuvre in order to demonstrate the consistent nature of this philosophical enterprise, and to attempt to systematize some of its results. Third, I further develop these concerns, especially insofar as they impinge on the problem of universality, by analyzing a series of Derridean concepts that have been absorbed into deconstructionist criticism, and I clarify their philosophical status in Derrida's work. This threefold intention broadly corresponds to the three parts of this book.

Unlike others who have attempted to situate Derrida's thought in the history of the grand disputes concerning the question of being (Gérard Granel), or in the apocryphal history of the grammatological (Jean Greisch), not to mention certain histories bordering on the phantasmic which some philosophers and critics have devised, I discuss Derrida's philosophy in terms of the criticism to which the philosophical concept of reflection and reflexivity has been subjected. The reasons for this choice are clearly circumstantial. Indeed the dominant misconception of Derrida is based on the confusion by many literary critics of deconstruction with reflexivity. Reflection and reflexivity, however, are precisely what will not fit in Derrida's work—not because he would wish to refute or reject them in favor of a dream of immediacy, but because his work questions reflection's unthought, and thus the limits of its possibility. This book's title, *The Tain of the Mirror*, alludes to that "beyond" of the orchestrated mirror play of reflection that Derrida's philosophy seeks to conceptualize. *Tain*, a word altered from the French *étain*, according to the *OED*, refers to the tinfoil, the silver lining, the lusterless back of the mirror. Derrida's philosophy, rather than being a philosophy of reflection, is engaged in the systematic exploration of that dull surface without which no reflection and no specular and speculative activity would be possible, but which at the same time has no place and no part in reflection's scintillating play.

Yet my history of the critique of reflection, outlined in Part I, is not a straightforward history. It does not describe the full range of answers suggested with respect to this question. Nor does it refer to Anglo-Saxon and American authors who have broached this problem, from Shadworth Hodgson to Sydney Shoemaker. By contrast, Hegel's speculative criticism of the philosophy of reflection is given what some may consider inordinate importance. But Part I is intended not as a total history of that problem, but merely as an oriented history that serves as a theoretical prelude to the systematic exposition of Derrida's thought, which I undertake in Part II. In spite of my contention that Derrida's philosophy must be related to the modern history of the concept of reflection and to the criticism it has drawn, I seek primarily to bring into view Derrida's debate with the traditional paradigms of philosophy in general. The speculative form in which Hegel cast the unvarying philosophical topoi, and even their Husserlian or Heideggerian phenomenological form, are, undoubtedly, because of their strategic importance for Derrida's writings as a whole, privileged means of access to this thinker's discourse. But neither Hegel nor Husserl is truly at stake, nor is any other regional or historically limited form of philosophy. At stake rather is what in these authors touches on the enterprise of philosophy as such. Indeed to interpret Derrida is to confront the whole tradition of Western thought, not so much as a cumulative series of philosophical figures, however, but as a tradition rooted in and yielding to a set of unsurpassable theoretical and ethical themes and demands. These are, as I have tried to show, the real terms of reference and the adequate horizon of thought of Derrida's philosophical enterprise, and they alone explain the radicality and contemporary attractiveness of his writings, however mis-construed they may have been.

In short, whether discussing Hegel, Husserl, or Heidegger, Derrida is primarily engaged in a debate with the main philosophical question regarding the ultimate foundation of what is. Contrary to those phi-losophers who naively negate and thus remain closely and uncon-trollably bound up with this issue, Derrida confronts the philosophical quest for the ultimate foundation as a necessity. Yet his faithfulness to intrinsic philosophical demands is paired with an inquiry into the inner limits of these demands themselves, as well as of their unques-tionable necessity.

My goal is to demonstrate that Derrida's philosophical writings display a subtle economy that recognizes the essential requirements of philosophical thought while questioning the limits of the possibility of these requirements. Deconstruction, as I show in Part II, is engaged in the construction of the "quasi-synthetic concepts" which account for the economy of the conditions of possibility and impossibility of the basic philosophemes. *Infrastructures,* a word used by Derrida on several occasions in reference to these quasi-synthetic constructs, seemed to represent the most economical way to conceptualize all of Derrida's proposed quasi-synthetic concepts in a general manner. "Undecida-bles" would have been an alternative, yet "infrastructure" has the supplementary advantage of allowing for a problematization of Der-rida's debate with structuralism and with the Platonism that it has inherited from conservative strata in Husserlian phenomenology. The notion of infrastructures has not yet been picked up by any of those who have written on Derrida. From the perspective of my analysis of deconstruction, however—its necessity, how it is carried out, and of what its conclusions consist—the occurrence of the word *infrastruc-ture* in Derrida's writings is more than a coincidence.

In Part III I inquire into the problems of philosophical generality and universality from a deconstructive point of view by way of a discussion of Derrida's use of the terms *writing, textuality,* and *met-aphor.* In each case I try to reconstruct the precise context in which these concepts become operational in Derrida's work, and thus to determine what philosophical task they are meant to perform. Here too I suggest some of the criteria that a possible deconstructionist literary criticism would have to observe.

As an investigation into the irreducibly plural conditions of pos-sibility of all major philosophical, theoretical, and ethical desiderata, deconstruction is eminently plural. Derrida's philosophy, as I shall show, is plural, yet not pluralistic in the liberal sense—that is, as Hegel knew, secretly monological. This plural nature, or openness, of Derrida's philosophy makes it thoroughly impossible to conceive of his work in terms of orthodoxy, not simply because, since he is a living author, his work is not yet completed, but primarily because it resists any possible closure, and thus doctrinal rigidity, for essential reasons. Still, such openness and pluralism do not give license to a free interpretation of Derrida's thought, or for its adaptation to any particular need or interest. Nor are all the interpretations of Derrida's thought that seek legitimacy in such openness equally valid. In this book I hope that I have found a middle ground between the structural plurality of Derrida's philosophy—a plurality that makes it impossible to elevate any final essence of his work into its true meaning—and the strict criteria to which any interpretation of his work must yield, if it is to be about that work and not merely a private fantasy. These criteria, at center stage in this book, are, as I shall show, philosophical and not literary in nature.

Some might want to call my efforts a retranslation of Derrida's writings back into the technical language of philosophy and its accepted set of questions. Indeed, in order to show at what precise point the questions and demands of philosophy are transgressed in Derrida's thought, I have had to emphasize their technical aspects. Yet such a procedure can hardly be called a literal retranslation, since "philosophy" is spelled out in capital letters throughout Derrida's work, his seemingly more playful texts included. If this is a retranslation at all, it is one that focuses on what Dupin describes, referring in *The Purloined Letter* to a certain game, as that which escapes "observation by dint of being excessively obvious."[4] Yet this excessively obvious aspect of Derrida's work, which so many readers have overlooked, is precisely what gives special significance to Derrida's so-called abandonment of philosophy and its technical language.

But in addition to the danger of being *too* obvious in demonstrating the philosophical thrust of Derrida's work, a more serious risk is involved in attempting a retranslation. Apart from the always looming danger of opacity and crudity owing to insufficient philosophical sensitivity on the part of the interpreter, the major danger is that this operation may be understood as an end in itself. Obviously this is the risk I encounter with the professional philosopher. Indeed, in referring Derrida's philosophy back to the classical and technical vocabulary in order to determine precisely the level, locus, and effect of a deconstructive intervention in the traditional field of philosophical problematics, one may well confound the assignment of that locus with the debate itself. In spite of all the precautions I have taken—regarding, for instance, my reference to such Derridean concepts as originary synthesis and transcendentality to indicate the level on which his debate with philosophy occurs—my determination of the level and the scope of the debate may be mistaken by some for that which is at stake in the debate itself. In this sense, rather than clarifying extremely intricate problems, my "retranslation" may even create a series of new obstacles to understanding Derrida's thought. Yet this is the risk any interpretation must take, a risk that, as Derrida's philosophy maintains, is *always possible* and thus a necessary possibility that has to be accounted for. And it is a risk that I happily assume, if I have been successful in providing some insights into a number of difficult matters not previously addressed, and especially if this book helps set forth more rigorous criteria for any future discussion of Derrida's thought.

PART ONE

Toward the Limits of Reflection

1

Defining Reflection

❧

Reflection is undoubtedly as old as the discourse of philosophy itself. A statement such as this, however, borders on the trivial, if one defines reflection in its most common sense, as meditation or careful consideration of some subject by turning or fixing one's thoughts on it. Without such action, no philosophical discourse could get off the ground. I am concerned here instead with the philosophical concept of reflection, which from the outset has turned away from the immediacy and contingency of the reflective gesture by which philosophizing begins in order to reflect on the beginning of philosophy itself. The concept of philosophical reflection is, as we shall see, a name for philosophy's eternal aspiration toward self-foundation. Yet only with modern philosophy—philosophical thought since Descartes—did reflection explicitly acquire this status of a principle par excellence.

Why, then, did reflection become an outstanding, perhaps an unsurpassed, principle of philosophical thinking, and in what way are we to understand it? First of all, from the moment it became the chief methodological concept for Cartesian thought, it has signified the turning away from any straightforward consideration of objects and from the immediacy of such an experience toward a consideration of the very experience in which objects are given. Second, with such a bending back upon the modalities of object perception, reflection shows itself to mean primarily self-reflection, self-relation, self-mirroring. By lifting the ego out of its immediate entanglement in the world and by thematizing the subject of thought itself, Descartes establishes the apodictic certainty of self as a result of the clarity and distinctness with which it perceives itself. Through self-reflection, the self—the ego, the subject—is put on its own feet, set free from all unmediated relation to being. In giving priority to the human being's determination as a thinking being, self-reflection marks the human being's rise to the rank of a subject. It makes the human being a subjectivity that has its center in itself, a self-consciousness certain of itself. This is the first epoch-making achievement of the concept of reflection, and it characterizes modern metaphysics as a metaphysics of subjectivity.

By severing the self from the immediacy of the object world, reflection helps give the subject freedom as a thinking being. From Descartes to Husserl, not to mention German Idealism, reflection as the self-thinking of thought, as self-consciousness, has had an eminently emancipatory function. It constitutes the autonomy of the *cogito*, of the subject, of thought. *Liberum est quod causa sui est.* Only the subject that knows itself, and thus finds the center of all certitude in itself, is free. But self-reflection in modern philosophy not only grounds the autonomy of the individual as a rational being; it also appears to be the very motor of history as progress toward a free society. Self-reflection has informed all philosophy of spirit since Descartes; indeed, it also constitutes the modern concept of history and is the alpha and omega of political philosophy.

Yet Descartes's attempt to doubt anything, and Husserl's eidetic bracketing of all thetical positioning of the world, acts of freedom by which the thinking subject reflects itself into itself, do not abandon the world of objects. Although the principle of self-reflection risks the danger of solipsism, it is the very condition by which the world can turn into a world of objects. Self-reflection, then (and this is another of its major modern characteristics), makes mastery of the world dependent on the status of the world as a world of objects for a free and self-conscious subject who bears the promise of a free world.

As I have mentioned, since the beginning of modern metaphysics reflection has represented the sole means by which an ego can engender itself as a subject. Because such a subject is seen as providing the foundation, the solid and unshakable ground of all possible knowledge, the theory of reflexivity also inaugurates the particular kind of philosophical investigation that with Kant came to be known as transcendental philosophy, "transcendental" referring to that sort of philosophical reflection that brings to consciousness the inner conditions that constitute the objects in general that present themselves to our experience. Indeed for Kant, transcendental philosophy not only thematizes the forms and categories that make objective knowledge possible but also makes the transcendental subject "not merely a logical condition of possible self-consciousness, but that which real consciousness knows to be the subject of all possible real consciousness."[1] From Descartes to Kant, self-consciousness as the ground of deduction of the systems of knowledge represents a still unanalyzed presupposition; the analysis of its structure becomes a central preoccupation of modern philosophy only with Fichte. Nonetheless, in the sort of investigation latent since Descartes and beginning with Kant—namely, transcendental philosophy—self-reflexivity remains an a priori structural precondition of what we understand by knowledge itself. As this implies, the implications of self-reflection go beyond subjectivity, freedom, and transcendentality.

To the extent that transcendental philosophy lays claim to reflecting the a priori conditions of all knowledge, it must also reflect on the ground proper of philosophy, and thus become the medium of the self-reflection of philosophy. In the thinking of thinking—what Aristotle called *noesis noeseos*—reflexivity serves at once as a medium, the method, and the foundation by which philosophy grounds itself within itself. Through such a reflection upon itself, in the philosophy of philosophy, the philosophical discourse seeks to achieve complete clarity concerning its own essence and complete freedom from any assumptions, thereby confirming its claim to be the "first" philosophy, the philosophy of philosophy, the philosophy capable of furnishing the foundation of all other sciences. In other words, self-reflection grounds the autonomy of philosophy as the knowledge that is most free. Here, one can best grasp that self-reflection is not only method or medium but foundation as well. All modern philosophy has an essential relation to itself such that all reflexive analyses are analyses of the essential nature of things themselves, as Husserl claimed with respect to phenomenological reflection; furthermore, all reflection by philosophy upon itself represents an essential act of freedom in which, as Fichte maintains, philosophy becomes its own content and returns into itself.[2] In short, self-reflection is not merely a key concept denoting a method specific to modern philosophy, nor is it simply one of philosophy's major concerns. The scope of reflexivity is not exhausted by its role in constituting subjectivity, freedom, transcendentality, and philosophy *as* philosophy. At the very heart of modern metaphysics as a metaphysics of subjectivity, reflexivity is the very medium of its unfolding; it is the method and substance, the very origin of philosophy itself as a discourse of radical autonomy. Yet, despite its capital importance, the task of determining rigorously what reflection is is not an easy one.

Since reflection is as old as philosophy itself, and gained systematic significance as early as Descartes, it is surprising that it has not been fully conceptualized. One can, of course, try to explain this incongruity by pointing at the in fact very different meanings of reflection throughout the history of philosophy, but one would still confront the necessity of conceptualizing these differences. Any attempt to circumscribe a definite meaning of these different uses of the term by tracing it back to its etymological roots in the Latin verb *re-flectere* is certain to be of little help. Still, such a procedure is not without merit as a beginning, since it will suggest some of the more formal characteristics of the movements that compose reflection, as well as some of the fundamental imagery associated with this concept. *Re-flectere* means "to bend" or "to turn back" or backward, as well as "to bring back." Yet this turning back is significant for understanding reflection only if one recalls that in both Greek and Latin philosophy the term has optic connotations, in that it refers to the action by mirroring surfaces of throwing back light, and in particular a mirror's exhibition or reproduction of objects in the form of images. In this sense, reflection signifies the process that takes place between a figure or object and its image on a polished surface. As a consequence of this optic metaphoricity, reflection, when designating the mode and operation by which the mind has knowledge of itself and its operations, becomes analogous to the process whereby physical light is thrown back on a reflecting surface. From the beginning, self-consciousness as constituted by self-reflection has been conceptualized in terms of this optic operation and, more generally, as we shall see later, in terms analogous to perception, with the effect that self-consciousness has come to suggest a beam of light thrown back upon itself after impact with a reflecting surface. In this vein the Stoics, and later the Neoplatonists, came to understand the *nous* as a self-reflecting and self-illuminating light, which sees itself by mirroring objects.[3] As soon as consciousness is said to reflect the world and itself by turning upon itself, and thus to be conscious of itself in this act of coiling upon itself, this metaphysics of light, or photology, is transposed to it. Unlike the common notion of reflection, reflection as a philosophical concept requires that the action of reproduction also be thrown back upon itself.

Recognizing the convergence of the word *reflection*'s etymological meaning with the metaphoricity of light, one could venture a preliminary definition: reflection is the structure and the process of an operation that, in addition to designating the action of a mirror reproducing an object, implies that mirror's mirroring itself, by which process the mirror is made to see itself. Such a minimal definition, apart from the formidable problems it poses, can hardly explain all the different theories or philosophies of reflection throughout the history of philosophy, although they may all share the optic metaphor predominant in the concept of reflection. This is particularly true of modern philosophy from Descartes to Kant, and to some extent Hegel.

What are the major events in this history of the philosophy of reflection? Although it is true that the Augustinian notion of *reditus in se ipsum*—a return upon and into oneself constituting the medium of philosophy—prefigures the modern concept of reflection, the philosophy of reflection is generally considered to have begun with Descartes's *prima philosophia*. There are good reasons for this assumption, for in Descartes the scholastic idea of the *reditus* undergoes an epochmaking transformation, whereby reflection, instead of being merely the medium of metaphysics, becomes its very foundation. With Cartesian thought, the self-certainty of the thinking subject—a certainty apodictically found in the *cogito me cogitare*—becomes the unshakable ground of philosophy itself. No longer does the essence of the human being reside primarily in grounds ontologically and theologically independent of him; Descartes discovers it in the logically and ontologically prior phenomenon of the *cogito me cogitare,* in which the thinking self appears to itself as *me cogitare*. With the ego as *cogitans* becoming its own *cogitatum,* a major paradigm of reflection, and of the ensuing philosophy, is set forth. In fact, one could schematically ascertain the different and often controversial forms of the philosophies of reflection in post-Cartesian philosophy up to Kant as different modes of determining the *me cogitare*.

The status of the founding reflexive act in Descartes retains, as Herbert Schnädelbach has convincingly demonstrated, a strange ambiguity, such that it is impossible to make out clearly whether this act is sensible or intelligible.[4] From here on, the history of the development of the philosophy of reflection becomes almost predictable. Take, for instance, the case of Locke, for whom reflection is also the fundamental method of philosophizing, inasmuch as it is the sole means of discovering logical categories. But for Locke, this source of cognition, by which the mind becomes aware of its own doings, is basically a sensible, empirical operation of internal perception or inner experience. Reflection here is *empirical* reflection, an *intentio recta* directed upon thought as an internal reality, belonging by right to psychology and not to philosophy. For Leibniz too, reflection is an attention directed upon self, but it is a process that takes place in turning from everything sensible toward an intellectual actualization of innate ideas. Unlike Locke's empirical reflection, Leibniz's reflection must be termed *logical*. A first synthesis of these opposite positions on the status of the *me cogitare* can be found in Rousseau, for whom self-consciousness is grounded in a state of emotional self-affection which stands as the precondition of all propositional activity—that is, of the passing of judgments. Needless to say, these characterizations are not straightforwardly historical but are schematic at best; yet I do not mean them to be more. All I am concerned with at this point is evoking this dominant motif of reflection as a founding principle of modern philosophy.

Now, as regards this history of the concept of reflection, what is Kant's position? As the famous addendum to *Transcendental Analytic*—the chapter entitled "On the Equivocal Nature of Amphiboly"—demonstrates, Kant is critical of both logical and empirical reflection. His criticism is made in the name of what could be considered a return to Descartes, yet which is, at the same time, a total innovation within the Cartesian paradigm of reflection. His criticism is a function of *transcendental* reflection. Kant writes: "*Reflection (reflexio)* does not concern itself with objects themselves with a view to deriving concepts from them directly, but is that state of mind in which we first set ourselves to discover the subjective conditions under which [alone] we are able to arrive at concepts."[5] As *transcendental* reflection, reflection examines and distinguishes the faculties of cognition with which conceptions of objects originate, and which determine whether a given conception belongs to pure understanding or sensuous intuition. Transcendental reflection is defined as the inquiry into the ground of possibility of sensible intuition in general and of the objective comparison of representations, and it is thus very different from empirical and logical reflection, neither of which accounts for the faculty of cognition to which the conceptions belong. Unlike inner or outer reflection, transcendental reflection anticipates the deeply concealed *transcendental unity,* to use Kant's words, of these two types of reflection.[6] Transcendental reflection grounds both empirical and logical reflection in the unity of a more fundamental reflection, which is the result of Kant's twisting the founding certainty of *cogito me cogitare* into the subjective dimension for the conditions of possibility of all knowledge. But what is most decisive for the turn reflective philosophy takes in post-Kantian thought is that transcendental reflection is also the thinking of the unity of the operation of reflection itself. With the pure synthetic unity of the *I think* that must at least virtually accompany all of the experiencing subject's representations, and which Kant was led to assume as a result of his transcendental deduction of the categories, he achieved a first, however hypothetical unification of the different moments that constitute the minimal definition of reflection as self-reflection.

Although since Descartes self-consciousness has been the ground of foundation and deduction for all systems of knowledge, not until Fichte did anyone begin to explore systematically the structure of self-reflexivity that constitutes self-consciousness. Since such an investigation into the structure of reflection, understood by Fichte as the being driven inward of the endlessly outreaching activity of self, became possible only after Kant had recognized the synthetic nature of reflection, Hegel could view Fichte's demonstration of a self-positing "I," the indispensable presupposition of any objective "I" or of any objective positing (Non-I), as a direct continuation of what he termed "speculative germs" in Kant's philosophy. While Fichte radicalized Kant's idea of the transcendental unity of apperception in terms of a subjective idealism, Schelling, in his philosophy of nature, developed an objective variation on the same problem. With Hegel's attempt to supersede these oppositions between subjective and objective solutions to the problem of self-consciousness and self-reflection, the philosophy of reflexivity reached a climax.

What this all too short outline of the history of reflection suggests is that we need to distinguish between different types of reflection. First are those we have already encountered: logical, empirical, and transcendental reflection. Empirical reflection, as bending in upon what takes place within us, is the source of all psychological knowledge. Logical reflection is a turning backward of thought, away from its relation to objects (including itself as an empirical reality) to the examination of the relations among objects, and the relations among the concepts of these objects. Since Kant recognized that neither empirical nor logical reflection accounts for the reasons that would prove their epistemological validity, or for the origin of the concepts they examine and compare, a new form of reflection—transcendental reflection—takes over the task of determining and securing the conditions of possibility of valid cognition. In this sense, transcendental reflection is an inquiry into the a priori principles of the cognition of objects in general. Of course, this is not the only meaning of transcendental reflection, which acquired a new and original meaning with Husserl's phenomenology in particular. Reflection for Husserl has a

"*universal* methodological function"; it is " 'consciousness' own method
for the knowledge of consciousness generally"—that is, a method
immanent to the sphere of being which it analyzes, and by which the
phenomena of this sphere can be grasped and analyzed in the light
of their own evidence.[7] Insofar as the fundamental methodological
importance of reflection for phenomenology is based on its investigation of the reflexive acts of consciousness—that is, of all the modes
of immanent apprehension of the essence and of all modes of immanent experience as well—it is a transcendental reflection. Yet, whereas
Kant's transcendental reflection is essentially concerned with the validity of reflections or thoughts, Husserl's assumption of a *reell* connection between reflection and what is reflected makes Husserlian
transcendental reflection an analysis of the production and constitution of thoughts by a thinking subject. Such reflection can be considered noematic reflection, turning on the acts constituting the
intentional objects of thought in general.

The last type of reflection, which will preoccupy us more extensively
than the previous four, is what Hegel called absolute and speculative
reflection. Hegel's notion of absolute reflection represents the most
complete type of reflection—the concept of reflection itself—reflecting
the totality of its formal movements. In addition, it is important to
note that it is a first critique of the paradigm of reflection.[8] Before
proceeding, let us first circle back for a moment to the minimal definition of reflection as the process and structure of the mirroring of
an object by a polished surface *and,* at the same time, a mirroring of
the mirror as well. Reflection thus seems to yield to a double movement, and to contain two distinct moments, but it is far from clear
how these two moments relate, how reflection as a unitary phenomenon can at once be reflection of Other and reflection of the mirroring
subject. Yet a philosophical analysis of reflection is bound to live up
to the universal requirement for unity. Kant's concept of transcendental reflection is a first attempt to realize this demand, whereas
Hegel's concept of absolute reflection fulfills this requirement. In what
ways must one determine the two distinct moments of reflection in
order to make them the living parts of a harmonious whole? As we
have seen, reflection as self-reflection coincides in modern metaphysics
with the powerful motif of subjectivity. Therefore, it is in subjectivity
that we must look for the source of unification of the reflexive process's separate elements, although this implies that the mirror's self-
reflection cannot be a part of that whole comparable to the moment
of objective reflection. The mirroring subject's self-mirroring is the
goal of the whole process. Consequently the question is, how can the

reflection of objects lead or be related to self-reflection? Obviously a third moment is required to unite all the elements of reflection into one whole. Thomas Aquinas had remarked in *De veritate* that reflection is directed both at the reproduced image or concept of an object and at the act of reflecting itself. Indeed, such a reflection provides the missing link; the third, in truth, first moment of reflection is found in the recognition that the object reflected by the mirroring subject is not just any object but rather this subject's symmetric Other— in other words, a representation of its alienated self. With such an alienating positing of itself as object, its reflection truly becomes an act of bringing back, a recapturing recognition. In the reflection of the mirror-subject as an annulment of the mirroring subject's former alienation, the reflection of Other becomes a reflection of self. The mirror's self-reflection is the embracing whole that allows it to release itself into Other, which explains why it faces an object in the first place and why it returns reflexively to itself.

In Hans Heinz Holz's analysis of the structure and logical meaning of this dialectical unity of self-reflection, in his essay "Die Selbstinterpretation des Seins," the mirror metaphor is shown to be constitutive of being, if the latter is understood in terms of subjectivity. Moreover, as metaphor, it is itself a moment in the process of the self-interpretation of the concept of being. In the metaphor of the mirror the concept of being can properly appear to itself. Holz concludes: "The doubling of what is mirrored in the mirrored, the latter being the same as what is mirrored and yet an other, hence represents the dialectical relation according to which the species encompasses itself and its opposite: being is the species of itself and of nonbeing, the One is species of itself and the manifold."[9] The paradigm of reflection thus requires, in addition to the two moments outlined in the minimal definition, a third element, which triggers the unifying dialectic between the mirror and its object, as well as between the mirror and itself. This dialectic, by means of which the mirrored object is seen to be that into which the mirror opens out as an image of the mirror itself, both the same as and different from it, allows for the integration of the two previously distinguished moments of reflection into the unity created by the self-revelation of the mirroring subject. The alienation of the mirror in its Other and the reflection of the object are linked together in such a way as to form a totality in which they are reflected into one another, leaving absolutely no remainder outside. This conceptual totality salvages even the reflective mirroring process as its alienating metaphoric detour to itself.

Although we now have a more complete minimal definition of

reflection, of its basic ingredients and their dialectic, it remains an abstract concept of reflection, and one that must be rendered more concrete. Such an abstract definition cannot serve to identify all the philosophies of reflection; it only encompasses other, more narrow definitions, to the extent that it represents a more complete exposition of reflection's formal movements. In historical terms, this definition can be found only in the philosophy of German Idealism after Kant. Hegel's critique of the philosophy of reflection was carried out in the name of this speculative definition of reflection. I hope to prove that most of the later criticism of reflection was carried out in the name of this definition as well. The irony, then, of this more encompassing definition of reflection is that it brings the problem of reflection to a certain end.

2

The Philosophy
of Reflection

❧

In the following three chapters I hope to clarify the concept of reflection by analyzing Hegel's notion of absolute reflection. This analysis should provide us with the totality of the formal movements of
reflection. It is important to note at the start that Hegel developed
the notion of absolute reflection, or speculation, as the result of his
confrontation with what he calls the *philosophy of reflection*. His
concept of absolute reflection represents the first attempt to address
a number of problems which were left unsolved by the pre-Hegelian
philosophers of reflection. Hegel's debate with these philosophers of
reflection—with Kant, Jacobi, and Fichte—is located in the two long
essays written in Jena between 1801 and 1802, *The Difference between Fichte's and Schelling's System of Philosophy* and *Faith and
Knowledge,* as well as later, in a different form, in *The Science of
Logic.* It is therefore only fitting that we should give these two essays,
and in particular *The Difference,* special consideration. A very succinct outline of the historical background and at least some of the
major theoretical stakes in that debate is indispensable before I elaborate what Hegel understands by "philosophy of reflection," what
his critique consisted of, and what concept of reflection he developed
to overcome its difficulties.

When Hegel arrived in Jena in 1801, the process of differentiation
within German Idealism was already well under way. Two years
before, Kant had published a declaration against his follower Fichte,
repudiating all affiliation between his own thinking and *Science of
Knowledge,* which pretended to be nothing other than a rigorous
explanation of the spirit of Kantian philosophy.

Although Schelling still conceived of his work as no more than a supplement to Fichte's philosophy, Schelling's *System of Transcendental Idealism,* which appeared in 1800, made his theoretical differences with Fichte quite clear. On his arrival at Jena, Hegel immediately became involved in the debate. He published *The Difference,* and then, in *Kritische Journal der Philosophie,* which he and Schelling founded as a forum for promulgating objective idealism, the essay *Faith and Knowledge.* Both texts represent a global and systematic settling of accounts between what was at that moment the position of subjective idealism, as opposed to that of objective idealism, a debate in which Hegel seems to have sided almost uncritically with Schelling. Although in his essay "Über die wissenschaftliche Behandlung des Naturrechts" he had already declared the superiority of the spirit to nature (by spirit I mean the intelligible reality of the moral world of freedom, and not the immaterial substance called spirit in pre-Kantian theo-rationalistic systems), the break with Schelling became effective and final only with the appearance, in 1807, of *Phenomenology of Spirit,* which Schelling rightly understood to be a categorial critique of his own thought.

In order to understand what Hegel means by philosophy of reflection, and in order to appraise the critical achievement of his notion of absolute reflection, the stakes in this process of differentiation must be summarized briefly. In *The Difference,* in explaining what distinguishes Kant, Fichte, and Schelling, Hegel makes use of a Schellingian formula which, in spite of its schematic character, describes the situation quite well. Hegel accuses Fichte of subjective idealism in *Science of Knowledge,* while valorizing Schelling's philosophy of nature and system of identity as objective idealism. Although Hegel seems entirely partisan, one cannot remain insensitive to his implicit declaration, in *The Difference,* that philosophy has to proceed beyond the difference between subjective and objective idealism toward a subjective-objective, or absolute, idealism. This tripartite idealism is rooted in the three philosophers' differing appraisals of their own critical developments of Kant's philosophy of reflection. As Hegel defines it in *The Difference,* the philosophy of reflection is the kind of thought that, by sharply distinguishing between thinking and being, determines objects through a subjective assessment of experience. By contrast, in the philosophy of identity, and even more so in Hegel's absolute idealism, being and thinking are one, only moments in the objective process of self-developing thought.

Now, when Kant denied all similarities between Fichte's philosophy and his own, he was both right and wrong. Indeed, *Science of Knowl-*

edge develops out of Kant but is, at the same time, an entirely new mode of philosophizing. In historical terms, the new kind of philosophy that starts with Fichte and leads through Schelling to Hegel, who brings it to fulfillment, takes its impulse from what in Kant reaches beyond a mere critique of knowledge and beyond his reflexive distinction between the thinking being and that which is being thought. Fichte's, Schelling's, and Hegel's philosophies develop the speculative and dialectical elements in Kant, promising that the gap opened up between thinking and being, sensibility and understanding, theory and praxis, and so on which Kant's philosophy appears unable to overcome might be bridged. This impossibility of coming to grips with dualism characterizes Kant's philosophy as a philosophy of reflection; consequently, any attempt to ground thinking in the speculative germs of Kant's enterprise must be viewed as a critique of reflexivity.

I hope to prove that this use of the term *reflection* to designate the duality of opposition is not at all incompatible with the methodological concept of reflection as previously outlined, which was shown to constitute modern metaphysics. By formulating the problem of reflection in terms of dualism, Hegel brought to the fore a logical inconsistency in the methodological concept of reflection, an inconsistency, however, that could be overcome only at the price of a radicalization of reflection that is itself a departure from the philosophy of reflection from Descartes to Kant. In order to make this argument, I shall have to explain what must be called reflexive in Kant's thought and what are in Kant the so-called speculative germs of the dialectical bridging of dualism. Before moving on, though, let us first consider some of Hegel's objections to Kant. According to Hegel, Kant's philosophy is a "metaphysic of reflection."[1] Before analyzing in some detail Hegel's determinations of reflection, let us for the moment define it as characterizing the act by which the ego, after having stripped away its natural immediacy and returned into itself, becomes conscious of its subjectivity in relation to counterposited objectivity, and distinguishes itself from it. For Hegel, such a characterization implies in general that Kant's thinking remains caught in a movement of endless duplication which it is unable to overcome. Furthermore, because the activity of doubling is the result of an act of separating, the philosophy of reflection is shown to be in essence a philosophy of understanding (*Verstand*), since "the activity of dissolution is the power and work of the *understanding*," as Hegel remarks in *Phenomenology*.[2]

But what are the major separations brought about by understanding? First and foremost, understanding separates itself, as thinking, from its own object, that is, from being. A philosophy of reflection is similarly marked by an unbridgeable gulf between reflection and that which it reflects. This opposition is coeval with that of subject and object, since reflection, which Hegel associates in *Faith and Knowledge* with Spinoza's concept of imagination *(Einbildungs- kraft)*—that is, with a mode of thought related to existing singular things yet lacking conceptuality—is subjective, an activity by a know- ing subject. Yet as subjectivity, as a movement of the ego, reflection is also self-knowledge and, in the last instance, knowledge of the transcendental presuppositions of knowledge and of what is given. As a transcendental inquiry, however, reflection is as antithetical as when it is seen as an activity by a subject upon the world. In both cases it departs from and fosters irreducible oppositions. Because reflection is unable to overcome the separation it presupposes, Hegel stigmatizes the knowledge of understanding as mere formal knowl- edge.[3] This knowledge splits into two irreconcilable forms: reflection leads either to empirical knowledge, void of concepts, or to an un- derstanding of the a priori conditions of knowledge, independent of what empirically exists. Reflection gives birth to an endless and un- determined multiplicity of facts and/or to a coherent system of a priori conditions; both forms of knowledge are in an antithetical relation. Reflection, as belonging to understanding, opens differences and per- petuates them as fixed and unalterable oppositions, because under- standing, or the intellect, is for Kant "the absolute immovable, insuperable finitude of human Reason."[4] To put it in the language of the greater *Logic,* Kant is unable to bridge the gap between reflection- into-self and reflection-into-other, and since reflection is at the heart of the ideas of subjectivity, freedom, and transcendentality, according to Hegel, it confers its own power of dissolution upon them, unable to overcome the mere abstraction of these concepts. Hegel, therefore, can speak of a failure of reflection owing essentially to its fundamental presupposition of an irreconcilable difference between the object to be explained and the explanation. Because of this gulf, reflection becomes enmeshed in unsolvable contradictions; wherever it tries to unite itself to its object (be it the given or the ego itself) in order to account for it, it necessarily fails to do so. Although reflection is critical of everything, it is unable to question its own premises. It cannot do so because, as Eugène Fleischman remarks: "Reflexion cannot rec- ognize that its objects exist in its imagination alone without at the same time giving itself up. And, on the other hand, it cannot give itself up, since—and always according to its imagination—cognition (or explication) would not be possible without the subject-object distinction."[5]

It must be emphasized here, however, that this failure is not simply a weakness of Kantian thought but is itself the result of the dissolving power of understanding, whose (relative) merit Hegel was the first to acknowledge. What, then, are the precise limits of reflection? For Hegel the limits of reflection are rooted in its neglecting to recognize that, logically speaking, doubling, separation, and dissolution are meaningful only with respect to a totality. The metaphysic of reflection, without its knowledge, presupposes an original unity within which the fragmenting and antithetical power of understanding can become effective. Kant, who was well aware of this exigency, could nonetheless conceive of such a totality only as a hypothetical necessity, or as an abstract and absolute beyond (*Jenseits*), that is, as an object only of human faith and strife. In thus removing the original unity from the realm of what can properly be known, Kant was again a victim of his philosophy of reflection. In short, one can conclude with Jean Hyppolite that Kantian thought, in its aborted attempt to reflect the very presuppositions of its dualistic philosophy, "*represents the deepening of reflection in all its dimensions.* This reflection penetrates indeed into what makes it possible—and that is its speculative side—but it refuses to give up its reflective rigor, and that is what Hegel credits it for; yet it proves unable to overcome reflection by reflection and, thus, remains chained to reflective opposition."[6] This judgment is confirmed by Fleischmann when he claims that "Kant's thought is full of unsuccessful mediations, since they are witness only to the artifice of separation that is at their basis."[7]

Still, although Kant's mediations are purely hypothetical, or have the character of an absolute and unfathomable beyond and are in essence reflexive, they are, to follow Hegel, the speculative germs within Kant's thinking that carry the promise of overcoming the metaphysic of reflection. What are these speculative germs in Kantian philosophy? There are many, among which one must mention schematism, which serves to mediate sensibility and understanding; faith, which mediates the world of the phenomena and the *mundus intelligibilis;* and others. Let us concern ourselves here with only two: the transcendental unity of apperception in *Critique of Pure Reason* and the assumption of an *intellectus archetypus* in *Critique of Judgment.*

When, toward the beginning of his First Critique, Kant contends that thoughts without content are empty, and intuitions without concepts blind, he implicitly suggests that a common tie must reunite the very different faculties of sensibility and understanding. The same sense of unity is at work in his inquiry into synthetic a priori judgments—that is to say, into the reasons that permit the base term, or the subject in its particularity in a *synthetic* judgment, to be characterized by *universal* predicates of thought. In order to be possible, synthetic judgments—the judgments by means of which nature becomes knowable to a subject—must presuppose a hidden ground, the originary synthetic unity of the transcendental ego, a unity that, as the highest reason and ground, explains the validity of scientific propositions. This unity, of course, must not be mistaken for the subjective unity of individual consciousness, which in itself has no necessity whatsoever. Hegel comments on this absolute identity in *Faith and Knowledge:* "This is how Kant truly solved his problem, 'How are synthetic judgments *a priori* possible?' They are possible through the original, absolute identity of the heterogeneous. This identity, as the unconditioned, sunders itself, and appears as separated into the form of a judgment, as subject and predicate, or particular and universal."[8]

But Kant explicitly broaches the idea of such an original identity only when discussing understanding *(Verstand)* with respect to the transcendental deduction of the categories. Indeed, what becomes obvious at this point in Kant's argumentation is that in order for there to be a coherence in the experience of the manifold, this experience must be one's own and must draw on a prior logical representation of unity made possible precisely by the ego's self-comprehension. The ultimate structure of synthesizing understanding, the most originary a priori of cognition, is the originary unity of the *cogito,* or what Kant calls in this context the originary unity of transcendental apperception. In developing this idea of pure self-consciousness as neither an inner nor an outer act—in short, as not belonging to sensibility—Kant reaches back to the common source of both intuition and understanding. As Hegel remarks, "This original synthetic unity must be conceived, not as produced out of opposites, but as a truly necessary, absolute, original identity of opposites" (p. 70). And in the greater *Logic:* "This original synthesis of apperception is one of the most profound principles for speculative development; it contains the beginning of a true apprehension of the nature of the Notion and is completely opposed to that empty identity or abstract universality which is not within itself a synthesis."[9] Kant's insight into the spontaneous a priori synthesizing faculty of pure self-consciousness, according to Hegel, implicitly overcomes the dualism inevitably connected with reflection. By opening up the dimension of transcendental imagination, Kant sets forth the very principle of speculation.

Apart from the fact that *Critique of Judgment* is itself conceived as a bridge linking the two heterogeneous worlds of the First and Second Critiques, the speculative germs of the Third Critique are to be found in the hypothesis of an immemorial identity of pleasure and cognition, and especially in the notion of a reflective faculty of judgment, a faculty that gives itself the transcendental principle of the unity of the manifold. Here, I will consider only the famous paragraph 76 of the Third Critique. Here Kant, after having recognized that ordinary human knowledge is reduced to subsuming the particular within the universal, and that this kind of knowledge, whereby the particular is condemned to remain contingent, is inadequate to nature as a whole, declares himself compelled to posit hypothetically the possibility of a higher form of cognition for which this opposition of the universal and the particular would no longer exist, a sort of *intellectus archetypus* anterior to the antinomies of understanding. Hegel notes in *Faith and Knowledge:* "It is an 'archetypal *(urbildlich)* intellect' for which 'the possibility of the parts, etc., as to their character and integration is dependent on the whole.' Kant also recognizes that we are necessarily driven to this Idea. The *Idea* of this archetypal *intuitive intellect* is at bottom nothing else but the *same Idea* of the transcendental imagination" (pp. 88–89). The *intellectus archetypus,* in contrast to the derivative mode of human intuition, is original. It is an intellect that itself gives existence to its objects. It is, in other words, a nondiscursive intellect, linking things as heterogeneous as the intellect and the intuition, which for Kant is the privilege of the primordial being alone. This intellect is characterized by intuitive intellection or intellectual intuition *(intellektuelle Anschauung),* a mode of intuition beyond the antinomies of understanding and reflexive thinking.

The idea of a transcendental imagination, of a pure apperception which *implicitly* serves to bridge intuition and understanding, as in *Critique of Pure Reason,* as well as the *hypothetical* assumption of an *intellectus archetypus* beyond the antinomies of reflection in *Critique of Judgment,* became programmatic for the whole of German philosophy in the wake of Kant's thought. Under the name of intellectual intuition (not to be mistaken for the homologously termed concept in Kant), the idea of an original and synthetic knowledge, of a sensible understanding—in short, of Reason—led to the development of the systems of Fichte, then Schelling, and finally Hegel. "The still purer Idea of intellect that is at the same time *a posteriori,* the Idea of an intuitive intellect as the absolute middle" (p. 80), to quote Hegel, becomes after Kant the identical subject-object, the foundation of all three idealisms. Because intellectual intuition—the principle of speculation—can be grounded in three logically different ways (in the self-positing self of Fichte's *Science of Knowledge,* in the objective dialectics of nature according to Schelling, and in the dialectics of an absolute subject-object identity à la Hegel), it gives birth to the three systems of German idealism, the last of which is the most complete, the most encompassing.

Since intellectual intuition is a key term in all of German Idealism, and since it is the germ of the speculative critique of reflection, we must further clarify this issue. Intellectual intuition overlaps with the original and synthetic unity of sensibility and understanding, which Kant was compelled to posit in order to be able to proceed to the categories of understanding or to the determination of the epistemological boundaries of the faculty of judging. Intellectual intuition is the unity of self-consciousness, pure apperception—that is to say, the self-reflection of the self as the possibility of a priori cognizance; it is the mode of cognition specific to *cogito me cogitare.* As a matter of fact, pure apperception is the Kantian figure for the Cartesian *ego cogito.* This becomes even more clear with Fichte, where intellectual intuition designates the inner state of the self and its ways of knowing itself which precede the separation into an objective self and a nonself. In *Faith and Knowledge,* Hegel refers to Fichte's concept of intellectual intuition in the following words:

The difficult requirement of intellectual intuition has aroused general complaint, and we have sometimes heard tell of people who went mad in their efforts to produce the pure act of will and the intellectual intuition. Both the complaint and the madness were no doubt occasioned by the name of the thing, not by the thing itself, which Fichte describes as common and easy enough, the only difficulty being perhaps to convince oneself that it really is just this simple everyday thing. The intuition of anything at all as alien to pure consciousness or Ego, is empirical intuition; though the Ego too is, as Fichte puts it, equally given in common consciousness. Abstracting from everything alien in consciousness on the other hand, and thinking oneself, is intellectual intuition. Abstracting from the determinate content in any sort of knowledge and knowing only pure knowing, knowing only what is formal in knowing, this is pure absolute knowledge. (pp. 157–158)

Intellectual intuition in Schelling's objective idealism becomes the "organ of all transcendental thinking," which means, in his *System of Tran-*

scendental *Idealism,* the organ of adequate comprehension and disclosure of objective reality, and of the demonstration of the Oneness
of nature and human knowledge. In contrast to Kant's hypothetical
assumption of an intellectual intuition, and to Fichte's limitation of
it to the realm of subjectivity, intellectual intuition for Schelling becomes an *objective* reality.[10] Although intellectual intuition is also the
starting point of Hegel's philosophy, it does not escape his criticism.
For Hegel, Kant's, Fichte's, and Schelling's treatments of intellectual
intuition fall short of solving the problems engendered by the metaphysics of reflection.

To summarize Hegel's criticism of Kant's theory of mediation in
an elementary way, Hegel's argument demonstrates that Kant's attempts to mediate apparently irreconcilable opposites falls prey to his
philosophy of reflection. For Kant, Hegel argues, the speculative Idea
which occurs in uncorrupted and pure form in the deduction of the
categories of understanding "becomes at once a pure [that is, abstract]
identity, a unity of the intellect," or "it occurs as a merely possible
thought which cannot acquire any reality in thinking because reflection is to be dominant without qualification" (p. 148). Furthermore,
in his critique of the unity of apperception as elaborated by Kant,
Hegel sides with Kant when the latter characterizes this original synthesis as the unity of the *I think,* or self-consciousness, but he objects
to Kant's reduction of this unity to the purely formal *I think* that
must accompany all representation. Hegel writes in *Faith and Knowledge:*

The whole transcendental deduction both of the forms of intuition and of
the category in general cannot be understood without distinguishing what
Kant calls the faculty of the original synthetic unity of apperception from
the Ego which does the representing and is the subject—the Ego which, as
Kant says, merely accompanies all representations. [Second] we must not
take the faculty of [productive] imagination as the middle term that gets
inserted between an existing absolute subject and an absolute existing world.
The productive imagination must rather be recognized as what is primary
and original, as that out of which subjective Ego and objective world first
sunder themselves into the necessarily bipartite appearance and product, and
as the sole In-itself.   (pp. 72–73)

Hegel's objections to Kant's handling of the "true a priori" is that
the latter's reduction of this a priori to the pure formal unity of the
I think not only robs the true a priori of its character as an original,
synthetic unity, but also fixes the formal Ego in an opposition with
an always unfathomable beyond. With this objection in particular,

Hegel's radical critique of reflection becomes manifest: although it retraces the original synthesis—a synthesis of which subject and world are the necessarily bipartite appearances and products—the metaphysics of reflection proves unable to lift the self-reflecting subject out of its opposition to the world of objects. To limit the idea of a pure apperception to an essentially accompanying phenomenon of a subject reflecting upon itself and upon a world of phenomena is not only to fall back into a Lockean critique of knowledge, but also to reinstate and even solidify the derivative moments of an opposition which the true a priori was meant to overcome.

In *The Difference between Fichte's and Schelling's System of Philosophy*, Hegel formulates the same objections. He argues that, although intuition and understanding are grounded in the course of the transcendental deduction in the original synthesis of apperception, one opposition remains intact: the opposition of intellectual intuition to other forms of intuition. Since the opposition that remains is that between self-consciousness and empirical or objective consciousness, the unsolved problem arises from turning the original unity of apperception into mere formal self-reflection. Although this sort of criticism also affects Kant, it is aimed here especially at Fichte. Hegel agrees that the idea of the absolute act of the free self-activity of a self-positing self-consciousness is indeed the condition of possibility of philosophical knowledge as such. But, since it is opposed to empirical consciousness, and thus remains abstract and formal, only a concept, it is not yet that knowledge itself. Such an opposition, like all oppositions, presupposes that its moments share a common higher sphere. If intellectual intuition as a formal activity remains opposed to other intuitions, such as those of empirical consciousness, then they must both partake in the communal sphere of thought as such. Thought as such—the totality of both empirical intuition and pure self-consciousness, a totality in which *all* separation and opposition is sublated—is philosophical knowledge itself. Unlike the unhappy syntheses of the metaphysics of reflection, philosophy *(Denken überhaupt)* becomes a reflection on reflection's unsolved oppositions, and thus, within the perspective of Hegelian thought, the end of reflection in absolute reflection or speculation.

Hegel's critique of Kant's and Fichte's interpretation of the intellectual intuition demonstrates that they had not understood this concept as a true totality. In identifying it as the self-knowing of self-consciousness, they abstracted intellectual intuition from its intrinsic relation to consciousness of Otherness, and as a result created the problem of reconnecting it to its Other again. Interpreted in this manner, intellectual intuition, rather than being a totality, is only part of a totality. The reasons for their failure to conceive intellectual intuition as the true a priori, as Hegel makes quite clear in *Faith and Knowledge*, lie in empirical—that is, nonphilosophical—experience: "Why does not this idea of the totality itself, the measure against which pure knowing shows itself to be incomplete, step forth as the Absolute? Why is the Absolute [in Fichte] something that is recognized as being only a part and as deficient? No reason can be found for it except that this part has empirical certainty and truth; of course everyone knows that he knows. Empirical truth of this sort is given preference over the absolute truth of the totality!" (p. 159). Genuine intellectual intuition would call for the sublation of empirical experience (of the givenness of objects or states of mind) and of analyzing thought, as well as of what makes such experience possible. True intellectual intuition requires that the reflexive oppositions of an experience, enmeshed in empiricist immediacy, be reflected back into the common ground from which these oppositions grow. Only through such a regrounding of the reflective oppositions as bifurcations of an original synthetic unity, which encompasses both the opposition of that unity and that which it reunites, can one prevent intellectual intuition from falling back again "into inert simplicity" and from depicting "actuality itself in a non-actual manner," as happens in Schelling.[11]

It is evident at this point that Hegel's critique of the metaphysics of reflection takes place under the aegis of the concepts of totality, ground, and unity. Hegel's principal objection to reflection is its inability to reflect itself—to reground its opposed moments—in the totality presupposed by the antithetical terms. These objections reveal that Hegel's critique of the philosophy of reflection questions the very titles of this philosophy. Because philosophy in general is most intimately determined by the quest for unity, he chastises the metaphysics of reflection for its inability to achieve that end.

According to Hegel, the only possible mediation—a mediation that leaves nothing unmediated—must be based on the idea of totality. Unlike Kant, whose major preoccupation is to establish a variety of autonomous unifying principles, Hegel radically reinterprets the speculative germs of Kant's philosophy in such a way as to show that all these principles, by entering into opposition with one another, constitute the unity formed by their dialectical relations. Since any separation is, for Hegel, always the result of a previous unity apprehensible through the opposing moments, this unity is the true ground of these moments. The passage from reflection to the thinking of totality is the passage from reflection to absolute reflection or speculation.

Reflection in Kant, insofar as it engenders and solidifies opposites, *is* the unity of the opposing terms, but in an immediate manner only. Yet since reflection does not reflect it, this unity remains purely formal. Consequently, one can contend that Kant's transcendental reflection, although a solely subjective reflection, anticipates and calls for the elaboration of an absolute reflection. Absolute reflection, to quote Hyppolite,

transcends reflection. Reflection coincides with mere human reflection on experience and on its constitution. Absolute reflection comprehends content itself as reflection. It is being that knows itself through man, and not man who reflects on being. This speculative reflection—or absolute reflection— replaces the old dogmatic metaphysics. Anthropology is overcome, yet the essence is not turned into a second world that would explain and ground the first. The immediate itself reflects itself, and this identity of reflection and the immediate corresponds to philosophical knowledge as such.[12]

The relation of philosophical knowledge, or absolute reflection, to reflection properly speaking is a relation of partial criticism and partial justification. Within absolute reflection, reflection properly speaking and transcendental reflection coincide with what as mere reflection they could not but presuppose: the infinitely reflected totality. Hegel's criticism of reflection puts reflection into the Absolute, thereby sublating the dualism which it seemed unable to overcome by itself. Reflection is no longer lost in the bipartite moments of its appearance or in the pure and transcendental a priori which the dualism of reflection necessarily presupposes.[13]

3

The Self-Destruction
of Reflection

❧

In order to understand what Hegel, in *The Difference between Fichte's and Schelling's System of Philosophy,* calls the self-destruction of reflection, it is necessary to study the passage from reflection proper to absolute or speculative reflection. Such an investigation requires us to distinguish clearly among the several types of reflection to which Hegel refers. Indeed in Hegel, the notion of reflection is not a unified concept. The word appears in a variety of contexts that determine its meaning and is used in at least three different ways. Absolute reflection, as characteristic of the speculative process as a whole, must be distinguished from rectified reflection, as outlined in the "Logic of Essence" section of the greater *Logic,* which is itself a speculative reinterpretation of the reflexive process of understanding.[1] Therefore, we can distinguish between reflection as (1) the dissolving force of understanding, (2) the totalizing power of the speculative process, and (3) one moment within that process. Each of these different notions of reflection is itself divided into a number of aspects. In outlining the logico-dialectical process of the passage of reflection from understanding to Reason, I shall skip the critical and dialectical reappropriation of reflection in the greater *Logic* and limit my discussion to the major features of this problem by following the distinctions Hegel made in *The Difference* between isolated and philosophical reflection.

ISOLATED REFLECTION

Isolated reflection, also called simple, pure, or common reflection, is the mode of thought characteristic of the positioning *(Setzen)* particular to understanding. Representing the force of limitation *(die Kraft des Beschränkens),* understanding only posits opposites *(Entgegen-gesetzte).* Isolated reflection thus perpetuates the dissolving activity of understanding by fixing those things that understanding posits as being in opposition to each other. In short, isolated reflection is a mode of thought that has no relation to the Absolute, that is, to the unity or totality of what the fixed opposites presuppose as their common medium or element. Lacking such a relation, isolated reflection remains incapable of raising itself above itself, or above what it is opposed to. Since it has no relation to the Absolute, it remains isolated.

PHILOSOPHICAL REFLECTION

Philosophical reflection, according to *The Difference,* is *"the instrument of philosophizing."*[2] Since the task of philosophy is the construction of the Absolute, or totality, for consciousness, philosophical reflection is called upon to mediate between isolated reflection and the divided totality that it produces. Yet in order to be able to render pure reflection fluid and thus overcome its obdurate oppositions, philosophical reflection must entertain some form of relation to the Absolute. How, then, does this relation to the Absolute become manifest in philosophical reflection, and what are the ways in which it surmounts the dualism of isolated reflection?

Whereas simple reflection, or reflection without relation to the Absolute, perpetuates the opposites posited by understanding, philosophical reflection conceives the totality or the Absolute; it does so, however, in a merely formal manner. Because philosophical reflection belongs to the realm of understanding, it can grasp the true and real synthesis of opposites only if it inverts *(verkehren)* that synthesis into something opposed to that which it is the synthesis of. According to Hegel, philosophical reflection inverts Reason as the unifying faculty into something merely reasonable *(Verständiges).* Philosophical reflection originates in opposites, and the formal insight into the necessity of a unity of opposite terms. It posits this unity in opposition to the initial dualistic structures, as their "beyond." When philosophical reflection expounds the true nature of this identity, it sets it forth *(Darstellung)* as the binding power of irreducible opposites. Consequently, it can conceive of the original synthesis as a union only in the form of an antinomy of absolutely dualistic terms. Because it is indebted to understanding, philosophical reflection continues the separating activity of this mode of thought: it can behold only the *analytical* form of absolute synthesis, or, as Hegel expresses it,

"the purely formal appearance of the Absolute." Indeed, for philosophical reflection, the Absolute is at most an antinomy, a synthesis
of opposites, a "nullification [*Vernichtung*] of the opposites in contradiction" (p. 109). The knowledge that flows from philosophical
reflection is "pure knowledge," a knowledge without true intellectual
intuition.

Yet the purely formal or antinomic synthesis to which philosophical
reflection raises itself is not just any unity. It is a unity thoroughly
determined in itself. It is a totality whose antinomic nature is grounded
in what Hegel calls reflective determinations *(Reflexionsbestimmun-
gen)*, or in what Kant calls the categories of *understanding*. These
reflective determinations, which arise through abstraction from absolute identity, help philosophical reflection set forth its antinomic
synthesis of opposites. But why do these reflective determinations lead
only to a purely formal and antinomic union?

At least two reasons must be mentioned here. Since the reflective
determinations are abstracted by understanding from the absolute
identity, they are thought to be irreconcilable. Hegel writes: "Infinity
and finitude, indeterminateness and determinateness, etc. are reflective
products of the same sort. There is no transition from the infinite to
the finite, from the indeterminate to the determinate. The transition
as synthesis becomes antinomy; for reflection, which separates absolutely, cannot allow a synthesis of the finite and the infinite, of the
determinate and the indeterminate to be brought about, and it is
reflection that legislates here" (pp. 158–159). By analyzing the specific
sort of contradiction that exists between these reflexive determinations, one can better grasp not only the exclusively formal quality of
the unity to which philosophical reflection is capable of raising itself,
but also the second reason for which this unity must remain contradictory.

All that is posited by understanding—that is, being and everything
limited—is determinate, since philosophical reflection "aims at tho-
roughgoing determination" (p. 95). But determination proceeds through
negation, that is, by positing an opposite to what is given. Being and
everything limited, because they are determinate, must consequently
have an indeterminate before and after, according to Hegel, for the
determinate must be bounded by an indeterminate. Yet in the perspective of understanding, that indeterminate is nothing; it is a mere
beyond. Thus the determinate rests on nothing. Hegel concludes, "Thus
its [understanding's] positings and determinings never accomplish the
task; in the very positing and determining that have occurred there

lies a nonpositing and something indeterminate, and hence the task of positing and determining recurs perpetually" (p. 95). Because philosophical reflection is "bound to fall into the making of endless determinations" (p. 146), a compulsion Hegel compares to the activity of policing, the totality to which it is able to raise itself is not solely the formal unity of antinomies, the simple abstract concept of a unity that, since it remains opposed to what it reunites, "kills the living element of true identity in it" (p. 149). It is also an abyssal concept of unity, that is to say, no concept at all. Indeed, by extending the process of determination to infinity, by reducing it to an endless process, philosophical reflection nullifies not only its own principle but also the idea of a unity itself.

With this failure to conceptualize the Absolute, philosophical reflection reaches the point where it begins to dissolve and pass over into its Other. "The highest maturity, the highest stage, which anything can attain is that in which its downfall begins," Hegel writes.[3] Having reached its inner limits with the impossibility of thinking the identity of the determinate, philosophical reflection faces the necessity of passing over into another mode of thought or reflection that will accomplish what it set out to do. Such a possibility arises, according to Hegel, as soon as philosophical reflection recognizes that the things it opposes in a dualistic fashion are only *ideal* factors, or opposites of thought alone. With this recognition that the opposites of understanding are thoroughly relative terms, as long as they are not understood with respect to the true absolute identity, that of thought itself, and with the determination of the opposites of philosophical reflection within the limits of the Absolute—that is, as *real* opposites—philosophical reflection becomes Reason and makes the leap into absolute or speculative reflection.

SPECULATIVE OR ABSOLUTE REFLECTION

In order to understand the nature of absolute reflection, and how it compares to the other forms of reflection, we must first understand the manner in which the transition of philosophical reflection to speculation occurs. What makes that passage possible is that understanding is already a fore-form of Reason. Without knowing it, understanding copies Reason, says Hegel. Indeed, it cannot keep Reason away: "it seeks to protect itself against the feeling of its inner emptiness, and from the secret fear that plagues anything limited, by whitewashing its particularities with a semblance of Reason" (pp.

92–93). It is seduced by Reason "into producing an objective totality" (p. 95). Although it is not conscious of doing so, understanding as the force of separation already presupposes an identity into which its dissolving power cuts. As philosophical reflection, understanding takes on the task of thinking the originary unity of the determinate in a formal manner, as we have seen. But understanding not only copies Reason unknowingly insofar as it sets forth a merely formal identity; it also lets itself be seduced by Reason into nullifying its own principle in the endless task of reflectively determining the formal totality in question. When philosophical reflection recognizes that its antinomic synthesis of opposites is only the explicit formula, the purely formal expression *(formellen Ausdruck)*, of truth, it makes a place for Reason. At that point Reason, as Hegel remarks, "has [already] brought the formal essence of reflection under its control" (p. 108). Indeed, what causes the downfall of philosophical reflection, the indeterminate that it must necessarily oppose to determinate being in order to determine it fully, the infinite that it cannot avoid juxtaposing to the finite—an opposition that throws philosophical reflection into the endless process of determination—"is [already] something rational [belonging to the order of Reason] as posited by the intellect," because "taken by itself . . . it merely expresses the negating of the finite" (p. 90). Although the infinite task of determination that ruins philosophical reflection is a characteristic of the lower standpoint from which the absolute synthesis is considered, it is a characteristic of Reason as well. This infinite task shows understanding to be manipulated by Reason, because it is Reason that "makes the intellect boundless, and in this infinite wealth the intellect and its objective world meet their downfall" (p. 95).

Let us recall that the opposites of philosophical reflection are only opposites of thought. Their merely ideal nature is a function of the indeterminate, conceptualized by philosophical reflection under the form of the Ego, which is turned into the correlate of the totality of the determinations of being. Yet, because "the Ego is [thus] placed in absolute opposition to the object, it is nothing real, but is something thought, a pure product of reflection, a mere form of cognition," Hegel argues (p. 158). Because it is indebted to understanding, philosophical reflection is unable to think an organic relation between the opposites it sets forth. As ideal opposites, whose objective pole, moreover, is determined by a host of additional ideal opposites, they remain in absolute contradiction to one another. Thus, the totality of philosophical reflection is composed only of "the Ego, i.e., indetermi-

nateness, or self-determination, and . . . the object, determinateness,"
beyond whose play of reciprocity it cannot reach (p. 139). In a clear
reference to Fichte's transcendental philosophy, Hegel shows the purely
formal and antithetical synthesis of understanding to be rooted in a
hypostasis of the Ego, or in a subject-object relation that is primarily
subjective. According to Hegel, Schelling opposes an objective subject-
object relation, an objective identity, to Fichte's subjective one in order
to overcome the subjective and merely ideal determination of the
opposites, and to overcome with the same stroke understanding and
philosophical reflection. With such an objective interpretation of absolute identity, the totality of moments at play in philosophical reflection begins to come into view. The hitherto ideal opposites, whose
signification now derives from the totality of which they are parts,
appear as real opposites in Schelling's philosophy of nature as the
theory of nature's self-construction. As soon as philosophical reflection turns to the conceptualization of the absolute identity of subject
and object, it becomes, in Hegel's terms, speculative.[4] But it truly
becomes speculation only when it conceives of the absolute identity
as the subjective and objective subject-object, because only this determination of absolute synthesis takes the totality of its logically
possible determinations into account. Needless to say, this concept
of the Absolute coincides with Hegel's philosophical enterprise.

Before analyzing absolute or speculative reflection in itself, and its
distinction from mere philosophical reflection, we must first consider
what happens to reflection in the transition to absolute reflection.
What takes place is the self-destruction of reflection. "Being the faculty
of being and limitation," reflection, says Hegel, "nullifies itself and
all being and everything limited . . . [as soon as] it connects [itself
and] them with the Absolute" (p. 94). The self-destruction of reflection
resulting from the reflection upon reflection takes place at the moment
at which the limited is related to the Absolute. "Like everything else,
reflection has standing only in the Absolute; but as reflection it stands
in opposition to it" (p. 96). The negative power of understanding, by
destroying itself in the process of self-reflection, is consequently the
manifestation of the positive power of Reason.

Let us analyze this process of self-destruction in more detail. By
conceiving of the totality of all determinations as an antinomic unity
in which the opposites are destroyed precisely to the extent that they
are in a relation of antinomy, reflection reveals itself as Reason by
pointing toward an absolute synthesis. Indeed, in the antinomic destruction of opposites, a destruction that leads to the establishment

of a formal totality, philosophical reflection "has not maintained but nullified the opposition and the standing of the two terms or of either of them, and it has not maintained but nullified [the claim] that it is itself the Absolute and the eternal; it has thrown itself into the abyss of its perfection" (p. 140). Since reflection, like everything else, has standing only in the Absolute, but stands as reflection in an adverse relation to it, then reflection, in order to be at once opposed to and ruled by Reason, "must give itself the law of self-destruction." This law, which is "its supreme law, [is] given to it by Reason and [is] moving it to become Reason" (p. 96). Because reflection is Reason only to the extent that it is connected to the Absolute, the reflection on this connection does away with all of reflection's work. The truth of reflection is thus "the truth of its nullification" (pp. 97–98). By destroying itself in making itself its own object, reflection throws itself, to use Hegel's words, into the abyss of its own perfection. But what does this colorful expression mean? The abyss is the negative image by which Reason appears to and in reflection. Reflection must become this abyss, in which alone it has a standing. Only by destroying itself can reflection achieve this goal. By working at its own destruction, "Reason thus drowns itself and its knowledge and its reflection of the absolute identity, in its own abyss: and in this night of mere reflection and of the calculating intellect, in this night which is the noonday of life, common sense and speculation can meet one another" (p. 103). The abyss is the abyss of Reason; in it, all opposites are reunited. It is the element in which reflection, common sense, and speculation first meet in indifference.

The abyss of Reason is destructive of *all* forms of reflection, insofar as the latter serves the opposing force of understanding. Thus, Reason is the abyss into which reflection throws itself as a self, that is, as standing in opposition to Reason. But it is also the abyss *of* Reason, as long as philosophical reflection and understanding are still its opposites. In short, the abyss of Reason, into which reflection throws itself in a gesture of self-destruction, is the medium of the sublation of all self and everything opposed to the self, that is, of *all* opposition. And since this sublation takes place when reflection destroys itself by making itself its own reflective object, the process of the becoming of Reason coincides with the overcoming of the last possible opposition, that of the self to itself. With this total identity of subject and object, an identity in which neither a subjective nor an objective synthesis of the subject-object relation prevails, all separation is overcome, and the realm of the Absolute is reached. The self-destruction of reflection represents a regrounding of reflection in the Absolute. This regrounding takes place in reflection's *self*-annihilation—that is, by its destruction of itself as standing in opposition to all objects, and to itself as well. The self of reflection, the hypostasis of the Ego or subject, is the main obstacle in the way of becoming speculation or absolute reflection. What, then, is speculation?

Speculation is a word that has fallen into deep disrepute since Martin Luther's criticism of system-oriented scholastic theology. Since then the pejorative sense of *speculative* has referred primarily to those propositions of Christian theology that evasively transcend the given, or reality, and, more broadly, to the construction of idle thoughts about idle subjects, of so-called a priori constructions or, of what is believed to mean the same, contrary-to-fact hypotheses. But speculation, or *speculatio*, which together with *contemplatio* makes up the Latin translation of the Greek concept of *theoria*, has little to do with that deforming representation meaning that which is mere fancy of thought, in thought alone. The term bears a connotation of recklessness only for thought that is caught in a "naturalistic" prejudice against thought itself. Undoubtedly scholastic philosophy and German Idealism have indulged in speculative aberration. Yet, since speculation as *theoria* means essentially the pursuit of knowledge for knowledge's sake, it is from that perspective that speculation must be understood and evaluated. Thus, for Thomas Aquinas, speculation coincides with the necessity of philosophical thought as such, to the extent that philosophical reflection transcends the factual given and moves toward its ultimate determining grounds.[5] Such speculation, since it was tied to the scholastic and theological form of philosophical thought, was of course restricted to the interpretation of all finite substances as deriving from the one divine substance. But since Descartes's recasting of the concept of truth, the meaning of speculation in Cartesian and post-Cartesian philosophical thought has not only signified the necessary transcendence of what is given in a sensuous manner, but has begun to signify as well the necessary demonstration of the givenness of being, of the cognitive objectivity of the world and its absolute ground.[6] It is in this amplified sense that Kant's positive use of the concept of speculation should be understood. The same applies to the German Idealist philosophers, Hegel included. The term *speculation* is rooted in the Latin *specio*, "to look," "to behold." The speculative discourse is, as Ricoeur remarks, the theoretical discourse par excellence—that is, "the discourse that establishes the primary notions, the principles, that articulate primordially the space of the concept"—and, since concepts cannot effectively be deduced genetically from perceptions or images, "the speculative is the condition of the possibility of the conceptual."[7] Because, with respect to ordinary and scientific languages, speculation offers the reflective distance that allows a conceptual space to constitute itself, and because it is thus first in the order of foundation, it appears as the very condition of the possibility of philosophical knowledge and thought. This must not be forgotten when, hereinafter, we review a series of critical positions on speculations and absolute reflection, positions which in essence represent radical attacks on what the tradition has meant by philosophical thought. Yet not all critiques of the essence of philosophical thought are of equal pertinence. The one I shall be most concerned with—Derrida's criticism of speculation and absolute reflection—is a position that recognizes the well-foundedness, the exigencies, even the absolute necessity of the speculative element of philosophical thought.

But what is it that makes speculation such a privileged discourse? Nothing less, indeed, than its mirroring function. Cicero, apparently erroneously, derived *speculatio* from *specularis,* "in the manner of a mirror" *(speculum).* Scholastic philosophy referred to *speculum* as well, in order to emphasize speculation's capability of indirect cognition of the Divine. But with post-Cartesian philosophy, the mirroring aspect of speculation takes on a new and additional meaning. Since Kant, but especially in German Idealism, *speculative* designates that kind of pure, or purely theoretical, knowledge—a knowledge free from all subjective and practical ingredients—that is also the knowledge of itself. Speculative knowledge is that sort of knowledge that constitutes itself in self-reflection. Since German Idealism, *speculative* has meant the process of constant exchange between a mirror and its mirror image. One calls a relation speculative when an object first remains fixed in a purely phenomenal state, but is then also recognized as being for a subject—an in-itself, or indeed a for-itself. Consequently, Hans-Georg Gadamer can write that "a thought is speculative if the relationship that it expresses is not conceived as the unambiguous assigning of a determination to a subject, a property to a given thing, but must be thought of as a mirroring, in which the reflection is the pure appearance of what is reflected, just as the one is the one of the other, and the other is the other of the one."[8]

But Gadamer's definition of speculative thought is not precise enough to account for what really distinguishes absolute reflection or speculation from philosophical reflection. When Hegel writes in *Science of Logic* that "*speculative thinking* consists solely in the fact that thought holds fast contradiction, and in it, its own self, but does not allow itself to be dominated by it as in ordinary thinking, where its determinations are resolved by contradiction only into other determinations or into nothing," it becomes obvious that speculative thought is concerned with reconstituting the unity of what is diverse.[9] In contrast to philosophical reflection, whose essence resides in opposing, and in this manner relating, one thing to another—and which therefore cannot conceptualize the unity of what is in opposition—speculative thought possesses, as Hegel puts it, the *boldness* to *think* contradiction, which according to traditional logic is unthinkable and should thus be nonexistent.[10] It has the boldness to conceive of opposites in their unity. Now, because the thought of such unity requires a beholding of what is opposite as such—that is, the being in opposition of the opposites as well as the mutual reflection by which these opposites become unified in the idea of the Spirit—speculative thought is grounded in this reflective mirroring of what is positively in opposition. It coincides with the reciprocal mirroring and unification of the conflicting poles. The mirroring that constitutes speculative thought articulates the diverse, and the contradictions that exist between its elements, in such a way as to exhibit the totality of which this diversity is a part. Speculation, then, is the movement that constitutes the most complete unity, the ultimate foundation of all possible diversity, opposition, and contradiction. The standpoint of speculation, unlike that of reflection, is a structured and absolutely encompassing totality, comprising both difference and unity. Its standpoint is that of absolute identity, and its mode of cognition that of pure reasonable *(vernünftige)* knowing of the Absolute. Its standpoint is thus the standpoint of Reason, and Reason itself is the Absolute under the form of knowing.

In *The Difference,* Hegel contends that "for speculation everything determinate has reality and truth only in the cognition of its connection with the Absolute" (p. 99). "To speculation . . . the finitudes are radii of the infinite focus which irradiates them at the same time that it is formed by them. In the radii the focus is posited and in the focus the radii" (p. 111). Speculative thought is the systematic accomplishment of the unity presupposed by reflection. It lifts, says Hegel, "the identity of which sound sense is not conscious into consciousness" (p. 100). But in the highest and most complete synthesis, speculation must also abolish the opposition between the conscious and the nonconscious, thought and nonthought, *cogitans* and *cogitatum.* Speculation consequently also demands the nullification of mere consciousness through the self-destruction of reflection. The higher unity of spirit is achieved only at the price of a suspension of all opposition. Only at this point does philosophical thinking achieve its telos, because the moment at which all opposition is abolished coincides with the total self-penetration and self-determination of thought. At this point of completion, speculative thought can conceive of the object of its thinking as nothing less than the self-determined movement of its own self-comprehension as thought. Indeed, speculation achieves its totalizing efforts when it recognizes its own achievement as the achievement of the self-determination of the Concept.

To sum up: Speculation, or absolute reflection, is a critique of reflection and, particularly, of philosophical reflection insofar as its mirroring function permits the overcoming of the major antinomy of reflection, that between the empirical, formal, or transcendental self-reflection of the subject of cognition (the thinking being) and the reflected object of this epistemological endeavor (what is thought). The determination of the object of cognition in terms of a self-alienation of the subject, as the image of the subject thrown back by the reflecting mirror (or, in Hegelian terms, as an itself that is in fact a for-oneself), is a movement of thought that permits at once the overcoming of the purely formal and constitutive function of self-consciousness in the process of knowledge, and the beyond of the object that for such a consciousness must always remain indecipherable. By establishing this speculative totality, philosophical thinking expounds and develops, explicitly and exhaustively, the logical presuppositions of dividing philosophical reflection itself.

Before we move on to further discussion of the philosophical achievements of this critique of reflexivity, it may be useful to assert that speculation is not a diffuse and occult enterprise. Speculation is rooted, as hermeneutic philosophers such as Gadamer and Ricoeur remind us, in language itself, or to be more precise, in the philosophical concept of language. At the very moment that language is understood as more than a pragmatic tool for representing what is (although this view does not escape the philosophical concept of language), it vouches for the possibility of articulating a relation to the whole of being, and of expressing it in language. Because language realizes meaning in speech or writing, because it makes communication and understanding possible, it must, in philosophical terms, be thought of as a totalizing medium. Undoubtedly Hegel, who brought the Greek philosophy of the *logos* to its full completion, at first conceived of speculative mediation as an operation of thought alone. But since speculation is effective or real only where it finds its exposition in the speculative proposition, it cannot be altogether severed from the medium of language. Indeed, it presupposes the *possibility* of linguistic utterance and exposition.

Let us look more closely at what Hegel understands by the "speculative proposition," which destroys the ordinary notion of the proposition. Although Hegel discusses the speculative proposition in the preface to *Phenomenology* and in the last pages of *Science of Logic,* as well as in a number of passages from his *Encyclopedia,* I shall consider only the discussion in the preface, since it is here that he is most explicit on this subject. Speaking of the speculative proposition, Hegel writes, "The general nature of the judgement or proposition, which involves the distinction of Subject and Predicate, is destroyed by the speculative proposition, and the proposition of identity which the former becomes contains the counter-thrust against that subject-predicate relationship."[11] The speculative proposition is thus said to alter radically the relation between subject and predicate in predicative sentences or empirical propositions. The common structure of judgments or propositions consists, from an Aristotelian and Cartesian perspective, of the predication of a subject within the horizon of a determination of truth as certitude. But why should it be important to overturn the structure of predication, and what happens to that structure in speculative propositions?

Ratiocinative thought, argues Hegel, is adequately expressed within the usual structures of the common proposition, because it conceives of the content of its thought in the same way as it conceives of the subject of the proposition—that is, as an underlying substance, a *hypokeimenon,* whose attributes are by definition clearly distinguishable. Yet the content of speculative thought is such that it destroys the structure of the ordinary proposition. As we have seen, differences in the content of speculation such as subject and object or subject and attributes are determined within the totality of which they are the bipartite manifestation. The content of the speculative proposition is the identity of the self-determining Concept and thought itself. Therefore, the common proposition, with its possibility of absolutely isolating and separating subject and predicate, seems an inappropriate form of expression for speculative content.[12]

But what, then, are the ways in which speculative content destroys the traditional form of judgment? First, despite the fact that the speculative critique of the form of predicative propositions is a critique

of Kant, Hegel's speculative reinterpretation of the structure of judgment is possible only as a result of Kant's insights into the ternary
structure of the proposition. "The germ of speculation lies in this
triplicity alone," Hegel writes in *Faith and Knowledge*.[13] Indeed, at
the beginning of paragraph 19 of the second deduction of "Transcendental Logic" in *Critique of Pure Reason*, Kant admits that he is
not satisfied with the logician's definition of judgment as a representation of a relation between two concepts. He recognizes that for a
judgment to be possible, a third element or medium must be added
to the two relating concepts. For Kant, this medium is self-consciousness, and it ties the relation between the two concepts to the originary
synthetic unity of apperception. This third term, according to Kant,
explains the synthetic character of propositions, or judgment. Even
if Hegel finds fault with this Kantian explanation of judgment—which,
since the medium of self-consciousness is not for Kant a concept,
remains formally a binary synthesis of subject and predicate—Kant's
hypothesis of a ternary structure of the proposition serves as the
starting point for Hegel's development of the speculative proposition.
Hegel develops the simple proposition of judgment into the syllogism.
His speculative interpretation of judgment, "his so to speak quaternary interpretation of triplicity"—quaternary because Hegel's replacing self-consciousness with a third concept does not do away with
self-consciousness but reinstates it as a fourth position from which it
grounds and animates the triplicity itself—is only a more consistent
development of Kant's own discovery.[14]

Yet it is important to realize, as Werner Marx has argued, that
despite the incongruity between the speculative content and the ordinary structure of the proposition, the form of the ordinary proposition is not overtly destroyed. At first, speculative thought is simply
projected into the traditional form of the proposition.[15] What, then,
does such an inner destruction of the traditional form of the proposition amount to? Hegel's own example of such an inner destruction
of the common figure of the proposition by a speculative content is
the statement "God is being." In contrast to the conventional relation
between subject and predicate in propositions, being, in the proposition "God is being," has acquired an essential substantiality, which
destroys its character as a predicate, and in which the subject, God,
becomes dissolved. According to this example, a speculative sentence
is one in which the predicate of the proposition is made a subject.
The speculative content of the proposition "God is being" reads "Being
is God." Speculative thought does not proceed by affirming or denying

predicates about a subject that would remain a stable and solid base throughout the process of determination. Hegel remarks:

Here thinking, instead of making progress in the transition from Subject to Predicate, in reality feels itself checked by the loss of the Subject, and, missing it, is thrown back on to the thought of the Subject. Or, since the Predicate itself has been expressed as a Subject, as *the* being or *essence* which exhausts the nature of the Subject, thinking finds the Subject immediately in the Predicate; and now, having returned into itself in the Predicate, instead of being in a position where it has freedom for argument, it is still absorbed in the content, or at least is faced with the demand that it should be.[16]

In other words, the inner revolution of the proposition, made possible by a speculative content, is not limited to a simple reversal of subject and predicate. The counterthrust of which Hegel speaks makes the speculative proposition a proposition of identity. Hence, what is changed by the speculative content in the usual subject-predicate relation of propositions is not only the respective positions of subject and predicate but the very status of the copula in the judgment. The *is* has radically changed meaning: it no longer secures the attribution of predicates to a subject, of universals to the particular; instead, it expresses an identity that is itself both passive and transitive.[17] The copula of the proposition thus becomes the real subject of the speculative proposition. It expresses the Absolute itself—the Absolute that is the totality of the Concept.

In what ways, then, is the speculative proposition different from the empirical proposition? Although a speculative proposition resembles the empirical proposition in appearance, it is destructive of the binary and reflective form of the relation of subject and predicate. In a speculative proposition, the predicate is no longer a class, a sensible generality, but a category, a universal determination. It is the very substance, the essence of the subject. The subject of the ordinary proposition becomes lost in the substantial essence of the predicate in the speculative proposition. With this identity of subject and predicate, an identity that makes the bounds of reflection disappear, mediation becomes the true subject of the proposition. Such mediation as a totalizing process of determination stands for absolute reflection. Within the speculative proposition, Hegel argues, the difficulties of reflection insofar as they pertain to the structure of judgment are overcome.

On the level of judgment, the speculative proposition represents the solution of the Kantian reflective difference between the empirical proposition as a formal relation of two concepts and self-consciousness as the judiciary medium of the synthetic function of judgment. In the speculative judgment, this solution is the result of the synthesizing function of the copula, of the dialectical self-reflection of mediation in which subject and predicate become identical.[18]

The solely inward destruction of the empirical proposition, however, is still insufficient. Hegel writes:

The sublation of the form of the proposition must not happen only in an *immediate* manner, through the mere content of the proposition. On the contrary, this opposite movement must find explicit expression: it must not just be the inward inhibition mentioned above. This return of the Notion into itself must be *set forth* [dargestellt]. This movement which constitutes what formerly the proof was supposed to accomplish, is the dialectical movement of the proposition itself. This alone is the speculative *in act* [wirkliche], and only the expression of this movement is a speculative exposition [Darstellung].[19]

Since the predicate in a speculative proposition must exhibit its nature as subject, and since this can occur only dialectically, through mediation, one proposition alone is incapable of explicitly expressing the speculative. This is why the true speculative, "the speculative *in act* [wirkliche]," requires what Hegel calls "speculative exposition." In speculative exposition not only is the speculative content devoted to the immediate or inward destruction of the common form of the proposition; the speculative expresses itself in an *effective* manner as well. As Werner Marx has shown, absolute reflection achieves its essence only in such a speculative exposition of the speculative content.

Within the presentation of the whole as truth, a singular proposition is something "fixed" and "positively dead," and hence something "wrong." The simple proposition can at best denote a "fixed result." In the portrayal of the life of truth, and completing itself as a whole, the proposition in its particularity is sublated. The single proposition becomes a link in a chain of propositions. The propositions are linked together as presupposing and as positing; therein lies the sole possibility of showing how the totality of determinations is fused into a true association. The speculative presentation must take command of an entire system of propositions.[20]

The passage from the structure of the single speculative proposition to the texture and totality of sentences marks the transition from speculation to dialectics. While the young Hegel used *speculation* and *dialectics* synonymously, in his later work he distinguishes between these concepts. Dialectics, in the preface to *Phenomenology*, signifies the mode of exposition of the speculative content. With dialectics, speculation turns from a purely inward revolution into an active demonstration of its content.

Yet since the dialectical exposition of the speculative in a system of propositions empties these propositions of everything that is not the Notion or Concept, or everything that the Notion does not comprehend, the passage to dialectics does not correspond to a simple exteriorization of speculation in the medium of language. Language is used in the dialectical exposition of speculative thought only to the extent that the proper meaning of the words is entirely superseded by the categories, which themselves form a "logical" totality, and in which they appear only as moments of the self-determining Notion or Concept. Although the dialectical mediation of the speculative takes place only in thought, its altered state, language, represents an essential moment in the completion of the totality of the Concept. Language thus becomes the privileged medium by which the Concept can acquire the total transparency, the absolute intelligibility that characterizes it as the totality of the reflected moments of the process of its own becoming.[21]

Despite the difference between the hermeneutic and the Hegelian concept of language, it is important to stress the essential link of language to both speculation and absolute reflection. In Hegelian and hermeneutic philosophy, language plays a fundamental role in establishing the speculative totality, or opening, as it is called today, within which philosophical reflection, be it empirical or transcendental, must be situated, that is, shown to be at once possible and limited in its scope.

This exposition of the speculative totality as the resolution of reflective oppositions can be taken one step farther. A useful starting point is Ricoeur's account of what makes the speculative discourse possible and of what it is to achieve. Ricoeur writes in *The Rule of Metaphor*:

Speculative discourse is possible, because language possesses the *reflective* capacity to place itself at a distance and to consider itself, as such and in its entirety, as related to the totality of what is. Language designates itself and its other. This reflective character extends what linguistics calls meta-linguistic functioning, but articulates it in another discourse, speculative discourse. It is then no longer a function that can be opposed to other functions, in particular to the referential function; for it is the knowledge that accompanies the referential function itself, *the knowledge of its being-related to being.*[22]

From a Hegelian perspective, Ricoeur's definition of speculation could easily be considered Kantian. One reason for this is that Ricoeur understands the speculative discourse itself as a discourse *about* language's discernible and multiple functions, as a discourse that thematizes and extends the meta-linguistic function that accompanies the function of reference. According to Ricoeur, each of these functions can be clearly and absolutely distinguished from each other. Although Ricoeur stresses that language's reflective character, when articulated in speculative discourse as language's consciousness of its openness to what is, can no longer be opposed to the linguistic functions, and that it is incommensurable with such functions, he seems to reduce the reflective character of language to a formal synthesis similar to the Kantian "I think," which must accompany not so much all one's representations as all one's linguistic acts. If Ricoeur escapes such criticism, it is because he also views language as a totality comparable to the Hegelian Absolute, which encompasses through sublation the two distinct linguistic functions of the meta-linguistic and the referential. But if this is so, Ricoeur would have to expound speculatively the ways in which the two functions within language are superseded by the totality of language itself. In any event, Ricoeur's discussion allows us to determine more clearly what Hegel achieves with absolute reflection.

In order to be all-encompassing, the speculative discourse cannot be *about* the functions of language. If the speculative discourse is restricted to the articulation of these functions, it remains, in Hegelian terms, opposed to language. Therefore, Hegelian speculative knowledge demonstrates the identity of self-cognition and the cognition of the world of objects. The identity of these two positions occurs at the moment when exterior reflection, or the reflection of objects, recognizes that it must presuppose *itself* as self-reflection, and that the immediate object of its reflection is merely the reflection of that which grounds exterior reflection. Through this gesture of thought, speculative or absolute reflection succeeds in reuniting both the dogmatic or naively empirical mode of thinking characteristic of empiricism— which consists of identifying absolutely a content prior to its formal reflection—and the critical attitude, presented by Kant's transcendental philosophy, in which thought knows itself to be in the position of a content for itself. Jean Hyppolite makes this quite clear when he writes that speculative knowledge

implies the synthesis of the dogmatic attitude and the critical attitude as presented in Kant's transcendental philosophy. The *intentionality* of consciousness, which is turned toward preexisting being and which relegates reflection to its subjectivity, and transcendental reflection, which reflects the self of knowing by relegating being to the thing-in-itself, must be confounded in *speculative knowing,* which is self-knowledge in the content, of the content as self, and for which the twisting of the soul, which in looking at being looks at itself and vice-versa, is itself expressed in a new logic.[23]

In empirical consciousness, intuition posits subject and object by opposing them absolutely to one another. For this reason intuition is, as Hegel states in *The Difference,* "empirical, given, non-conscious" (p. 110). Transcendental intuition, by contrast, "enters consciousness through free abstraction from the whole manifold of empirical consciousness, and in this respect it is something subjective" (p. 173). It is, above all, nothing but "pure knowledge, which would be knowing without intuition, [as] is the nullification of the opposites in contradiction" (p. 109). Speculative reflection is not the mechanical synthesis of the two previous positions on intuition, reflection and cognition. Only by reflecting those two positions into identity can the synthesis of absolute reflection be brought about. This is done by demonstrating that empirical consciousness presupposes *itself* in transcendental consciousness, and that the subjective aspect of transcendental consciousness has its truth in the objectivity of the thing-in-itself. As a result of such a mediation of the two opposed and contradictory positions of empiricism and transcendentalism, speculative or absolute reflection becomes, as Hyppolite notes, "the a priori *spontaneity* that both presuppose, and which one discovers in them . . . This a priori synthesis is that of the self-positing Absolute that enlightens itself by its own light."[24] Hegel's speculative reflection thus gathers *into one* what Kant had conceptualized under the title of the transcendental and formal unity of apperception *and* the empirical consciousness made possible by the latter. Speculative reflection is the analysis *sub specie aeterni,* so to speak—that is, here, in the perspective of the entirety of logical determinations—of the still reflective opposition of empiricism and transcendentalism. Hegel writes in *The Difference:* "In order to grasp transcendental intuition in its purity, philosophical reflection must further abstract from this subjective aspect so that transcendental intuition, as the foundation of philosophy, may be neither subjective nor objective for it, neither self-consciousness as opposed to matter, nor matter as opposed to self-consciousness, but pure transcendental intuition, absolute identity, that is neither subjective nor objective" (pp. 173–174). The task of speculative philosophy is, consequently, "to suspend the apparent opposition of transcendental and empirical consciousness" (p. 120). This suspension is achieved in the truly a priori synthesis of absolute reflection, which is a truly a priori spontaneity because it contains in itself both the a priori as a purely formal identity and the very possibility of an a posteriority, which in it are no longer absolutely opposed. This true a priori spontaneity of absolute reflection also represents the overcoming of the absolute reflective opposition of subject and object. Empirical subjectivity as a subjectivity riveted to objects, as well as transcendental subjectivity, is overcome in this true a priori, which coincides with the self-determination of the Concept or Notion in the exposition of the process of its logical unfolding.

The suspension of the empirical and the transcendental is achieved in speculative reflection by means of the dialectical exposition of the identity of understanding, or reflection, and intuition. "Speculation," writes Hegel, "produces the consciousness of this identity, and because ideality and reality are one in it, it is intuition" (p. 111). Speculation, then, is the true fulfillment of transcendental imagination or of what, since Fichte, and in distinction from Kant's homologous use of the term, has become known as intellectual intuition. Speculation is absolute intuition. In *The Difference* Hegel writes:

In empirical intuition, subject and object are opposites; the philosopher apprehends the activity of intuiting, he intuits intuiting and thus conceives it as an identity. This intuiting of intuiting is, on the one hand, philosophical reflection and as such opposed both to ordinary reflection and to the empirical consciousness in general which does not raise itself above itself and its oppositions. On the other hand, this transcendental intuition is at the same time the object of philosophical reflection; it is the Absolute, the original identity.   (p. 120)

When transcendental intuition as the intuition of intuition becomes the object of philosophical reflection, philosophical reflection is raised to the status of a transcendental intuition, because "philosophical reflection makes itself [in this manner] into the object and is one with it: this is what makes it speculation" (p. 173). In other words, absolute reflection or speculation is "the activity of the one universal Reason directed upon itself," grasping "its grounding within itself" (p. 88). Or, as Hegel also notes, it is "the pure thinking that thinks itself, the identity of subject and object" (p. 81).

To sum up: speculation or absolute reflection resulting from the self-destruction of reflection—the annulment of such reflexive oppositions as the *tautological* knowledge of formal thinking and the *heterological* knowledge of empirical thought, of the a priori of the transcendental and the a posteriori of the empirical, of subjectivity and objectivity, of freedom and necessity, of theory and praxis, as well as of the *last* logically possible oppositions, the opposition of the self to itself and to what it is not—is the self-intuition of Reason in "absolute indifference," as the young Hegel called it, using a Schellingian term. The self-destruction of reflection in absolute reflection coincides with the self-begetting of Reason in infinite intuition. Absolute reflection is the full exposition of all the logically possible moments of the *logos,* a process that is completed as soon as the *logos* is folded back into itself.

4

Identity, Totality, and Mystic Rapture

Unlike reflection, which, as a function of understanding, perpetuates division and absolutely fixed opposition, absolute reflection, or speculation, deliberately pursues a totalizing goal. Nevertheless, speculation is not in a relation of opposition to reflection. Speculation simply articulates and develops what reflection, as the activity of dividing, must itself presuppose—the prior wholeness of the divided. This idea of totality whereby absolute reflection measures itself up to the idea proper of philosophy—that is, its claim to completeness—has constituted philosophy since its inception in Greece. The best way to expound the Hegelian concept of totality is to demonstrate that the passage from philosophical reflection to speculation is also a passage from one way of mediating opposites to another. Yet this is also to acknowledge that the difference between reflection and speculation is based on the different wholes they promote. Indeed, philosophical reflection, to the extent that it is philosophical, is also based on this totality. But in contrast to absolute reflection, philosophical reflection only presupposes such a totality, or knows of it only in an instinctive way, whereas speculation throws this regulating idea of philosophy into relief and elaborates on it.

Let us first negatively determine the true synthesis at which speculation aims. An absolute synthesis, says Hegel, "must be more than a mere fitting together . . . for the Absolute is no [mere] juxtaposition."[1] Because it is not supposed to be a whole composed of discrete parts, the mode in which its parts relate to one another cannot be one of reciprocal determination (*Wechselbestimmung, Wechselwirkung*). Such an interplay of mutual conditioning would in no way reduce the opposition of the opposites. Nor is this a whole in which parts are connected in conformity with the law of causality, for such a synthesis would be a "synthesis by way of domination," in which one of the poles would be placed "in subservience to the higher," thus making lordship and bondage absolute, and infinitely extended (p. 138; see also p. 146). A true synthetic totality is not characterized by an infinite or endless process of either mutual determination or subservient domination of the parts. A totality of that sort would only prolong the reign of reflection. But more important, a true totality cannot be constructed from mere products of reflection. Hegel writes in *The Difference,* "Out of products of mere reflection identity cannot construct itself as totality; for they arise through abstraction from the absolute identity which can only relate itself to them immediately through nullification, not through construction" (p.158). As long as the "products of mere reflection" are not related to the absolute identity, as long as they remain pure determinations of understanding, they appear incapable of engendering a true totality. What, then, is a true synthetic totality? While philosophical reflection and its exclusively formal concept of unity are characterized by discontinuity, absolute reflection is based on a demonstration of the continuity of its constituting elements. A true totality is a medium of continuity in which hitherto opposed terms, by being related to the Absolute and by being destroyed in their isolated one-sidedness, are lost in each other. But such a totality is also differentiated in itself, "so that unity and manifold do not supervene each to the other in it; rather they detach themselves from one another within it, and are held together forcefully, as Plato says, by the middle."[2]

Discussing, in *The Difference,* the idea of complete totality in terms of the two sciences of the Absolute—that is, the transcendental science (of Kant and Fichte) and the science of Nature (of Schelling) which have to be reunited within it—Hegel remarks: "Inasmuch as both sciences are sciences of the Absolute and their opposition is real, they are the poles of the indifference [point] and cohere with one another at this point itself; they are themselves the lines which link the pole with the center. The center is itself doubled, however, identity being one, and totality the other, and in this perspective the two sciences appear as the progressive evolution, or self-construction, of identity into totality" (p. 170). Identity and totality are not the same. The identity of opposing poles does not suffice to make a totality. Identity is only one aspect of totality. In order for a totality to be complete, "the claims of separation must be admitted [within the totality itself] just as much as those of identity" (p. 156). For Hegel, absolute totality is the result of a self-construction in which identity turns into totality by maintaining the identical poles' nonidentity. Indeed, as Hegel remarks in *Science of Logic*, "*truth is complete only in the unity of identity with difference*, and hence consists only in this unity." He continues:

When asserting that this identity is imperfect, the perfection one has vaguely in mind is this totality, measured against which the identity is imperfect; but since, on the other hand, identity is rigidly held to be absolutely separate from difference and in this separation is taken to be something essential, valid, true, then the only thing to be seen in these conflicting assertions is the failure to bring together these thoughts, namely, that identity as abstract identity is essential, and that as such it is equally imperfect: the lack of awareness of the negative moment which, in these assertions, identity itself is represented to be.[3]

In order to achieve the continuity that constitutes true totality, totality must, as the substratum, embrace both identity and nonidentity. This is why Hegel makes use, in *The Difference*, of the following formula, which brings together the conflicting thoughts on unity: "the Absolute itself is the identity of identity and non-identity; being opposed and being one are both together in it" (p. 156). With this inclusion of nonidentity, of the negative moment presupposed by identity, the totality encompasses the last logically possible moment without which the passage from identity to totality would not be complete. Totality, then, is the unity of itself and of the disunion that such a unity must presuppose. By including that moment of negativity, no other negative determination remains possible, and the totality is thus complete. Since everything that is in counterposition to something else is also opposed to itself in this developed whole, and thus destroyed in its singularity, everything singular, to the extent that it has standing in the Absolute, is nothing but a point at which "relations" cross. Everything is at once pole, line, and center. To quote again: "Since a duality is now posited, each one of the opposites is opposed to itself and the partition goes on *ad infinitum*. Hence, every part of the subject and every part of the object is itself in the Absolute, an identity of subject and object; every cognition is a truth just as every speck of dust is an organization" (p. 157). A totality in which the poles "are themselves the lines which link the pole with the center" amounts to a medium of mediation, a middle of intersecting lines. In its full exposition, this medium is the very completion of Reason, the ultimate ground of everything singular.[4]

Now, let us elaborate, at least briefly, on a major difference between the concept of totality as employed by Hegel and (the later) Schelling. Although Hegel seems, in *The Difference,* to endorse fully Schelling's idea of totality as an objective subject-object identity, it follows from everything we have seen that, to conform with Hegel's radical critique of the philosophy of reflection, a true synthesis has to be a synthesis of a subjective and objective subject-object, to use his language of that period. Despite the fact that Hegel refers to totality in Schellingian terms as a "point of indifference," he also evokes the "true point of indifference"—that is, a totality that, unlike Schelling's, does not imply the complete annulment or extinction of all opposition (p. 172). For Schelling, the critique of the rigidity of the reflective determinations and the categories of understanding led to their complete dissolution in the categories of Reason, understood as immediate and unmediated intellectual intuition. In Hegel, by contrast, the mediation of the opposites replaces Schelling's originary synthetic unity. Therefore, Hegel's concept of totality contains the nonidentity as well as and apart from the identity of the opposites. He writes in *The Difference:* "In the absolute identity subject and object are suspended, but because they are within the absolute identity they both have standing too. This standing is what makes a knowledge possible; for in knowledge their separation is posited up to a point" (p. 156).

A totality such as Schelling's, which excludes all negativity and has no room for that which is limited, is, according to Hegel's later language, an *abstract* totality. In *Phenomenology of Spirit* he refers to it as the night in which all cows are black. Such a philosophy is satisfied "by simply penetrating to the principle of nullifying all fixed opposition and connecting the limited to the Absolute" (p. 112). The "colorless light" of such an intuition confined to the abstract side of cognition culminates in "the mystic rapture" so familiar to the Romantics. Indeed, Hegel's critique of the abstract totality aims not only at Schelling's philosophy but, in *The Difference,* at Jacobi, and at Schlegel and Novalis as well. By heavily relying on Fichte's notion of a self-positing self, the early Romantics developed a conception of the Absolute in terms of what Walter Benjamin calls the "medium of reflection." Although Schlegel and Novalis were not entirely without pretensions concerning the systematic exposition of their philosophy, they contented themselves with what Hegel calls, in *The Difference,* the "negative side, where everything finite is drowned in the infinite" (p. 156). What Hegel objects to in such an understanding of the Absolute is its lack of internal coherence, and thus the Romantics' failure to achieve an objective totality of knowledge.

Although such an abstract notion of totality could, of course, be made concrete, Hegel claims that, for the Romantics, it is merely "a matter of subjective contingency whether this kind of philosophizing is bound up with the need for a system or not" (p. 156). In other words, Romantic philosophy, although no longer "abstract reasoning," and already a form of overcoming the reflective determinations of understanding, falls back again into the rigid Kantian oppositions by leaving the opposition of the Absolute and the manifold intact, or the object of a (merely) contingent, subjective act of mediation. A philosophy, however, that aims at a radical critique of the metaphysics of reflection cannot be satisfied with the mystic rapture that the all-devouring Absolute of the Romantics invites; it must expound the intrinsic links between the Absolute and its content, and it must try to posit this manifold as internally connected to the Absolute. Yet such internal connection coincides with producing a totality of knowing, that is, a system of science. A "philosophizing that does not construct itself into a system is a constant flight from limitations" (p. 113); true philosophy, according to Hegel, renders the Absolute concrete in the form of the system. Such an exposition of the content of the Absolute, however, cannot remain dependent on a subjective and contingent act, as is the case in Romanticism, since it corresponds to an objective need of the Absolute itself. The system must be understood as the "pure self-exposition" of the absolute totality. Hegel states, "In this self-production of Reason the Absolute shapes itself into an objective totality, which is a whole in itself held fast and complete, having no ground outside itself, but founded by itself in its beginning, middle and end" (p. 113).

The self-production of the Absolute requires, moreover, that "the philosophy of the system and the system itself do . . . coincide" (p. 114), that "the product . . . correspond to the producing" (p. 131), and that "the result of the system . . . return to its beginning" (p. 132). Having failed to mediate these oppositions, Fichte, Schelling, and the Romantics have not escaped the metaphysics of reflection. Only absolute reflection or speculation can be consistent and successful in surmounting the aporias and antinomies of reflection manifest in philosophy from Descartes to Kant.

5

Post-Hegelian Criticism
of Reflexivity

※

Reflection, according to Hegel's critique, is an almost entirely negative concept. As the mode of thinking particular to understanding, it is a force of separation incapable by itself of thinking the unity presupposed by this activity. For the critic of Kantian philosophy—that is, Hegel—everything dependent on the notion of reflection—subjectivity, freedom, transcendentality, and so on—is also affected by the inability of reflection to meet the most fundamental of all philosophical demands, that of unity. In distinction from other representatives of German Idealism and early Romanticism, who also conceived of themselves as followers and critics of the Kantian philosophy of reflection, only Hegel succeeded in overcoming the Kantian dichotomies. Hegel indeed liquefies even the ultimate reflective distinctions left standing by both Fichte and Schelling.

As we have seen, Hegel is critical of the metaphysics of reflection because it leaves the demand for totality unanswered. Hegel's speculative dialectics might be called a first critique of the philosophy of reflection, but not because he opted for an immediate response to the question of unity and totality, thereby relegating reflection with all its problems to the trash heap of thought. Unlike some of the Romantics Hegel does not discard this idea, so fundamental to modernity, but, by historicizing the logical categories constituting reflexivity, he shows reflection to be tied up in a process in which its own aporias are overcome by reflection itself. His critique culminates in a demonstration of reflection's development towards its own sublation. Rooted in the unthought of the metaphysics of reflection—that is, the idea of totality—Hegel's critique is made in the name of a reflection that has overcome its shortcomings: absolute reflection, or speculation, which Hegel opposes to the narrow philosophical concept of reflection. Critical of the metaphysics of reflection and yet containing it insofar as it brings the unthought of the philosophy of reflection to bear on that very concept, absolute reflection represents the fulfillment of reflection, its completion, its coming into its own.

It is important to note that the concept of reflexivity found in contemporary philosophical debates or in the discourse of literary criticism rarely refers to the pre-Kantian or Kantian definition of reflection. Rather, the concept of reflection in contemporary debates, which surfaces in an affirmative or critical manner, is basically indebted to the speculative critique of the metaphysics of reflection. Indeed, what is generally meant by the terms *reflection* and *self-reflection* is either absolute reflection or its Romantic sense—what Benjamin called "the medium of reflection."[1] This implies that the critique of what is called, in contemporary German philosophy, the "theory (or philosophy) of reflection" is either tributary to or critical of the speculative project or of the idea of Romantic absolute reflection. In any case, whatever direction this sort of criticism takes, for historical and systematic reasons, it raises itself, unlike the positivist critique of reflection, to the heights of speculation, which is as we have seen distinguished by its awareness of the problems posed by reflexivity. Yet what is true of the German critique of the philosophy of reflection—namely, its consciousness of the philosophical exigencies of speculation, whether or not Hegel's own solution to the problems of reflexivity are seen to have lost their persuasive power—is even more true of the debate with reflexivity that stretches from Heidegger to Derrida. This debate takes off against the backdrop of Hegel's speculative thought.

Before I embark on a review of both types of criticism, it seems fitting to refine the minimal definition of reflection, outlined at the beginning of Part I. It now appears that this definition, which unites the most important formal movements of reflection, corresponds to the speculative notion of reflection. To recapitulate: The pre-Kantian theory of reflection is characterized by the assumption that the cognitive subject becomes a self-relating subject by making itself an object for itself. The identity that springs forth from such an activity is a result of turning that kind of attention originally directed upon objects back upon the knowing subject itself. This act of throwing the subject of representation back onto itself is the act of reflection. By detaching reflection from human reflection, Kant elevates transcendental reflection to the rank of a constituting principle of all the forms of thinking and experience. Reflexivity thus becomes an essential characteristic of thought itself. Yet Kant's transcendental ego is dominated by the dualism characteristic of reflective metaphysics from Descartes on—the dualism of an active subject and a passive object. Only when reflection is raised to the rank of the Concept or Notion, and thus radically separated from the realm of human self-relation and its attention to objects—in other words, when thought as such becomes the subject of thinking—is the dualism of reflection overcome.

How does Hegel bring about the reflection of the absolute subject, or spirit? The possibility of a sublation of the dualism of reflection becomes a reality only at the moment at which the thesis of an object and the antithesis of a subject can be viewed as partaking in a totality. As we have seen, Hegel's criticism of the metaphysics of reflection is guided by the notion of totality. If reflection is an operation produced *between* a figure and its image in the mirror, *between* a subject and an object, then the poles or extremes of the process of reflection are no longer the essential part of that process but its mean, or the whole of all of the relations of the process between them. The medium in which reflection takes place, this middle which splits into opposed poles and from which they borrow their meaning, becomes the real subject of reflection. This subject, the spirit or Concept, is what, as pure activity, produces both the opposed moments of subjective reflection—the subject and the object—*and* itself as the totality of the medium of reflection. To the extent that this medium gathers into one synthesis the whole of the moments that characterize reflection *and* itself as the mean of these moments, it is the true Subject, absolute reflection. Its achievement is to unite in one whole that which is opposed.

This unity as a developed whole is the radical answer to the *quaestio iuris,* which, with the inception of the idea of reflection in Descartes, was reflection's guiding idea, but which had not yet revealed all of its consequences. In the same way, Hegel's critique of reflection, and his intensification of it to absolute reflection by elevating the major themes of reflection to the level of the Concept or Notion, represents a radical completion of subjectivity, freedom, autonomy, self-certitude and certitude, transcendentality, and so on. The speculative determination of the meaning of these concepts takes place in the development of a philosophy of absolute subjectivity and absolute reflection that breaks away from the theories and philosophies of cognition and knowledge, and from the dualisms with which they are beset: empirical and transcendental experience, apriorism and aposteriorism, subject and object. In overcoming these conceptual dyads, which arise from the kind of positing that characterizes understanding, Hegel's critique of the philosophy of reflection and his development of a philosophy of absolute reflection try to achieve the goal of philosophy itself, the goal of a totality of knowledge, itself free of contradictions, that accounts for all contradictions and oppositions.

Let us consider this totality and its essential constituents one last time. It is a unity of self-relation and Otherness, of immanent reflection and reflection-into-Other. A "metatheory" of reflection of sorts, the theory of absolute reflection restores the immediacy of being that is lost at the moment when immanent reflection severs the subject from the world. This immediacy is reestablished as the movement of the reflection of the antagonistic modes of reflection—that is, reflection-into-Other and reflection-into-self. Absolute reflection—"the movement of reflecting itself into itself," as Hegel remarks in *Phenomenology*[2]—becomes the totality embracing both types of reflection, which thus remain entirely immanent and interior to one another, to the extent that it also reflects itself in the form of the reflection-into-self it now comprises. With this self-inclusion of absolute reflection, which escapes any further reflection, not only is reflection overcome, for it is comprised, but also absolute reflection becomes the ultimate totality of all possible relations, the relation to self included. Because what is reflected within it has lost its power of separation and fixation, it has become, so to speak, a self-relating relation without related poles. It is identical to Reason, or logos; it is Reason in its completion.

To circle back, then, to the minimal definition of reflection, let us add that such a definition must contain, in addition to the three moments already distinguished, the thought of reflection's own reflection in the form of that mode of mirroring that is opposed to objects or images. To achieve the totality of all the movements of reflection, it is not sufficient to point to the dialectics of self and Other which take place between mirror and object. This dialectic is possible only on condition that the mirror of self and Other is itself only a form of absolute reflection. Reflection's reflection requires that reflection be contained within reflection, that mirroring itself include the mirror's mirroring. This can be achieved only by demonstrating that the mirror's mirroring of itself and Other is a still insufficient reflection and that in its fixation, which opens a process of endless self-mirroring, the mirror's mirroring is dependent on a positing by absolute reflection, which at the same time makes this mirroring process an alienated, and thus recuperable, moment of absolute reflection.

Only at this point is the totality of reflection's constitutive features defined. Reflection is completed—that is, inclusive of all its constitutive moments—when it includes itself in that form of reflection which is reflection of self in opposition to reflection of Other.

In the aftermath of Hegel's speculative overhauling of the metaphysics of reflection, all rigorous debate with reflection has been a debate with this concept of reflection, in which self-reflection is also the reflection of that sort of self-reflection that still faces objects. But since Hegel's critique of the philosophy of reflection addresses the demand that characterizes philosophy as philosophy, the demand for unity or totality, a debate with his speculative concept of reflection is a debate not only about the fundamental themes of modern philosophy—subjectivity, freedom, autonomy, transcendentality—but also about the themes constituting the very project of philosophy since its inception in Greece. Indeed, when Hegel subjected the most important methodological concept of modern philosophy, as well as the themes coeval with the birth of this concept, to his speculative critique, he measured the achievements of reflection against the demand for a totalizing understanding of thought and being, a demand as old as philosophy itself. Any rigorous critique of reflexivity must face this challenge to values, without which there would be no such thing as a discourse of philosophy, ethics, or politics.

But are these not the difficulties faced by any critique of reflection and reflexivity? Such a critique must recognize that reflection is an unsurpassed principle of philosophy for which naive resistance is certainly no match. This is even more true of absolute reflection. The traditional arguments against absolute reflection or speculation do not seriously affect such reflection, even where one would be inclined to acknowledge that some of its historical consequences have been aberrant. Total dialectical mediation as it characterizes absolute reflection, is, in principle, of unequaled superiority. As a result of this logical preeminence, all polemics against it would seem to be without ground. Absolute reflection, as articulated in the greater *Logic*, for instance, anticipates all the logically possible adverse stands and integrates them as moments within its speculative totality. Gadamer expresses this very well in *Truth and Method:* "The Archimedean point from where Hegel's philosophy could be toppled can never be found through reflection. This is precisely the formal quality of reflective philosophy, that there cannot be a position that is not drawn into the reflective movement of consciousness coming to itself."[3] This superiority of absolute reflection is one of principle. It cannot be challenged by the aberrational consequences to which it has led, and which are to a great extent responsible for bringing speculation into discredit. Nor can absolute reflection's superiority be challenged by a demonstration of its imperfections or alleged indefensibilities, as, for example, in Hegel's *Phenomenology, Science of Logic,* or *Encyclopedia.* Such deficiencies become manifest if one attempts to penetrate the microstructures of the argumentation that develops absolute reflection. Subjected to close scrutiny, the passage from one logical moment to another often appears imprecise. But, as Dieter Henrich has most convincingly demonstrated, "the deficiencies in the development . . . are not harmful to the firmness or soundness of the architecture of the original draft [of Hegel's *Science of Logic*] nor as far as the fundamentally important outlines of its execution are concerned."[4] What Henrich has been able to show in a most persuasive manner, in what he calls "corrections" or "reconstructions" of Hegelian argumentation, is that Hegel in fact had all the means necessary to make his arguments logically faultless, and that one can supply certain weak microstructures with more powerful reasonings that remain entirely within the spirit of Hegelian thought.[5] These deficiencies, consequently, have no impact on the actual concept of absolute reflection. If it is true, as Henrich contends, that the degree of perfection that Hegel actually achieved in his major work diverges quite a bit from the ideal, but that it can nevertheless be measured up to Hegel's own exigencies, then the work's imperfection can be accounted for, as Henrich shows, by the discrepancy between Hegel's virtuosity in developing logical relations and his methodological reflections on this development.

Where, then, does this leave us with regard to the problem of absolute reflection? If absolute reflection cannot be radically put into question by reflection itself, because all possible points of criticism are already moments of reflection, and if actual deficiencies of the system of absolute reflection pale into insignificance when compared to its potential elaboration, does this mean that reflection cannot be critically evaluated, and that Hegel's speculative critique and interpretation of reflection are the only ones possible? Does the success of the principle of absolute reflection close off all further questioning?

Let us step back for a moment into history. As early as Plato, reflection, in the sense of self-reflection, has been subject to criticism. In the dialogue *Charmides,* a part of Plato's critique of the Sophists, Socrates makes the at first surprising move of declaring that *sophrosyne* cannot exist because it is a contradictory notion.[6] *Sophrosyne,* an ideal second to none in importance for the Greeks, was held to be a science or knowledge distinct from all other knowledge since, compared to other sciences, which are sciences only of something else, *sophrosyne* was a science both of other sciences and of itself. *Sophrosyne*—wisdom, temperance—corresponds essentially to self-knowledge. But Socrates' argumentation shows that a relation to self is altogether inadmissible, and hardly credible, because it is impossible for a property of something to relate to itself. One example is the impossibility of a seeing that would be the seeing of itself. Socrates asks Critias: "Suppose that there is a kind of vision which is not like the ordinary vision, but a vision of itself and of other sorts of vision, and of the defect of them, which in seeing sees no color, but only itself and other sorts of vision. Do you think that there is such a kind of vision? Certainly not."[7] For the same reason, Socrates believes a knowledge of knowledge—that is, a knowledge that would not relate to anything in particular—to be impossible. He even goes so far as to question the use of this knowledge of knowledge if it were to exist, a use he declares null because such knowledge would be empty knowledge, relating to nothing. Indeed, if knowledge is always relational, knowledge of knowledge would have to be knowledge of knowledge of, a structure which, epistemologically speaking, is void.

Socrates' demonstration is surprising at first because it seems to contradict other passages in Plato in which a *dynamis* is shown to relate not only to what its power is the power of but also to itself. These passages, however, concede self-relationality only to the soul, which, as the *primum movens* of the cosmos, is determined by the property of self-movement, and has little in common with what is understood by soul in modern philosophy.[8] Consequently, although Plato recognizes a self-relationality of the soul, or of divine being, he denies such a possibility to the knowledge of knowledge. Indeed, instead of anticipating the Cartesian self-relationality of reflexivity, *sophrosyne,* in the context of *Charmides,* is at best a knowledge of good and evil. Socrates' arguments, therefore, do not impinge on the possibility of conceiving of absolute reflection, in particular since, on other occasions, he recognizes self-relationality as that which constitutes the soul.[9] As a matter of fact, Socrates' questioning of *sophrosyne,* by presupposing the possibility of the self-relationality of the soul, is a kind of criticism that would not be possible without the higher form of a *dynamis* by which the soul relates to itself. It is in this sense that we understand Socrates' critique of the knowledge of knowledge to be implicitly speculative. Socrates' interrogation of the reflexivity of *sophrosyne*, by implying that reflection is truly possible only in the form of the self-movement of the soul, leads us directly back to Hegel's speculative correction of the contradictions of reflection in absolute reflection. In contrast to skeptical or empirical criticism of reflexivity, which concludes from the aporetic nature of self-reflection its thorough impossibility, the sort of criticism Plato directs against self-reflection—which informs many later objections to the philosophy of reflection, Hegel's objections included—is, in essence, speculative. It points towards the aporias of self-reflection in the name of a higher form of self-reflection.

It is important to recognize that where the criticism of reflection is not simply skeptical, it is overtly or latently speculative. But what if all genuine skepticism must also presuppose what it puts into question? To outline an answer to this question, we must first establish the nature of the authentic criticism that skepticism levels against reflection. Sextus Empiricus formulates these objections in the following passage:

For if the mind apprehends itself, either it as a whole will apprehend itself, or it will do so not as a whole but employing for the purpose a part of itself. Now it will not be able as a whole to apprehend itself. For if as a whole it apprehends itself, it will be as a whole apprehension and apprehending, and, the apprehending subject being the whole, the apprehended object will no longer be anything; but it is a thing most irrational that the apprehending subject should exist while the object of the apprehension does not exist. Nor, in fact, can the mind employ for this purpose a part of itself. For how does the part itself apprehend itself? If as a whole, the object thought will be nothing; while if with a part, how will that part in turn discern itself? And so on to infinity.[10]

The aporia is obvious: either reason knows itself as Other, and this means that it does not know itself, or it becomes caught in a never-ending process of self-approximation.

Yet these contradictions are not final obstacles to elaborating the self-reflection of the Absolute, because they can be seen to be moments in self-knowledge as a process. The Other, which the self can only know itself as, thus becomes the result of a self-alienation of the self before it recognizes this Other as itself again. The skeptical contradictions in this perspective are seen *sub speciae aeterni,* that is, with regard to the unity they presuppose. Certainly one cannot refute this skeptical doubt concerning the possibility of self-knowledge or self-reflection in the same way that one refutes skepticism's calling into question the epistemological signification of reflection in general. Indeed in refuting self-knowledge, it does not presuppose what it is doubtful about in the same way that it must presuppose the signification of reflection when putting, in a reflective manner, reflection into question. But it remains to be seen whether the skeptical evidence concerning the impossibility of self-knowledge must not, in the last resort, also be grounded in the evidence of a self-knowing subject. Hegel's speculative criticism, as we have seen, displaces the question of the aporias by admitting that they can certainly not be solved on the level of psychological and epistemological self-reflection, but only on the higher level of absolute knowing. Such a totality of the Notion or Concept is something that the skeptical argument, at least from a speculative perspective, must presuppose, since it serves as the unity in the light of which its aporetic demonstrations make sense in the first place. The same is true of a variety of other objections to the possibility of self-reflection. We shall consider several of these objections in a discussion of the critique of the philosophy of reflection as it has been developed in contemporary German philosophy.

This critique branches out into two different sets of arguments. The first set is heavily indebted to Russell and Whitehead's demonstration of the formal antinomies that characterize the idea of self-reference or reflexiveness, as well as to Wittgenstein's theory of types. Among this set of objections is Dieter Henrich's demonstration of the inevitably circular construction of self-reflection. This type of argument was first raised by Fichte's disciple Friedrich Herbart, whose polemic against his master demonstrated not the impossibility of self-consciousness but the inadequacy of the model of self-representation to describe it. Henrich follows this line of thought inasmuch as his whole argumentation concerning self-reflection is a function of his desire to show that self-reflection is an inappropriate tool for explaining self-consciousness. Yet, is that not precisely what a theory of reflection hopes to achieve?

With basically two arguments, Henrich demonstrates the circularity of all the forms of the theory of reflection up to Kant, including transcendental reflection. He borrows his first argument from Fichte, whom he considers to be the first to have felt the inadequacy of the theory of reflection to cope with the problem of self-consciousness. This argument may be summarized as follows: The theory of self-reflection contends that a Subject-Self comes to know itself when it turns its reflection upon itself. Yet, since one can speak of a Subject-Self only where there is already self-consciousness, the theory of reflection presupposes what it hopes to explain. Indeed, the act of reflecting must be the act of a self in possession of itself. Henrich writes in "Fichte's Original Insight": "Thus anyone who sets reflection into motion must himself already be both the knower and the known. The subject of reflection on its own thereby satisfies the whole equation 'I = I.' Yet, reflection alone was supposed to bring about this equation."[11] From this the corollary follows that reflection of the self will never produce self-consciousness if that self is something other than a self-consciousness. "If the Subject-Self is not the Self, then neither can the Self, of which we come to have knowledge, that is the Object-Self, ever be identical with it."[12] In short, a theory of reflection that pretends to explain the origin of self-consciousness must presuppose what it is supposed to explain. If self-reflection is to lead to self-consciousness, the reflected self must necessarily already be conscious of itself. At best, a theory of reflection can account for an explicit self-experience of a self, but it is unable to explain the self-knowledge of a knowing subjectivity. Compared to this primordial phenomenon, reflection is only a secondary phenomenon.[13]

Henrich's second objection takes off from the theory that reflection assumes that the self-knowledge of a subject originates in an act of self-reversion. Yet in order for such self-knowledge to be possible, the subject must know *in advance* that the object reflected is its own self, identical with itself. It is just that identity—that is, the knowledge that the object turned upon in reflection is oneself—that the theory of reflection is supposed to account for. Henrich writes: "But how can self-consciousness know that it has grasped itself, if an Object-Self had come about only via the Self's act of reflection? Obviously it can know this only if it already knew itself before. For only on the basis of previous knowledge is it possible for self-consciousness to say: 'What I am grasping is I myself.' But, if it already knows itself, then it already knows that 'I = I.' "[14] This second objection reaches the same conclusion as the first: the theory of reflection already presupposes the solution of the problem it sets out to explain. The theory of reflection is based on a *petitio principii*.

Now, what is important here is that Henrich's critical arguments concerning the circularity of reflection, as well as his confining reflection's epistemological significance to a secondary phenomenon, do not at all discredit self-consciousness itself. Self-reflection only seems an inadequate tool with which to think self-consciousness proper. As a matter of fact, the attempt to exhibit reflection's antinomical properties is grounded in the assumption of a primordial identity of self-consciousness. It is in the very name of self-consciousness that

Henrich's whole argument takes place, especially since he shows that the theories of reflection presuppose, in their very failure, such an originary self-identity. It is this intimacy with oneself—that is, this intimate knowledge of oneself, as Henrich calls it—that makes the secondary, reflexive mode of self-relation possible, for this secondary mode is itself derivative, and cannot serve as its own origin.[15] In "Fichte's Original Insight," he writes: "This primordial selfhood first allows a Self to work itself free from its connection with the world and to grasp itself explicitly as what it must have been previously, namely, knowledge that what it is, is knowing subjectivity. The possibility of reflection must be understood on the basis of this primordial essence of the Self."[16]

Despite its prereflexive connotations, which bring it near to Husserl's and Heidegger's attempts to circumvent radically the *regressus ad infinitum* caused by the idea of self-relation, which I discuss later in this chapter, such a notion of the original identity of selfhood, based on an intimacy with oneself and presupposed by self-reflection, is perhaps, with its insistence on genuine identity and totality, the major theorem of speculative philosophy. Henrich seeks to conceptualize this originary identity in the inevitably paradoxical terms of "an (implicitly) self-less consciousness of self," precisely to avoid the circularity of reflexive theories.[17] Primordial selfhood is to be thought of as a nonreflexive identity.[18] Thus, although Henrich's critique of the theories of reflection cannot be called speculative in the sense of an attempt to solve the aporias of reflection by absolutizing reflexivity, it is nonetheless an attempt to solve these aporias by deducing reflection from an original totality of which it would be a secondary mode. Henrich does not explain the nature of the nonreflexive relation which constitutes the fundamental fact of such an original identity. Thus, as long as this nonreflective totality is not expounded explicitly, its connotation of identity and totality brings it near to what Hegel calls a speculative germ. Although a nonreflective totality, this original identity is, with respect to reflection, in a relation of constitution and derivation similar to that between absolute reflection and the sphere of essential reflection. In short, Henrich's critique of reflection—a critique that seeks not to rid itself of consciousness or the subject, but rather to think such phenomena by avoiding the classical aporias of thought—abandons reflection on the ground of arguments that are basically skeptical. Yet he does so to the benefit of a different and, because it avoids the antinomies of thought, higher mode of relation to self. Although this higher mode of identity to self, of a selfless consciousness of self, would not coincide with what the Idealists called "intellectual intuition," the critique is indubitably speculative in nature.

The same observations can be made in the case of Ulrich Pothast's attempt to come to grips with the aporias of self-relation conceptualized reflexively. By making use of the tools developed by analytical philosophy, Pothast shows, even more clearly than Henrich, that the aporias that result from the attempt to think consciousness with the help of concepts of reflexivity are analogous to the antinomies of logic. Not only does a relation of reflexive turning upon oneself lead to an infinite regress, but it is also semantically void. What is important for us is what follows from such a basically skeptical and even empiricist approach to the problem of reflection. Toward the end of his study, Pothast remarks that his critique does not, for principal reasons, exclude all turning backward of attention. Self-reflection is possible in the sense of an attentional experience; but this is not to be conceived as self-perception, that is, in terms of cognitive self-relation. As Pothast has demonstrated with great accuracy, the major aporias that haunt the reflexive model of consciousness are due to a projection of analogies of perception onto psychic relations. Because consciousness is thus interpreted in terms of spatiality, making self-relation a function of a prior dichotomy of subject and object (the subject as object), it is logically impossible to avoid the *regressus ad libitum*. Yet, says Pothast, such an interpretation is illegitimate, because within consciousness there are no perceptions properly speaking. If self-reflection as attentional experience, in short consciousness, is thus to be thought without contradiction, consciousness cannot be a (reflexive) self-relation. As Pothast puts it, a bit ambiguously, it can only be thought of as "an entirely 'objective' process, in the sense that it is not accompanied by a knowing self-relation at any moment." Consciousness becomes, in short, a predicate, or a propriety that refuses all further analysis.[19]

At this point one may object that there is no reason to view a critical approach such as Pothast's as implicitly speculative. Yet Pothast links the concept of consciousness, as a predicate developed in the process of what he understands as a destruction of the traditional philosophical theories of subjectivity, to one area of that tradition which has become questionable in almost every regard, and which he wants to defend against any further attempts at destruction. This issue is nothing less than the synthetic unity of apperception. Although Pothast does not want to understand this originary unity, as did Kant, as the highest point in the sense of a deduction, and although he claims that it need not always already be inhabited by a representation of its own self nor be composed synthetically of discrete and singular things, he holds that "probably, it alone explains how a being can develop a structure as differentiated and as far removed from its initial nature as a happening, as the structure of our 'knowing.' "[20] The idea of a synthetic unity of apperception is not simply, in Pothast's argument, a piece of the tradition to be saved; the entirety of Pothast's reasoning takes place in its name. Yet, like intellectual intuition, the idea of an originary unity of consciousness is a speculative germ, and thus Pothast's skeptical arguments against reflection, like Henrich's, appear to be functions of a speculative understanding of philosophy. This remains the case even if speculation is no longer understood as the reflection of reflection. Indeed, Henrich's and Pothast's discussions of the aporias of reflection suggest a non-Hegelian mode of speculation, in which the demand for unity and deduction is to be achieved on nonreflective grounds.

The second type of criticism of reflexivity proceeds from the assumption that reflexivity is not to be relinquished but must be saved by reflection itself. Even though Hegel's reflection of reflection is not itself sufficient to overcome all the problems inherent in reflection, it is nonetheless an explicitly speculative approach to the aporias of reflection. To begin, let us turn to another aporia, this time concerning the self-engenderment, by and through itself, of the absolute subject. This aporia has been pointed out by Walter Schulz in his study entitled *Das Problem der Absoluten Reflexion*. It affects the very possibility of absolute reflection's achieving a grounding function, which is the purpose for which it was developed in the first place. Paradoxically, because this grounding function of absolute reflection (of self-consciousness, of the self-positing Self, Reason, Spirit) is of prevailing importance to thought, its very possibility is never examined as such within the tradition. According to Schulz, the aporia is that absolute reflection, although it is supposed to function as the principle of a transparent construction of what is, cannot be conceived in itself, since, according to its nature, it must not be derived from anything else. But if absolute reflection cannot be fixed, cannot possibly be conceived, because it is in itself a continuous self-transgression that endlessly presupposes its own self-positing, then it cannot serve as a grounding principle. Ungraspable because it escapes all fixation, it cannot serve as the ground of all that is. Schulz writes: "Absolute reflection is indeed superior to mundane beings, but this superiority exists only if one accepts the Absolute to be what it is, that is, the principle that repeatedly and continuously transgresses itself, and whose essence thought cannot, in truth, hope to think in a satisfactory manner."[21]

In addition, Schulz points out that such an Absolute, as the ground of all being, also undercuts the possibility of deducing being from it, since such a deduction would equal a limitation of the Absolute, and would indeed cancel out the privileged status of absolute reflection as a principle:

One who posits a limitation, with respect to the world, in the Absolute as the true beginning is not only incapable, as Kant has already demonstrated in the antithesis of the third antinomy, of rendering this step toward limitation intelligible but, above all, he contradicts the pure thought of the principle which—because absolutely unconditional—cannot even be subjected to the form of self-limitation. Indeed, self-limitation hides the fact of the present world, and it is this fact which calls for self-limitation as the restriction of the Absolute. But what this means is that the insights that the absolute principle cannot be made into what is conditioned by that principle, *and* that being cannot be derived from it, belong together.[22]

This awareness of the aporetic nature of the concept of absolute reflection as a grounding principle leads Schulz to criticize reflection's claim to absoluteness without, however, opting for the polar opposite of reflection, for the immediate, or so-called reality. Schulz wants to contain the idealist gesture that brings about the absolute self-positing of reflection as the principle of all things, while at the same time keeping the antithetical anthropological option in check, since the latter is as metaphysical as that which it attempts to dislocate. Schulz writes, "Neither absolute reflection nor an unreflected being, but reflection as the self's confrontation with what is, makes the essence of man."[23]

Yet, in describing absolute reflection in the absolute fashion mentioned earlier, as a principle of all beings yet so absolute that it is entirely beyond comprehension, Schulz merely summarizes a position of speculative thought that was held by Schelling, whose Romantic and abstract tendencies Hegel had radically criticized in the preface to *Phenomenology*. Hegel was concerned with Schulz's attempt to overcome the unhappy choice between absolute reflection and anthropological immediacy. Hegel's own notion of absolute reflection, which, as we have seen, avoids the aporias Schulz has pointed out by understanding and developing the Notion or Concept as the concrete totality of all the logically possible relations between the abstract and the particular, is precisely that kind of dialogue between the self and what is, between the ego and being, that Schulz promotes. The "critical reduction" of Idealism that he proposes is nothing short of what Hegel has in mind in *Science of Logic,* where he develops his concept of absolute reflection. Like Schulz, Hegel was unwilling to consider the unity preceding the dissension in question as a state of unity that "really" and "actually" precedes the given state as its metaphysically original beginning. Hegel thought that the totality of the possible relations between polar oppositions are immanent in them. If there is any difference between Hegel's critical account and speculative appraisal of the aporias of reflection, and that of Schulz, it is that for Schulz, the dialogue seems to be an open debate, with no internal boundaries. This is to say that although Schulz's critique of the aporias of absolute reflection is in essential agreement with the mediating speculative solution of these contradictions, it is also critical of the subjectivity constituting the modern metaphysical solution of that essentially speculative and philosophical problem. In other words, while Schulz's critical account of the aporias of reflection avoids the pitfalls of a philosophy of immediacy, or philosophical anthropology, it is nonetheless very much a speculative account, in a Hegelian sense, yet negatively so.

Any attempt to challenge absolute reflection through some notion of immediacy is bound to fail. For instance, the reproachful argument that immediate perception dissipates when reflected upon, an argument that ascribes, in Hegel's words, "everything bad to reflection generally, regarding it and all its works as the polar opposite and hereditary foe of the absolute method of philosophizing," disregards the fact that such a reflection, which starts with something alien to it, is what Hegel called external reflection, and thus one moment in the dialectics of reflection, which develops into absolute reflection where that dualism is superseded.[24] It becomes obvious that the insistence on the immediate, since it is not itself an immediate kind of relating, always already refutes itself. Indeed, insisting on the immediate is itself a reflective act. Thus, even this sort of naive criticism of reflection is latently speculative, because it admits as its unthought premise what it tries to put into question: reflection itself. Let me emphasize, then, that it appears impossible to bypass the Hegelian speculative solution to the difficulties of absolute reflection. If one is to address the principal deficiencies of the theories of subjectivity, of consciousness and self-consciousness—that is, of reflection—recourse to Hegel's speculative and dialectical solution is unavoidable, not only for all post-Hegelian theories of reflection, as Konrad Cramer strongly suggests, but for the pre-Hegelian attempts to cope with this problem as well.[25] As Cramer notes, "The systematic place in which, and in which alone, the possibility opens up of avoiding the fundamental deficiencies of the theory of reflection as it concerns self-consciousness as well as the embarrassed and meaningless response by the thesis of immediacy, is a science of pure meanings that proceeds according to the dialectical method."[26]

As we have seen, this is implicitly the case with the sort of criticism that makes reference to skeptical arguments concerning the aporetic nature of reflection. It is all the more the case for those attempts that aim at saving reflection by trying to assign it a proper function, such as constituting what Schulz calls the dialogue between the self and the world. It is also necessarily the case with all attempts to overcome the difficulties in thinking reflection by reflection as a method itself. Yet it would be erroneous to believe that the inevitable pathway through Hegel means that one has no choice but to accept the Hegelian solution. It is to affirm, for the moment only, and foremost, that all criticism of reflection, all attempts to come to grips with what has traditionally been viewed as reflection's aporetic structure, must take its standards from the Hegelian project, and second, must, whatever its answer to these problems may be, measure up to the speculative solution given by Hegel. This means that no critique of reflection, or, for that matter, of absolute reflection, can legitimately try simply to destroy reflection, or to declare it, as did the logical positivists, null and void. Turning to Hegel prompts us to give sharpened attention to problems unthought of in reflection and in the speculative solution as well. This sort of problematic is an intraphilosophical demand and calls for a radical deepening of the reflection of reflection. Yet, as we shall see in the next chapter, an entirely different approach to the problem of reflection is possible. It is an approach that takes the Hegelian solution most seriously and is highly conscious of the philosophical exigencies translated into the speculative overcoming of the deficiencies of reflection. This particular approach seeks to account for reflection *and* absolute reflection from "presuppositions" of both that traditional philosophical thought has not found it necessary to thematize.

Exorcising reflexivity from the discourse of philosophy through positivistic or analytic arguments could only be a short-lived and short-sighted way of dealing with the problem of reflection. Russell and Whitehead's phobia of what Russell termed the paradoxes of reflexivity—that is, of the semantic and logico-mathematical conflicts that result from propositions that speak of themselves, from predicates that apply to themselves, or from classes that contain themselves— led to the banning of the very concept of reflexivity from much of the philosophy to which they gave rise. But the "pseudoproblems" they had hoped to eliminate by strictly prohibiting the use of linguistic reflexivity soon crept back, disguised by a new terminology, into the discourse of analytic philosophy. Thus, Austin's so-called revolution of analytic philosophy amounts to nothing more nor less than the surreptitious reintroduction of the problem of reflection in order to solve the problems left in the wake of logical positivism. His revolution consisted of hinging the entire representational function of language, with which Russell and Whitehead were exclusively concerned, on a constituting self-reflexivity of the linguistic act. To speak of the "performative function" of speech acts is to apply a new word to a very old problem.

Before turning to a discussion of the type of criticism of reflexivity that I characterized as dealing with certain unthought "presuppositions" of reflection, let me mention briefly two attempts to cope with the problem of reflection and absolute reflection, which, in spite of being inspired by the analytic perspective in philosophy, do not altogether sacrifice the philosophically fundamental aspects of that problem.

The first concerns Ernst Tugendhat's critical appraisal of the aporias of reflection as pointed out by Henrich and Pothast. Tugendhat argues that these aporias, and the impossibility of solving them, are a result of the absurd starting point that informs traditional theories of reflection. Following Henrich's and Pothast's analyses, Tugendhat argues that the following three models animate these theories: (1) the ontological model of a substance and its modifications, a model deeply rooted in the subject-predicate structure of (ordinary) language; (2) the subject-object relation, which characterizes consciousness as a representational structure, with the result that self-reflection is understood as a relation in which the subject turns upon itself as upon an object; and (3) the assumption that all immediate knowledge is rooted in perception, and that self-reflection must therefore be understood as inner self-perception.[27] The interplay of these three models required by the idea of self-consciousness, self-reflection, and absolute reflection as an identity of the knower and what is known, of the subject and itself as object is, says Tugendhat, a priori impossible. In addition, to speak of immediate identification as a cognitive achievement is sheer nonsense. Indeed, if the three models can, under no circumstances, produce self-consciousness, and if, moreover, identity cannot be taken as knowledge, it is because for Tugendhat and the analytic tradition he represents, knowledge and truth can only be propositional, and are thus incommensurable with any form of self-identification. He concludes that "a structure of the form 'I know myself' is in itself impossible and contradicts the very meaning of 'knowing.' "[28] Yet it does not follow from all this that self-consciousness itself would be an impossibility. On the contrary, Tugendhat accuses Henrich of disposing of self-consciousness, despite the fact that Henrich's regress from self-consciousness to consciousness is a step toward the deduction of self-consciousness as a secondary phenomenon from what he calls "selfless consciousness of self." Instead of relinquishing self-consciousness, Tugendhat intends to give an analytic account of what he calls "self-less consciousness of self." Instead of relinquishing self-consciousness, Tugendhat intends to give an analytic account of endhat concedes, is entirely linguistic. It is grounded in the immediate knowledge one has *of having* certain states. It is a knowledge not of oneself or of one's states in themselves but only a knowledge that one has those states. Tugendhat contends that this kind of self-consciousness can be thought without aporias, since its concept can be elaborated without the three models that inform traditional theories of self-reflection.

It is not my intention to discuss in detail Tugendhat's theory of epistemic or theoretical self-consciousness, or to ponder its speculative echoes. What I want to stress here is that the theoretical ascetism that springs from confining oneself to linguistic and propositional truth is self-defeating. By eliminating altogether the ontological dimension of self-identity in self-consciousness (and, for that matter, in absolute reflection), one deprives oneself of the possibility of thinking the very foundations of propositional knowledge and truth, as well as of the very idea of epistemic self-consciousness. The very possibility of propositional truth requires that kind of immediate identification Tugendhat rejects as contradictory to all cognitive achievement proper. Without the presupposition of ontological or formal-ontological identity of being and thought, of subject and object, of the knower and what is known, there is no ground for any propositional attribution whatsoever. To reject the concept of self-reflection or absolute reflection on the basis that it leads to contradictions is precisely to reject that kind of necessary ground. Since one cannot abandon such a ground without hesitation, one must embark on a critical inquiry into the nature of that ground, an inquiry capable of accounting for the aporetic structure of the ultimate principle, without necessarily yielding to the Hegelian solution of these aporias.

This is what Herbert Schnädelbach seems to have achieved in his superb study *Reflexion und Diskurs, Fragen einer Logik der Philosophie*. While contending that the problems affecting traditional theories of reflection are rooted in their "mentalistic" terminology, and thus subject to the danger of psychologism and solipsism, Schnädelbach embarks on a new explication of the concept of reflection by translating the phenomenon of reflection into linguistic terminology while at the same time conserving the full scope and depth of the traditional problem of reflection. Schnädelbach's attempt to reformulate the traditional problem of reflection linguistically does not consist of confounding it with metacommunication. If reflection were to be translated into metacommunication, one would miss the specificity of reflection while at the same time projecting on it a number of unsolvable problems that beset the theory of metalanguages. Schnädelbach writes: "Merely metalinguistic speech is . . . *per definitionem* nonreflexive. The attempt to grasp its constituting rules in a metatheoretical fashion leads to the well-known endless hierarchy of metalanguages, in which reflexivity has no place."[29] In order to translate the traditional problem of reflection into linguistics, Schnädelbach chooses a modified version of Habermas's pragmatic theory of discourse, in which the reflective structure of discursive modes of thematizing does not entail an endless progression of superimposed levels of speech. What Habermas, and even more so Schnädelbach, understand by discourse is precisely a language game which is simultaneously a process of communication and metacommunication. On the historical premise that reflection has been the major methodological concept of philosophy since Descartes—the very means by which philosophy must seek to ground itself as philosophy—this characterization of philosophical reflection as discourse leads Schnädelbach to call for the development of a philosophy of philosophy which "seeks to clarify the conditions of the *logon didonai* in philosophy and to secure them from a normative point of view."[30] With this theory of discourse, Schnädelbach reestablishes reflection as the medium of self-foundation of philosophy. He succeeds while warding off the pitfalls of mentalism that affect the traditional concept of reflection, in fully reinstating this notion to its speculative heights and to its role as a principle free of the aporias its critics have pointed out. Schnädelbach's reformulation of the problem of reflection is a most persuasive demonstration that within traditional philosophy, and within its rules and standards for an ultimate overcoming of contradictions, such a solution can be satisfactorily reached.

6

Beyond Reflection:
the Interlacings of Heterology

※

Up to this point I have discussed a mode of dealing with the aporias of reflection that still seems to prevail, in which a return to Hegel's speculative thought is seen as the only way to come to grips with the shortcomings of subjectivity. Let us now turn to a different approach to the problems of self-consciousness and, *mutatis mutandis,* absolute reflection. It is an approach that recognizes the previous one as philosophically well founded, and recognizes as well the logical superiority of speculative thought over all attempts to criticize it in a reflexive mode from a position erroneously considered to be outside it. But this approach also grants the possibility that the aporias of reflection, at least as far as the horizon of expectation of philosophy is concerned, are susceptible of being successfully overcome in absolute reflection, or in a modified speculative theory of discourse. Whether or not these would be *definite* solutions is not really the question. Such an approach concedes that, within the limits of the standards of philosophical problem solving, a common ground capable of superseding aporetical propositions can be found. This does not, of course, imply that success is taken for granted or left unquestioned. On the contrary, I shall question the very successfulness of successful philosophical solutions to the aporias of reflection. If Aristotle, discussing form as primary being, could state that to ask why something is itself *(ti auto estin auto)* is to inquire into nothing or not to inquire in the first place, then one can just as easily contend that to question the success of the speculative solutions to reflexivity is not to question at all.[1] From a traditional philosophical perspective, an approach of this sort makes no sense. Indeed, as we shall see, the approach I shall be concerned with escapes the norms and expectations classically associated with the discourse of philosophy. It is an approach that is attentative to a set of what one could call "presuppositions," "pre-positions," or better yet "structures," which inform, without philosophy's knowledge, its treatment of the problem of the aporetic nature of reflection and its possibly successful sublation by absolute reflection.

First we must evoke yet another type of criticism directed against the philosophy of reflection, as well as against Hegel's speculative solution, a criticism from which the approach to be presented derives some of its major impulses. When, in the aftermath of Kant's transcendental solution to the problems of rationalism and empiricism, the tradition begun by the Cartesian philosophy of subjectivity experienced a certain dampening, in an effort to avoid the aporias that such a philosophy carries with it, Hegel's radically immanent philosophy emerged as the major challenge to the philosophy of reflection. Yet, although Hegel attempted to overcome the reflexive aporias of the Cartesian and Kantian paradigm of thought through a return to the Greek concepts of being and substance, this return took the form of a total subjectivization of these concepts. For this reason, Hegel's philosophy must be viewed above all as the completion of Cartesian thought. Therefore, although Hegel's immanent and, in his sense, nonreflexive philosophy can be seen as originating the type of criticism on which I shall elaborate, it also elicited this criticism as a reaction to itself.

I do not mean this to be a straightforward historical presentation of the antecedents of the approach now to be discussed, namely, that of Jacques Derrida. Those landmarks can be found in the philosophies of Nietzsche, Dilthey, the later Husserl, and the early Heidegger—in short, in a type of philosophy that cannot comfortably be placed within the usual philosophical classifications. These are philosophies that unwind out of the philosophy of subjectivity. The critique of reflexivity and speculation enacted by these philosophies (which at their best house a philosophically irreducible and radical "empiricism" unlike the philosophical doctrine of empiricism grounded in experience, and which can be easily accommodated by traditional philosophy as its nonphilosophical Other) is mingled with much more traditional themes. And yet new and unwonted motifs also make themselves heard in these philosophies. Take, for instance, Nietzsche's critique of reflection and self-consciousness, which places a *necessary gap* between knowledge, on the one hand, and, on the other, self-cognition. He writes at the beginning of *On the Genealogy of Morals:*

"We are unknown to ourselves, we men of knowledge—and with good reason. We have never sought ourselves—how could it happen that we should ever *find* ourselves? . . . So we are necessarily strangers to ourselves, we do not comprehend ourselves, we *have* to misunderstand ourselves, for us the law 'Each is furthest from himself' applies to all eternity—we are not 'men of Knowledge' with respect to ourselves."[2] The same motif can be said to underlie his "autobiography," in which Nietzsche declares that to become what one is, one must avoid knowing oneself: "Where *nosce te ipsum* would be the recipe for ruin, forgetting oneself, *misunderstanding* oneself, making oneself smaller, narrower, mediocre, become reason itself."[3]

Self-reflection is seen in both cases as a flower of decadence and mundanity, as a phenomenon deriving from a primary state free of self-awareness, with respect to which self-consciousness is a falling away; but it is also seen as the necessary gap between oneself and one's knowledge, which breaks radically with the philosophically consecrated mode of accounting for the knowledge that one claims to possess by grounding it in the self-conscious and publicly accountable subject. Here, self-reflection loses all foundational capacity with respect to knowledge. It is not my purpose to evaluate the extent to which such a turn in interpretation remains indebted to the tradition under attack. I mean rather to emphasize that the noncognitive and nonreflexive state, of which self-knowledge is an alienated product, cannot simply be conceptualized in terms of the irrational, emotional, and intuitive. What Nietzsche and Dilthey thematize as life is something that escapes, at least up to a certain point, the classical opposition of the rational and the irrational. Is it not after all because he called the vital link between understanding and lived experience irrational that Dilthey's concept of life has been greatly misunderstood? In many ways merely a substitute for what Hegel called objective spirit, life, in Dilthey, is essentially the nonreflexive source of reflection and self-reflection. As the source of all reflexivity, it forever escapes reflection. This also explains why life, for Dilthey, lacks the aspect of totality, which is so decisive for all self-reflective entities: "The realm of life, treated as a temporal and causal construction objectified in time, is history. It is a whole which can never be completed."[4] Whether Dilthey can really conceptualize the essential incompleteness of the whole of life is not the point here. What concerns us is only Dilthey's, as well as Nietzsche's, suggestion that life and lived experience—in other words, something of an order other than that of self-consciousness (individual or cultural)—serve as the ground of self-consciousness. Self-consciousness can never hope to encompass that ground, because it is not simply a more true, more fundamental, more essential self-consciousness, such as intellectual intuition, but also because it is incommensurable with all reflexive appropriation. What Dilthey calls life is undoubtedly another name for spirit, counterposed to the isolating and abstract operations of reflective life; but at the same time, it is also *heterogeneous* to that which depends on it for its possibility, without, however, serving merely as what I have hitherto called a ground. The thought of such a *constitutive heterogeneity* of self-reflection and self-consciousness inaugurates the type of criticism to which I refer here.

By drawing on such issues as Brentano's claim that predication is not the essence of judgment; Husserl's critique of the abstract nature of the Cartesian *cogito,* his opening of the stream of experience to inactualities, and his general return from logic to the prepredicative; Scheler's phenomenological analyses; and Jaspers's investigations into the psychology of world views, Heidegger in *Being and Time* powerfully continues this type of criticism of the philosophy of reflection. Let us consider briefly his analyses of the modes of understanding proper to *Dasein,* modes that structurally precede all thematic, propositional, and reflexive cognition. Heidegger's concern in *Being and Time* is to demonstrate that man is never simply a subject relating to objects, that the essence of man does not lie primarily in the subject-object relation. Analyzing the existential structures of *Dasein,* Heidegger comes to assume, on the contrary, that man's relation to the world is constituted, first and foremost, by a disclosure not of objects but of what is ready-to-hand within-the-world *(innerweltlich Zuhandenes),* not to a reflecting subject but to a being characterized as being-in-the-world. This disclosure, which takes place through states-of-minds *(Stimmungen),* is an unconcealing in a primordial sense. It is presupposed by all immanent reflection, which, as a "kind of apprehending which first turns round and then back," can only come upon "experiences" "because the 'there' has already been disclosed in a state-of-mind."[5] The states-of-mind that characterize man primordially, by first disclosing the world as a whole, effect the required opening within which subject-object relations, and hence reflexive operations, can take place. Heidegger characterizes the knowing peculiar to states-of-mind as follows: "This 'knowing' does not first arise from an immanent self-perception, but belongs to the Being of the 'there,' which is essentially understanding" (p. 184). Hence, it is a knowing by the *Dasein* that is not grounded in a subject's relating to itself in the mode of a subject-object relation. It is not a knowing that would arise primarily from a lone subject's self-reflection. To cite again: "In existing, entities sight 'themselves' [sichtet 'sich'] only insofar as they have become transparent to themselves with equal primordiality in those items which are constitutive for their existence: their Being-alongside the world and their Being-with-Others" (p. 187).

Self-reflection, one's relating to oneself in the mode in which a subject relates to an object, presupposes the pre-reflexive transparency of man's viewing "himself" in contemporaneity with the world. The *Dasein*'s self, its identity, cannot be understood as that of a self-knowing, self-conscious being. In *The Basic Problems of Phenomenology,* his lectures at Marburg following the publication of *Being and Time,* Heidegger made this quite clear: "Self-understanding should not be equated formally with a reflected ego-experience."[6] Indeed, *"the associated unveiling of the self"* accompanying the *Dasein*'s relation is not a given "as might be thought in adherence to Kant—in such a way that an 'I think' accompanies all representations and goes along with the acts directed at extant beings, which thus would be a reflective act directed at the first act" (p. 158). In what sense, then, is the self given to itself? Heidegger answers: "The self is there for the Dasein itself without reflection and without inner perception, *before* all reflection. Reflection, in the sense of a turning back, is only a mode of self-*apprehension,* but not the mode of primary self-disclosure" (p. 159). The *Dasein* does not find itself within itself; on the contrary, it finds itself in the things by which it is surrounded in the world of what is ready-to-hand. This also explains why *Dasein*'s self-understanding takes on many different forms in conformity with the things by way of which it encounters itself, and by way of which it is disclosed to itself in its own self. These multiple means of self-understanding cannot be equated with what, since Descartes, has been conceived of as "the ontological constitution of the person, the ego, the subject" (p. 174), in short, as self-consciousness. Self-consciousness and its constituting self-reflection relate to these more primary forms of prereflexive self-disclosure as to their lost foundation. To conclude his development of this subject, Heidegger writes: "We cannot define the Dasein's ontological constitution with the aid of self-consciousness, but, on the contrary, we have to clarify the diverse possibilities of self-understanding by way of an adequately clarified structure of existence" (p. 174).

Heidegger entirely excludes the possibility of making an appropriate theoretical response to the question of existential self-understanding by reflecting on it in terms of a reflexive relation to self. Only by regressing toward the prereflexive structures of understanding characteristic of the *Dasein* as being-in-the-World can one account for primordial self-sighting. Self-consciousness as a self-reflexive state can then also be derived through abstraction from the initial disclosure of the world and the self in state-of-mind.

Even in a brief outline of this other type of criticism of reflexivity, it becomes obvious that the philosophies of Nietzsche, Dilthey, and Heidegger before the *Kehre* are attempts to account for the problem of subjectivity. In this sense, they carry on the philosophy of subjectivity typical of modern philosophy since Descartes. Yet the manner in which these philosophies account for subjectivity is no longer subjective. They are philosophies, in a manner substantially different from that of Hegel, of the "object," the *world*, life, the life-world, and, finally, Being. If Hegel's turn toward the philosophy of being resulted in an absolute subjectivization of being, here, on the contrary, we find that the orientation toward the object, the world, or Being serves to desecrate the concept of the subject. More precisely, these are philosophies of finitude, understood as the radical concretion of the universal and abstract metaphysical concept of subjectivity. Nonetheless, even finite concepts of the subject such as *Dasein,* of self-reflexivity such as *Dasein*'s self-disclosure, of the transcendental such as the existential structures of *Dasein,* of freedom such as the concept of *Sein-können,* and so on, do not radically break with the paradigm of subjectivity. It is true that the traditional problems of reflexivity and self-reflexivity—that is, their constitutional role with regard to the subject and object—are overcome by grounding these modes of knowing in primary and prereflexive modes of disclosure, a solution independent of the question of whether the aporias of reflection have been solved. It is for this reason that Heidegger's circumscription of self-consciousness and self-reflection has justly been considered a relinquishing of the Cartesian opening of the problem of reflection and of the questions to which it is linked. But is Heidegger's concretion of the subject in terms of *Dasein* really as radical a break with the Cartesian paradigm as is believed? That Heidegger borrows all the conceptual tools with which he criticizes reflection, or rather puts it in its proper place, from within the tradition itself is not insignificant, especially in light of the fact that Descartes himself conceived of the *cogito* not merely as the pure act of a reflexive recoiling upon one's thought, but also as a collection of complexes of various and changing spontaneities of consciousness. It is thus not astonishing that Heidegger's exploration of the structures of consciousness in daily life could produce only a more original and primordial concept of re-flection, namely, the *Dasein*'s prereflexive self-understanding. Last but not least, it is Heidegger's insight into the unsatisfactory nature of this handling of the problem of subjectivity and self-consciousness that triggers the *Kehre*—that is, Heidegger's turning away from the analytics of *Dasein* toward the question of Being. With this he begins an entirely new way of questioning the phenomenon of reflection.

Heidegger's theory of self-consciousness is not concerned with the aporias of reflection. Self-consciousness is a mode of self-apprehension in terms of a reflexive subject-object relation. If it is problematic for Heidegger, it is not because such a relation could not be thought without our becoming enmeshed in unsolvable problems. The manner in which the tradition has conceptualized self-consciousness is per-suasive, and Heidegger does not question what was, for philosophers from Descartes to Husserl, a good enough solution in terms of what the philosophical discourse expects of itself. What he objects to are not logical deficiencies in a narrow sense, but rather that these phi-losophies erect only one mode of self-apprehension, and one that is moreover historically limited, as the very essence of man. In *Being and Time* this particular mode of relating to oneself is grounded in the original mode of *Dasein*'s self-disclosure. But by deliberately turning to the question of Being, Heidegger grounds the *Dasein*'s self-under-standing more fundamentally, by making it a function of the history of Being, and the very nature of the things now thematized under the title of Being even more radically displace the traditional problems concerning the aporias or antinomies of reflexivity. Heidegger's later philosophy reaches out under the name of Being toward structures of thought that are not easily recuperable in terms of semantics and that are, indeed, more originary than the classical objects of thought. Instead of synthesizing the manifold, the contradictory, the aporetic into one speculative whole or totality, these structures (such as *Zug, Fuge, Geviert, Unter-Schied,* and so on) serve as path-breaking, breaching traces, according to which the manifold, the contradictory, is laid out (and held together). They offer the primal matrix for the irreducible difference between subject and object constituting the de-rivative mode of that sort of self-apprehension that is self-reflection. These structures are the incommensurable, heterogeneous "beyond" of the aporetic or antinomic, without corresponding to the truly syn-thetic and speculative. From the perspective of Being, therefore, self-reflection, and absolute reflection as well, do not fail simply because

they cannot be properly thought. The structures of Being offer themselves to the confining abstraction that leads to the historical event
of the surge of self-consciousness. These structures account for the
possibility of self-reflection, its aporias, and their speculative solution,
but they also show it to be a reductive figure of the modes in which
relation to self takes place. From the perspective of Being, the synthetic
unity of apperception is itself foregrounded in the structures of Being,
instead of representing a reflexive or speculative solution to the problems of self-reflection. As the opening for any originary self-perception, these structures remain strangely external to it.

By freeing the structural articulations of Being, Heidegger paved
the way for Derrida's even more effective accounting, beyond traditional aporetics and speculation, for the problem of reflexivity. Concerned with demonstrating both the possibility and essential limits—
that is, ultimate impossibility, of self-reflection—Derrida's approach
aims neither to dismantle nor to annul reflection in a skeptical, empiricist, or positivist manner; nor does it aim to solve reflection's
notorious problems in a speculative fashion. Like Heidegger, Derrida
is not concerned with dialectically solving intraphilosophical problems
according to the canonized forms of philosophical procedures.

Since Plato, and especially since Aristotle's *Metaphysics,* the philosophical method has consisted in starting off from difficulties and
conflicting arguments that seem to offer *no way out*—in other words
from *aporias*—and exploring various routes, assuming the features
of a dialectical process, until a way out *(euporia)* is found. The passage
through the hopelessness of aporetic situations or propositions in
search of philosophy's own way constitutes the philosophical *method.*
To relinquish all efforts to master these situations or propositions—
setting aside the problem of the aporetic—is also to relinquish method.
But to put method aside does not necessarily imply that one rambles
arbitrarily. Although Derrida is not interested in (dialectically) finding
the way out of hopeless situations, without of course declaring these
situations unsolvable, like Heidegger, he focuses on an entirely new
set of issues on the margin of the philosophical path that leads from
aporias to their harmonious unity. The manner in which he tackles
the problem of reflexivity thus takes the form of an investigation into
the "pre-suppositions," "pre-positions," or "structures" to which the
exposition of this problem, as well as its eventual speculative solution,
must necessarily yield. It is not easy to define the nature and the status
of what I have called, for better or worse, "pre-suppositions." The
term *pre-supposition* is not to be understood to mean mere assump-

tions that the philosophical discourse would have allowed to pass
without demonstrating their truth. Nor is pre-supposition to be taken
to mean logical presupposition, a necessary truth that is either implicit
or explicit in the philosophical discourse. As far as its ontological
status is concerned, it cannot have the status of an effective actuality,
either real or ideal, beyond the omnipotence of reflection, since both
types of actuality, and actuality itself, are themselves reflexive concepts.

Since, as I have suggested, all new accounts of reflexivity must
measure up to Hegel's speculative and absolute reflection, and since
this is even more the case for the approach that I am outlining (and
which is concerned with the entirety of the argumentive structures
that lead from the aporias to the dialectical fluidization), let us take
as a starting point the methodological directions that Dieter Henrich
has shown to characterize the position of idealist philosophy. Henrich
writes:

(1) The first task of philosophy, from whose solution one obtains the
solution of all its other tasks, is the correct comprehension of the difference
that still breaches the idea of self-relation.
(2) One cannot expect to be able to think a self-relation that would be
the result of a simple difference, or even of an exclusion of all difference.
There is nothing such as an immediate and yet closed self-relation. Real self-
relation includes, on the contrary, the development of the difference that it
contains into a form which is so complex that it can no longer be distinguished
from the totality of what is.[7]

The position of idealist philosophy is to capitalize on the difference
within self-relation at the benefit of a whole for which difference,
rather than irremediably dividing it, becomes, in its speculative layout,
that very whole itself. As Heidegger has pointed out, the insurmount-
able reverse of speculation is a theology of the Absolute.[8] What distinguishes Heidegger's and Derrida's positions from that of idealist
philosophy is primarily their inquiry into what may be called the
difference between identity and difference, between the totality of
what is and the difference that inhabits self-relation. What sounds at
first like a parody of speculative thought is not, however, its negative
counterpart. It is not an inquiry in the service of a greater difference.
What distinguishes the positions is that Heidegger's investigation is
into difference *itself*, into the true *essence* of difference, not into difference that would simply be the same as the whole of Being (let us
not forget that the later Heidegger relinquishes the name of Being)

and that would unite what is set forth within it, whereas Derrida's inquiries are concerned with a difference that is no longer phenom-enologizable, that has no "itself" to itself but that, in its irreducible plurality, ceaselessly differs from itself. In Derrida, this difference links identity based on self-relation to difference, each time in a different manner, and in such a manner that what is held together does not form a whole. Within the network of relations of this difference, wholes can be set out, but because they are inscribed within that difference, they remain forever incomplete. In other words, the difference Derrida is concerned with is a condition of possibility constituting unity and totality and, at the same time, their essential limits.

Both Heidegger's and Derrida's approaches could therefore be viewed as inquiries, in a new sense, into the principles of the ultimate foundation of all possible knowledge. Yet, of the pre-suppositions or structures that both philosophers build upon—structures concerning the passage from difference to identity, from the aporias of self-reflection to absolute reflection, and so forth—Derrida's appear the most remote from the logos of philosophy, which, as a discourse that is an argumentative enterprise within the horizon of totality, must nonetheless, although unwittingly, combine with these pre-suppositions or structures.

As the contemporary neo-Kantian German philosopher Werner Flach has pointed out, all inquiry into the *truly ultimate* principles of the foundation of knowledge is of necessity a "pure heterology." Derrida's philosophy can be viewed as a heterology as well, especially since the structures treated in his writings are, as we have said, strangely extraneous to the discourse of knowledge. But what are we to understand here by heterology? Is Derrida's philosophy a heterology because it would reveal the fundamental grounds of knowing, or rather because the structures it develops are in a relation of a certain alterity to the discourse of philosophy? To give a satisfactory answer to these questions it is necessary first to establish firmly what heterology means in terms of traditional philosophy itself. Toward that end, let us consider the unjustly ignored work of Werner Flach entitled *Negation und Andersheit: Ein Beitrag zur Problematik der Letztimplikation.*[9] Flach's development of heterology is one of the most radical attempts possible within the traditional boundaries of philosophy's thinking of Otherness. This detour through Flach's study, which will reveal a variety of striking resemblances to certain topoi of Derrida's thought, will have the additional advantage of providing the necessary foil against which the radicality of Derrida's heterology can be clearly set off.

It is important to note from the outset that Flach's pure heterology, as an investigation into the final implications of logic, conceives of itself as a critique of Hegel's notion of absolute reflection. Pure heterology, as Flach understands it, is aimed at demonstrating that Hegel's interpretation of synthesis as reflection, or as reflection of reflection, falls short of establishing the ultimate ground for determining thought *(bestimmendes Denken)*. Flach's enterprise elaborates on the structural moments of the absolute relation *(absolutes Verhältnis)*, which, as the principle of thought, cannot be grasped by methodical reflection since, as a principle, it is supposed to account precisely for the nature of reflection. Flach's enterprise is geared toward a more radical understanding of reflection, toward grounding it in an absolute principle whose self-relationality is no longer of the realm of reflexivity. Flach is compelled to follow such a direction because he recognizes that Hegel's determination of the ground of reflection—of the originary synthetic unity—is not accompanied by a determination of that ground as ground. Instead of determining that ground as radically heterogeneous to what, as ground, it is supposed to make possible, Hegel's concept of the reflection of reflection understands ground in the sense of homogeneity, that is, in the sense of what the ground is to account for.

Yet if a ground is to be an absolute ground, it must be heterogeneous. "Pure heterogeneity," Flach notes, "contains nothing less than the thought of the principle, of what can, and can alone be understood by 'principle.' "[9] Through his pure heterology, Flach purports to achieve the goal of establishing the ultimate and radical ground of determining thought. He writes: "The caesura lies in thought itself: with the thinking of the meaning of meaning (total reflection), a heterogeneous sphere of conditions must be at issue that precedes thinking as the thinking of meaning (determinate reflection) and the thinking as the thinking of being (external reflection), as well as the thinking as being (positing reflection). It is the sphere of 'pure heterogeneity' which constitutes itself in itself as the logical beginning" (p. 64). Like both Heidegger's and Derrida's critiques of reflexivity, Flach's heterogeneous and principal conditioning relation of thought, which grounds reflection more radically, does not issue from a debate over the aporetic nature of reflection but is based on a rigorous understanding of what a ground is supposed to achieve. Since Flach's enterprise does not start as either a skeptical, irrationalist, or rationalist critique of reflection (it takes speculation in a Hegelian sense very seriously indeed) but as an accusation against Hegel for having failed to give a radical solution to the problem of originary synthesis, it is a sort of debate with reflection that does not try to get rid of the latter. In claiming that the different forms of reflection cannot be logically accounted for by a reflection of reflection, but only by a pure heterology, Flach aims only at a more originary understanding of the structural characteristics of the absolute relation that makes reflection possible in the first place.

Let us see how Flach determines the pure heterogeneity of the absolute relation, and how he conceives of its intercourse with determining thought and reflection. By pinpointing the various motifs shared by Flach's and Derrida's philosophies, we shall see beyond doubt that Derrida's philosophy must also be understood as a heterology. But this comparison will also demonstrate the essential differences between the two types of heterologies. From the pure heterology of Flach, we shall have to distinguish Derrida's philosophy as an unconditionally pure *and* impure heterology.

In demonstrating what he terms the "reflexive constitutivity" of the heterological principle, Flach, in order to determine the absolute synthetic unity of this originary correlation, questions the originarity of negativity and contradiction constituting the relation between moments within reflection. Flach recalls that negation is a structural concept of reflection, an index of determining thought characteristic of the sphere of judgment. The same is true of contradiction, which, because it is connected to predication, belongs to the sphere of judgment as well. Hence, dialectics must also be situated in the sphere of determining thought, in the sphere of knowing. It follows from this that if a heterology is to establish the identity of the absolute ground as the pure logical beginning, it cannot achieve this goal by determining the absolute ground in terms of negation, contradiction, or dialectic, for these concepts are inadequate for formulating the pure structure of heterogeneity. Since the Hegelian concept of negation links moments in a relation of self and Other, the inevitably contradictory nature of such a relation necessarily anticipates its dialectical sublation in a third term, by which synthesis the homogeneity of the sphere of reflection is established. Thus, the terms required to conceptualize the ultimate structure of thought must be very different from those of negation, contradiction, and dialectics, yet must be capable of accounting for those principles, which govern the homogeneous domain of reflection and judgment.

If the absolute synthesis is to account for the play of the moments in which reflection and dialectics are grounded, and which they mediate into an undivided whole, it must be divided in itself. The absolute synthesis, according to Flach, can fulfill this task only if it is divided to such a degree that all mediation is radically excluded from the realm of pure logic. Hence, the moments that enter the originary synthesis must be irrevocably disjunctive—their nature must be one of "full disjointedness" (p. 45)—if they are to furnish a justifying explanation for the duplication constituting unifying reflection. Although this originary division of the pure logical beginning is inseparable from the dividedness at the base of reflection that it makes possible, it is also very different and thus cannot be thought in terms of reflection: "One thing is the inseparability of this 'duplication' from reflexivity, another the determination of this 'duplication' by reflexivity. The inseparability of 'pure heterogeneity' from reflexivity is a necessary determination of its structure, and this precisely insofar as 'pure heterogeneity' makes reflexivity possible in an originary manner" (p. 44).

In order to subtract this originary division and duplication from the principles that reign in the homogeneous realm of reflection, yet without hampering its originary constitutivity with respect to reflection, Flach, with recourse to Rickert's development of the notion of heterothesis, as well as to a controversy that took place in the twenties between Rickert and Kroner, determines the structure of that division to be heterological. What this means is simply that the coupled moments of the absolute relation stand in a relation of mutual exclusion, in which the opposite moments, without negating one another, complete each other to form a totality. Following Rickert's determination of the heterothetical principle, Flach sees the absolute relation as comprising the one and the Other, in which the Other is not the negation of the one but an exclusive Other of the same. In this minimum of the pure logical relation, both the one and the Other are equiprimordial. Neither has any ascendancy over the other; it is a relation of the one to the Other, and vice versa, in which negativity plays as yet no part. Since there is no negativity in the one's relation to its complementary Other, they do not stand in a relation of contradiction. As a result, the originary synthesis of the absolute relation appears to be irretrievably divided.

Having banned contradiction from heterology, Flach also empties it of the unifying and homogenizing possibility of reflection and dialectics. Yet it is precisely because it does not contain contradiction that the absolute relation can become a genuine principle of thought and reflexivity. Flach remarks: "Otherness is not a 'plus' but a 'less' than negation; indeed, it belongs to the minimum of what can theoretically be thought. This is what makes its originarity, and grounds its character as a moment" (pp. 36–37). As Rickert had insisted, Otherness logically precedes the possibility of negation. No negation would be possible without a prior Otherness; and since not all Otherness lends itself to negation, negation is doubly derivative. Instead of being a fundamental principle of thought, it is, in spite of its importance, a particular principle of thought. Notwithstanding the formidable role played by negation as a methodical tool of reflection, this role does not suffice to endow negativity with any priority regarding Otherness. Negation and contradiction belong to the sphere of reflection—that is, to that of cognition—whereas the heterothetical principle of Otherness is a function of pure positing. As a pure, minimal principle of thought, it belongs to the heterological medium of the originary relation. That sphere, unlike the sphere of cognition, determination, and reflection, is one of pure positing thought.

At this point we should be in a position to assess the implications of Flach's concept of heterology. It must be noted that his concept of pure heterogeneity as bearing upon the originary structures of thought— upon thought's heterothetical positings—has a very distinctive and singular meaning. It is certainly not to be mistaken for that sort of heterogeneity grounded in homogeneity that stems from the structural leveling of pure heterology to the Otherness required in determination.[10]

But in truth, how heterological is Flach's heterology? Flach leaves no doubt as to his heterology's also being a heautology, a science or a logic that thinks *itself (heauton)* and not exclusively Otherness. In a manner similar to Hegel, whose philosophy of spirit is an attempt to subsume under the One the thinking of the self and the thinking of the Other, Flach's heterology becomes a heautology not only insofar as the originary and absolute relation to itself is concerned, but also insofar as the heterogeneity that characterizes that primary relation is linked in an embrace with the principles governing the realm of cognition, determination, and reflection. The heterology of the originary logical sphere does not merely ground the homogeneous sphere of judgment. Between these two distinctive logical domains also reigns a communion of being, what Flach calls a constitutive *koinonia,* by which or in which very different principles come together to form the unified nature of thought: "das *eine* Denken." Flach's heterology is a unified and unifying science of the Other. It hinges on the essential Oneness of thought, whereas this originary Oneness is itself a function of its embracing noncontradictory and contradictory Otherness. To cite again from *Negation und Andersheit:* "In the communion, in the *koinonia,* in the *symploke* alone of the heterothetical and the principle of contradiction as well as of the other principles of thought, the *one* thought becomes constituted." And, "The one thought is constituted by all the principles of thought" (p. 54).

As a result of the nature of the originary relation as one to Otherness in general, the heautology in question can only be a heterological whole itself. It is in itself, as a whole, opposed to itself, irretrievably divided, and since its parts are complementary only to the extent that they are mutually exclusive, its unity is not dialectical. Oneness of thought, for Flach, is not equal to identity or indifference; on the contrary, it is one in its very division. The unity that holds thought together in its primary principle, as well as in thought as a whole, is that of "a functional closure of the principles," as well as of the whole of thought" (p. 60). This unity of the heterological is the result of an encompassing bond of union that weaves the very different moments and principles together into one totality that preserves difference— the difference of the Other—as complementarity in the whole. The unity of that whole stems from an articulation *(Gefüge)*, a relationship and connection of the parts. No wonder, then, that Flach stresses the themes of combination, communion, or interlacing—in technical terms, *koinonia* and *symploke*—and that he conceives of his heterology as an essential freeing of the idea of *symploke* to include Otherness, in this case linking into One the heterological and the homogeneous realm of judgment, the domain of the absolutely different ground and the domain of what is grounded, as well as the idea of unity itself. Flach asks: "In what manner does the heterology come to grips with the problem of *symploke?* In the only sufficient one, namely by con- ceiving of unity, difference, totality and foundation (in their unifia- bility) as the uniform and unified speculative character of the absolute relation." (p. 45).

Flach's ambition is clearly to bring to a fulfillment what Hegel began: the linkage of the entirety of all principles. But in distinction from Hegel, who set out to ground reflection in the homogeneous (non)ground of the reflection of reflection, Flach, by tying into one whole the ground *as* ground to what this ground in its very Otherness makes possible, opens the meaning of *symploke* to the heterogeneous, to the heterogeneity of the ground as the *radical* Other, and to the heterogeneity of the noncontradictory Other. But apart from this narrowing down of Otherness—of the heterological—to these two forms of Otherness, the opening of the question of *symploke* to Oth-

erness remains itself a function of the idea of the totality of all relations. *Symploke* becomes subject in this manner to a telos of all-compre-
hensive inclusion as far as the principles of thought are concerned.
Although it may be a Oneness no longer owing to dialectical mediation
of opposites, Oneness nonetheless is the horizon of Flach's heterology,
and of the corollary problem of *symploke*.

I do not mean to engage in a detailed comparison of Flach's determination of nondialectical Otherness with Derrida's heterological
venture, although such a comparison would help clarify many details.
I mean only to outline the similarities and differences between their
concepts of heterology. It remains unclear whether Flach really does
justice to Hegel when, in interpreting the Hegelian concept of negation
as belonging to the sphere of judgment alone, he is compelled to
restrict the realm of dialectics to determining thought alone, to the
sphere of knowledge based on judgment, neglecting in this manner
the all-important objective dialectics, or dialectics of the real. But in
spite of Hegel's most powerful elaboration of the entirety of the logical
senses of Otherness, Flach's concept of an Otherness logically anterior
to negation, and thus his heterology as well, is in principle capable
of accounting for Hegelian dialectics and speculative thought to the
extent that it does not fall under the jurisdiction of what Hegel calls
the abstract or even harmless Other. Flach's Other does not yield,
from a speculative viewpoint, to such a logical determination of simple
Otherness, because the relation of the one to its complementary Other
in the absolute relation is not conceived, however negatively, in terms
of a logic of determination. It is not a relation of mediation, and thus
the Other is not the Other *of* the one in spite of their complementarity.
What makes the absolute relation different from all simple Hegelian
Otherness is that its relation between the equiprimordial one and
Other is a relation of pure difference, or originary duplication, which
cannot be turned into a moment of the process of determination
whether or not it is limited to the sphere of judgment, because it is
itself a *logical* presupposition of the logic of speculative determination.
Yielding nonetheless to the imperatives of Hegelian thought, in particular inasmuch as Hegelian thought exemplifies the requirements of
philosophy as such, his inquiry into what I have called pre-suppositions or structures of reflection and the reflection of reflection represents a standard against which Derrida's heterology can be measured
and thus determined in what one can no longer call its *radical,* because
unheard of, specificity.

In a manner similar to Flach, Derrida acknowledges an irreducible doubling of the logical origin, a caesura at the heart of the grounding principles and of the principal conditioning relation of thought. Like Flach, he conceives of this caesura in terms of alterity rather than in terms of negativity and contradiction. Both philosophers question the fundamentality of negativity and contradiction as structural concepts of absolute reflexivity, compared to relation to Otherness in general. Both also share the insight into the solidarity between the terms of negativity, contradiction, sublation, dialectics, and homogeneity, a solidarity in the service of the evacuation of the heterological from the speculative unity of the totality of all oppositions. In addition, both Flach and Derrida open up the concept of *symploke* to include the heterogeneous.

But this is as far as the similarities go. As we have seen, in Flach the heterological is basically limited to the Otherness of the principles and to the Other which, in the One, complements the one. Flach's heterogeneity is an *essential* heterogeneity, whereas, as I shall try to prove, Derrida's heterogeneity is not confined to the essential. Consequently, his heterology is not a heautology either. Although one may at first justly compare the pre-suppositions exhibited by Derrida's philosophy—in other words what he calls "infra-structures" or "undecidables" such as "arche-trace," "differance," and "supplementarity," to name only a few—to founding principles, their own nature, as well as the relation they entertain with what they constitute, can no longer be thematized in terms of essence. Unlike Flach's, Derrida's treatment of the problem of *symploke* is not governed by totality and Oneness, values the German philosopher rightly holds to constitute thought as such, following in this a philosophical theme as old as philosophy itself. But is it not precisely *thought as such* that is the issue in the second type of criticism of reflexivity to which I have alluded? And are not the "pre-suppositions" of reflexivity in particular presuppositions of thought's Oneness, of the generality of Oneness, and not only of the one of speculative thought? But if this is the case, then Flach's recasting of the traditional definition of *symploke* remains a revolution within the conceptual limits of the tradition itself.

Let us consider for a moment the classical treatment of the problem of *symploke*. The dialogue on the *Statesman* is one of the most important Platonic dialogues dealing explicitly with this problem.[11] The objective of this dialogue is to determine the activity of the true statesman as "a kingly weaving process" *(basiliken symploken)* (306a). Yet, compared to the craftsmanship of the weaver, which serves in this instance as the leading paradigm to define such kingly activity, the statesman's task is a much more formidable challenge. Whereas the weaver combines threads into cloth, thus exemplifying the many in the One and the One in the many, the sort of plaiting together that awaits the kingly weaver is much more complex, for unlike the weaver, the statesman cannot limit himself to combining what already lends itself through its inherent substance *(auto autois syndeta)* to combination. What the weaver weaves together is compacted in its own substance *(eautois syndoumenon)* (279e–280a). The kingly weaver, in contrast, is supposed to plait together opposites that are at war with one another. But what are these opposites that, because they are mutually exclusive, find themselves in inevitable conflict?

The examples to which Plato refers are different kinds of virtues that clash with one another, such as moderation and courage. The task of the statesman consists of tying together these inimical values, caught up in a family quarrel, with what Plato calls a "supernatural link" or bond *(theio sunargmosamene)*, which "unites the elements of goodness which are diverse in nature and would else be opposing in tendency" (310a). In doing so, the statesman makes sure that the gentle virtues are never separated from the brave ones, and that they combine in such a manner as to form one organic whole. Compared to the cloth woven by the craftsman, the kingly weaver's web is smooth and close woven; it is "the finest and best of all fabrics" because "in its firm contexture" it weaves together hitherto opposed strands into a unified character (311b–c).

To understand fully Plato's handling of the problem of *symploke*—and by extension its interpretation throughout the tradition—it is imperative to realize that the unity, or the *one* name, into which the opposites or extremes are plaited together *(tis auto onoma sunago-gein)* is a function of the extremes' negative determination with respect to one another (267b–c). Each of the extremes is a negation of the other. This is the condition under which they can be dialectically linked together by the divine bond that the statesman draws between them. Obviously, to restrict the operation of the *symploke* to the weaving together into one totality of what must, with respect to its opposite, be determined as negative leaves a variety of other possible relations unreckoned. Or rather, they become violently excluded from the scope of the *symploke*. No artist who works by combining materials would deliberately choose to make any of his products out of a combination of good materials and bad, asserts the stranger in the dialogue. On the contrary, he rejects the bad material as far as possible. Similarly, a statesman would never "choose deliberately to con-

struct the life of any community out of a combination of good characters with bad characters" (308d). *Symploke* can achieve its goal
only if it expels from the envisioned totality those opposites that
cannot be determined in terms of negativity, that is, in terms of dialectical Otherness. The true statesman, in order to achieve the finest
and best of all fabrics in which opposed strands are unified in one organic whole, is bound to eliminate those irreducible Others that do not
bend to negativity. Thus, for instance, those children who "cannot be
taught to be courageous and moderate and to acquire the other vir-
tuous tendencies, but are impelled to godlessness and to vaunting pride
and injustice by the drive of an evil nature. These the king expels from
the community. He puts them to death or banishes them or else he chastises them by the severest public disgrace" (308e). The totality woven
by the *symploke*—a totality of concurring and complementary opposites—is thus a function of the expulsion of absolute heterogeneity.

In distinction to this Platonic interpretation of *symploke,* Flach
seems at first to broaden the spectrum of what lends itself to forming
a part in a whole. The heterogeneous that he includes in the minimal
unit of the absolute relation is of the order of an Other that is not in
a negative opposition to the one (or same), but that is a complementary
Other.[12] Yet, since the heterogeneity that he includes within the totality of the Oneness of thought is that of the principles, it is a heterogeneity that, in spite of all the difference between ground as ground
and what it makes possible, is *in pari materia* with what follows from
these principles. Indeed, the equality of matter is the condition on
which a complementary Other, as well as a principle, can contribute
to forming a whole, although this whole will not be the result of a
dialectical process of sublation of opposites. But above all, what keeps
Flach's interpretation of *symploke* within the limits of its Platonic
determination is the teleology (and theology) of Oneness, unity, and
organic totality. As we have seen, these values are intrinsically part
of the traditional understanding of the concept. As a result, Flach's
pure heterology, despite its stress on a heterogeneity beyond mediation
and reflection—a heterogeneity constituting thinking, reflection, and
determination—remains an attempt at establishing the (however nondialectical) identity of the Absolute. It culminates in a heautology of
all the principles of thought.

But in what ways is Derrida's work concerned with the problem
of *symploke?* Any attentive reader will notice that the problem of
symploke is a major *fil conducteur* in Derrida's writings. In *La Vérité
en peinture* he claims that "c'est vers la pensée du *fil* et de l'*entre-*

lacement que . . . je voudrais vous conduire" (VP, p. 24). From his first work to his most recent publications, the topoi of *Verflechtung, Geflecht*, interlacing (in the writings of Husserl, Heidegger, Freud, and others), the bond (*la bande* in *Glas*), grafting (*greffe*), and so forth have been the focus of his attention.[13]

The discussion of the art of weaving of the statesman shows that *symploke* is dialectical in essence. The opposite moments that it plaits together are not moments in a relation of capricious or contingent exteriority, consequently lacking any meaning. From Plato to Hegel such relations were considered arbitrary and lawless. Dialectical interlacing takes place between terms that, because they are at war with one another, are also posited in the Absolute. Real opposites are absolutely identical. Only between real opposition does the dialectical art of *symploke* weave what Plato, at one point in *Timaeus*, calls "the fairest bond," and which, by the way, Hegel also refers to in *The Difference* at the precise moment at which he describes the dialectical identity of opposites.[14] Plato writes:

The fairest bond is that which makes the most complete fusion of itself and the things which it combines, and proportion is best adapted to effect such a union. For whenever in any three numbers, whether cube or square, there is a mean, which is to the last term what the first term is to it, and again, when the mean is to the first term as the last term is to the mean—then the mean becoming first and last, and the first and last becoming means, they will all of them of necessity come to be the same, and having become the same with one another will be all one. (31c–32a)

The fairest bond is not only the fundamental bond of essence that penetrates and unites a plurality of predicates. It is not only the bond created by the interlacing par excellence that is being. As Plato indicates, the fairest bond is that of continued geometrical proportion—in short, the union according to analogy. Such a bond alone effectuates the true *koinonia* with the Other, as a communion in which the one encroaches upon the Other, unifying itself and the Other in One whole. In this unity, caused by the fairest bond, the Other (and Otherness) find their rightful place as they become justified in their role of an Other to the one, to the same, which assumes the function of legitimizing itself and the Other dependent on it.

Derrida recognizes this essentially dialectical nature of *symploke* when he writes in *Dissemination* "that dialectics is also an art of weaving, a science of the *symploke*" (D, p. 122). That the interlacing of dialectics is eminently, and preferably, analogical, and thus one of being, is at least implicitly assumed in such essays as "White My-thology" in *Margins of Philosophy,* and in *The Archeology of the Frivolous.* But this recognition that dialectics is an art of interlacing also implies that dialectics, and with it analogy, are somehow only forms of *symploke* among others, and, as Flach has contended, that there is a nondialectical form of linkage. Indeed, this is what Derrida sets out to prove in "Plato's Pharmacy," but with clearly different results from Flach's opening of *symploke* to a more fundamental, more originary form of plaiting together.

As Derrida demonstrates, in analyzing Plato's distinction in *Theae-tetus* between the science of grammar and dialectics, the science of interlacing represented by dialectics—a science guided by the value of truth—instead of being able to distinguish itself clearly from gram-mar, must, in fact and always, compound with relation, nonpresence, and thus with the nontruth of the *other* science of *symploke,* a science traditionally seen as inferior to dialectics, the science of grammar. Indeed, as one can gather from the *Sophist,* "the very condition of discourse—*true or false*—is the diacritical principle of *symploke*" (*D,* p. 166).

With this insight into the structural dependence of dialectics as one art of weaving on the science of grammar as another, not only does the distinction between the two sciences begin to waver, but the ne-cessity of a *generalization* of *symploke* also begins to be felt. Since both sciences, dialectical and grammatical interlacing, are linked to each other—interlaced—a meditation on the generality of *symploke* becomes inevitable. This meditation can no longer choose between one of the two sciences of interlacing. Focusing on what ties them together and what unties them into their unstable difference, the med-itation must articulate them as a *double science,* a science simulta-neously playing on *two stages* during *two sessions.* As we shall see, the generalization of *symploke* by this double science is nothing other than the production, through interlacing, of *generality.*

The new art of weaving suggested by Derrida's heterology is thor-oughly different from that of Flach. It is no longer governed by truth values, and it escapes regulation by the ideas of totality and unity. Derrida's deconstruction of *symploke*—his generalization of inter-lacing, and his thinking of radical alterity—are subversive of thought itself, of what has been called by that name in the tradition, namely the thinking not only of something specific but of *one* determined thing, of a thing in its Oneness. Aristotle set the standards of thought when he stated that one does not think at all if one does not think *one* thing—the thing in its essential unity.[15] From this perspective, Derrida's heterology is not only different from the *pure* heterology of Flach; it is, strictly speaking, no longer a philosophical enterprise (nor is it, for that matter, a literary undertaking), since the force of knotting the manifold is no longer that of thought. In an Aristotelian view, this heterology does not think anything at all.

Focusing in a nondialectical manner on the ways in which truth compounds with nontruth, on how principles and nonpresence are welded together, Derrida's heterology is not to be seen as a search for more fundamental principles of thought and cognition, unless the nature of both were to be radically redefined. The sort of syntheses produced by Derrida's heterology—consider the "arche-syntheses" of the arche-trace, differance, supplementarity, and so on—are not cumulative operations of totalization. The Other tied into the arche-syntheses would not find its justification by being embraced by the One. These "syntheses," on the contrary, "account" for structurally nontotalizable arrangements of heterogeneous elements, with the result that the system of predicates that they form is also essentially incomplete. Thus, these "syntheses" do not belong to the register of the grounds; theirs is an alterity beyond that which characterizes the relation of principles to what they rule. It is, one could venture to say, an alterity that separates the principle from what it is supposed to account for, and *from itself,* by demonstrating how it is breached by that which it makes possible. It is thus an alterity that represents both a condition of possibility and one of impossibility, of principles and what they justify, that is, *their* Other. It follows from this that the interlacing produced by this unheard-of heterology does not stand in a relation of constitutive *koinonia* to what it "accounts for." It is, therefore, also incorrect to speak of its interlacing simply as one of founding, grounding, accounting, and so on.

But the question to be raised at this point is whether this unheard-of heterology can still be called by that name, especially if one takes into account that the pure heterology we have examined deals exclusively with the Otherness of the absolute relation constituting knowledge and the self-knowledge of knowledge. Heterology is indeed a highly charged term, and by itself does not adequately designate what I want it to say in this context. *Heterology* means "science of" or "discourse on" the Other. But first, is a *science* or *theory* of "arche-syntheses" possible, since all such science or theory presupposes them? Second, considering the significance of the concept of the Other in the philosophical tradition, can one conceptualize the infrastructural syntheses in terms of Otherness? And third, since heterology is not only the science of the Otherness of the *logical* principles of thought, but also the science of a more radical *content* than the one with which the discourse of knowledge is believed to be concerned (one thinks here in particular of that irrationalist movement of thought which leads from the Romantics to Rudolf Otto's determination of what he called "the Absolute Other" in terms of the sacred or *numinous*) might it not be advisable to avoid the word *heterology* altogether? Still, since Western philosophy is in essence the attempt to domesticate Otherness, since what we understand by thought is nothing but such a project, *heterology,* for both intrinsic and strategic reasons, seems an adequate name for the investigation of the "pre-suppositions" of Western philosophy, of what is understood by *thought* and by what is called *noesis noeseos,* the thinking of thought. If one avoids the danger and the almost inevitable temptation of construing heterology as the *truth* of philosophy—that is, as another, more true mode of philosophy—and if one remains aware of the fact that the alterity with which heterology is concerned is not a positive Other given in any way, whose enigma could be solved once and for all (as we shall see, this is not because the Other in question would be ineffable, but for reasons of structure, which make it always other than itself), such a heterology would not only help to understand thought; it would also, and especially, open thought—which could then no longer be called by that name—to a confrontation with Otherness that would no longer be *its own.* Indeed, such a possibility hinges on the inscription within thought of its structural limitations—limitations that do not result from the deficiencies of the cognizing subject as a finite being. Thought, or rather "thought," would in this manner become able, perhaps for the first time, to think something other than itself, something other than itself in *its* Other, or itself in itself.

To circle back to the problem from which we set out—the problem of reflexivity—it must be said that, unlike Flach's pure heterology, Derrida's heterology does not function as a reflexive constitutivity. In *Of Grammatology* we read:

There are things like reflecting pools, and images, an infinite reference from one to the other, but no longer a source, a spring. There is no longer a simple origin. For what is reflected is split *in itself* and not only as an addition to itself of its image. The reflection, the image, the double, splits what it doubles. The origin of the speculation becomes a difference. What can look at itself is not one; and the law of the addition of the origin to its representation, of the thing to its image, is that one plus one makes at least three. (*OG*, p. 36)

Derrida's unconditional heterology questions the very possibility of a source of reflection, of a constituting homogeneous principle, or of a heterogeneous principle à la Flach. The alterity that splits reflection from itself and thus makes it able to fold itself into itself—to reflect itself—is also what makes it, for structural reasons, incapable of closing upon itself. The very possibility of reflexivity is also the sub-version of its own source. Derrida's critique of reflexivity must there-fore at first take the paradoxical turn of a generalization of reflection, of infinitely reflecting mirrors. But, since such a reflection is caught up in an endless process of reference to Other, preventing all ultimate recoiling into self, the generalization of reflexivity becomes at the same time the end of reflection and speculation. It opens itself up to the thought of an alterity, a difference that remains unaccounted for by the polar opposition of source and reflection, principle and what is derived from it, the one and the Other.

Before I engage in a detailed exposition of such an unconditional heterology, and of the "method" of deconstruction associated with it, it is appropriate to insist once more on the fact that Derrida's unconditional heterology, like Flach's pure heterology, is concerned with Otherness not exclusively elicited in terms of negation. For this reason the sphere of heterology must, for both, be clearly distinguished from that of reflexive determination. As we have seen, Hegel deter-mines difference—that is, meaningful difference—exclusively as con-tradiction. Difference, or the relation to Otherness, becomes, therefore, relation to the negative. The difference that such negatively charac-terized Otherness makes to thought is that it allows for reflexive determination in a developing dialectical system. Difference, under-stood as contradiction, makes negativity one face of positivity within the process and the system of the self-exposition of absolute knowl-edge, or of the absolute idea. As the underside and accomplice of positivity, negativity and contradiction are sublated, internalized in the syllogistic process of speculative dialectics. The dialecticization of negativity, by which negativity remains within the enclosure of meta-physics, of onto-theology and onto-teleology, puts negativity to work. As Derrida demonstrates in *Writing and Difference*, "negativity is a *resource*. In naming the without-reserve of absolute experience 'ab-stract negativity,' Hegel, through *precipitation*, blinded himself to that which he had laid bare under the rubric of negativity. And did so through precipitation toward the seriousness of meaning and the security of knowledge" (*WD*, p. 259).

Derrida expresses reservations as to the use of "the metaphysical or romantic pathos of negativity," fearing "that the category of 'negation' reintroduces the Hegelian logic of the *Aufhebung*" (*P*, pp. 86, 95). Instead of determining negativity as only a facet, a moment, or a condition of meaning—as work—Derrida's philosophy, like Bataille's, pushes the negative to its logical end, to that point where the negative seems an afterimage of something that resists all salvage by the system of meaning. In his essay on Bataille, Derrida formulates the task in the following way:

It is convulsively to tear apart the negative side, that which makes it the reassuring *other* surface of the positive; and it is to exhibit within the negative, in an instant, that which can no longer be called negative. And can no longer be called negative precisely because it has no reversed underside, because it can no longer *collaborate* with the continuous linking-up of meaning, concept, time and truth in discourse; because it literally can no longer *labor* and let itself be interrogated as the "work of the negative."   (*WD*, pp. 259–260)

The Otherness with which unconditional heterology is concerned is not even a negative. Unlike Flach's Other, which is only Otherness *in general,* the *essence* of Otherness, a logically more fundamental Otherness compared to negativity, Derrida's Other—let us call it the *general Other*—is an alterity that has nothing of an essence or truth. Instead of being *one* essential alterity, it is irretrievably plural and cannot be assimilated, digested, represented, or *thought as such,* and hence put to work by the system of metaphysics. Rather than being a more profound ground of the systems of what can be known and thought, of what is meaningful, it is precisely the alterity of the structural conditions of that which is determined as knowledge and its grounds within the tradition.

Derrida's Otherness is, consequently, neither a lack, a substantial void, an absence susceptible of determination, nor the still meaningful reverse side of the positivity of the Hegelian Concept or Notion. The Otherness of unconditional heterology is more and less than negativity. It is *less* because it has no meaning, no signification; it is a "negativity without negativity," to quote Derrida (*VP*, p. 147). It is *more* than negativity because it is the "medium" (the nonmediating medium) in which philosophy comes to carve out its (dialectical, and

hence sublatable) contradictions. The Otherness of unconditional heterology is the undecidable reserve of negativity. Speaking of the *pharmakon* as one other name for this Otherness, Derrida remarks:

> Contradictions and pairs of opposites are lifted from the bottom of this
> diacritical, differing, deferring, reserve. Already inhabited by differance, this
> reserve, even though it "precedes" the opposition between different effects,
> even though it preexists differences as effects, does not have the punctual
> simplicity of a *coincidentia oppositorum*. It is from this fund that dialectics
> draws its philosophemes. The *pharmakon*, without being anything in itself,
> always exceeds them in constituting their bottomless fund.   (*D*, p. 127)

Such an Otherness, which is referential to other, more alien modes
of difference, conflictuality, contradiction—modes of difference that
cannot be made meaningful by bringing them to a stop in negativity—
is not merely of the order of what Flach calls the heterogeneity of the
principles. It is an Otherness that divides the principle against itself,
that is more originary than it, that even divides a double principle
like that of Flach, the minimum of the absolute relation. For the radical
alterity that Derrida thematizes, and that we call radical only for
reasons of convenience, there is no place either as an essential moment
of the principles, or as that which these principles shape or constitute,
or in the totality of what Flach calls the *one* thinking. The Otherness
of unconditional heterology does not have the purity of principles. It
is concerned with the principles' irreducible impurity, with the non-
negative difference that divides them in themselves against themselves.
For this reason it is an impure heterology. But it is also an impure
heterology because the "medium" of Otherness—more and less than
negativity—is also a mixed milieu, precisely because the negative no
longer dominates it. Open to heterological modes of relating, this
milieu does not homogeneously knot or interlace. It is distinguished
by "syntheses" that, by soldering and grafting predicates, concepts,
instances, or levels of various orders onto one another, must necessarily appear contradictory, even irreducibly aporetic. But these categories, born from philosophy and its logic of contradiction, do not
apply here, because the syntheses in question are nothing less than
the conditions of possibility and impossibility of such logic.

The impure and unconditional heterology focuses on an alterity
that does not lend itself to phenomenologization, that escapes presentation of itself *in propria persona*. This "radical" alterity thus
marks a "space" of exteriority at the border of philosophy, whether
or not philosophy is explicitly phenomenological. It is situated on the

margin of what can be meaningfully totalized. Yet, although it does not bend to the concept of presence, neither does it for that matter lend itself to the conceptual grip of absence, since, lacking all meaning, it is also void of the meaning conferred by an absence of meaning.

But as we shall see, this border is not simply external to philosophy. It does not encompass philosophy like a circle but traverses it within. Although this "radical" alterity does not present itself *as such*, the history of philosophy in its entirety is, indeed, the uninterrupted attempt to domesticate it in the form of its delegates. In presenting it in negative images—as the opposites of valorized metaphysical concepts—specular reflection seeks to account for, and do away with, the sort of alterity that subverts its hope of reflexive or speculative self-foundation. This alterity forever undermines, but also makes possible, the dream of autonomy achieved through a reflexive coiling upon self, since it names a structural precondition of such a desired state, a precondition that represents the limit of such a possibility.

PART TWO

On Deconstruction

7

Abbau, Destruktion, Deconstruction

❦

Before engaging in a detailed analysis of Derrida's philosophy and determining in what manner his "method" of deconstruction is critical of reflexivity, let us first examine the conceptual filiation of this notion of deconstruction, which for many has come to designate the content and style of Derrida's thought. Such an inquiry into the provenance of what seems to be a methodological concept of sorts should provide the historical and systematic background for the subsequent attempt to demarcate "deconstruction" radically from its antecedents. The main concepts to which deconstruction can and must be retraced are those of *Abbau* (dismantling) in the later work of Husserl and *Destruktion* (destruction) in the early philosophy of Heidegger.[1]

Although Husserl's notion of *Abbau* appears for the first time in *Experience and Judgment* (1938), and thus later than Heidegger's notion of *Destruktion* in *Being and Time* (1927), it should be discussed first, for, in spite of some essential differences, it is in large part another name for phenomenological reduction. Since Heidegger's method of destruction in *Being and Time* must be viewed against the backdrop of the epochal process of discovery, it is certainly legitimate to discuss the method of *Abbau* first, in particular since those features that distinguish it from orthodox phenomenological reduction make it part of the history of the critique of reflexivity.

It is important to understand the context in which Husserl speaks of *Abbau* in *Experience and Judgment* if one is to assess the meaning of this notion. Engaged in a genetic exploration of the conditions of the validity of judgment, Husserl contends that neither logic nor psychology is capable of revealing the true foundations of predicative evidence. This would require a "necessary retrogression to the most original self-evidence of experience," to a stratum of experience that is never thematized by either logic or psychology.[2] To achieve this goal, Husserl proposes a double retrogression: one that leads from the pregiven and "objective" world to the original life-world, and another that reaches through the life-world toward the transcendental subjectivity constitutive of both life-world and "objective" world. The objective world "is there as that on which contemporary science has already done its work of exact determination." In fact, it is the "theoretical world," a world inseparable from the natural sciences, whose tradition determines its mode of givenness and informs the way one experiences it. A retrogression to the original life-world, to the pretheoretical world and prepredicative experience by which it is characterized, thus requires a radical dismantling of the theoretical world, an undoing of the idealizations out of which it is woven. This dismantling, which Husserl refers to as *Abbau*, is supposed to produce a "breakthrough to the concealed foundation" of these idealizations or "sense-sedimentations" in the most original experience. This foundation represents the source, according to Husserl, of "the origination of this garb of ideas thrown over the world."

In paragraph 11 of *Experience and Judgment*, Husserl explains that the original life-world, as well as transcendental subjectivity, do not "lie open to the view of reflection." In other words, the operation of retrogression through dismantling is not a reflective operation. It cannot be performed by psychological reflection, which is an aspect of what Husserl also calls "theoretical convictions," and which must be dismantled if one wants to gain access to that more "effective subjectivity" that "is not the subjectivity of psychological reflection" but that, on the contrary, grounds it. Consequently, reflection appears to be not only an inappropriate mode of access to the life-world and the constituting subjectivity, but also one of those idealizations that conceal the originary foundation of all sense-sedimentations. Yet perhaps Husserl rejects psychological reflection only because its scope does not go beyond that of which it is itself a part. It may well be that, in a manner thoroughly consistent with the whole of his phenomenological enterprise, Husserl rejects psychological reflection in the name of a more radical reflection, that is, transcendental reflection. In that case, of course, it would be a mistake to conclude that the method of *Abbau* is nonreflexive. The retrogression that it achieves would have to be understood simply in terms of a more fundamental mode of reflection.

And yet, as David Carr has argued in *Phenomenology and the*

Problem of History, a strange ambiguity sets the operation of dismantling apart from all other forms of phenomenological reduction.
On the one hand, *Abbau* seems to stand for a nonreflexive way of
reaching the roots of the pregiven world, its idealization, and the
sense-constituting structures of transcendental subjectivity. On the
other hand, as a nonreflective approach to the origins of the idealizing
superstructures of the pregiven world, it is not an *unmediated* approach. The very idea of dismantling is clearly "a far cry from the
phenomenological insistence on grasping in original intuition the thing
itself," remarks Carr.[3] Obviously the paradox Carr refers to results
from the traditional equation of nonreflexivity with immediacy. But
since Husserl's procedure in *Experience and Judgment* consists of
dismantling the idealizations that cover up the original life-world, a
world with which our historical world has lost all contact, the operation of *Abbau* in its paradoxically mediated nonreflective gesture
is particularly suited to achieve what is at stake: to reach back to
origins that must remain essentially concealed if they are to function
as the original historical premises of history. The method of dismantling is nonreflective because it allows for a retrogression to something
that cannot *in principle* be given as such. Because the conditions of
predicative evidence with which it attempts to make contact cannot
be beheld in an intuiting act, *Abbau* is a mediated approach. *Abbau,*
then, is precisely the kind of retrogression required for a reactivation
of origins, such as historical origins, which must remain *essentially*
dissimulated, in order to achieve the sort of grounding one expects
from them. Therefore, it is no contradiction if the method of retrogression through dismantling is at once mediated and nonreflective.[4]

It is, consequently, appropriate to assume that, in *Experience and
Judgment,* Husserl repudiates both psychological and transcendental
reflection. Unlike all previous forms of reduction, or what Husserl in
Ideas calls mental destructions *(gedankliche Destruktion),* which operate in concert with a nonpsychological mode of reflection, the operation of *Abbau* is not informed by a fully reactivatable end point
of the retrograding process.[5] *Abbau* is certainly a method of transcendental investigation, but in a sense thoroughly different from that
of Kant, as well as from that of the early Husserl. In this sense it can
be said to anticipate deconstruction. It is a nonreflective turning back.

The nonreflexivity that characterizes Husserl's notion of *Abbau* is
undoubtedly a major feature of what in 1927 Heidegger called *Destruktion.* Heidegger may have borrowed this concept from Husserl,

who referred to the forms of reduction, bracketing, or *epoche* as "mental destructions." But it is only with *Being and Time* that destruction acquired the status of a philosophical concept. It is interesting too that, in his 1927 lectures, Heidegger speaks of destruction as a "critical dismantling" *(kritischer Abbau)*, thus anticipating the concept that Husserl was not to make his own until 1938.[6]

The concept of destruction, as coined by Heidegger, issues from a debate with Husserl's early philosophy, and especially with the method of phenomenological reduction. Whereas phenomenological reduction, as Husserl had first developed it in *Ideas* (1913), represents the method of bracketing the natural attitude toward the world in order to focus on the transcendental subjectivity that constitutes it, Heidegger comes to see it as "leading phenomenological vision back from the apprehension of a being, whatever may be the character of that apprehension, to the understanding of the being of this being," as he explains in his 1927 lectures entitled *The Basic Problems of Phenomenology*.[7] This retrogression, no longer toward the sense-constituting structures of a transcendental ego or the prepredicatory experience of evidence in the original life-world, becomes for Heidegger a means of regaining the original metaphysical experience of Being. As a consequence of the more fundamental understanding of this phenomenological gaze, destruction serves to level off not only the force of tradition to the extent that it is dominated by the sciences, but also the entire philosophical tradition since antiquity. Indeed, once Heidegger establishes in *Being and Time* that the trancendental horizon for the explication of Being is time, the whole history of ontology—that is, of the previous doctrines of Being—appears to have determined Being in the perspective of *one* singular mode of time, the mode of the present. In the projected second part of *Being and Time* he intended to outline the "basic features of a phenomenological destruction of the history of ontology, with the problematic of Temporality as . . . [the] clue," in order to reestablish the elementary conditions under which the question of Being could be taken up again in a productive manner.[8] Heidegger writes: "We understand this task as one in which by taking *the question of Being as our clue,* we are to *destroy* [*Destruktion*] the traditional content of ancient ontology until we arrive at those primordial experiences in which we achieved our first ways of determining the nature of Being—the ways which have guided us ever since."[9]

As orthodox phenomenological reduction goes hand in hand with a (transcendental) reflection concerning its goals, the end terms of the operation of retrogression, similarly this "guidance of vision back from beings to being require[s] at the same time that we should bring ourselves forward to being itself."[10] Heidegger calls this movement of projection of what is pregiven toward its Being and its structures not reflection but *"phenomenological construction."*[11] According to Heidegger, the phenomenological method is distinguished by three related moments: reduction or retrogression from what is to Being, construction of Being, and destruction or the dismantling of tradition. Destruction is the necessary correlate of both reduction and construction: "It is for this reason that there necessarily belongs to the conceptual interpretation of being and its structures, that is, to the reductive construction of being, a *destruction*—a critical process in which the traditional concepts, which at first must necessarily be employed, are de-constructed *(kritischer Abbau)* down to the sources from which they were drawn. Only by means of this destruction can ontology fully assure itself in a phenomenological way of the genuine character of its concepts."[12]

This unavoidable loosening up of a hardened tradition, and the dissolution of the concealment it has brought about, are not, as Heidegger often insists, violent acts. Nonetheless, it is interesting to note that in the context of the public debate between Cassirer and Heidegger in April 1929 at Davos, Switzerland, Heidegger employed the much more forceful German word *Zerstörung,* as opposed to its Latinization in *Being and Time,* to designate the radical dismantling of the foundations of Occidental metaphysics (the Spirit, Logos, Reason).[13] At any rate, the destruction of the history of ontology that he calls for in *Being and Time,* or the overcoming *(Verwindung)* or detachment *(Loslösung)* from the tradition, as he would later call it, "must not be forced, because the tradition remains rich in truth."[14] Heidegger remarks, "To bury the past in nullity is not the purpose of this destruction; its aim is *positive;* its negative function remains unexpressed and indirect."[15] This positive intent of destruction consists of a systematic removal or dismantling of the concealments *(Verdeckungen)* of the meaning of Being by the history of ontology, a meaning with regard to which traditional ontology does not simply become relativized but in which it is rooted and from which it acquires its own epochal meaning. Such a destruction, says Heidegger, must "stake out the positive possibilities of that tradition, and this always means keeping it within its *limits.*" The loosening of the hardened tradition, as well as the dissolution of the concealments it necessarily produces, is positive, as long as it is carried out along the guidelines of the question of Being. At the same time, this question—the on-tologically fundamental investigation into the meaning of Being—gains its true realization only in the performed destruction. In short, destruction is the necessary reverse of the reductive construction of the question of Being in philosophy. The leveling off that it accomplishes equals a positive appropriation of the tradition, such that the philosophical inquiry into Being is, in a specific and important way, historical knowledge. Destroying what conceals the original experience, releasing the first and subsequently guiding determinations of Being, paves the way for a transsubjective beginning of a meaning of Being, through which ontology from antiquity to the present finds its possibility, insofar as that ontology represents the oblivion of that first gaze into the destiny of Being.

I have already stressed the necessary correlation between destruction and reductive construction. Although this correlation seems to parallel Husserl's correlation between reduction and transcendental reflection, it may well be of a different nature. First, reduction in Heidegger seems to refer to nothing more than a qualification of a construction that takes place within the space created by the leveling off of the traditional interpretations of Being. Reductive construction would thus appear to correspond to Husserlian transcendental reflection, as it sets limits and a goal to the movement of destruction. But what distinguishes reductive construction from reflection is that instead of providing a level that no longer needs to be dissolved, such as the Husserlian essences and forms, it constructs a radically original ground. By avoiding the terminology of reflection with respect to reductive construction as it relates to destruction, Heidegger emphasizes a fundamental shift from a subjective transcendental perspective toward the question of Being as the transcendental question par excellence, giving *transcendental* a historically new meaning. What takes place in the passage from phenomenological reduction to Heidegger's concept of destruction of the history of ontology is a decisive turning away from the question of reflexivity. This shift from egological thinking, transcendental or not, can be grasped in Heidegger's turn toward the question of Being, as well as in the very conception of the modalities of his phenomenological method.

Instead of further engaging in a demonstration of the nonreflexivity of the operation of destruction, I want to comment briefly on three other methodological notions in the later work of Heidegger that clearly support the nonreflexive conception of destruction: *Schritt zurück, Andenken,* and *Besinnung.* The movement that characterizes these three notions involves a certain obscurity, which necessarily baffles both the philosopher of reflection and the empiricist. The question that these three "methodological" devices answer is, How can the ontological tradition be dismantled without recourse to a concept such as reflection, which, as part of that tradition, would provide a present ground for the operation of retrogression? The movement that distinguishes the three notions of *Schritt zurück, Andenken,* and *Besinnung* must ensure that the detachment from tradition makes contact with the hidden and essentially withdrawing ground of that tradition, with a ground that is thus not simply forgotten but whose oblivion is forgotten as well. The gesture of such a reaching out cannot but appear suspicious to reflective and empirical thought, as it seems to rely on a *petitio principii.*

Let us recall that what is being turned to in the operation of dismantling is not of the order of the subject, however transcendental it may be, nor of the order of anything constituted by such a subject. It is not something that would come into view through reflecting on oneself. On the contrary, as Heidegger puts it, "it is what we ourselves are not and least of all could ever be."[16] Yet at the same time it is not only within our confines; it is as near to us as the unthought of our forgetting of it. The movement characteristic of this reaching back to the withdrawn ground resembles that of the Greek *epagoge,* as analyzed by Heidegger in his essay on *physis. Epagoge,* often misleadingly translated as "induction," does not mean the scanning of a series of facts in order to induce what they have in common, an abstract universal. Instead, "*Epagoge* means 'leading towards' that which comes into view insofar as we have previously looked *away,* over and *beyond* individual beings. At what? At Being. For example, only if we already have treeness in view can we identify individual trees. *Epagoge* is seeing and making visible what already stands in view—for example, treeness. *Epagoge* is 'constituting' in the double sense of, first bringing something into view and then likewise establishing what has been seen."[17]

Now, the universal that the *epagoge* brings into view, to which it leads, is never given in the mode of the present. For instance, being in motion is the fundamental mode of being of *physis* as it comes into view in *epagoge.* As such, the retrogression toward it does not assume a definite end point of the turning back, since *physis* is not to be understood as motion per se but as *being in motion.* The *epagoge* does not lead to a definable essence and therefore does not imply a *petitio principii.* Yet the very movement of the *petere principium,* as "the reaching out to the supporting ground," is, according to Heidegger, "the only move that philosophy makes. It is the 'offensive' that breaks open [*der eröffnende Vorstoss*] the territory within whose borders science can first settle down."[18] The retrogression does not hinge on the prior assumption of a present term of its movement but is itself the reaching out for a ground, its positing, which it constructs as it retrogrades. *Schritt zurück, Andenken* and *Besinnung* are the different modes in which that which shows itself in and by itself becomes the object of the retrogressive reaching out for the grounding ground. All three are modes of disclosure of this ground; they occur as one makes the step back through recollective thought, or *Besinnung* (a term which I prefer to leave untranslated), toward what we ourselves are not.

Let me try to describe these three movements more succinctly, according to their differences and to the manner in which they complement each other. First, the step back from traditional ontology—that is, from metaphysics as a whole—toward its hidden essence does not signify a return to the past. It is not an attempt to revive the past artificially. The misinterpretation particularly to be avoided is that of a historical return to the earliest Occidental philosophers, for, as Heidegger notes in *Identity and Difference*, "the 'whither' to which the step back directs us, develops and shows itself only in the execution of the step."[19] What, then, is the step back? It is a mode of dealing with the history of philosophy conceived by Heidegger in opposition to Hegel's process of the sublation of the truth-moments of that tradition. It undoubtedly represents a return to a beginning; but it is a beginning that never occurred as such, and that is the realm, "which until now has been skipped over," of the essence of metaphysics, which comes into view only by means of retrogression.[20] What is constructed in the step back from metaphysics is "that locality (the oblivion of Being), from out of which metaphysics obtained and retains its origin."[21] By unwinding out of representing, reflecting, and explicatory thinking, the step back *lets* that locality and what characterizes it—the ontico-ontological difference, or the question of Being—appear face to face with thought. Through this stepping back, that which is worthy of being questioned is set free into a confrontation with thought, and thought can enter into a questioning that experiences or lets itself be addressed by what it confronts face to face, instead of making it the object in the habitual opining that characterizes philosophy. This is how the step back turns thinking into "recollective" thinking, a thinking which, as Heidegger puts it, "may well remain wholly without an object."[22]

The qualitative difference of thought in the step back from all subsequent presentation *(Vorstellung)* of recollection's facing its opposite is that this face-to-face confrontation to which it leads back, and by which it lets itself be addressed, is something to which it itself belongs as recollection. Heidegger formulates this relation as follows: "Such thinking is, insofar as it is, recollection of Being and nothing else. Belonging to Being, because thrown by Being into the preservation of its truth and claimed for such preservation, it thinks Being."[23] Recollective thought, which frees that toward which one steps back into an opposite for thought, belongs to what it constructs in the very movement of retrogression. What is being reached out for in both the step back and in recollection does not exist independently of these movements. It is achieved in the process of being posited, although this process is itself a function of that which is constructed in this manner.

Now, if recollective thought brings what is constructed into a position face to face with thought, what, then, is *Besinnung*? It must not be translated as "reflection," a concept that presupposes the subject-object division, since we have here neither a subject nor an object but rather recollective thought and its opposite. *Besinnung* corresponds to the movement by which thought becomes involved in what it belongs to—that is, in its opposite, which it meets face to face—"instead of objectifying it through subject presentation." "*Besinnung*'," writes Heidegger, "is calm, self-possessed surrender to that which is worthy of questioning."[24] *Besinnung*, like the step back and the idea of recollective thought, thus articulates a different moment in the operation of retrogression: "Through *Besinnung* [since 'reflection' is misleading, I have substituted the original German word] so understood we actually arrive at the place where, without having experienced it and without having seen penetratingly into it, we have long been sojourning. In *Besinnung* we gain access to a place from out of which there first opens the space traversed at any given time by all our doing and leaving undone."[25] *Besinnung*, consequently, is the term by which Heidegger calls the nonreflexive capturing of what is turned back to through a destruction of the history of ontology, not only insofar as its representations of Being are concerned, but also as concerns its major methodological concept of reflection.

Here, one is able to grasp how the movement of retrogression beyond the tradition of ontology is at the same time the construction and the *letting be* of the hidden ground of that metaphysical tradition. As we have seen, it is not a reflective return to something that, as the origin of that tradition, would be of the same order—an essence, a

past-present or a pregiven, for instance. Retrogression is the very
movement of differentiating *(krinein)* between what shows itself in
and by itself and what does not—*what is* in all its forms. As such a
differentiation, a retrogression manages the radical space of the ultimate ground of what is. That ground is a "function," so to speak,
of the regressive differentiation and dismantling of the tradition. More
precisely, it is itself of the order of that dismantling retrogression, of
an appearing through retreat; moreover, the operation of dismantling
is itself grounded therein. This ground grounds when it is set free in
the very act of returning to it. Such a ground, since it can never be
given, cannot become the end point of a reflection. As one reaches
out for it reflectively, it withdraws.

To the extent that Heidegger's concept of destruction appears to
be a nonreflexive concept, it can be said to prefigure, as does Husserl's
concept of *Abbau*, Derrida's concept of deconstruction. Before discussing the similarities, and especially the differences, between deconstruction on the one hand and *Abbau* and destruction on the other,
however, let us first consider what Derrida himself has said about the
word *deconstruction*. In the debates following the presentation of
"L'Oreille de l'autre" in 1979 in Montreal, Derrida recalled that when
he employed the word *deconstruction* in his early writing, he did so
only rarely, and with the understanding that it was only one word
among others, a secondary word, translating Heidegger's terms for
destruction and dismantling.[26] It is a word, he has said elsewhere, that
he has never liked, and whose fortune has disagreeably surprised
him.[27] Only after others valorized the word in the context of structuralism—which, Derrida claims, did not primarily determine his usage
of the word—did Derrida try to define *deconstruction* in his own
manner.[28]

In this short inquiry into the origin of the concept of deconstruction
I have already hinted at the level of abstraction required to understand
the concept and the problems it is meant to confront. But by outlining
this history I do not mean to blur the fundamental differences between
deconstruction, destruction, and dismantling. All three are nonreflective methodological devices; all three are in essence positive movements, never negative in the usual sense, and certainly not "purely
negative"; and all three attempt to construct, in a more or less systematic fashion, grounds of greater generality for what is to be accounted for. Yet, although Derrida's notion of deconstruction continues
to address the questions raised by the philosophies of Husserl and
Heidegger, his critique of the basic tendencies of their work also

touches on their notions of dismantling and destruction. Like Heidegger, Derrida criticizes Husserl's phenomenological reduction, but he also questions Heidegger's interpretation of that method as a method of inquiring into the meaning of Being. If, as Derrida writes in *Writing and Difference,* referring to the *Cartesian Meditations,* that "in criticizing classical metaphysics, phenomenology accomplishes the most profound project of metaphysics" (*WD,* p. 166), then the same can be said of Heidegger's destruction of the Occidental tradition of ontology and of his focus on Being.

Derrida's objections to Heidegger's destruction of traditional ontology (as well as to Heidegger's "solution" of the problem of reflexivity by taking it back to the more radical idea of a prereflexive understanding) are perhaps most forcefully expressed in "Ousia and Gramme." Here Derrida argues that Heidegger's break with metaphysics remains, for systematic reasons, faithful to metaphysics. He writes, "At a certain point . . . the destruction of metaphysics remains within metaphysics, only making explicit its principles" (*M,* p. 48). In fact, what Derrida tries to demonstrate in this essay is that Heidegger's destruction in *Being and Time* of the metaphysical concept of time borrows *uncritically* from the discourse of metaphysics itself, the very conceptual resources that he uses to criticize and delimit metaphysics' naive concept of time. This is possible because "every text of metaphysics carries within itself, for example, *both* the so-called 'vulgar' concept of time *and* the resources that will be borrowed from the system of metaphysics in order to criticize that concept" (*M,* p. 60). Thus any concept of time that one would wish to oppose to a naive one remains metaphysical, because the very idea of a more fundamental, more universal, more radical concept of time belongs to the very possibilities of metaphysical conceptuality. "In attempting to produce this *other* concept, one rapidly would come to see that it is constructed out of other metaphysical or onto-theological predicates." As a consequence, "the extraordinary trembling to which classical ontology is subjected in . . . [the destruction of that tradition] still remains within the grammar and lexicon of metaphysics" (*M,* p. 63).

The phenomenological reduction of which Heidegger's destruction aimed to be a more radical interpretation led Heidegger, as it had led Husserl, to an ever more fundamental notion of the essence of what is under consideration. The very concept of essence that accompanies the operation of destruction is only a more radical, more original concept of essence than the naive onto-theological concept of it. Phe-

nomenology in general, whether in its Husserlian form or its more
radical Heideggerian form, is by definition a methodical passage to
essentiality. Reduction, dismantling, and destruction are in agreement
with such a systematic transition toward essences.

Here the differences between deconstruction, destruction, and dismantling start to come to light. Surely deconstruction shares with
Abbau and *Destruktion* the goal of attaining the "ultimate foundation" of concepts (OG, p. 60). Yet these foundations, as we shall see,
are no longer essences, however radical. For the same reason, these
ultimate reasons are no longer primordial, and the operation of deconstruction that reaches out for them is no longer phenomenological
in any strict sense. The Husserlian notion of *Abbau* already seemed
to preclude reflection, since the latter represents a methodological
concept that belongs precisely to that tradition beyond which the
operation of dismantling tries to reach in its search for an original
life-world (and for the transcendental egological structures that constitute both that original world and its transformation into the world
of the natural sciences), and thus for a world and for structures of
which there is no experience within that tradition. The Heideggerian
notion of destruction is manifestly nonreflective, because it retro-
gresses to something that is not present in any way whatsoever, but
that constructs itself in the very process of stepping back. Deconstruction is, in an even more radical manner, nonreflexive. The resources
necessary to conceive of the ultimate foundations that deconstruction
seeks are not a positive part of metaphysical conceptuality but are
given in metaphysics in a negative manner. The "rationality," so to
speak, of the "ultimate foundations" to be discovered by deconstruction "no longer issues from a logos. Further, it inaugurates the
destruction, not the demolition but the de-sedimentation, the deconstruction, of all the significations that have their source in that of
the logos" (OG, p. 10). In other words, the ultimate foundations for
which deconstruction reaches out are no longer simply part of the
grammar and lexicon of metaphysics. They are in a certain way, as
we shall see, *exterior* to metaphysics. For this reason, neither reflexivity nor any more radical concept of it is capable of disclosing such
foundations, because reflection can reflect only what is immanent to
the logos. But for the same reason, it may well be that deconstruction
cannot be termed nonreflexive, in the sense that I have applied this
term to *Abbau* and destruction. In what follows, we shall address
these questions specifically.

8

Deconstructive Methodology

If deconstruction reaches out for "ultimate foundations," it may be said to represent a methodical principle of philosophical foundation and grounding. Such a statement, however, must be rendered more precise and secured against a number of misunderstandings. All the concepts implied in this statement will have to be put in quotation marks.

Methods are generally understood as roads (from *hodos:* "way," "road") to knowledge. In the sciences, as well as in the philosophies that scientific thinking patronizes, method is an instrument for representing a given field, and it is applied to that field from the outside. That is, it is on the side of the subject and is an external reflection of the object. It is an instrumental approach to knowledge from an entirely subjective position. Yet such a relation of scientific representation as a form exterior to a given content is in principle extraneous to any thinking philosophy. This, however, is not to say that methodical thought should be replaced "by the non-method of presentiment and inspiration, or by the arbitrariness of prophetic utterance, both of which despise not only scientific pomposity, but scientific procedure of all kinds," as Hegel puts it.[1] For genuine philosophical thought, methods are always *determined* methods, which have their source in the region to which they apply and which are dependent on the nature and specificity of that region. For this reason the ultimate method—that is, the method that represents the philosophical itinerary to truth—must be one that describes the intrinsic and spontaneous movement of truth itself. The philosophical method, as the road toward truth in a domain that is itself determined in terms of truth, implies philosophy's self-implication, and the necessity to reflect itself into self-consciousness. Since Plato such a method has been called *dialektike*, the science of dividing *(diairesis)* and reunification *(synagoge)*. Such a method is nothing other than the patient pursuit of the conceptual activity of truth as it develops its own coherence. It is thus not a formal procedure or rule separate from the content of truth. Method, then, is no longer simply the way to truth; it is truth itself. This is what Hegel means when, in the last chapter of the greater *Logic,* entitled "The Absolute Idea," he finally thematizes the concept of method: "From this course the method has emerged as the *self-knowing Notion that has itself,* as the absolute, both subjective and objective, *for its subject matter,* consequently as the pure correspondence of the Notion and its reality, as a concrete existence that is the Notion itself."[2] What is called "method" in Hegel is thus the totalizing dynamic description of the intellectual activity that, as "the soul of being," attains its most complex and complete fulfillment in the Notion or Concept wherein that activity achieves full self-determination. In other words, method for Hegel is identical to the structure of thought, insofar as thought is also the systematic and genetic exposition of the successive moments that constitute it as a whole. In Hegel it coincides with the self-experience of thought.

To the extent that Derrida's work is a genuinely philosophical inquiry that takes the standard rules of philosophy very seriously, its "method" is certainly not characterized by any exteriority to its object. But is this to say that, in the last resort, it would tend to coincide with the movement of the self-exposition of truth as Concept? Undoubtedly not, since deconstruction also manifestly includes the deconstruction of dialectics, in both a Platonic and a Hegelian sense. As a method, deconstruction is very much determined by the region and the regions of philosophy to which it applies. Yet Derrida has argued that deconstruction is exorbitant to the totality of philosophical knowledge, in particular as that knowledge culminates in the Hegelian Concept. It proceeds from a certain point of exteriority to the whole of the region of all regions of philosophy so as to reinscribe or reground that totality in or with regard to what is exorbitant to it. Obviously, such a procedure not only makes it impossible to give the usual methodological or logical intraorbitary assurances for an operation such as deconstruction, but it also raises the question whether deconstruction can be thought of in terms of method.

Taking off from a certain point outside the totality of the age of logocentrism,—that is, the totality constitutive of philosophy, and in particular speculative philosophy, which claims to have achieved that totality—deconstruction seems to flirt with the scientific idea of method that is characterized precisely by its exteriority to its object. But as we shall see, this point of exteriority to the totality is not that of the subject. Deconstruction is never the effect of a subjective act of desire or will or wishing. What provokes a deconstruction is rather of an "objective" nature. It is a "must," so to speak. "The *incision* [*l'entame;* also 'opening,' 'beginning,' 'broaching'] of deconstruction, which is not a voluntary decision or an absolute beginning, does not take place just anywhere, or in an absolute elsewhere. An incision, precisely, it can be made only according to lines of force and forces of rupture that are localizable in the discourse to be deconstructed" (*P,* p. 82).

Deconstruction, as a methodical principle, cannot be mistaken for anything resembling scientific procedural rules, in spite of its departure from a certain point outside philosophy, nor does it yield to philosophy's classical definition of method, according to which the method must not be irreducibly alien to the field through which it leads. Although deconstruction is an eminently philosophical operation, an operation of extreme sensibility toward the immanence or inherence of the ways of thought to that which is thought—the subject matter (the identity of method and concept, as Hegel would say)—it is not *strictu sensu* methodical, since it does take place from a certain point outside such an identity. Therefore, deconstruction is also the deconstruction of the concept of method (both scientific and philosophical) and has to be determined accordingly.

As in Heidegger, the scientific and philosophical concepts of method are reductive concepts for Derrida. According to Heidegger, the concept of method, by inaugurating the technologization of thought, has radically disfigured the essence of the road *(hodos)* as the proper mode of philosophical thought. In his debate with method, however, Derrida does not attempt to oppose a more fundamental notion of method to scientific or philosophical method. If method for Derrida is a reductive concept, it is so in a different sense than for Heidegger. For Derrida, method is by nature reductive, whether it is fundamental or only derived.[3] Yet it would be a great mistake to conclude that because deconstruction is critical of the discourse of metaphysics and its concept of method (scientific or philosophical), it would, in total disrespect of all levels, indulge in uncontrollable free play. Although a deconstruction of method, deconstruction is not a nonmethod, an invitation to wild and private lucubrations. The rigor of deconstruction is exemplified, for example, by the discrete steps it takes to

deconstruct method. Like those of dissemination, the steps of deconstruction, says Derrida, "allow for (no) *method* [*pas de méthode*]: no
path leads around in a circle toward a first step, nor proceeds from
the simple to the complex, nor leads from a beginning to an end . . . We
here note a point/lack of method [*point de méthode*]: this [however]
does not rule out a certain marching order" (D, p. 271).

It is therefore important to emphasize the systematism of deconstruction. It represents a procedure all of whose movements intertwine
to form a coherent theoretical configuration. Thus deconstructive
"methodology" as a whole cannot be characterized by any impres-
sionistic or empiricist appropriation of one or two of its "moments."
A mere evocation of some of these moments, or of some of the themes
with which deconstruction is concerned, will never lead to any true
insight into what deconstruction purports to achieve.

Derrida makes varied use of the term *deconstruction*. In the early
writings especially, *deconstruction* sometimes merely translates *Abbau*
or *Destruktion*; at other times it metonymically names its own different movements or steps as well; and finally by appositional qual-
ifications it now and again appears to differentiate between a multiplicity
of operations. Yet for the most part, the term has a very definite
meaning. Even if the operation of deconstruction also affects the
concept of method, nothing prevents our formalizing to some extent
the different theoretical movements that make up one rigorous notion
of deconstruction. Before we can discuss the methodical aspect of
deconstruction, however, we must clarify its theoretical presuppositions, determining the specific point at which it becomes compelling
and operational, the different steps that lead up to that point, and
finally the aims of deconstruction. Only against such a background
can the formal characteristics of deconstruction be fully understood.

THE PROPAEDEUTICS OF DECONSTRUCTION

Let us recall Gadamer's contention that absolute reflection as it is
articulated by Hegel anticipates all logically possible reflective stands
on the speculative totality of philosophy by turning them into particular moments of that totality. More generally speaking, Hegel's
discourse is thought to have taken account of all possible Otherness
to that totality, including the concept of Otherness and exteriority,
of a remainder or a beyond to the system, by making them simple
elements in the process of the self-elaboration of truth. With this, of
course, philosophy reaches its completion and its end. Derrida rec-

ognizes this completion of philosophy in speculative thought as well when he writes that "in completing itself, [philosophy] could both include within itself and anticipate all the figures of its beyond, all the forms and resources of its exterior; and could do so in order to keep these forms and resources close to itself by simply taking hold of their enunciation" (WD p. 252).[4] The compelling problem at that moment is how to break the silence without falling back behind the logical achievements of Hegel's position when in the end there is nothing left to be said.[5] Like all other philosophies, starting with the Hegelian left, which in the wake of Hegel's completion of the meta-physical project of philosophy became aware of the dilemma posed by Hegel's thought, Derrida acknowledges that Hegel's superior so-lution of the traditional problems of philosophy is a terrible challenge to philosophical thought. Obviously that challenge cannot be met either through a deliberate decision to overcome Hegel's completion of metaphysics or by simple indifference. That brief segment of the history of the tradition of contesting metaphysics in the aftermath of Hegel, which, as I have shown in Part I of this study, began with Nietzsche, clearly shows what is at stake. Instead of ignoring the task, such a tradition, on the contrary, testifies to the increasing urgency of meeting that challenge, as well as to an equally increasing vigilance concerning all the methodological tools and themes that purport to unhinge the discourse of absolute knowing. After Heidegger's destruc-tion, Derrida's deconstruction is the latest and most complex devel-opment of that tradition.

How, then, are we to characterize, in as succinct a manner as possible, Derrida's approach to the problem? Hegel's philosophy must be described as an attempt to overcome the aporias of traditional philosophical positions, which arise from a naive adoption of a set of inherited conceptual oppositions, by constructively destroying them in a purely conceptual genesis. Derrida's concern is with a naivety unthought by philosophy in general, a blindness constitutive of phil-osophical thought, Hegel's speculative system included. This naivety is an *essential* one and is a function of the logical (dialectical or not) consistency sought and achieved by the philosophical discourse. It is not a naivety that would hamper the solution of traditional philo-sophical problems; on the contrary, it is a blindness without which there may be no hope of ever solving them. This naivety is that of the philosophical *discourse,* of its practice of arguing toward and exposing its concepts. Derrida, who is particularly concerned with the discursive strategies constitutive of the speculative solution (in all its forms) of the aporias to which the traditional formation of concepts leads, has described the approach of singling out this discursive naivety as follows:

A task is then prescribed: to study the philosophical text in its formal structure, in its rhetorical organization, in the specificity and diversity of its textual types, in its models of exposition and production—beyond what previously were called genres—and also in the space of its *mises en scène*, in a syntax which would be not only the articulation of its signifieds, its references to Being or to truth, but also the handling of its proceedings, and of everything invested in them.   (*M*, p. 293)

The naiveties brought to light by such a study—a study that is *not yet* the deconstruction of the philosophical text but only its negative and *prior* moment—are not, properly speaking, logical deficiencies. Thus, after pointing out in "The Double Session" that, for organizational reasons concerning the text of *Philebos*, Plato's contention of a priority of the imitated over imitation is problematic in the text itself, Derrida warns us "not to be too quick to call [it] contradictory" (*D*, p. 190). Contradictions are in principle susceptible to a (dialectical) solution. What Derrida is pointing out here is an inconsistency on the level of philosophical argumentation that cannot be mended, but that nevertheless makes it possible to obtain the desired authoritative results. The very success of Plato's dialogue hinges on such inconsistencies.

These naiveties are contradictions owing neither to an inconsistency in logical argumentation nor to the rhetorical force of the discourse of philosophy. To call these naiveties logical deficiencies or to make them dependent on the inevitable rhetorical use of language in philosophy is to describe only very approximately the sorts of problems exhibited in what may be called the propaedeutics of deconstruction. It is even misleading, because the logical and the rhetorical are, precisely, corresponding intraphilosophical norms of the coherence and cohesion of the philosophical discourse, whose unthought is being focused upon here. In its apparent contradiction to the logical exigencies of philosophical discourse, the rhetorical, figural, and improper use of language combines with the logical use of language to achieve the desired conceptual transparency.

In order to understand the full impact of the shift from one sort of criticism of naivety to another—from the philosophical criticism of the unscientific and unphilosophical consciousness and its "natural attitude" (from Parmenides to Husserl) to the critique of the naiveties implied by the discursive pragmatics of the first type of criticism (speculative or not)—it is necessary to recall that at least since Plato, all major philosophical concepts have represented desiderata, values not of what is but of what *ought* to be. As Derrida has shown, since its inception philosophy has been conceived of as an antidote to the Other of philosophy, either in the form of the masters of illusion, the charlatans and thaumaturges (in the *Republic* for instance), or in the form of the unrepresentable and unnameable, which in Kant's Third Critique is thematized under the name of the disgusting, against which it is said that we strive with all our might (see *D*, pp. 137– 138).[6] Moreover, all of philosophy's concepts and values are *dreams* of plenitude. It would be simplistic to retort that such would be true only of idealist philosophy, since even the most empirical description in philosophy of what is is normative, even were it only for the inevitably axiological dimension of the concepts used in description. As desiderata, all philosophical concepts are in a way utopian and atopic; they represent what Derrida calls ethico-teleological or ethico-ontological values (*LI*, pp. 217, 236). Hence the history of philosophy is the expression of the need to think these concepts, again and again, in a satisfactory and desirable manner—satisfactory, that is, according to the principle of noncontradiction. All these desiderata of philosophy are thus concepts of unity, totality, identity, cohesion, plenitude, states of noncontradiction, in which the negative has been absorbed by the positive, states that lack, and by all rights precede, all dissension, difference, and separation, states of peace and reconciliation. Yet Derrida's contention is not simply that it would be impossible to think noncontradiction in a noncontradictory way. By focusing on the formal, organizational, and textual production of noncontradiction in the philosophical discourse, he shows that, on the contrary, what makes noncontradiction possible and successful within the limits of philosophy's expectations is precisely the evasion of insight that results from the failure to question the discrepancies and inconsistencies of philosophy's *mise en scène*. This is the naivety that is thematized in Derrida's writings.

This inquiry into the process of philosophical conceptualization, as well as into the practice of discursive exposition and the structures of philosophical argumentation, brings to light a whole new field of "contradictions" and "aporias," which, instead of simply belying the philosophical enterprise, are rather constitutive of its successful completion. If one could venture to say that Heidegger reveals a *theme* unthought by metaphysics—the question of the ontico-ontological

difference—one could certainly say that Derrida discloses the unthought *syntax* (a word that I shall have to render more precise) of
philosophical conceptualization and argumentation. Since the "contradictions" and "aporias" that spring from this unthought dimension
of philosophical practice have never been thematized by philosophy
itself and are thus in a certain way exterior to the traditional and
coded problems of philosophy, they cannot be construed as contradictions or aporias proper. Therefore, rigorously speaking, it is misleading to define deconstruction as an operation that, as Ricoeur puts
it, "always consists in destroying metaphysical discourse by reduction
to aporias," without further clarification.[7] Derrida's own occasional
use of the words *aporia* and *contradiction* (see, for instance, *M*, p.
50) does not render such an effort toward clarification dispensable,
since understanding deconstruction depends on it. As we shall see,
Derrida does not limit the notions of aporia and contradiction to
fallacies of philosophical description and predication. Neither are
these concepts borrowed from the conceptual arsenal of the skeptical
tradition in philosophy, a tradition that throws doubt upon philosophical knowledge only from the perspective of a higher mode of
truth. *Aporia* and *contradiction* must be understood in Derrida as
referring to the general dissimilarity between the various ingredients,
elements, or constituents of the discourse of philosophy as such. Indeed, Derrida's parallel inquiry into the formation of philosophical
concepts and the argumentative, discursive, and textual structures of
philosophy leads to the recognition of an essential nonhomogeneity
between the concepts and philosophical texts or works themselves.
All major philosophical concepts, he contends, are ethico-teleological
values of unbroached plenitude and presence. But, as respectable as
they may be, they "live on a delusion and nonrespect for . . . [their]
own condition of origin" (*OG*, p. 139). They exist precisely on a
disregard for their own bipolar opposite, to which they deny a value
similar to their own. Philosophical concepts would be entirely homogeneous if they possessed a nucleus of meaning that they owed
exclusively to themselves—if they were, in other words, conceptual
atoms. Yet since concepts are produced within a discursive network
of differences, they not only are what they are by virtue of other
concepts, but they also, in a fundamental way, inscribe that Otherness
within themselves.

Let us outline several ways in which the teleological value of the
homogeneity of concepts is disproved by the very process of the formation of concepts. First, since a concept is not a simple point but a

structure of predicates clustered around one central predicate, the determining predicate is itself conditioned by the backdrop of the others. Second, each concept is part of a conceptual binary opposition in which each term is believed to be simply exterior to the other. Yet the interval that separates each from its opposite and from what it is not also makes each concept what it is. A concept is thus constituted by an interval, by its difference from another concept. But this interval brings the concept into its own by simultaneously dividing it. The property of a concept depends entirely on its difference from the excluded concept. No concept, including the concept of ethics ("There is no ethics without the presence *of the other* but also, and consequently, without absence, dissimulation, detour, differance, writing," OG, pp. 139–140), can be thought rigorously without including the trace of its difference from its Other within itself. Yet that is as much as to say that the concept—of ethics, for example, but all other concepts as well—includes within itself the trace of that to which it strives (teleologically) to oppose itself in simple and pure exteriority. As a result of this law constitutive of concepts, all concepts are in a sense paradoxical. Take, for instance, the concept of the center:

It has always been thought that the center, which is by definition unique, constituted that very thing within a structure which while governing the structure, escapes structurality. This is why classical thought concerning structure could say that the center is, paradoxically, *within* the structure and *outside* it. The center is at the center of the totality, and yet, since the center does not belong to the totality (is not part of the totality), the totality *has its center elsewhere*. The center is not the center. The concept of centered structure—although it represents coherence itself, the condition of the *episteme* as philosophy or science—is contradictorily coherent. And as always, coherence in contradiction expresses the force of a desire.   (WD, p. 279)

Third, concepts are always (by right and in fact) inscribed within systems or conceptual chains in which they constantly relate to a plurality of other concepts and conceptual oppositions from which they receive their meaning by virtue of the differential play of sense constitution, and which thus affect them in their very core. And fourth, one single concept may be subject to different functions within a text or a corpus of texts. It may function as a citation of itself as well as of another meaning that this same concept may have in a different place or stratum or on another occasion. This citational play, far from being innocent, also affects the ideal closure of the concepts. True, the different meanings to which any one concept may be subjected within the same context are not a problem for philosophy. If philosophy does not simply ignore the question, it solves it hermeneutically, as an index of a more profound and hidden meaning, or it solves the question of relating the two kinds of meaning of one concept by elevating one of these meanings into the more true, complete meaning, of which the other is but a derivation. As an example, let us refer to Kant's distinction between *pulchritudo vaga* and *pulchritudo adhaerens*. Although these two determinations of beauty are of a predicating nature, the question of beauty in general—that is, of the common root that would precomprehend the two concepts and make them communicate—is denied consideration. The essence of beauty is understood in terms of one of the determinations only. For Kant there is no single common source of the two forms of beauty: "We do not pre-understand the essence of beauty in the commonality of the two types, but rather from the perspective of the free beauty that gives rise to a pure aesthetic judgement. It is the pure that gives us the meaning of beauty in general, the pure *telos* of beauty (as a *non-telos*). It is the most beautiful that allows us to think essential beauty and not the less beautiful, which remains a groping approximation *en vue de l'errance*" (*VP*, p. 114).

In short, then, philosophical concepts are not homogeneous. Their nonhomogeneity is manifold, caused by the very process of concept formation and concept use. Yet the variety of dissimilarities that turn concepts into paradoxical structures must not concern us further, since at this point I am interested only in accentuating the generality of their contradictory and aporetic nature. We must note, however, that these different incoherences constituting concepts, which are either absolutely fundamental insofar as concepts are formed within a differential play, or seemingly contingent if they stem from a varied, if not contradictory, usage within a single context, are overshadowed by philosophy's desire for coherence. What Derrida calls the "regulated incoherence within conceptuality" (*OG*, pp. 237-238) cannot, therefore, be thematized in philosophy. But the motive of homogeneity—a teleological motive par excellence (*P*, p. 86)—not only blurs the incoherence within concepts but also organizes the philosophical conception of texts. Let us first consider how philosophy regulates differences in homogeneity relative to philosophical description and the construction of an argument. Derrida's investigation of philosophical works (and of literary texts as well) brings into view a variety of discrepancies between the various strata that make up a work's argumentation and description, and that make it thoroughly illusionary simply to maintain the metaphysical desire for the pure coherence of their volume.

Let us dwell for a moment on the specific nature of what, in the light of Althusser's concept of uneven development, I have chosen to call discursive inequalities or dissimilarities, which are due to these conflicting strata within the coherence of texts or works.[8] Their nature is manifold too. One example of such a disparity between levels of argumentation is Derrida's demonstration of a contradiction within Saussure's scientific project. This contradiction stems from the fact that Saussure, in determining the object of structural linguistics according to the principle of differentiality as a system of marks comparable to writing, belies his strong condemnation in *Cours* of writing as harmful to speech. Both a logo- and a phonocentric valorization of speech cohabit in this discourse, as well as another scientific stratum that is a radical questioning of the former orientation. Another example is the tension between gesture and statement in Rousseau's discussion of the origin of language. In *Of Grammatology,* Derrida distinguishes between Rousseau's explicit declarations as to how he *wishes* to think the origin of language and his matter-of-fact *description* of it. Rousseau's declared intention is to think the origin as a simple one unbroached by any difference. "But in spite of that declared intention, Rousseau's discourse lets itself be constrained by a complexity which always has the form of the supplement of or from the origin" (*OG,* p. 243). Yet instead of concluding, based on what follows from his own description of the origin, that from the outset difference has corrupted the origin, Rousseau prefers to believe that the supplement *"must (should) have"* been enclosed in, in the sense of being confused with, the origin. "There *must (should) have* been plenitude and not lack, presence without difference" (*OG,* p. 215). As a result of this ethico-theoretical decision, which valorizes originarity as a desideratum, everything that had emerged in the description of the origin as already broaching it—that is, as being more originary than the origin—is turned into secondariness, into something that *"adds itself from the outside as evil and lack* to happy and innocent plenitude." The dangerous supplement, then, "would come from an outside which would be simply the outside" (*OG,* p. 215). Consequently, the tension between gesture and statement, description and declaration, far from resulting in mutual annihilation contributes to the coherence of the text by means of the grid of the "ought to be," or the conditional mood. "*Should* [*devrait*]: it is the mode and tense of a teleological and eschatological anticipation that superintends Rousseau's entire discourse," writes Derrida (OG, p. 295). Through this mood the contradiction is made to be no more than apparent, and Rousseau can think the two incompatible possibilities, the origin and the supplement, simultaneously. As the conditional mood reveals, it is itself the unity of a desire. Derrida writes, "As in the dream, as Freud analyzes it, incompatibles are simultaneously admitted as soon as it is a matter of satisfying a desire, in spite of the principle of identity, or of the excluded third party—the logical time of consciousness" (OG, p. 245). These discursive contradictions are united by desire into a contradictory coherence regulated by what Freud calls the sophistry of the borrowed kettle.[9] Derrida sums up this kind of reasoning, which according to Freud is supposed to illustrate dream logic, in the following passage: "In his attempt to arrange everything in his favor, the defendant piles up contradictory arguments: (1) The kettle I am returning to you is brand new; (2) The holes were already in it when you lent it to me; (3) You never lent me a kettle, anyway" (D, p. 111; see also S, p. 67).

The various arguments concerning the origin and the supplement, speech and writing, are organized by Saussure and Rousseau in a similar manner: (1) The supplement and writing are totally exterior and inferior to the origin and to speech, which are thus not affected by them and remain intact; (2) they are harmful because they are separate from the origin and thereby corrupt living speech, which otherwise would be intact; and (3) if one needs to fall back on the supplement or on writing, it is not because of their intrinsic value but because the origin was already deficient, and because living speech was already finite before it became supplemented by writing. Hence, supplement and writing do not harm origin or speech at all. On the contrary, they mend the deficiencies of origin and speech (D, p. 111).

Because of this logic within discursive contradiction, or contradictory arguments held together by the desire for unity, it is insufficient simply to say "that Rousseau thinks the supplement without thinking it, that he does not match his saying and his meaning, his descriptions and his declarations" (OG, p. 245). Rather, the contradiction is regulated, which gives these texts their very coherence and totality. Instead of permitting these contradictions to cancel each other out, Rousseau, like Saussure "accumulates contradictory arguments to bring about a satisfactory decision: the exclusion of writing," difference, or the supplement (OG, p. 45). But this organization of incompatibles into a unity dominated by ethico-teleological values, which maintains and contains the adverse arguments and strata in the very act of decision by which philosophy institutes itself, is possible only through the evasion of a number of questions and implications that follow from the fact that "Rousseau, caught, like the logic of identity, *within* the graphic of supplementarity, says what he does not wish to say, describes what he does not wish to conclude" (*OG*, p. 246).

A last example of such contradictions concerning the gap between declaration and, this time, factual practice concerns the often perceived contradiction in the Platonic condemnation of writing in writing. How could Plato, Rousseau, and others subordinate writing to speech while writing themselves? Derrida asks:

What law governs this "contradiction," this opposition to itself of what is said against writing, of a dictum that pronounces itself against itself as soon as it finds its way into writing, as soon as it writes down its self-identity and carries away what is proper to it *against* this ground of writing? This "contradiction," which is nothing other than the relation-to-self of diction as it opposes itself to scription, as it *chases* itself (away) in hunting down what is properly its *trap*—this contradiction is not contingent.   (*D*, p. 158)

The sort of discursive inequalities that I have pointed out concern contradictory strata of description within the argumentation of a single work, discrepancies between explicit statements and the desiderata of thought, between declaration and factual practice. But the analysis preceding deconstruction—the propaedeutics of deconstruction—is not limited to bringing into prominence conceptual aporias on the one hand and, on the other, discursive inequalities of all sorts. There is a third type of discursive heterogeneity which in fact defies categorization properly speaking. In each instance it comprises a multiplicity of very different and radically incommensurable layers, agencies, or sediments that invariably make up discursive wholes. Through thematizing this kind of contradiction or aporia in the philosophical text, it becomes evident that the philosophical concept of contradiction or aporia is incapable of covering and comprehending these types of inconsistencies, not only in isolation but especially when taken together. Indeed, these discrepancies stem from differences in the importance, scope, and status of parts or elements of philosophical discourses, as well as from the irreducibly disproportionate and dissimilar nature of various constituents of these parts or elements. Let us, then, look at some paradigmatic types of this sort of discursive inequality, which, contrary to appearances, have not been problematized in the perspective outlined above.

The analysis of philosophical discourses reveals that they are com-

posed not only of pure concepts and philosophemes but also of metaphors and mythemes. As discursive elements, the last two are of an
entirely different status from that of concepts, yet they necessarily
combine with concepts, whose purity as to mythical and figural residues should be beyond all question. Certainly the relation between
myth and logos is a philosophical problem of long standing; the same
must be said of the relation between concept and figure. But what
Derrida is concerned with—in "Plato's Pharmacy," for instance—is
not so much the way in which philosophy tries to master its relation
to myth or to figures as the manner in which this intimate combination, within a whole of such dissimilar elements as concepts and
nonconcepts, philosophemes and mythemes, instead of simply resisting absorption into the homogeneity of the concept contributes to the
creation of an effect of such purity. In other words, Derrida's concern
is with the irreducibility and inevitability of the combination of opposite genres in the philosophical discourse.

Such an analysis may also accentuate a lexicological inconsistency
arising from the different and repeated use of one particular so-called
key word or key signification in a text. The emphasis of such an
analysis is on the singularity and inextricability of the juxtaposition
of these significations in one ensemble. The different citations of one
and the same word within one text or context can be *opposed* to one
another, but they can also be simply dissimilar and irreducible to
one another, in which case they resist all hermeneutical solution.
"There cannot be any such thing as key words," writes Derrida (*D*,
p. 256). These multiple different usages of the same term in one work
or textual unity must thus be analyzed as the background against
which the hermeneutical search for an ultimate signified takes place.

The analysis may also focus on a chain of words similar to one
another, which may have the same etymological root but are nonetheless not supposed to communicate within the text. *Pharmakeia–
pharmakon–pharmakeus* in Plato's *Phaedros,* which Derrida analyzes
in "Plato's Pharmacy," is an instance of such a chain.

This sort of analysis may also throw into relief unsublated and
unmediated statements or propositions about one particular theme
within a text or a corpus of texts, for instance the theme of the
"woman" in Nietzsche, analyzed by Derrida in *Spurs.* It may also
point out the cohabitation in one text or corpus of two or more
irreducible types of one general thing (such as *pulchritudo adhaerens*
and *pulchritudo vaga* in the Third Critique, analyzed by Derrida in
"Parergon"); of a variety of information in a text and a context;[10] or

simply of the repeated and dissimilar functions within one text or context of mere signifiers, such as the letters *i* and *r* in Mallarmé (see *D*, p. 282).

Other such discursive inequalities can be found between parts of a text, for example a preface and the main body of a text, as discussed by Derrida in "Outwork, Prefacing"; between the title and the main part of the text, as thematized in "Titre à préciser"; or between two segments of a text divided by an intermediary space which is marked either by a blank, as in Blanchot's *L'Arrêt de mort,* analyzed in "Living On: *Border Lines,*" or marked by an interpolated text as in Nietzsche's *Ecce Homo,* treated in "L'Otobiographie de Nietzsche."[11] For present purposes, it is not necessary to accumulate further evidence of such discursive discrepancies arising from a grafting of thoroughly heterogeneous elements upon one another. Let us recall for the moment that they are multiple, different in status, and different in essence. The analysis presupposed by all deconstruction, properly speaking, consists of such an assessment of the various heterogeneous levels of philosophical discourse, as well as of the heterogeneous elements or agencies that combine on these levels. It is not a question of reducing these variegated discursive and conceptual disparities to one model of divergency, especially not to that of contradiction as the major criterion of the necessary falsehood of statements. Nor is the question one of how to reduce these disparities, inconsistencies, and dissimilarities through any of the traditional procedures. What is at stake is the assessment of the generality and irreducibility of these various inequalities. Under this condition only can the second step of deconstruction take place. Deconstruction is thus the attempt to account for the heterogeneity constitutive of the philosophical discourse, not by trying to overcome its inner differences but by maintaining them.

To sum up: deconstruction starts with a systematic elucidation of contradictions, paradoxes, inconsistencies, and aporias constitutive of conceptuality, argumentation, and the discursiveness of philosophy. Yet these discrepancies are not logical contradictions, the only discrepancies for which the philosophical discourse can account. Eluded by the logic of identity, they are consequently not contradictions properly speaking. Nor are these necessary inconsistencies the result of inequality between form and content. Their exclusion from the canon of philosophical themes is precisely what makes it possible to distinguish between form and content, a distinction that takes place solely against the horizon of the possibility of their homogeneous reunification.

As its first step, deconstruction thus presupposes a concretely developed demonstration of the fact that concepts and discursive totalities are already cracked and fissured by necessary contradictions and heterogeneities that the discourse of philosophy fails to take into account, either because they are not, rigorously speaking, logical contradictions, or because a regulated (conceptual) economy must avoid them in order to safeguard the ethico-theoretical decisions that orient its discourse. These fissures become apparent when we follow to its logical end that which in the process of conceptualization or argumentation is only in a certain manner said. Deconstruction thus begins by taking up broached but discontinued implications—discontinued because they would have contradicted the intentions of philosophy. In the case of Rousseau's text, Derrida formulates this procedure as follows:

> Rousseau's text must constantly be considered as a complex and many-leveled structure; in it, certain propositions may be read as interpretations of other propositions that we are, up to a certain point and with certain precautions, free to read otherwise. Rousseau says A, then for reasons that we must determine, he interprets A into B. A, which was already an interpretation, is reinterpreted into B. After taking cognizance of it, we may, without leaving Rousseau's text, isolate A from its interpretation into B, and discover possibilities and resources there that indeed belong to Rousseau's text, but were not produced or exploited by him, which, for equally legible motives, he *preferred to cut short* by a gesture neither witting nor unwitting. (OG, p. 307)

The demonstration of these unexploited possibilities and resources, which contradict the ethico-theoretical decisions characteristic of conceptualization and philosophical argumentation and haunt the concepts and the texts of philosophy, corresponds to the thematization of a naivety unthought by discursive philosophical practice. Such naivety complies with and is a function of the ethical orientation of theorizing and is in no way a naivety or deficiency owing to the finitude of the philosophizing subject, Rousseau or Saussure, for instance. On the contrary, such naivety is the very possibility of theory.

AGAINST NEUTRALITY

Although philosophy's blind spot may be located in the discrepancies constitutive of the philosophical discourse, it does not necessarily follow that the philosophical project itself would be unsettled by attempts to show that these contradictions or aporias cancel each other out. Exactly the opposite is true. Such a purported demystification of philosophy amounts to nothing more (nor less) than the Romantic attempt to realize philosophy's dream of homogeneity by a shortcut. Deconstruction begins with demonstrating such inequalities within concepts or texts, but it aims as little as the texts themselves at an annulment of that which is in opposition. That deconstruction has nothing in common with such an operation of annulment is spelled out in capital letters in Derrida's work. The primary reason for this is that the contradictions, oppositions, and dyadic structures of concepts, texts, and their multiple argumentational levels are never symmetrical. Derrida insists time and again that "in classical philosophical opposition we are not dealing with the peaceful coexistence of a *vis à vis*, but rather with a violent hierarchy. One of the two terms governs the other (axiologically, logically, etc.), or has the upper hand" (*P*, p. 41). Indeed, "there is no dualism without primacy," as even Friedrich Schlegel well knew.[12] Thus, no simple collapsing of opposite terms is possible. But this dissymmetry is not only one of concepts opposed binarily within the discourse of philosophy; it is also true of the aporias, paradoxes, and contradictions that constitute the concepts themselves, or that exist between suppressed possibilities, resources, or implications and that which is valorized or explicitly developed within discursive totalities. In the latter case they cannot be collapsed, because they belong to entirely different levels of thought and argumentation. To mistake deconstruction for an operation aiming at an annulment of these conceptual or textual discrepancies is to confound levels of thought and texts, to overlook the axiological and logical subordination of its concepts, and to demonstrate an insensibility to what texts, and particularly philosophical texts, are meant to achieve. Even if deconstruction's intention, in the last analysis, is to expose the impossibility of clear-cut genres, and thus the ultimate failure of a distinct genre such as philosophy, its point of departure remains an extreme awareness of the project particular to the genre of philosophy, as opposed to literature in particular.

"Deconstruction," writes Derrida, "cannot limit itself or proceed immediately to a neutralization" (*M*, p. 329). Such an annulment or neutralization of conceptual or textual inconsistencies, by overlooking the conflictual structure of oppositions, would *in practice* "leave the previous field untouched, leaving one no hold on the previous opposition, thereby preventing any means of *intervening* in the field effectively" (*P*, p. 41). Such neutralization would not only renounce all active intervention in the texts to be deconstructed, but would even serve the purposes and interests of traditional interpretation. In a long footnote to "The Double Session" he writes, "Just as the motif of neutrality, in its negative form paves the way for the most classical and suspect attempts at reappropriation, it would be imprudent just to cancel out the pairs of metaphysical oppositions, simply to *mark off* from them any text (assuming this to be possible)." (*D,* p. 207). In the case of Mallarmé, for example, a deconstruction, in the sense of a neutralizaton or annulment, of oppositional dyads would serve only to confirm the hitherto idealist interpretation of that author. Indeed, by annulling and equalizing all oppositional forces in the mode of pro and contra, such an operation would not only stabilize these forces in an economy of decidable polarities, but would also be a "free shot which aims nonetheless to collect its interests" (*S,* p. 63). Therefore, Derrida insists on a *dissymmetric strategy* in deconstruction in order to control and "counterbalance the neutralizing moments of any deconstruction" (*D,* p. 207). Deconstruction is not neutral; neutrality "has a negative essence *(ne-uter),* is the negative side of transgression" (*WD,* p, 274). As such, it is produced within discursive knowledge, in which ultimately all the contradictions and all the oppositions of classical logic are overcome in the work of neutralization. Neutralization, then, is a negative image of deconstruction *within* discursive knowledge. What Derrida says in *Writing and Difference* of Bataille's sovereign operation is valid for deconstruction too: "The sovereign operation is not content with neutralizing the classical operations *in discourse;* in the major form of experience it transgresses the law or prohibitions that form a system with discourse, *and even with the work of neutralization*" (*WD,* p. 274).[13]

Since the identifying of deconstruction with the neutralization or mutual annulment of contradicting concepts or textual strata is still one of the dominant misconceptions about deconstruction, it may be useful to pursue its implications. This misconception has informed most deconstructive literary criticism, whether of literary, philosophical, or critical texts, and it has come to be known as the theory of self-reflection or self-deconstruction of texts. This self-reflection is understood to take place by a mutual annulment, neutralization, or cancellation of all bipolar oppositions within these texts. Such a principle of annulment also informs critical enterprises that oppose conflicting and mutually exclusive positions within critical theory or philosophy in order to demonstrate their identity, by showing that one position partakes in the other it opposes (and vice versa), in this manner pointing out the inadequacy of either as a universal statement.

Whether this mutual neutralization is seen as a final coming to rest of the antagonistic positions or as an endless conflict between the two positions, the principle is the same. But what theoretical presuppositions do these different critical enterprises share, whether they deal with texts of literature, philosophy, or criticism? First, the suspicion that antagonistic positions or opposite concepts are identical arises from a neglect of the historical and pragmatic aspects of the contexts in which they are expressed. Only through such a simplification or reduction of this context—that is to say, only when historical and theoretical displacements within a tradition are no longer seen as corresponding to real theoretical problems, forces, ideologies, and so on—is such a dramatization of antithetical positions of criticism possible. By neglecting the pragmatic and historical context of the utterance of what is dramatized in such a manner as to cancel it out, the criticism in question reveals its origins in Romantic (as well as, in a certain interpretation, Idealist) philosophy. It is a suprahistorical criticism that pretends to speak from a position free of ideology—that is, from an absolute point of view.

This last point needs to be developed a bit further. First, let us remember that this kind of criticism originated in early German Romanticism. The reciprocal dissolution of opposing concepts or contradictory strata within a text, which this criticism promotes, must be traced back to the Romantics' attempt at a transcendental poetry that was to represent an amalgam not only of all different genres but also of all the hitherto separate disciplines. Such a poetry was to be created through a fluidization or liquefaction *(Verflüssigung)* of all oppositions and particularities by means of objective irony. The result was to be a *medium of reflexivity,* in which all individual, and thus opposite, stands would achieve total reciprocity.[14] Second—and this point too can only be presented schematically—it is necessary to recall Hegel's criticism of Romanticism, both in general and in particular of the ideas of reciprocity, annulment, and neutrality. The medium of neutralization or dissolution *(menstruum universale)* was thought to result from the reciprocal determination of all the terms that partake in it. In their attempt to define this medium, the Romantics singled out Fichte's synthetic concept of interdetermination *(Wechselbestimmung)* and turned it into the one constitutive movement of annulment. But interdetermination in Fichte's *Science of Knowledge* is not the only form, however major, of determination. In order to break the idealist circularity of such an interaction, he established the necessity of a further determination of interdetermination through self-deter-

mination.[15] This speculative concept of determination is the very back-
bone of Hegel's critique of Romantic philosophy.

Especially in his *Logic*, Hegel develops this Fichtean critique of a
self-contained reciprocity, a reciprocity that avoids its own determination. This further determination of reciprocity and interdetermination takes place in "The Doctrine of Essence" in the second book
of the first part of *The Science of Logic*. The problem of reciprocal
determination, which constitutes the Romantic medium of reflection
as much as the contemporary idea of a self-destructing text, is dealt
with in "The Logic of Reflection." While discussing the penultimate
reflexive determination—in other words, contradiction—Hegel concludes that the reflective dissolution of contradiction, the "ceaseless
vanishing of the opposites into themselves," in which each of the
polar oppositions "is simply the transition or rather the self-trans-
position of itself into its opposite," serves to produce a *unity (Einheit)*
created precisely by the self-destruction of the opposed terms. "*They
destroy themselves [sie richten sich zugrunde]* in that they determine
themselves as self-identical, yet in this determination are rather the
negative, an identity-with-self that is a relation-to-other."[16] This unity
in which the contradictions mutually dissolve is therefore a unity of
nullity *(Null)*. As a matter of fact, representing *(vorstellendes)* consciousness, unlike speculative consciousness, "stops short at the one-
sided *resolution* of it into *nothing,* and fails to recognize the positive
side of contradiction where it becomes *absolute activity* and absolute
ground" (p. 442). How are we then to think the positive side of
contradiction, and in what way can a self-dissolution of opposites
lead to a positive unity? Hegel writes: "But contradiction contains
not merely the negative, but also the positive; or, the self-excluding
reflection is at the same time *positing* reflection; the result of contradiction is not merely a nullity. The positive and negative constitute
the *positedness* of the self-subsistence. Their own negation of themselves sublates the positedness of the self-subsistence. It is this which
in truth perishes in contradiction" (p. 433).

Indeed, from the perspective of speculative consciousness—that is,
from a determination of interdetermination in self-determination—
the mutually derestricting play of opposites does not simply result in
a zero outcome. Instead of destroying themselves in a unity of nullity,
the contradictory terms that "fall to the ground" *(zugrundegehen)* in
self-liquefaction articulate a unity of reflection in which the opposed
terms are rooted and of which they are the bipolar representation.
As Hegel puts it, the dissolved contradiction, the canceled-out op-

position, is "ground, essence as unity of the positive and negative" (p. 435). But this can be recognized only if consciousness does not stop short at the concept of interdetermination but determines it further:

The self-contradictory, self-subsistent opposition was therefore already itself ground; all that was added to it was the determination of unity-with-self, which results from the fact that each of the self-subsistent opposites sublates itself and makes itself into its opposite, thus falling to the ground [*zugrunde geht*]; but in this process it at the same time only unites with itself; therefore, it is only in falling to the ground [*in seinem Untergange*], that is, in its positedness or negation, that the opposite is really the essence that is reflected into and identical with itself. (p. 435)

In short, Hegel's speculative critique reveals that both the shortcomings and ambitions of the Romantic dissolution of contradiction, a dissolution that *presupposes* difference and results only in the *negative unity of the neutral* (a unity of nullity), were within the realm of truth. Unless one recognizes with Heidegger that nihilism is the very essence of metaphysics and that consequently all the concepts of essence, ground, and unity as thought within onto-theology are nihilistic—concepts to which both Romanticism and contemporary literary criticism and those ideological positions that accuse them of being nihilistic are indebted—Hegel's critique of the medium of reflexivity shows that what the Romantics aimed at was not so nihilistic after all. As this discussion of reciprocal determination or the self-canceling of bipolar oppositions has demonstrated, the Romantic idea of the medium of reflexivity, as well as that of the text as a medium of neutralization and annulment of concepts and strata, fails to achieve what it seeks: a unitary ground or essence in which all self-subsistent opposites dissolve in order to ground themselves. Were they to achieve this goal, Romantic self-reflection and deconstructive criticism would represent a fulfillment of the telos of metaphysics. But Hegel's speculative critique of the movement of contradiction, which applies both to Romanticism and to contemporary deconstructive literary criticism, shows that this movement produces only the simple or abstract idea of such a ground. As Hegel shows, such a unity cannot be achieved in a logically satisfactory manner within a logic of essence or reflection but only in the logic of the Concept or Notion, since only here can the determination of interdetermination by self-determination be completed.

Let me repeat, then, that deconstruction has nothing in common with this sort of philosophical or critical practice, although it is often confused with it. Deconstruction does not engage in the annulment or neutralization of opposites. It is not a practice in search of an essence, ground, or unity beyond all singular and opposite terms or beyond the historical and pragmatic aspects of the concepts or positions whose dramatization is staged in Romantic philosophy and in related literary criticism. We have seen that this cannot be the case. The propaedeutics of deconstruction reveal that it is not concerned with what has hitherto been called contradictions or aporias, which lend themselves to a mutual self-destruction or to dissolution in an all-embracing ground or essence.

INFRASTRUCTURAL ACCOUNTING

If deconstruction, consequently, cannot be mistaken for such a metaphysical operation, regardless of the way in which neutralization or annulment of differences is understood—as a conciliatory putting to rest or as the opening of an infinite war between them—how then is deconstruction different? What does it do with the contradictions, aporias, and inconsistencies that it so eagerly points to in the formation of concepts or the argumentative and discursive structures of texts of all sorts? A first schematic answer is that deconstruction attempts to "account" for these "contradictions" by "grounding" them in "infrastructures" discovered by analyzing the specific organization of these "contradictions." In addition to Derrida's philosophical style and the multifarious infrastructures to which his analyses lead, the very concept of infrastructure, as the *formal rule* that each time regulates differently the play of the contradictions in question, is an intrinsic part of his original contribution to philosophy. It is a contribution that displaces the logic of philosophy and inscribes it within a general heterology.

Let us address specifically the three general concepts that I have put in quotation marks in this definition of deconstruction: "accounting for," "grounding" (as it differs from the metaphysical operation of grounding), and "structure."

Since Plato, all reasonable speech has been held to be that which not only asserts but also always accounts for what is asserted, by stating the grounds or reasons for it. Yet such a substantiation, by reasons or grounds, of what is asserted, and hence the claims to knowledge of reasonable speech, does not proceed exclusively by empirical and logico-mathematical justification. It must also take place, as Kant writes at the beginning of *Critique of Pure Reason,* in a "free and public examination."[17] As *logon didonai,* or a rendering of accounts, all accounting—that is, all stating of the grounds of what is asserted—comprises a practical and public aspect in which the thinker justifies himself before others. Just as in ancient Greece the individual laid his entire life bare in the public square of the *agora* to receive the civic stamp of approval of the whole community, without which his life as a citizen would have been incomplete, so too the appeal to public approval is a necessary and intrinsic element of philosophical accounting, without which philosophy could not claim universality. In this process the individual's self-consciousness coalesces, and the legitimacy of the grounds of explanation receives its official stamp of recognition from the public. The concept of accounting for, then, which ultimately hinges on the *logon didonai,* involves much more than merely stating grounds in the process of substantiating what is asserted. The individual also responds to the demand of accounting for himself before the community in order to receive recognition of his status as a self-conscious public being. Only in unison can all these moments of accounting establish the certitude of truth. They show the process of accounting to be a unitary process, in which the substantiation of truth claims hinges on the public constitution of the individual as a self-conscious, reasonable being, capable of demonstrating philosophy's claim to self-legitimization.[18]

Derrida's attempt to "ground" the contradictions in concept formation as well as in the argumentative and textual strata of philosophical ensembles in "infrastructures" has many consequences for the traditional concept of accounting and its structure of wholeness—more consequences than can be analyzed here. Although it is important to realize that Derrida does not simply erase the metaphysical concept of accounting and of a last instance, if only because to do so "would run the risk of defusing the necessary critique it permits in certain determinate contexts" (*D,* p. 208), it will soon become clear that the infrastructural grounds that account for the differences in question and correspond to problems that do not belong to the classical canon of philosophy are no longer simply grounds in the philosophical sense. Consequently, establishing such nongrounds can no longer be viewed as an act of philosophical accounting.

I have maintained that deconstruction consists of establishing "infrastructures" to account for differences as far as they pertain to concepts and texts. Clarifying what *structure* and *infrastructure* mean in this context may give us a better grasp of the epistemological achievement of deconstruction. Throughout his writings Derrida has acknowledged the pertinence of the structuralist enterprise. But he has also regularly pointed out its ethico-metaphysical provenance, especially in phenomenology, in whose shadow modern structuralism has grown and flourished. He has insisted on the affinity between structural and eidetic reduction and on the problem that follows from both: the systematic privileging of one of the two series that characterize the system of metaphysics—the series concerned with form, quantity, internal organization, closure, static analysis, and so on as opposed to that concerned with content, quality, history, openness, genetic analysis. Therefore, Derrida concludes, "it would not be difficult to show that a certain structuralism has always been philosophy's most spontaneous gesture" (WD, p. 159). Yet he also claims to have developed "the most legitimate principled exigencies of 'structuralism' " (P, p. 28), as far as a notion such as "differance" is concerned, that is, as one example of "infrastructures." Consequently, it is all the more urgent to clarify the concept of structure as used by Derrida.

Whether one retraces the traditional meaning of *structure* back to the origin of its present usage in the calculus of variations of the 1870s and in topology at the turn of the century, or to its synonyms in Greek thought, it always refers to a constructed system functioning perfectly within itself. Yet in this sense the term *structure* borrows heavily from several other traditional concepts. Thus, an analysis pretending to exhaust the meaning of the modern concept of structure would have to begin by explaining why it seemed necessary at one point to replace more traditional concepts with this new term. "To know why one says 'structure,' is to know why one no longer wishes to say *eidos*, 'essence,' 'form,' *Gestalt*, 'ensemble,' 'composition,' 'complex,' 'construction,' 'correlation,' 'totality,' 'Idea,' 'organism,' 'state,' 'system,' etc. One must understand not only why each of these words showed itself to be insufficient but also why the notion of structure continues to borrow some implicit signification from them and to be inhabited by them" (WD, p. 301). What the notion of structure shares with all these concepts is closure, according to which the passage from one structure to another can be thought only in terms of chance, hazard, or catastrophe. It is important to note that this closure is due not only to the bracketing of facts that a structuralist perspective requires, but also to the fact that the traditional concept of structure is always thought to be centered. The concept of structure has always been thought with regard to a point of presence or fixed origin which turns its borders into the circumference of a totality. This aspect of a closed totality, withdrawn from all possible change from outside, which thus makes the structure an ideal *model* rather than a de facto construction, is also emphasized by the metaphorical origin of structure in the concept of spatiality.

In *Writing and Difference,* Derrida reminds us that

> strictu sensu, the notion of structure refers only to space, geometric or morphological space, the order of forms and sites. Structure is first the structure of an organic or artificial work, the internal unity of an assemblage, a *construction*; a work is governed by a unifying principle, the *architecture* that is built and made visible in a location . . . Only metaphorically was this *topographical* literality displaced in the direction of its Aristotelean and *topical* signification (the theory of commonplaces in language and the manipulation of motifs or arguments) (*WD,* pp. 15–16)

In short, the concept of structure is a highly charged and ambiguous one. Consequently, "everything depends upon how one sets it to work," as Derrida says in *Positions* (*P,* p. 24). The kind of work to which Derrida refers is located, first of all, in the spatiality evoked by the metaphor of structure. The task is to interrogate the metaphoricity of the term *structure* in order to prevent its geometrical and morphological connotations from taking the upper hand. Subsequently, a certain nonspatiality or original spatiality of the concept of structure comes into focus. Derrida writes in *Writing and Difference:*

> As long as the metaphorical sense of the notion of structure is not acknowledged *as such,* that is to say interrogated and even destroyed as concerns its figurative quality so that the nonspatiality or original spatiality designated by it may be revived, one runs the risk, through a kind of sliding as unnoticed as it is *efficacious,* of confusing meaning with its geometric, morphological, or, in the best of cases, cinematic model. One risks being interested in the figure itself to the detriment of the play going on within it metaphorically. (*WD,* p. 16)

By bracketing in this manner all the figurative connotations of the original model of structure—that is, by thematizing and excluding from the term its geometrical representation of a unified and centered space—the "structurality of structure" may come into view. As a matter of fact, the predominantly figurative spatiality associated with the term *structure* neutralizes and obliterates the thought or structurality of structure and what it is to achieve. The morphological and geometric metaphoricity of the notion of structure not only fails to exhaust the meaning of the term but also depends on the structurality of structure for its very meaning.

The thought of the structurality of structure, a thought that becomes possible as soon as the originary metaphorical meaning of *structure* is recognized and put between quotation marks, is the thought of the law according to which the notion of structure has always been subjected to a center. It is also an attempt to decenter structure, to think its openness, or to think what remains open in an otherwise closed structure. The structurality of structure seems, thus, to be another name for the essence of structure, which comes into view as soon as the spatiality that informs the metaphor of structure is set aside. Why essence is not the proper name for the structurality of structure will become obvious as we go on. For the moment it should be clear that when Derrida operates "positively" with the concept of structure, he aims at the structurality of structure. To speak of the structurality of structure is to speak on a level entirely other than the level on which the concept of "the (necessarily closed) minor structure" exists. This structurality of structure is the "fundamental structure" (*WD*, pp. 155, 26); it allows a closed-off totality to open itself, if only in the mere anticipation of its subsequent reclosure. But this "fundamental" or "essential" structure is in truth "the structurality of an opening," a transcendental of sorts that allows the minor structures to come to the fore (*WD*, p. 155). It is an opening that is structural, or the structurality of an opening. Yet each of these concepts excludes the other. It is thus as little a structure as it is an opening; it is as little static as it is genetic, as little structural as it is historical. It can be understood neither from a genetic nor from a structuralist and taxonomic point of view, nor from a combination of both points of view.

What, then, is this more "fundamental" structure? What is its structurality? It is the opening or possibility of what opens up closed structures, and what closes structures off against any exterior interference. It is the principle that guides the decentering and centering of structures. "This opening is certainly that which liberates time and genesis (even coincides with them), but it is also that which risks enclosing progression toward the future—becoming—by giving it form. That which risks stifling force under form" (*WD*, p. 26). The transcendentality of this structurality of an opening is therefore both the condition of possibility of a systematic structuralism and "the principled, essential, and structural impossibility of closing a structural phenomenology" or any systematic structuralism of whatever kind (WD, p. 162). To sum up: *structure* in Derrida has the meaning of a nonregional and transcendental opening that represents the condition of possibility of the minor structures and the accidents that they suffer. *Structure,* as used by Derrida, is an infrastructure.

In *Positions,* Derrida notes that the concept of infrastructure, as he uses it several times in *Of Grammatology,* corresponds to a "transformed concept of 'infrastructure,' . . . an 'infrastructure' of which the *general text* would no longer be an effect or a reflection," that is to say, to a non-Marxist notion of infrastructure (P, p. 90). Since Derrida has never explicitly outlined this particular transformation, we may immediately proceed to a characterization of the major features of the notion of infrastructure.[19]

With regard to concepts in bipolar opposition—that is, to metaphysical concepts, to the aporias that become visible in the formation of concepts, and to the conflicting strata of argumentative and discursive totalities—the infrastructure is the "open matrix" in which these oppositions and contradictions are engendered.[20] Derrida defines *infrastructure* when he writes, "Here structure means the irreducible complexity within which one can only shape or shift the play of presence or absence: that within which metaphysics can be produced but which metaphysics cannot think" (OG, p. 167). The infrastructures, which as we shall see are irremediably plural, represent the relation—connection, *ratio, rapport*—that organizes and thus accounts for the differences, contradictions, aporias, or inconsistencies between concepts, levels, argumentative and textual arrangements, and so on that characterize the discourse of metaphysics.

Now, I have claimed that by means of such infrastructures deconstruction accounts for the differences that fissure the discourse of philosophy, and any other discourse dependent on it. Putting aside for the moment the questions concerning the technicalities of such a way of accounting, we must first of all come to an understanding of the philosophical titles of such an operation. Indeed, what makes the infrastructures in general capable of explaining and judicially grounding the aporias and contradictions of philosophical discourse? Let us consider three reasons indicative of the exceptional rank of these infrastructures: (1) their preontological and prelogical status, (2) their synthetic character, and (3) their economical and strategic nature. All these qualities are, of course, linked, so that in expounding one, we may have to presuppose another.

Preontological and Prelogical Status of Infrastructures

Because of the strategic predicament of the infrastructures—that is, because of their contextual and historical determination—it is, rigorously speaking, improper to refer to infrastructures *as such,* as I have done until now. The infrastructure, as the specific complex organization responsible for the philosophical opposition of structure and genesis, is only one possible infrastructure, in the sense in which I use the term here. For reasons of exposition, however, I shall have to continue to speak of infrastructures in general in order to name everything that can account for the differences that I will be addressing. Now, in establishing the preontological status of infrastructures in general, one encounters the same problem, owing to the fact that the qualification *preontological* refers, rigorously speaking, to the character of one particular infrastructure with regard to the opposition in philosophy of being and nothingness, presence and absence. In spite of these strategic limits, the determination *preontological* will nonetheless help us characterize infrastructures in general. But let me caution against any misunderstanding of *preontological* either in terms of temporal anteriority or in terms of Heidegger's fundamental ontology.

What, then, does *preontological* mean in terms of infrastructures? As a judiciary ground, an infrastructure must not be of the nature of the opposites for which it accounts; otherwise it would belong to the order of what it comes to explain. With regard to the traditional and canonical oppositions of presence and absence, of being and nothingness, infrastructures must not be described in terms of these bipolar oppositions, or of other oppositions derivative of them. Only by putting the authority of presence and its simple symmetrical counterpart, absence or lack, into question can an infrastructure achieve what it is supposed to achieve. The infrastructure, consequently, must be thought of as preceding, in a nontemporal way, the alternative of being and nothingness, of presence and absence, and of the ontico-ontological difference as well, as Derrida shows in "Differance." If an infrastructure is to assume the explicatory status of a ground, it must be a radical alterity in excess of that which it accounts for. For the same reasons, the infrastructure must be prelogical. The laws that it formulates for the discourse of philosophy must be laws that account for the difference between the philosophical logos and all its Others, and for that very reason it cannot have the simplicity of a logical principle. Of course this is not to say that the infrastructure would be irrational, since the irrational as one of the many Others of philosophy is also only "the abortive offspring of the unthought rational," as Heidegger puts it.[21] The infrastructural analysis concerns both the deciding instance of the logos and that which is derivative of it. As Derrida has made amply clear in "Limited Inc.," the infrastructural laws are those that govern the possibility of every logical proposition. Therefore, "no constituted logic nor any rule of a logical order can . . . provide a decision or impose its norms upon these prelogical possibilities of logic. Such possibilities are not 'logically' primary or secondary with regard to logic itself. They are (topologically?) alien to it, but not as its principle, condition of possibility, or 'radical' foundation" (*LI*, p. 235). It follows from this that:

1. An infrastructure is not an existent. It *is* not. Nor, however, is it simply absent. "It is not a being-present, however excellent, unique, principal, or transcendent one makes it," writes Derrida in "Differance" (*SP*, p. 153). Although not a being *(on)*, it is not a nonbeing *(me on)*. Being present in neither a sensible nor an intelligible manner, and thus belonging to no region whatsoever, the infrastructure belongs to a space "logically" anterior and alien to that of the regulated contradictions of metaphysics. To quote again: "We must let ourselves be referred to an order that no longer refers to sensibility. But we are not referred to intelligibility either, to an ideality not fortuitously associated with the objectivity of *theorein* or understanding. We must be referred to an order, then, that resists philosophy's founding opposition between the sensible and the intelligible" (*SP*, p. 133). By this deontologization of the infrastructures, all realism with regard to them is avoided. As it will become clear, the concept of infrastructure escapes all nominalist philosophy as well.

2. Its preontological nature aside, the infrastructure acquires its interpretive efficiency with regard to the specific problems it clarifies through being in excess of the opposition of sense and non-sense, meaning and the absence of meaning. Having no meaning in itself (in contrast to the fundamental Heideggerian question concerning the ontico-ontological difference as a question about the "meaning" of Being), it is in a position of anteriority to the epoch of meaning and the loss of meaning.

3. An infrastructure, moreover, is not an essence, since it is not dependent on any category of that which is present or absent. Nor is it a supraessentiality beyond the finite categories of essence and existence. It does not call any higher, inconceivable, or ineffable mode of being its own. It has no stable character, no autonomy, no ideal

identity, and is thus not a *substance,* or *hypokeimenon.* Its "essence" is to have no essence. And yet an infrastructure is endowed with a certain universality. The relations of irreducible complexity to which it refers are not merely fortuitous; but this is not to say that an infrastructure is for that reason an idealization. By accounting for the metaphysical opposition of the ideal and the nonideal, infrastructures are, as Derrida insists, in a position to render "the *project* of idealization possible without lending . . . [*themselves*] to any pure, simple, and idealizable conceptualization" (*LI,* p. 210).

If infrastructures are not essences, then they cannot be the object of even the most refined form of the intuiting of essences that is the Husserlian *Wesensschau.* They are not a correlate of phenomenologically reduced perception, and they do not yield to the "principle of all principles," that is, to the archetypal form of evidence of the immediate presence of the thing itself *in propria persona.* There is no *as such* to the infrastructures. They are not *noema* of perception. In other words, they escape phenomenologization to the extent that they refuse to appear in person or present themselves to a phenomenological gaze. The infrastructures dissolve the comprehension of the thing itself. Instead of offering themselves, they withdraw. They efface themselves, constantly disappearing as they go along. "They cannot, in classical affirmation, be affirmed wihout being negated" (*D,* p. 157). What thus makes its entrance into philosophy is the very possibility of a disappearing of truth, as Derrida has illustrated it, under what he names "women" in *Spurs* (*S,* pp. 48-51). Hence, what Derrida asserts of "differance" is true of all other infrastructures as well. "There is no essence of the differance; not only can it not allow itself to be taken up into the *as such* of its name or its appearing, but it threatens the authority of the *as such* in general, the thing's presence in its essence" (*SP,* p. 158).

Infrastructures appear or manifest themselves only *as the difference* of, say, structure and genesis, but never in person, never *as such.* One could venture the following definition: *infrastructures* are the "essences" of the structural-genetic difference. But since such an explanation makes illegitimate use of the concept of essence, as well as of the practice of *Wesensschau* in general, Husserlian or not, it is clear that the qualification *essence* cannot be bestowed on infrastructures. Infrastructures do not offer themselves as such to any *theorein,* be it that of traditional metaphysics, of Husserlian phenomenology, or of fundamental ontology. Yet it is precisely this alterity, which prevents them from ever presenting themselves in person, that qualifies the infrastructures as an explicandum of the difference between the thing in general and its essence, and of the differences crucial to phenomenology, the differences of appearance and appearing, of perception and what is perceived (independently of the existence of the perceived), of the noetico-noematic difference, and so on.

Synthetic Character of Infrastructures

The infrastructural process of accounting is distinguished from the speculative mode of resolving contradictions insofar as it maintains contradiction and resists its sublation into a higher unity. It is also distinguished from the Romantic fashion of eliminating contradiction in terms of a reciprocal self-destruction and annulment of oppositions within the sphere of, on the one hand, concordant fictions and, on the other, fictions of eternal strife between pairs of opposites. No difference-erasing complementarity or ontologization or idealization of the war between opposites—both Romantic alternatives to speculative sublation—is sought in infrastructural grounding. Hence, deconstructive interpretation of the contradictions, aporias, inconsistencies, and so on that are revealed in a scrutiny of the formation of concepts and the discursive structures of philosophy will speak within contradiction without contradiction. Indeed, in establishing the infrastructures as instances that account simultaneously for both poles of a bipolar opposition, conceptual or discursive, without eliminating that difference, one thinks of them without contradiction—that is, without considering such contradictions to be pertinent—as present *and* absent, sensible *and* intelligible, empirical *and* transcendental, and so on, precisely because the infrastructures are neither present *nor* absent, sensible *nor* intelligible, empirical *nor* transcendental. Infrastructures, as we shall see, are instances of an intermediary discourse, concerned with a middle in which the differends are suspended and preserved, but which is not simply a dialectical middle. What explains this strange logic is that the infrastructures must be original syntheses if they are to live up to their judiciary task. Yet, compared to the original syntheses at work in the discourse of metaphysics, and in particular in German Idealism as a whole, these syntheses can only be "unities by simulacrum" (P, p. 58). They cannot be seen as third terms that eventually initiate solutions in the form of speculative dialectics. Rather, these original syntheses, says Derrida, are analogous to what in traditional philosophy, especially in Kant, has been relegated to transcendental imagination, whose art does not simply belong to the realm of the sensible and the intelligible, the passive and the active (see *D*, p. 126). They do not simply carry implications of positing, activity, or agency of any sort; nor are they merely passive, constituted syntheses. They are, on the contrary, more "originary" syntheses than any classical origin. They represent a mode of synthesis that is older, or more "simple," than the mode of uniting that is characteristic of philosophical synthesizing. Synthesis, with respect to the infrastructures, involves a complicity and coimplication that maintain together an undetermined number of possibilities, which need not necessarily be in a relation of antithetical contrast with one another, as is the case in the classical concept of synthesis. The achievement of these original syntheses is that they tie together a variety of "contradictory" or heterogeneous concepts, instances, strata, significations, and so on, and that they make these communicate in a minimal organizational unit, thus accounting for their contiguity in a given context while also maintaining their irreducible difference. For these reasons, the infrastructural syntheses can be compared to scenes, stagings, and synopses (rather than to tableaux) to the extent that they do not eliminate difference, spatiality, or arrangement to the benefit of homogeneous unity.

The infrastructure is what knots together all the threads of correspondence among certain heterogeneous *points of presence* within a discourse or text. It must be understood as the *medium of differentiation* in general of the heterogeneous possibilities, contradictory strata, lexicological disparities, and so on. This medium of all possible differentiation—the common element of all the oppositions, contradictions, and discrepancies—is not a medium that would precede, as an undifferentiated plenitude, the differences into which it fragments itself. The adverse terms are not liquefied or mixed within it. As the medium of differentiation in general, it precedes undifferentiated unity and the subsequent bipolar division. It is a unity of combat, "the combat zone between philosophy and its other" (*D*, p. 138). It is the locus of what Heidegger calls the *same*, as distinct from the identical. Thus, what makes the originary syntheses of the infrastructures only simulacra of syntheses is not merely their nature as arrangements of possibilities, as opposed to what Hegel calls speculative germs, but their task of accounting for contradiction as such, without turning it into the force of the negative in the service of totality, whether speculative or not. An infrastructure, notes Derrida,

holds in reserve, in its undecided shadow and vigil, the opposites and the differends that the process of discrimination will come to carve out. Contradictions and pairs of opposites are lifted from the bottom of this diacritical, differing, deferring, reserve. Already inhabited by differance, this reserve, even though it "precedes" the opposition between different effects, even though it preexists differences as effects, does not have the punctual simplicity of a *coincidentia oppositorum*. It is from this fund that dialectics draws its philosophemes. (*D, p. 127*)

But the reserve of the infrastructures as the medium of all possible differentiation is also distinct from the Romantic medium of reflexivity, in which everything communicates with everything within the full presence of the soul of the world.

We must recall at this point that the contradictions among concepts or argumentative patterns that the infrastructures explain are contradictions to which philosophical totalizations are oblivious, and that survive in spite of the unity of the concepts, in spite of successful discursive totalization. The original synthesis of infrastructures must thus explain the possibility of unity, speculative totality, and synthesis against the backdrop of these nonsublimated, nonsublated, nonrecollected contradictions—that is, as syntheses that do not erase contradiction and aporia. Such a synthesis is originary precisely *because* it is not closed, and because it maintains contradictory possibilities together. Such a "synthesis" must explain synthesis.

Economical and Strategic Nature of Infrastructures

The last explanation I shall consider for the judiciary privilege of the infrastructures concerns the specific nature of the arrangement of the contradictory possibilities in original syntheses. These originary arrangements or compositions of conflicting possibilities are economical, in every sense of the word. They are economical syntheses according to the sense of *oikonomos* as "arrangement." They are economical insofar as they represent clusters of possibilities indicating "that the kind of bringing-together proposed here has the structure of an interlacing, a weaving, or a web, which would allow the different threads and different lines of sense or force to separate again, as well as being ready to bind others together" (*SP, p. 132*). Infrastructures fulfill the economic principle of successful explanation by accounting for a maximum of phenomena with a minimum of concepts and logical traits. Their syntheses are economical too, in that they are characterized by a certain calculus whereby the possibilities to be accounted for are summed up by being put aside, in the same way that one puts money aside as a reserve. The infrastructures reveal this general economy as organizing the relations between heterogeneous possibilities, such that they constitute, in a sense still to be elaborated, the last instance.

In addition, what makes the infrastructures economical—as the consideration of *all* the factors of possibility present within a certain theoretical configuration—is also what limits both the nonethical, nonidealizing explanatory scope of deconstruction and the intervention of its strategic dimension to only one particular discursive space and time. Yet what may appear to be a limitation is actually what makes deconstruction, contrary to the ahistoric and purely aesthetic practice of annulment and neutralization of opposites, an active historical form of intervention in historically specified contexts.

Considering deconstructive interpretation as the production of infrastructures capable of grounding contradictions and inconsistencies, deconstruction, far from being nihilistic, destructive, or negative, is, on the contrary, affirmative. In *Spurs,* Derrida insists that deconstructive interpretation is affirmative interpretation (see *S*, p. 37). Indeed, everything that Heidegger stated in his antinihilistic stand on destruction in "The Letter on Humanism" can be repeated with regard to deconstruction. The affirmative character of deconstructive interpretation, however, is not to be confused with positivity. Deconstructive interpretation is affirmative in a Nietzschean sense (see *SP,* pp. 159–160). In the context of the present attempt to define it as the production or reconstruction of infrastructures, this means that deconstructive interpretation affirms the play of the positive *and* and the negative, and thus it wards off the ethical temptation to liquidate negativity and difference.

THE MARGINAL INSCRIPTION OF THE GROUND

At this point we must ask ourselves whether, rigorously speaking, infrastructures can be called grounds, and we must question as well whether that which deconstruction achieves can in fact be comprehended and comprised by the traditional operation of grounding. No doubt, if deconstruction is described as an attempt to account by means of infrastructures for the contradictions and differences that the traditional discourse of philosophy accepts without question, then this enterprise documents precisely the earnestness and rigor characteristic of the philosophical operation of foundation. But in order to assess the true nature of deconstruction, the similarity between deconstruction and the philosophical operation of grounding must not be overemphasized, since this similarity is no more than a resemblance. Deconstruction repeats or mimes grounding in order to account for the difference between a ground and that which is grounded, with what can no longer be called a ground.

Since it is in the very nature of a ground to be in excess of what it accounts for, the infrastructure—the difference between the ground and what is grounded—cannot be understood simply as a ground. Nor for these same reasons are the infrastructures deep, as opposed to surface, structures; there is nothing *profound* about them. They are not, strictly speaking, *deeper* grounds, which would be in opposition to what they make possible. In *Spurs* we read: "In its turn, the opposition between metaphysic and non-metaphysic encounters its limits here, the very limit *of* that opposition and of opposition's form . . . But, if the form of opposition and the oppositional structure are themselves metaphysical, then the relation of metaphysics to its other can no longer be one of opposition" (*S*, pp. 117–119). The infrastructure, or what I shall call the space of inscription, is not in a relation of opposition to that which it makes possible. The relation of alterity between infrastructures and that which they account for is not the relation of opposition between the ground and the grounded.[22] The hierarchical relation between infrastructures and what they make possible (insofar as they also make it impossible) is not that of a hierarchy based on opposition and contradiction. Hierarchy is not, however, absent; it is differently structured. For all these reasons, an infrastructure is not what is called a ground in traditional philosophical language. It is, on the contrary, a nonfundamental structure, or an abyssal structure, to the extent that it is without a bottom. Yet it is not itself the bottom of anything either: "In such a structure, which is a non-fundamental one, at once superficial and bottomless, still and always 'flat,' the property [*propre*] is literally sunk. Even as it is carried away of itself by its desire, it founders there in the waters of this its own desire, unencounterable—of itself. It passes into the other" (*S*, p. 117).

Infrastructures, consequently, must be understood in a necessarily equivocal manner—that is neither as the result of florid language nor of fallacious reasoning—as simultaneously grounds and ungrounds, as conditions of possibility and impossibility. The necessity of such hybrid or spurious reasoning, of what Plato would have called *logismo tini notho*, stems from the effort to think into "one" the metaphysical opposition of the ground and that which it grounds, without, however, turning it into an identity.[23] The necessity of the apparently incongruous statements to which such reasoning leads can be fully accounted for only by considering what in Derrida corresponds to a general theory of duplication.

As we have seen, the infrastructure is not a subject or a cause, a thing in general, or an essence to which everything that is could be retraced, as to an origin present to itself. But more important, neither does the infrastructure designate the process of division and separation constitutive of differends and difference, because such a process still presupposes a prior, unbroached origin. Thus, although deconstruction, with its emphasis on the infrastructure, resembles what is called in traditional philosophical language a search for a constituting, producing, and originary causality, the reconstruction of infrastructures does not fall simply under philosophical jurisdiction. By tying together in an infrastructure things as different as a ground and that which is grounded, deconstruction does not proceed according to a strategy of finality. Infrastructures are only "general and formal predicative structures" that represent the "common root" for all predicates characterizing opposing terms. This explains why infrastructures cannot be concepts, but rather have the status of "philosophical quasiconcepts" (VP, p. 64). Moreover, it shows that the infrastructure is no more than the open but comprehensive fund—the system of predicative differences—in which the opposition between ground and that which is grounded is carved out. The infrastructure is therefore also the system of differences from which all constituting finality draws its resources. For this very reason, the infrastructural accounting does not correspond to an operation of grounding; on the contrary, this "operation which is not an operation" (SP, p. 137) questions the very values of origin, archae, and telos. In what terms, then, are we to understand the achievements of deconstruction? If the infrastructures do not constitute, engender, or produce these differences or contradictions, how, then, do they relate to them? If the infrastructures are not to be understood as causalities, active or passive, if they are neither of the order of subjectivity or essentiality nor, rigorously speaking, conditions of possibility, how, then, are we to think their intercourse with that of which they are infrastructures?

In his early work, such as Of Grammatology, Derrida at times speaks of the relation between the infrastructures and that which they are infrastructures of in terms of constitution and production, thus meeting all the requirements of traditional philosophizing. For instance, he invites us "to speculate upon the power of exteriority as constitutive of interiority: of speech, of signified meaning, of the present as such" (OG, p. 313). Hence, there cannot be any doubt as to the level on which infrastructures have to be situated or as to the goals toward which deconstruction is aimed. Derrida's hints, in Of Grammatology, at "a new transcendental aesthetic" (OG, p. 290) strongly support the view that deconstruction aims at a theory of originary constitution; but at the same time, *Of Grammatology* as a whole consists of a deconstructive critique of the philosophical concept of origin, and thus of the idea of a linear genesis. Let us also recall that in the earlier *Speech and Phenomena,* Derrida had written that "the very concept of constitution itself must be deconstructed" (*SP*, p. 85). In *Of Grammatology* the notion of "inscription" (of both the origin and what is derived from it) displaces the concepts of production, engenderment, genesis, constitution, and so on, which are tributary to and characteristic of metaphysics and transcendental phenomenology. After *Of Grammatology,* Derrida encloses all these terms in quotation marks.

Inscription is one of the terms that both continue and break with the transcendental question of production or constitution, of genesis and history. *Inscription* is another name for constitution, or more precisely, "for the constitution of *subjects* and, so to speak, of *constitution* itself" (*OG*, p. 281). In what ways, then, does the notion of inscription both continue and displace the transcendental question of constitution? First, what does the word *inscription* designate? *Inscription,* or rather, *inscription in general,* is the name for a *possibility* that all speech must presuppose—that marks all speech—before it can be linked to incision, engraving, drawing, the letter—in short, to writing in the common sense of the term. Without inscription *in general,* without an *instituted trace,* without arche-writing or proto-writing affecting speech as the possibility of its notation, whether or not that possibility is ever actualized, no actual notation would be possible. Without the possibility that an origin can be lost, forgotten, or alienated into what springs forth from it, an origin could not be an origin. The possibility of inscription is thus a necessary possibility, one that must always be possible. Derrida writes: "A new transcendental aesthetic must let itself be guided not only by mathematical idealities but by the possibility of inscription in general, not befalling an already constituted space as a contingent accident but producing the spatiality of space. Indeed we say of inscription *in general,* in order to make it quite clear that it is not simply the notation of a prepared speech representing itself, but inscription within speech and inscription as *habitation* always already situated" (*OG*, p. 290).

Inscription, consequently, designates the possibilities that necessarily affect all origin insofar as it can factually be the origin *of* something, or insofar as it can engender or constitute something, actively or passively. Inscription *in general* is the mode in which infrastructures *qua* necessary possibilities relate to that of which they are infrastructures. Thus inscription is what "constitutes" origins as possible constituting origins. Yet such an investigation into the "conditions of possibilities" of origins, into the space of inscription beyond such oppositions as sensible and intelligible, as Derrida remarks, "ought no longer to call itself a transcendental *aesthetic,* neither in the Kantian, nor in the Husserlian, sense of those words" (*OG,* p. 290). Indeed, deconstruction is an inquiry neither into the a priori forms of sense perception and object constitution characteristic of a subject in general nor into the meaning of the prepredicative and preobjective spatio-temporality that Husserl envisioned in the conclusion of *Formal and Transcendental Logic* as well as in the *Cartesian Meditations.* *Inscription* is only one name for the way in which infrastructures ground or constitute. It describes only one cluster of determinations according to which this particular mode of founding is to be thought. This one cluster of determinations must, however, suffice here to characterize the differences·between the philosophical operation of constitution and that of deconstruction.

Inscription, says Derrida at the end of *Positions,* "is not a simple position: it is rather that by means of which every position is *of itself confounded*" (*P,* p. 96). *Position* here translates the Hegelian concept of *Setzung,* the determination of one with regard to an Other, or to something in contrast with it. Position is thus a form of constitution by means of which something becomes what it is through its relation to something other. *Inscription,* however, does not signify such a relation; on the contrary, it is the determination of positional constitution, of the relation of the same and the Other, for it demonstrates that this relation refers to something that cannot in any case be posited—the alterity of the Other—since this alterity is itself the ground of possibility of a positing self. Inscription in this sense refers to an irreducible reference to Other, anterior to an already constituted subject that presupposes this reference as well as that which such a subject constitutes through positioning. This implies that the relaton of philosophy to its Others cannot be one of opposition.

How, then, are we to characterize the achievements of inscription? The alterity *in general* to which inscription refers is the possibility of sameness. For that very reason it is also the possibility of becoming different, other; and indeed, such a possibility must affect all self-present and selfsame origin if it is to be the origin of something. Indeed, an origin is an origin only if it can possibly be the origin *of* something, whether or not that possibility is actualized. An origin has no meaning whatsoever without such a possible space that it engenders and orients. It follows from this that an origin is necessarily an inscribed origin. In order to be a selfsame origin, it must irreducibly relate to an Other in general, and in order to be the origin *of* something, it must harbor the possibility of becoming other. In *Writing and Difference,* Derrida concludes, "The *inscription* is the written origin: traced and henceforth *inscribed in* a system, in a figure which it no longer governs" (*WD,* p. 115). Inscription, consequently, does not imply the annulment or destruction of the origin. On the contrary, the origin or constituting principle is put into relation with the infrastructural possibilities of an origin, with alterity *in general,* which must be presupposed if the origin is to be the origin of something. Inscription is a gesture of comprehension which comprises the origin, or any constituting principle, within a configuration of marks or infrastructural possibilities, a function of which the origin then appears to be. In a certain way one could speak of inscription as an *epoche* of the origin; but it would be the opposite of a phenomenological *epoche,* since it would represent a bracketing of the function of origin and of the meaning that origin confers on what derives from it. In contrast to the phenomenological *epoche,* which is carried out in the name of and in view of origin and meaning, inscription is the reduction of the phenomenologicl reduction. The infrastructures related to the origin, the principle, or the a priori through inscription are in excess of phenomenality in general—that is, in excess of what represents the absolute possibility of the meaning of what is, of what exists; they are more and less than an origin. The infrastructural possibilities represent an irreducible plurality in contrast with the uniqueness of the origin that they make possible but also impossible, since the origin can never dominate their system. The origin and its constitutive operation are themselves "situated within a syntax without origin" (*OG,* p. 243). Since an origin, or any function of origin, is inscribed within such a system of infrastructures, a system that is not a *topos noetos* or a *topos ouranios,* the relation of this system to what it constitutes can no longer be described as a linear genesis. Indeed, how could a *play* or *system* of possibilities engender *one* line, flow, or beam? How, moreover, could a system of inscription "engender" in the first place? What Derrida claims of dissemination is true of inscription in general: it only *affirms,* but does not produce or constitute, the play or system of possibilities that any function of origin must presuppose (and that therefore limit its possibility as well).

Thus inscription, instead of engendering, contextualizes that which claims uniqueness and oneness. Deconstruction reinscribes the origin into the context or text of its infrastructural possibilities. To speak the language of philosophy, one could say that this context of infrastructures—the space of inscription of the function of origin—is an *absolute passivity,* if it did not also anticipate the metaphysical difference between active and passive. But because of the irreducible plurality of these infrastructures, they could also be said to represent an *absolute activity,* if they did not subvert such an idea as well. Yet to mention these possible determinations in order to discard them immediately is not without purpose, for they give a hint of how inscription is to be understood. Indeed, it is now clear that inscription as the relation entertained by a function of origin to the context of its structural possibilities reveals repressed presuppositions and non-thematized conditions of possibilities. Moreover, since a function of origin is passively inscribed within a system of structural possibilities, it follows that the system of structural possibilities does not control or command the origin, which is precisely to be expected of grounds, foundations, origins, or conditions of possibility, in the strict sense. The system of infrastructural possibilities inscribes both the origin and its function of command, and even though this system of possibility does not control or command the origin, the origin presupposes it as its (limiting) possibility. An origin presupposes this play as a text presupposes its context, a book its margins, a painting its frame, or any unity its border. The relation to the Other of philosophy is one of a certain exteriority; yet the specificity of that relation, its transcendentality so to speak, is no longer of the order of production, engenderment, command. Throughout his works, under the name of the margin, the frame, the borderline, and so forth, Derrida has thematized this relation. Of "differance," which is one such structural possibility of origin—an infrastructure in short—Derrida contends: "It commands nothing, rules over nothing, and nowhere does it exercise any authority. It is not marked by a capital letter. Not only is there no realm of differance, but differance is even the subversion of every realm" (*SP,* p. 153).

Inscription is not a relation instituting the dependence of the origin or of any principle on another, more fundamental principle of responsibility, which would serve exhaustively as the primary cause of causes. Derrida's assessment of Bataille's notion of sovereignty is also true of inscription: it does not command in general. Rather, inscription puts the origin, or the causes liable to be called upon, in relation *(en rapport)* to the bundles of infrastructures that they presuppose, yet to which they are not subordinate. Inscription puts the origin in relation to that which is not controlled by its judiciary function, yet without which it could not pretend to responsibility in the first place. By inscribing a function of origin, infrastructures do not simply represent transcendentalia that, as a priori conditions, would rule over origins. Infrastructures are not deeper, supraessential origins. If they are said to ground origins, it must be added that they unground them at the same time. Infrastructures are conditions as much of the impossibility as of the possibility of origins and grounds. Infrastructures are structures, clusters of marks, without which grounds and transcendental a prioris could not exist and could not exercise the constitutional function expected of them. Yet if, instead of constituting or producing origins, infrastructures were seen to inscribe them, then the deconstructive explication of the fissures and cracks that characterize the philosophical discourse would no longer simply be thought of as an enterprise of accounting. Let us, therefore, circle back to the problem of accounting.

Inscription has been called a putting into relation, or rather *en rapport*. In the essay on Bataille, the term *rapport* serves to link two forms of writing, minor and major; two economies, restricted and general; as well as the known and the unknown, knowledge and the *non-savoir*, meaning and nonmeaning, mastery and sovereignty. None of the terms of these relations, however, dominates the other; none is the principle or ground of this inscription, or *mise en rapport*. Yet what does *rapport* mean? In English it means a relation marked by harmony, accord, or affinity. In French it has additional meanings, some of which we must take into consideration. First of all, it signifies a report, information, or account, as well as the revenue, profit, or return on a successful operation. It signifies such an operation insofar as it is productive. Finally, it refers to the *ratio* or proportion characterizing a relation. Consequently, *rapport* is characterized by semantic ambiguity as to its activity or passivity.

Inscription, or *mise en rapport,* the operation of deconstruction par excellence, is thus a form of accounting. By bringing the origin or a priori principles in relation to what exceeds them, the *mise en rapport* states its reasons. It accounts for them by relating the traditional principles of accounting to the infrastructures, which discount, or subtract, from these principles what they have necessarily left out of account. Through inscription, the traditional modes of philosophical accounting—that is, the modes by which philosophical discourse is repaid for its investments *(retrouver ses comptes)*—are shown to have been accounted for by that which exceeds them. The economy of the infrastructures takes into account that which exceeds accounting, that which, as a result, is never repaid in accounting (*manque à retrouver son compte,* see *SP,* p. 151). For the infrastructures to which the origin is accountable or owing, no account or reason can be given; they cannot be accounted for, and they represent a capital that cannot be cashed in or turned into an account, since they cannot be counted in the first place. They are, as I have mentioned, irremediably plural but, as we shall see, abyssal and undecidable as well.

It follows from this that inscription, or *mise en rapport,* is not a mode of accounting that, like the principles it inscribes, would account for itself. Indeed, in contrast to origins or principles of legitimacy, the infrastructures do not command themselves; indeed, they do not command in general. "At stake in the operation, therefore," writes Derrida, "is not a self-consciousness, an ability to be near oneself, to maintain and to watch oneself. We are not in the element of phenomenology" (*WD,* p. 264). Precisely by refusing to command itself or anything else, this operation can function as that alterity that absolutely escapes the logic of philosophical accounting while at the same time "accounting" for it. As soon as the infrastructures, or the deconstructive operation of inscription, or *mise en rapport,* tries to subject something to itself, itself included, it turns into what it purports to account for. "In order not to govern, that is to say, in order not to be subjugated, it *must* subordinate nothing (direct object), that is to say, be subordinated to *nothing or no one* (servile mediation of the indirect object)" (*WD,* p. 265).

To inscribe, or *mettre en rapport,* is thus to speak without any philosophical security. The action seems to resemble Plato's *logismo tini notho.* That is why Derrida can say that this is a *rapport* in the form of nonrapport (*WD,* p. 268). It is also a *rapport* that does not tolerate any *rapport,* because what the philosophical mode of accounting is being related to is beyond accounting. There cannot be the slightest symmetry between inscription and what is inscribed, between an origin and the syntax of the infrastructures against which it comes into relief. It is impossible to account for something that inscribes the operation of accounting in a cluster of structural possibilities that exclude their own self-domination and self-reflection. Yet it is precisely this impossibility of accounting that allows inscription, or *mise en rapport,* to explain what it inscribes—the origins, the principle of legitimacy and responsibility, the *de jure* conditions, and so on. The explicatory power of inscription springs from the radical Otherness of the infrastructural marks to the philosophical economy of accounts.

Inscription, as I have said, is beyond accounting, because what the origins refer to—the systems of infrastructural possibilities—are not supraorigins, nor do they account for themselves. Inscription is beyond reason, because the philosopher who puts origins into relation with what they presuppose as clusters of unthought possibilities speaks beyond the security that philosophy can, and must, confer through the self-reflection of its discourse. Thus to deconstruct, or inscribe, or put into relation the transcendental conditions of possibilities with their structural possibilities is to displace radically the *logon didonai* that is the ground of reasonable speech. This is not, however, to annul or discard reasonable speech; nor does it entail any flirtation with irrationalism. On the contrary, it is an attempt, paradoxically speaking, to "account" for the *ratio,* for the difference between rationality and irrationality, in a gesture that both fulfills and transgresses the most insistent and intimate goal of philosophy.

THE BIPARTITE OPERATION OF DECONSTRUCTION

I have characterized deconstruction as an attempt to account by way of infrastructures for a variety of essential differences and contradictions within the philosophical discourse. Let us now consider the way in which an infrastructure—or as Derrida also calls it a signifying structure *(structure signifiante) (OG,* p. 158)—is produced. Derrida provides a primarily negative elucidation of such an exorbitant production in the chapter entitled "The Questions of Method" in *Of Grammatology,* in which he emphasizes that a transgression of the contradictions, discrepancies, and differences in question toward their unifying infrastructure, or signifying structure, does not aim at something outside the discourse or text in which they are encountered. Deconstruction must be intrinsic; it must remain within the texts or discourses under examination. Since the interpretive efficiency of the infrastructures or signifying structures depends on their *insistence within* a given text or discourse, one need not stress Derrida's ultimate justification—the absence of any transcendental referent or signified— for the requirement that deconstruction take the classical discourse or the text as its point of departure. It may, however, be useful to emphasize that the determination of deconstruction as an operation immanent or inherent in the discourses or texts does not necessarily imply their thematic or formal closure. Deconstruction is a production that avoids both traditionally opposite but complicitously linked methods of reading. *"The security with which the commentary considers the self-identity of the text, the confidence with which it carves out its contour, goes hand in hand with the tranquil assurance that leaps over the text toward its presumed content, in the direction of the pure signified"* (OG, p. 159). The deconstructive production of signifying structures, which accounts for the problems it sets out to tackle, is thus an operation that remains intrinsic to the classical discourses and texts without, however, positing the formal identity or closure of the texts, as does all formalist criticism, New Criticism included.

Perhaps at this point it would be useful to address the argument, raised by some uninformed readers of Derrida, that deconstruction is a self-defeating method since it can transgress metaphysics or logocentrism only by continuing to speak the language of that tradition. Derrida has formulated the problem to which these critics refer in the following way:

But all these destructive discourses and all their analogues are trapped in a kind of circle. This circle is unique. It describes the form of the relation between the history of metaphysics and the destruction of the history of metaphysics. There is no sense in doing without the concepts of metaphysics in order to shake metaphysics. We have no language—no syntax and no lexicon—which is foreign to this history; we can pronounce not a single destructive proposition which has not already had to slip into the form, the logic, and the implicit postulations of precisely what it seeks to contest.   (WD, pp. 280–281)

But what does this insight into the inevitable involvement of deconstruction in metaphysics mean? For the moment let us note only that Derrida calls it a circle *of sorts,* not merely a circle, and that he links the very meaning of deconstruction to this kind of circularity. Thus the circularity of logocentrism and deconstruction may well be akin to Heidegger's hermeneutic circle, which, far from being a *circulus vitiosus,* to be avoided at all costs, is a circle into which one has to come in the right way if one wants to think *at all.*

It is true that Derrida himself may have encouraged his critics to conclude that deconstruction is self-contradictory, for example by speaking of the "aporias that appear to engage anyone who takes on the task of defining the constraints which limit philosophical discourse; for it is from the latter that the noncritical notions which are applied to its delimitation must be borrowed" (*M*, p. 180). But the critics ought to have been aware that these aporias are aporias only as long as the concepts borrowed from the discourse of metaphysics go uncriticized.

"Deconstruction," says Derrida, "does not consist in passing from one concept to another, but in overturning and displacing a conceptual order, as well as the non-conceptual order with which the conceptual order is articulated" (*M*, p. 329). This reversal and displacement require that one be solidly installed within traditional conceptuality, so that one sets out with an awareness of at least three principles: (1) that concepts in metaphysics are viewed as self-sufficient units; (2) yet they appear only in oppositions, which are never simply juxta-positions of terms but hierarchies and orders of subordination; and (3) that furthermore, all concepts stand in relations of solidarity. As a result of this last determination, concepts in philosophical discourse cannot be innocently separated. Instead of being discrete elements or atoms, the concepts and gestures of thought are taken in a syntax and system. Because of this systematic and historical solidarity, "every particular borrowing brings along with it the whole of metaphysics" (*WD*, p. 281). The awareness of these three aspects of concepts implies that a concept can never be a self-sufficient unity, as metaphysics claims. "Every concept is necessarily and essentially inscribed in a chain or a system, within which it refers to another and to other concepts, by the systematic play of differences," with the result that a concept "is never present in itself, in an adequate presence that would refer only to itself" (*SP*, p. 140). Two consequences follow from this. First, there are no metaphysical concepts in themselves. As Derrida writes in *Positions:* "I have never believed that there were *metaphysical* concepts *in and of themselves.* No concept is by itself, and consequently in and of itself, metaphysical, outside all the textual work in which it is inscribed" (*P*, p. 57; see also *M*, p. 329). And second, deconstruction cannot simply represent a shift from one con-cept to another, since the infrastructures with which it aims to account for the specific aporias and differences between the concepts must also account for the inability of concepts to be purely metaphysical concepts, that is, to be concepts at all. The infrastructure produced by deconstruction is, then, no longer a concept.

Now, because these infrastructures, which are the outcome of de-construction, have sometimes been designated by a word or concept that belongs to the tradition to be deconstructed, the critics have charged that deconstruction is inefficient and futile in its attempt to reach beyond metaphysics. This is not the place to review the different forms this argument has taken and to retrace it to an inability to understand the stakes of deconstruction. All I shall try to clarify is the specific manner in which an old concept can come to designate something entirely different from its previous signified, as well as the theoretical and practical impact of such a designation. Derrida calls the provisional and strategic reasons for which an old name is retained to designate infrastructures the "logic of paleonymics." First, it must be noted that, although deconstruction does not aim at something outside the discourse of metaphysics, such as a last signified, still, the old name that is retained serves to designate something that is of a certain exteriority to the discourse of metaphysics, to the extent that it is of the order of an unthought structural possibility of that discourse. Although there is simply no name for what the infrastructures designate, this is not to say that such an unnamable would not be represented in one way or another in the discourse of metaphysics. Since the infrastructures are implicitly presupposed by that discourse, the representatives of these structural complexities can be identified more or less easily. Derrida at one point calls these representatives "phantoms" or "ghosts." Phantoms are the shapes of that from which logic proceeds. As merely the shapes of the infrastructures, these representatives betray their subjection to the logic that they unground (D, pp. 103–104). The ghosts representing the excluded Other from the system are always constructed within the system in a tautological and symmetric form as "the negative key *(le propre négatif)* to the system," in short, as *its* Other.[24] The names of these ghosts, of the schemes under which the infrastructures abandon themselves to the discourse of logic, are the only names according to which that which exceeds metaphysical conceptuality can be named within the historical closure or limits of science and philosophy. The reasons for which the X designated by the infrastructures is given a particular name are entirely strategic, that is to say historical. Although the old name that is mobilized to name the infrastructural X initially designates something entirely different from it, it nevertheless is entitled to do so if the name communicates in an essential way with that X. *Writing* is an old name for such an infrastructural cluster of possibilities. Derrida justifies the use of the name *writing,* in the sense of arche-writing, as follows:

An arche-writing whose necessity and new concept I wish to indicate and outline here, and which I continue to call writing only because it essentially communicates with the vulgar concept of writing. The latter could not have imposed itself historically except by the dissimulation of the arche-writing, by the desire for a speech displacing its other and its double and working to reduce its difference. If I persist in calling that difference writing, it is because, within the work of historical repression, writing was, by its situation, destined to signify the most formidable difference.   (OG, p. 56)

Writing is thus a phantom name for the structural X, despite the fact that it is very different from what has always been called writing. What makes it susceptible to being named X is that, within the discourse of metaphysics, it marks the repression of that X and therefore essentially communicates with it. The reasons for retaining an old name to name the entirely new reality of the infrastructures is, consequently, historical, yet it is also a function of the singularity of a topic. The justification for its use "corresponds to a condition of forces and translates an historical calculation" (OG, p. 70).

Deconstruction, therefore, borrows its notions, names, or "concepts" from philosophy in order to name what is unnamable within its closure. Yet such an operation of borrowing is instantly followed by an effort to mark this operation as plagiarism. Demarcated in this manner, the borrowed concepts not only designate something entirely different from what they referred to before but also suffer a mutation of meaning. And since deconstruction's concepts have been taken from the given discourse of philosophy, it will permit an intervention within this discourse. In *Positions*, Derrida formalizes the logic of paleonymics as follows:

What, then, is the "strategic" necessity that requires the occasional maintenance of an *old name* in order to launch a new concept? With all the reservations imposed by this classical distinction between the name and the concept, one might begin to describe this operation. Taking into account the fact that a name does not name the punctual simplicity of a concept, but rather a system of predicates defining a concept, a conceptual structure *centered* on a given predicate, we proceed: (1) to the extraction of a reduced predicative trait that is held in reserve, limited in a given conceptual structure (limited for motivations and relations of force to be analyzed), *named X;* (2) to the delimitation, the grafting and regulated extension of the extracted predicate, the name X being maintained as a kind of *lever of intervention,* in order to maintain a grasp on the previous organization, which is to be transformed effectively. Therefore, extraction, graft, extension.   (P, p. 71)

What follows from this description of the formal modes in which an old name is transformed so as to designate precisely what it represses—modes I shall later discuss in themselves—is that the use of traditional language by deconstructive interpretation is much more complex than its critics believe. Indeed, the necessity of borrowing one's resources from the logic to be deconstructed is not only no inconvenience or calamity, as some have believed, but is rather the very condition of finding a foothold in the discourse to be deconstructed. It is the very condition under which deconstruction can be successful and effectively intervene in the discourse of metaphysics. "We cannot give up this metaphysical complicity without also giving up the critique we are directing against this complicity," writes Derrida (WD, p. 281). The necessity under which deconstruction borrows its notions from the discourse of philosophy secures the very possibility of a subversive foothold—always strategic and thus historical—within the historical closure of that discourse. Generally speaking, Derrida's attempt at developing a heterology—that is, a nonhomogeneous discourse—can be effective only if this discourse constantly compounds with the forces that tend to annul it. It must do so because deconstruction is an operation that situates itself in a historical manner with regard to the different forces that, at each particular moment, produce the closure of its conceptuality. It must do so precisely because it is a heterology, which as such must include, or inscribe within itself, that which it tries to displace or unhinge, and that which also tries powerfully to annul it. This heterological dimension of Derrida's work is undoubtedly one of the main obstacles to its assimilation by either the philosopher or the literary critic, whose discourses are teleologically bound to achieve homogeneity. Yet the contradictions that arise in a discourse critical of the premises of metaphysics from the necessity of inscribing within itself these very same premises are not all of equal pertinence. In *Writing and Difference,* Derrida remarks:

> But if no one can escape this necessity [of accommodating within his own discourse the premises he is denouncing], and if no one is therefore responsible for giving in to it, however little he may do so, this does not mean that all the ways of giving in to are of equal pertinence. The quality and fecundity of a discourse are perhaps measured by the critical rigor with which this relation to the history of metaphysics and to inherited concepts is thought. (WD, p. 282)

A heterological enterprise that compounds with the forces that try to annul it while simultaneously unhinging them by inscribing or generalizing them differs from a contradictory discourse—that is, from one that, owing to theoretical weakness or to deliberation, accommodates contradictions in an otherwise homological discourse—

in that it explicitly assumes a critical responsibility by unflaggingly problematizing its own status as a discourse borrowing from a heritage the very resources required for the deconstruction of that heritage itself.

One of the ways in which deconstructive interpretation assumes its responsibility as a discourse is to question unremittingly the solidarity and systematic relation among concepts in metaphysics:

> Within the closure, by an oblique and always perilous movement, constantly risking falling back within what is being deconstructed, it is necessary to surround the critical concepts with a careful and thorough discourse—to mark the conditions, the medium, and the limits of their effectiveness and to designate rigorously their intimate relationship to the machine whose deconstruction they permit; and, in the same process, designate the crevice through which the yet unnameable glimmer beyond the closure can be glimpsed. (OG, p. 14)

What, then, is the meaning of such a transgression of the discourse of metaphysics? It should be obvious that deconstruction cannot be an attempt to reach a simple outside or beyond of philosophy and metaphysics. Deconstruction is neither neutralized by the annulling force of the concepts it borrows from the tradition it deconstructs, nor deluded by the illusionary possibility of simply stepping outside of philosophy. In any case, deconstruction is profoundly suspicious of the cavalier assurance of those who think they have successfully crossed the line. Deconstruction as an attempt to step outside the always historical closure of philosophy not only produces this "outside," to speak the language of traditional philosophy, in a finite fashion; but since it is also, and in particular, the deconstruction of the genuinely metaphysical opposition of inside and outside, the operation by which it must produce this "outside" of the discourse of philosophy can no longer be understood as a passage from an interior to an exterior. Nor can such an outside be itself an outside with regard to an inside. Now, since a transgression must, in order to affirm itself *as transgression,* conserve and confirm in one way or another that which it exceeds, insofar as it *is* only with respect to the limit it crosses, it can only consist of a sort of displacement of the limits and closure of the discourse. To exceed the discourse of philosophy cannot possibly mean to step *outside* the closure, because the outside belongs to the categories of the inside. The excess or transgression of philosophy is, therefore, decided at the margins of the closure only, in an always strategical—that is, historically finite—fashion.

For this reason it is incorrect to speak of a transgression or excess at all. In *Positions,* Derrida remarks:

There *is not* a transgression, if one understands by that a pure and simple landing into a beyond of metaphysics, at a point which also would be, let us not forget, first of all a point of language or writing. Now, even in aggressions or transgressions, we are consorting with a code to which metaphysics is tied irreducibly, such that every transgressive gesture reencloses us—precisely by giving us a hold on the closure of metaphysics—within this closure. But, by means of the work done on one side and the other of the limit the field inside is modified, and a transgression is produced that consequently is nowhere present as a *fait accompli.* One is never installed within transgression, one never lives elsewhere. Transgression implies that the limit is always at work. Now, the "thought-that-means-nothing," the thought that exceeds meaning and meaning-as-hearing-oneself-speak by interrogating them— this thought, announced in grammatology, is given precisely as the thought for which there is no sure opposition between outside and inside. At the conclusion of a certain work, even the concepts of excess or of transgression can become suspect.   (*P*, p. 12)

With this clarification of the way in which we are to understand how deconstruction transgresses the discourse of philosophy, we can return to analyzing the modes in which the "outside" of metaphysics—that is to say, the infrastructures—are produced. As I have emphasized, a deconstruction is not a function of a subjective desire or act of will, nor is it an absolute act capable of providing the totality of its methodological justifications. Deconstructive interpretation, in its search for what exorbitantly exceeds the totality of the conceptual oppositions constitutive of metaphysics, proceeds in a radically empiricist manner—that is, in a manner incapable of justifying itself entirely—but not because of empiricism's recognized philosophical inability to do so. "We must begin *wherever we are,*" says Derrida. Nonetheless, the admitted lack of an absolute beginning does not mean that the beginning is arbitrary or subjective. Derrida continues, "*Wherever we are:* in a text where we already believe ourselves to be." In other words, broaching a deconstruction depends on a historical hermeneutics that justifies its beginning as "subject to a certain historical necessity" (*OG*, p. 162). Derrida summarizes these arguments in *Positions,* when he writes:

The *incision* of deconstruction, which is not a voluntary decision or an absolute beginning, does not take place just anywhere, or in an absolute elsewhere. An incision, precisely, it can be made only according to lines of force and forces of rupture that are localizable in the discourse to be deconstructed. The *topical* and *technical* determination of the most necessary sites and operators—beginnings, holds, levers, etc.—in a given situation depends upon an historical analysis. This analysis is *made* in the general movement of the field, and is never exhausted by the conscious calculation of a "subject." (*P*, p. 82)

Generally speaking, one could say that deconstruction starts within the texts to be deconstructed by focusing on traits within conceptual structures, or on concepts within conceptual dyads that, for reasons to be historically determined, have been confined to a secondary role, or put, so to speak, on reserve. Writing, for instance, is such a concept within the bipolar opposition speech/writing, whereas the concept of supplementarity relies on philosophy's refusal to give equal consideration to the totality of its traits or predicates. The general strategy of deconstruction, at least as it pertains to the discrepancies and differences affecting concepts and philosophical argumentation, is characterized first by a phase of *reversal* of these binary oppositions. This is a structurally necessary gesture, since a mere neutralization of the dual oppositions, which are de facto and de jure hierarchical structures, would leave the field intact and confirm what is to be deconstructed. Nor can the reversal simply limit itself to reestablishing an inverse hierarchical order. The operation of reversing the given hierarchies does not consist "in a renewal of the hierarchy or the substance of values, but rather in a transformation of the very value of hierarchy itself" (*S*, p. 81). In clarifying this issue, Derrida approvingly quotes Heidegger's discussion of Nietzsche's problematics of a reversal *(Umdrehung)* of Platonism. Heidegger writes in *Nietzsche*, "A new hierarchy and new valuation mean that the ordering-structure must be changed."[25] This transformation of the hierarchical scheme is not aimed at bringing about an inverse order or a total neutralization of the opposite terms in an anarchical state free of all hierarchy, but at a recasting of the traditional concept and structure of hierarchy: "What must occur then is not merely a suppression of all hierarchy, for an-archy only consolidates just as surely the established order of a metaphysical hierarchy; nor is it a simple change or reversal in the terms of any given hierarchy. Rather, the *Umdrehung* must be a transformation of the hierarchical structure itself" (*S*, p. 81). The phase of reversal of the hierarchy of predicates or concepts is only the first step; the second step consists of what is called a reinscription, displacement, or reconstruction. This second phase is necessary because the first operates solely within the conceptuality of the system to be deconstructed. Without such a second movement, the reversal would be "nothing more than a clamorous declaration of the anti-thesis" (S, p. 95).

What, then, is the function of reinscription, or displacement? In this second phase the hitherto repressed traits of concepts, or traits held in reserve, are restored to their generality, to their power of generalization, and to their generative force. With this liberation of the traits held in reserve by the concepts within philosophy, new "concepts" erupt into the territory of philosophy. These concepts refer to something that could never be comprehended, that could never have been an "object" within the discourse of philosophy. These repressed traits, leading through their generalization to the formation of new "concepts," can be *grafted* onto the traditional concepts or names privileged in the first phase of reversal. But since the newly privileged terms of reversed conceptual hierarchies are only the ghosts or spurious images of a beyond within the discourse of philosophy, deconstruction cannot stop with them. It is only by grafting onto their names the meaning of which they are the repression that the operation of deconstruction becomes complete. This step produces concepts previously unheard of in the tradition and in the discourse of meta-physics. These "philosophical quasi-concepts" are what I have up to now termed infrastructures.

Deconstruction, consequently, in Derrida's words, proceeds by a "double gesture," a phase of reversal and a phase of reinscription or displacement.[26] To speak of phases here could, however, be mislead-ing, since the word suggests a chronological sequence. It is not to be understood as such; rather, the double gesture that characterizes de-construction is to be conceived of as a systematically unified operation that simultaneously marks the difference between its two gestures. Derrida writes, "We must proceed using a double gesture, according to a unity that is both systematic and in and of itself divided, a double writing, that is, a writing that is in and of itself multiple" (P, p. 41). It is in this sense that Derrida speaks of deconstruction as a double science or a double staging. Within the unity of such a practice, deconstruction traces the irreducible difference between its two ges-tures.

In *Positions* the relation of these two gestures is further determined in terms of a chiasmatic doubling or crossing: "The form of the chiasm, of the X, interests me a great deal, not as the symbol of the unknown, but because there is in it, as I underline in 'La dissémi-nation,' a kind of fork (the series *crossroads, quadrifurcum, grid, trellis, key,* etc.) that is moreover, unequal, one of the points extending its range further than the other: this is the figure of the double gesture, the intersection" (P, p. 70). Determined as chiasmatic, the double gesture appears to maintain the distinction between its two movements because of their dissymmetrical communication. Instead of being simply a mixture that confounds the two gestures, the two phases of deconstruction participate in one another in a crosswise manner, thus emphasizing their sameness despite their difference. But sameness, since it does not mean identity, is precisely the opening for the difference between the two gestures. Yet what interests us here in particular is the fact that this chiasmatic structure of deconstruction is not symmetric. It is "a kind of fork . . . moreover, unequal, one of the points extending its range further than the other." The formal dissymmetry of deconstruction makes it radically dissimilar from reflection. This need for dissymmetry, however, is not only formal. Indeed, the two gestures of deconstruction are incommensurate. They are heterogeneous gestures, grafted upon one another in the "one" but irreducibly split operation of deconstruction. Whereas the first gesture plays entirely within the closure of metaphysics, the second attempts a breakthrough toward a certain outside of philosophy. These two gestures are of different bearing and scope. Compared to the conceptual hierarchies, reversed or not, the infrastructures produced during the second phase of deconstruction are unheard-of concepts within the limits of philosophy. The relation of the conceptual dyads to these infrastructures is one of presuppositions, "in dissymmetrical fashion, as the general space of their possibility" (M, p. 327). As the operation that leads to the production of that space of possibility, the second movement of deconstruction is entirely heterogeneous to the first movement, which remains within the boundaries or closure of what is to be deconstructed.

The chiasmatic relation of the two heterogeneous gestures of deconstruction is characterized by a structural asymmetry that defies all reflection; it is the matrix of both the possibility and impossibility, the ground and unground, of reflection. As I have mentioned, this dissymmetry is essential in preventing any neutralization of the bipolar oppositions of the aporias or other contradictions resulting from discursive inequalities and disparities. The dissymmetry, as well as the heterogeneity of the two movements of this double-pointed operation of deconstruction, ensures the reinscription—that is, the "regrounding"—of the concepts of metaphysics in what represents the generality of its Other. This space of inscription of the symmetrically organized binary concepts is the space of the infrastructures, which occupies a lateral and asymmetric relation with respect to the realm of the concepts. Although entirely different, the two orders communicate in various ways. As the notion of the old names of the infrastructures has demonstrated, infrastructures maintain a foothold in the conceptual order, and must continue to do so if they are to intervene in it effectively. And yet, as the open matrix of the conceptual differences, the infrastructures function as their grounds of possibility. Yet since these infrastructures are a sort of repressed reserve, they also by virtue of their encompassing power delimit the concepts of metaphysics, making them, rigorously speaking, impossible. They represent the *surplus* of the conceptual dyads or of the totality of a discourse as well as what prevents them or that totality from achieving closure. They are, in other words, a *lack*. As such, they are without the stability and plenitude "of a form or an equation, in the stationary correspondence of a symmetry or a homology" (*P*, p. 46). The space occupied by the infrastructures, the space of inscription, is thus in no sense an opening into an inexhaustible realm of meaning, of transcendental forms, or of a transcendental semantic excess.

As a way of summing up, let us review the problems that distinguish deconstruction, and that make it a significant undertaking. Deconstruction *starts* with an interrogation of a variety of contradictions and aporias in the discourse of philosophy. These are not contradictions and aporias proper, however, since the discourse of philosophy accommodates them without difficulty. In addition to these contradictions and aporias, which pertain to the formation of concepts and to the development of philosophical arguments, deconstruction addresses many other discursive and conceptual inequalities that have never before been questioned by philosophy. All these aporias, differences of levels, inequalities of developments, and disparities characteristic of the discourse of philosophy, yet which do not seem to disturb the logic of philosophy, also contribute to the establishment of that logic. All the gestures of philosophy—reflection and transcendentalization, all the themes of philosophy, but primarily those of subjectivity, transcendentality, freedom, origin, truth, presence, and the proper—are impossible without the differences and discrepancies that permeate philosophical texts. Yet these same disparities also limit the scope of these gestures and of the purity and coherence of the philosophical concepts or themes.

Deconstruction is an attempt to account for these various and essentially heterogeneous aporias and discursive inequalities with what I have called infrastructures. These minimal structures are both the grounds of possibilities of the canonical philosophical gestures and themes and their ungrounds, that is, that which makes them impossible. These structures limit what they make possible by rendering its rigor and purity impossible. The infrastructures are the internal limit from which classical philosophical concepts and themes take their force and necessity. Deconstruction does not merely destroy metaphysical concepts; it shows how these concepts and themes draw their possibility from that which ultimately makes them impossible. The infrastructures achieve this double task.

Since philosophy has grown out of these infrastructures of the formation of concepts, of the development of philosophical arguments, of the textuality of the discourse of philosophy, it cannot dominate these infrastructures with either its gestures or its themes. The infrastructures are in a dissymmetrical and heterogeneous relation to what they make possible. No reflection can reach out for them, return to them as to something that, like a solid and present ground, would make reflection possible. In contrast to the founding concepts of metaphysics, the infrastructures are incapable of accounting for themselves. They are not reflected into themselves; they do not relate to themselves in an identity-producing manner. Lacking the ability to justify themselves or answer for themselves, they are akin to writing as it has been determined by Occidental philosophy since Plato. This is one of the reasons why Derrida can say that they all entertain a certain essential relation to writing.

In addition the infrastructures are heterogeneous, and although they form chains, the space they occupy is not uniform or homogeneous. As an investigation of these irreducibly heterogeneous infrastructures, deconstruction is in essence a heterology. Extending the requirement of philosophy that a ground must be different from what it grounds, deconstruction exhibits such an absolute other ground as "constitutive" of the canonical philosophical problems. As a solution of sorts to traditional philosophical problems, such as, for instance, the problem of how something absolute can possibly have a generating, engendering, or constituting function, deconstruction both conserves the immanence of philosophical argumentation and concept formation while simultaneously opening it up to that which structurally disorganizes it. As in Hegel's speculative thinking, where "dialectic has been separated from proof," and where, thus, "the notion of philosophical demonstration has been lost," deconstruction, by reinscribing philosophical argumentation, radically displaces it.[27] As a critique of philosophical argumentation and of reflection as the major methodological concept of modern philosophy, deconstruction is consequently also a critique of the Cartesian dream of a self-foundation and self-justification of philosophy. Deconstruction traces the inner limits of the project of a philosophy of philosophy. Yet without in the least trying to do away with philosophy, its style of argumentation, with the rigor of classical logic, and without ever dreaming the empiricist—that is, the symmetrical—dream of a final impossibility of accounting and founding, deconstruction pursues the formulation of problems that, although apparently more easily accommodated by the discourse of literature and critical stylistics, are nonetheless not of that order. Deconstruction opens philosophy to its Others. Literature is only one of these necessarily plural Others. It is an Other which is not simply beyond, nor simply to the side. It is, *within* philosophy, the margin of infrastructural possibilities. This quest into the infrastructures is a philosophical quest, although it proceeds in a new way.

9

A System beyond Being

❦

As we have seen, infrastructures are the "grounds" by means of which deconstruction attempts to account for the "contradictions" and dissimilarities in, from a philosophical standpoint, successful concept formation, argumentation, and the production of discursive totalities. The "nature" of the infrastructures can be further clarified by exploring the "system," or rather the chains in which they are linked together, which, opened up in a deconstructive vista, form an irreducible "space"—in Platonic terms, *epekeina tes ousia*—beyond being. Traditionally it is assumed that when Plato refers in the *Republic* to the *idea tou agathou,* to that idea (of all other ideas) that is to the objects of cognition and to knowledge itself what the sun is to all visible objects, he thinks of the Good as the source of all possible knowledge. This source is itself "not essence but still transcends essence in dignity and surpassing power."[1] It is something more exalted than being *(ousia)*; it is the idea of all ideas, which thus becomes the ultimate source of being. Yet it is doubtful whether one can call it a form or idea in the first place. Furthermore, because of its fundamental indeterminacy, the *agathon,* as Heidegger has pointed out, cannot be hastily determined in ethico-metaphysical terms either.[2] Derrida follows Heidegger's lead as well as his warning when, for instance in "Plato's Pharmacy," he demonstrates that the "source" of all being beyond being is *generalized,* or rather *general,* writing, whose essential nontruth and nonpresence is the fundamentally undecidable condition of possibility and impossibility of presence in its identity and of identity in its presence (*D*, pp. 167–168). The "source" of being and beingness is, for Derrida, the system or chain beyond being of the various infrastructures or undecidables. Conversely, the idea of a *general system* is inseparable from this space, which is beyond the traditional oppositions of concepts and of the argumentative and discursive discrepancies to which deconstruction has made us sensitive. Yet the claim that Derrida's philosophical efforts are not without systematical intentions needs immediate clarification, owing to the general assumption that his philosophy is antisystematical.

In order to come to grips with Derrida's thought, one must reject the temptation—made possible by resources within the codified interpretive possibilities of philosophy itself—simply to determine it as antisystematic. From its inception in Greek thought, philosophy has contained the two absolutely symmetrical alternatives of a systematic and a nonsystematic approach to truth. As proved in particular by the later renewal of antisystematic thought in Hamann, the Romantics, Nietzsche, and others, the aesthetic of the fragment presupposes the early determination of philosophy as *episteme,* and hence the systematic exposition and construction of systems. This antisystematic, fragmentary practice is in no sense radically subversive of the idea of science or of systematicity as characteristic of the philosophical enterprise; it is, rather, a genuine possibility *within* philosophy itself, and it carries out the systematic requirements of philosophy in its own way. We have already seen that Derrida's efforts to reach a beyond of the classical opposition of logic and alogic do not lead him to abandon all rigor in argumentation. Neither does his critique of the idea of rigorous science as the timeless telos of all genuine philosophy entail a mere renunciation of scientificity and systematic intentions. Given the complicity between pretentions to systematicity and the antisystematic practices in philosophy, we must presume that Derrida's exploration of the infrastructures both continues the systematic telos of philosophy and attempts something entirely different, of which fragmentation gives at best a very oblique image.

Let us first briefly examine the ways in which Derrida assumes certain systematic intentions without, however, yielding to the intraphilosophical determination of the fragment. Take, for instance, the beginning of *Positions,* where Derrida refers to "a certain system [of his work] somewhere open to an undecidable resource that sets the system into motion" and determines it to be an interrogation of the order of reasons that traditionally informs systematic enterprises. Yet at the same time, he admits his reluctance "for obvious reasons, to call [the text of that system] fragmentary" (*P,* pp. 3–4; see also *S,* pp. 124, 134). Among the numerous instances of the concept of system in the texts of Derrida, with or without quotation marks, I shall mention only the following passages from the essay "Differance," where he speaks of the space of the infrastructures as "a system which is no longer that of presence but that of differance" or as "a system of ciphers that is not dominated by truth value, which in this manner becomes an included, inscribed, circumscribed function" (*SP,* pp. 147, 149; translation slightly modified). Derrida's intention must thus be viewed as aiming at a more encompassing system which inscribes the value of systematicity while criticizing that very value, but without asserting the opposing (and contemporaneous) value of the fragment. Derrida's philosophy is often seen as indiscriminately critical of the epistemic and systematic exigencies of philosophy, for deconstruction is an operation that also questions the possibility of totalization. As we have seen in Hegel, legislation by totalization is the speculative answer to the aporias of reflection; only by means of a faultless exposition of the system of totality of all determinations of thought could Hegel hope both to overcome the antinomies of reflection, which had become obvious with Kant, and to carry out and fulfill radically what had until then been only reflection's promise. As an interrogation of the totality of reflection, deconstruction also represents a critique of the concept and possibility of system, without reverting to a Romantic gesture of fragmentation, which is itself dependent on the possibility of apprehending totality and system in a pointlike, punctual, and immediate intuition.

Deconstruction has been explicitly construed by Derrida as an attempt to shake totality, to make it tremble in its entirety. Derrida's undertaking is to be viewed as "broaching the deconstruction of *the greatest totality*—the concept of the *episteme* and logocentric metaphysics" (*OG,* p. 46), insofar as that totality is constituted by the value of the system. Yet this critique of the limits of totalization does not proceed by means of a classical refutation, which judges totalization impossible on account of man's finitude: "One then refers to the empirical endeavor of either a subject or a finite discourse in a vain and breathless quest of an infinite richness it can never master. There is too much, more than one can say" (*WD,* p. 289). This classical rejection of totalization underlies the Romantic theology of the fragment. Derrida outlines a different objection to the possibility of totalization:

Nontotalization can also be determined in another way: no longer from the standpoint of a concept of finitude as relegation to the empirical, but from the standpoint of the concept of *play.* If totalization no longer has any meaning, it is not because the infiniteness of a field cannot be covered by a finite glance or a finite discourse, but because the nature of the field—that is, language and a finite language—excludes totalization. This field is in effect that of *play*, that is to say, a field of infinite substitutions only because it is finite, that is to say, because instead of being an inexhaustible field, as in the classical hypothesis, instead of being too large, there is something missing from it: a center which arrests and grounds the play of substitutions.   (WD, p. 289)

But this deconstructive interpretation of totality and system, at the benefit and in the perspective of the nontotalizable field of the infrastructures, does not preclude all systematicity. The deconstructive undoing of the *greatest totality,* the totality of onto-theology, faithfully repeats this totality in *its* totality while simultaneously making it tremble, making it *insecure* in its most assured evidences. The mimicry of totality and of the pretension to systematicity is an inseparable element of deconstruction, one of the very conditions of finding its foothold within the logic being deconstructed. Moreover, the space opened up by the deconstruction, that of the infrastructures, despite what fundamentally inhibits its eventual totalization is not without structure or systematicity. As we shall see, the infrastructures form chains; they can and must be systematized, up to a certain point. But because it is situated beyond the common opposition of structure and genesis, the space of infrastructures, as the space of structurality in general, is also the space of the general system. Since it lies beyond the opposition of system and fragment, whole and part, infinity and the finite, it also constitutes the systematicity of systems.

As I have suggested, the infrastructures do not form a homogeneous body. Their space has no simple structure, is not uniform or formed from one substance, and is not composed throughout in the same manner; it is a heterological space of an irreducible multiplicity of infrastructural instances. Here, perhaps, one can best begin to understand deconstruction's critique of the classical concept of origin as a point of presence and simplicity to which reflection tries to return as to an ultimate ground from which everything else can be deduced. The pluralization of the origin is a first step toward a deconstruction of the value of origin. This deconstruction begins with the recognition that the source or origin is characterized by a certain heterogeneity: "at first, there are sources, the source is other and plural" (M, p. 277). Only by abstraction from that plurality, from one source's referral to another, can a single origin be rigorously delimited. Deconstruction does not, however, satisfy itself with the mere intuition of originary plurality; it does not content itself with opposing the manifold to the one, but begins to determine the law of the complicity of origins. When Derrida writes, in *Of Grammatology,* that this complicity of origins may be called arche-writing, he is manifestly referring to the infrastructural chain, to the general system in which single origins are carved out.

Derrida is not alone in this effort to formulate an organized multiplicity of origins (which is not, of course, the same thing as an absence of origins). He is continuing a tradition that starts with Husserl and Heidegger, and he carries it up to a decisive turning point. Both Husserl and Heidegger introduced the idea of *Gleichursprünglichkeit,* a simultaneity of equally original instances or structures, in the context of a polemic against German Idealism's pretentions to having deduced the oneness of origin.[3] Let us restrict ourselves to one example of this "equiprimordiality" in Heidegger alone. In *Being and Time,* Heidegger introduces this concept in order to describe, in a fundamental and ontological perspective, the multiple and constitutive existential characteristics *(Seinscharaktere)* of an underivable and thus irreducibly original phenomenon such as *In-sein,* "Being-in." He writes: "The fact that something primordial is underivable does not rule out the possibility that a multiplicity of characteristics of Being may be constitutive for it. If these show themselves, then existentially they are equiprimordial *(gleichursprünglich).* The phenomenon of the *equiprimordiality* of constitutive items has often been disregarded in ontology, because of a methodologically unrestrained tendency to derive everything and anything from one simple 'primal ground.' "[4]

The irreducibly multifarious characteristics of Being that simultaneously constitute an underivable phenomenon like Being-in, or Being-in-the-World, make these phenomena structural phenomena. Indeed, what is comprised by equiprimordiality can be understood only under the title of structure; multiplicity, underivativeness, and structurality are the prime characteristics of equiprimordiality. In his lectures of 1925–26 entitled *Logic: The Question of Truth,* Heidegger further refines the concept of equiprimordiality:

In a general mode we say that the so-called structures that show a plurality [Heidegger refers to *Besorgen* and *Fürsorge* as equiprimordial possibilities of *Dasein*] are equiprimordial. In this way, we have already warded off the possibility of deriving one from the other, of constructing one on top of the other, but as yet we have not said anything about the unity of this plurality . . . Above all, nothing has been decided regarding the question whether there is only one kind of unity of this plurality or whether unity is not again the title for certain possibilities that belong to *Dasein* itself. In a negative fashion, all one can say regarding the question about the unity of these plural structures is that this unity is not a sum total in the sense that, as a unity, it would follow its parts as their result, so to speak. On the contrary, the unity of this plurality is a totality that, as a beginning, precedes plurality and, first and foremost, frees, so to speak, parts from itself.[5]

The plurally structured origins are thus characterized not only by the fact that they cannot be derived but also by the fact that the elements that enter their composition cannot be derived from one another. Equiprimordial structural phenomena are therefore heterogeneous. Yet for Heidegger these simultaneously coeval and originary structures are still contained within a unity. For Heidegger, in other words, the irreducibly heterogeneous structural possibilities form a totality that, in an originary fashion, precedes its severance into a multiplicity. It seems that the unity and totality of the multiplicity are not put into question as such, even by the possible plurality of the unities to which the multiplicities may give rise.

In spite of their plurality, coeval origins, are, consequently, contained in oneness. But this can also be seen in Flach's heterological foundation of the fundamental principles of logic, which I discussed toward the end of Part I. In his investigation of the ultimate principles of thought, Flach comes to the conclusion that these principles cannot be unities of identity, of general simplicity, in which the elements would be at once themselves and their opposites. The ultimate principle, according to Flach, can only be thought heterologically, that is, as a unity of one *and* the Other. The absolute minimum of the purely logical object is the unity of the equiprimordial moments of the one and the Other. Moreover, because the one and the Other are simultaneously original in the last principles of thought, the one is not distinguished by priority over the Other. Quoting Rickert, Flach writes: "The One and the Other are logically equiprimordial, 'they do not only logically belong to one another, they are also logically totally equivalent' . . . With this it is shown, in a well-founded manner, that what we can think as the last instance represents at least a duplicity."[6] But although these principles are determined as pairs in a process of *limiting exclusion* between complementary alternatives such as the one and the Other, and although one must recognize a multiplicity of such principles, and hence the plurality of thought, they must also be related as moments to a totality—the totality of the originary sphere—in which they receive their final determination. Plurality, as Flach remarks, is a positively infinite thought. As a result, the plurality of the in themselves heterothetical, ultimate principles of thought is synthetic. "The absolute is therefore this absolutely synthetic unity," writes Flach, in conclusion.[7] Yet if the equiprimordiality of the one and the Other lends itself to such a synthesis, it is because Flach's heterological principle implies a homogeneity of that which enters into conjunction. It presupposes not only the equivalence of the one and the Other but also their similarity in nature. What is equiprimordial thus also appears to be of the same ontological order.

Now, in distinction from Flach's contention that principles are endowed with a constituting function only if they are linked together in the totality of the originary *oneness* of thought, and also in distinction from similar statements by Husserl and Heidegger, Derrida's heterological doctrine of infrastructural grounds radically questions the philosophical gesture by which the structural multiplicity of the coeval and underivable originary phenomena is tamed into one whole. Indeed, if Flach's ultimate principles contain the one *and* the Other, unity *and* multiplicity, what allows him (or Husserl or Heidegger) to raise any of these principles to a position of dominance over all the other principles? One principle, none of whose components has any priority over the others, is raised nonetheless to a principle of principles; one heterothetical opposition of the system of the equiprimordial structural and minimal principles of thought is turned into the possibility of the system of all principles, in which it also partakes. By this paradox, the initially heterological multiplicity of fundamental principles is turned into a synthetic unity.

Precisely because of this paradox, constitutive of the very notion of equiprimordial principles, which raises one of the dually structured, heterological principles (one/multiplicity) to the status of a matrix for all principles and thus confers unity upon their plurality, one must distinguish Derrida's investigation into the heterological infrastructural grounds, which proceeds from an awareness of this paradox, from the positions discussed up to this point. Undoubtedly the infrastructures resemble the Heideggerian structural possibilities, or Flach's heterological principles, multiple and underivable, that is to say, ultimate structures. Yet precisely because they cannot be dominated, either by what they make possible or by themselves, their system cannot be absolutely closed off into a unity. As we shall see, each of the infrastructures can claim to represent all the others and thus to function as the matrix of possibility for them all. This possibility, however, which also undermines all domination of the system by one single infrastructure, consequently prevents its eventual closure. Although the plural infrastructures' lack of final unity indicates that they are not principles properly speaking, this is not a privation, for it allows the infrastructures, as we have seen, to account for the "antinomies" of philosophical discourse. One such antinomy is the paradox constitutive of a doctrine of last principles.

The concept of equiprimordiality is thus not sufficient to comprehend the irreducible multiplicity of the universality of the infrastructures. The system of the infrastructures is not a unity or totality; it is an open system, although not in the sense of an endless infinity, that is, what Hegel called bad or spurious infinity.[8] Nor is it a finite system, since the infrastructures are not simply principles, simple elements, or atoms. Derrida notes in *Positions:* "By definition the list [of the infrastructures] has no taxonomical closure, and even less does it constitute a lexicon. First, because these are not *atoms,* but rather focal points of economic condensation, sites of passage necessary for a very large number of marks, slightly more effervescent crucibles" (*P,* p. 40). The system is best conceived of as one of chains. The infrastructures can be linked together in different ways, and their chains too can enter into multiple combinations. Each infrastructure partakes in a chain or in several chains, but which it never dominates. In such a chain—arche-trace/arche-writing/differance/supplementarity, for example, or *marge/marque/marche,* or reserve/remark/*retrait/ restance/retard*—each term can be replaced by or substituted for the other. Yet these substitutions are not synonymous substitutions. Although the terms of the chains are *analogous* to each other, they are not synonyms for one identical term. The substitutions within chains, which, Derrida contends, become necessary according to context, are not simply metonymic operations "that would leave intact the conceptual identities, the signified idealities, that the chain would be happy just to translate, to put into circulation" (*P.* p. 14). It is more appropriate to understand this process of substitution as one of supplementation.

Because the infrastructures are not atoms, because they have no identity in themselves, the irreducibly multiple chains cannot be gathered once and for all upon themselves in some ideal purity. Let us not forget that the infrastructures are the conditions of possibility (and impossibility) of the conceptual differences as well as of discursive inequalities; thus, they are what makes the project of systematization possible, without, however, being systematizable themselves. Yet this is not to say that a certain systematization cannot apply to them; it simply means that their system cannot be closed upon itself by means of some dominating center. Strictly speaking they form no system; therefore, their "system" cannot be formalized. The infra-structures, Derrida remarks, "can never be stabilized in the plenitude of a form or an equation, in the stationary correspondence of a sym-metry or a homology" (P. p. 46). The system of the infrastructures cannot be formalized, idealized, or systematized because it is precisely its play that makes those projects possible. What the infrastructural chains, the chains of a number of "sites of passage necessary for a very large number of marks," demonstrate is the *general system.*

Let us now inquire into some infrastructural examples in order to demonstrate that systematic intentions are not foreign to the field of infrastructures. I shall also characterize the field of infrastructures as a space of repetition and self-doubling, in what I shall call a *general theory of doubling;* and I shall show that deconstruction is a medi-tation on the *general system,* or on what makes systematicity as such both necessary and impossible.

THE INFRASTRUCTURAL CHAIN

The concatenation to which the infrastructures lend themselves is not the result of an alleged plenitude or abundance of transformations. In what follows, my discussion of infrastructure *as* arche-trace, *as* differance, *as* supplementarity, and so on entails no predication or limitation of the infrastructure *itself.* I have already insisted on the purely expository grounds for my generalization of the term *infra-structure.* Indeed, the infrastructure is not a leading concept or genus which could be distinguished from its subordinate species. The *as* of these individualizations is meant to bring to the fore different grades of the breadth, clarity, and certitude of the infrastructure, appearing each time as different unities reflected into themselves. Infrastructure is to be thought of in the plural; the conjunction *as* serves to restore this irreducible singularity and plurality. Although *as* traditionally serves as an operator of phenomenologization, of the revealing of an essence, it serves a very different purpose here, where it is meant to indicate specific infrastructural syntheses or "functions" that are irreducibly singular. As a result, an investigation of the *general system* amounts to a sort of classification of a variety of such syntheses. To say that they are irreducibly singular, and not the expressions of a prior infrastructural essence, does not impinge on their universality. Compared to the universality to which philosophical concepts must pretend, infrastructural legitimation hinges, paradoxically, on the universality, or rather the generality, of something I shall initially refer to as a radical empiricity.

If, then, the infrastructural syntheses often appear complementary or overlapping, one must keep in mind that they are not aspects or facets of a unity that offers itself as such in their disguise; there is no such prior unity. Moreover, the infrastructural syntheses are not phenomena in the first place but represent an articulation "older" than the difference between being and appearance, appearance and appearing. The infrastructural traits are not the traits *of* something, nor can they be tied together retrospectively, *après-coup*. The concatenations between various infrastructures—between, for example, archetrace, differance, supplementarity, iterability, and re-marking—do not obey the linearity of logical time, or for that matter of dialectical time. The signifying chains of the infrastructures are voluminous; they have the appearance of scenes, stagings, synopses, and their organization changes according to what they are supposed to account for.

For *essential* reasons, I cannot hope to achieve any definitive presentation of the "system" of the infrastructures. My goal here is more limited. All I want to show is that the infrastructures lend themselves to a certain systematicity, to a certain stratified systematization. This can be achieved by setting side by side a limited number of these undecidables and exploring some of the ways in which they implicate one another.

The Infrastructure as Arche-Trace

In *Of Grammatology*, Derrida indicates a number of givens in the contemporary discourse of philosophy that motivated his choice of the word *trace* to designate a specific infrastructural articulation. The word *trace* makes reference to Nietzsche's and Freud's, Levinas's and Heidegger's preoccupation with a critique of the value of presence as constitutive of classical ontology. It must be noted that trace is a metaphysical concept on the same ground as the concept of presence as self-presence, from which it is derived. Yet for Derrida, the word designates something of which the metaphysical concepts of trace and presence are the erasure. From Derrida's analysis of Heidegger's concept of *die frühe Spur,* it follows that trace is the necessarily metaphysical concept that names an originary tracing and effacement, of which the traditional conceptual dyad of trace and presence within the metaphysical text is the trace of effacement (M, p. 66). What, then, does the word *trace* signify?

As I have indicated, it names something of which presence and trace, or more generally self and Other, are the erasure within the discourse of philosophy. Whereas philosophy traditionally considers the Other to be secondary to the self, the Other *of* the self, thus annulling the Other in its own right, Derrida's inquiry into their difference leads to the recognition of a certain irreducibility of the Other with respect to the self. Indeed, despite the self's traditional subjection of the Other to itself, its own identity is a function of its demarcation from the Other, which thus becomes endowed with an essential autonomy. The arche-trace is the constituting possibility of this differential interplay between self and Other, in short, of what is traditionally understood as difference.

Most generally speaking, the originary trace designates the *minimal structure* required for the existence of any difference (or opposition) of terms (and what they stand for), that is, for any relation to alterity. Within metaphysics, the difference between two terms is invariably perceived from the perspective of one of the terms, the term of plenitude, from which the second term of the opposition is held to derive; the first term is not taken to be affected by the fact that it appears in opposition to another, less valorized term. In contrast, the arche-trace stems from an insight into the constituting function of difference, the *holding-against-another,* of perspective variations *(Abschattungen),* to use a Husserlian term. The problematic of the arche-trace articulates the recognition that the privileged term in a difference of opposition would not appear as such without the *difference* or *opposition* that gives it form. Consequently, the arche-trace is a reflection on the form that a term or entity of plenitude must take, insofar as it can appear only in oppositions or dyadic structures; it is a meditation upon the indissociable *appearing* of what comes to the fore with another, lesser term or entity. The arche-trace explains why a concept of plenitude or presence can be thought only within dyadic conceptual structures.

Let us attempt to imagine a concept that has never been held against another in a dichotomous relation. Entirely undetermined, it would be altogether unintelligible; moreover, it would not yet be a concept. Now, suppose it appeared once and only once, as if by accident, in a differential relation to another term or entity; then, the very possibility of that accident would have to be accounted for by demonstrating what made it possible for *it* to suffer such an accident. Such a demonstration would reveal that that concept or entity includes, in one way or another, what it is opposed to, and also includes, most fundamentally, the mark of the negativity characteristic of difference. Yet conceptualized entities appear always simultaneously with other concepts in hierarchically determined (conflictual) oppositions. To say that a concept appears simultaneously with its polar opposite, which is usually in the lower position, designating the simulacrum of the value referred to by the first, is to admit that that concept can be what it is supposed to be only in distinguishing itself from another term that it adds to itself. The identity of the leading term, therefore, requires that the possibility of its own duplication and of its reference to another be inscribed within itself. Otherwise it could not enter into opposition with another term, in comparison with which it is what it is. *Arche-trace* is the name for the universality of this *difference,* for the *necessary possibility* of inscription in general, which must affect a concept and value of plenitude insofar as it appears as such only within a difference or opposition. Since a conceptual entity is, by right, self-identical only insofar as it calls upon its lower self in a dyadic structure, this *difference* is not accidental but is the possibility of both its identity and its difference from an Other. Any difference or opposition between terms, concepts, things, and so on presupposes this *difference,* which intimately affects everything that enters into a relation of difference or opposition—that is to say, everything—because it is the condition as such of the possibility of entering into a relation.

Since, within the sphere of metaphysics, a trace is derivative of, and opposed to, an instant or instance of full presence, the trace that names the *difference,* and that must inhabit that agency of full presence in order to distinguish it from its trace, must be called *arche-trace.* It is a trace of which the trace is only a trace, and it has breached the moment of full presence, which can thus appear in all its plenitude, in opposition to the lack of plenitude conceptualized by the conventional trace. What the arche-trace thus allows to appear in a difference of values, concepts, or entities is its own effacement in the form of the valorized value and in the form of the absence of that value, an absence which is the only possible representation of the arche-trace within the realm of appearances. The trace is indeed constituted by the possibility of such an effacement. "The trace is the erasure of selfhood, of one's own presence, and is constituted by the threat or anguish of its irremediable disappearance, of the disappearance of its disappearance. An unerasable trace is not a trace, it is a full presence, an immobile and uncorruptible substance, a son of God, a sign of parousia and not a seed, that is, a mortal germ. This erasure is death itself" (*WD,* p. 230).

The possibility of erasure constitutive of the trace shows itself in the trace's effacement of what could maintain the trace in presence. The tracing of the trace is identical with that effacement, and thus with the self-erasure of the trace. Through the effacement of what could maintain it in presence, the trace constitutes itself as relation to another trace. Hence, "since the trace can only imprint itself by referring to the other, to another trace . . . by letting itself be upstaged and forgotten, its force of production stands in necessary relation to the energy of its erasure" (*D*, p. 331). Tracing and effacing are not simply in a relation of exteriority; what constitutes the trace in depth is precisely the relation to Otherness by which the trace's self-identity and self-presence are marked, and thus effaced, by the detour through the Other. Also, because of this solidarity between tracing and effacing, the arche-trace can never be presented *as such* outside the differences that it makes possible and as which it itself disappears. "It is itself a trace that can never be presented, that is, can never appear and manifest itself as such in its phenomenon. It is a trace that lies beyond what profoundly ties fundamental ontology to phenomenology. Always deferring, the trace is never presented as such. In presenting itself it becomes effaced" (*SP*, p. 154; translation slightly modified). Indeed, if the trace is relation to another trace in self-effacement only, then it has nothing that could be called its own or that could, as its proper essence, be made to appear as such. For essential reasons, nothing of the infrastructure arche-trace as such can become present.

It follows that it is impossible to ask what the arche-trace *is,* because this would imply that it could appear, come into view, in its essence. To ask what the arche-trace *is* is to presuppose a difference, between appearance and essence for instance, which the arche-trace is intended to explain. Although this infrastructure cannot, for these reasons, be fixed within the definite and fully decidable contours of an *eidos,* a description of its main features is not thereby precluded.

No one would challenge the nuclear physicist's assumption of the theoretical "existence" of such particles as quarks or gluons, an assumption required by quantum chromodynamics to explain certain properties of matter on the subatomic level. Such a hypothesis could never be substantiated through the perception of such a single, uncombined particle, although its "existence" can be indirectly inferred from experience, since it leaves detectable signatures. Yet since these signatures do not stand for the existence of the particle as such, as the self-present entity, but only justify its assumption as that of a necessary possibility or mathematical function, the ontological status of these particles is most peculiar. In an analogous way, an infra-structure such as the arche-trace must be assumed if one is to explain the difference associated with concepts and entities. We begin to see, writes Derrida, that "difference cannot be thought without the *trace*" (*OG*, p. 57). The arche-trace, or difference in itself, is not a difference with respect to an already constituted presence. On the contrary, as "an originary synthesis not preceded by any absolute simplicity," it is before all determination of a particular difference "the *pure* move-ment which produces difference" (*OG*, p. 62). Since it produces dif-ferends as an effect, the arche-trace is thus more originary than the differends it constitutes. As the origin of difference, however, the arche-trace also undermines the value of origin, for reasons discussed in previous chapters. "The trace is not only the disappearance of origin—within the discourse that we sustain and according to the path that we follow it means that the origin did not even disappear, that it was never constituted except reciprocally by a non-origin, the trace, which thus becomes the origin of the origin" (*OG*, p. 61).

Similarly, and for the same reasons, the arche-trace is no longer a principle properly speaking. If the trace cannot be submitted to the onto-phenomenological question of essence, it is because in its case one can "no longer trust even the opposition of fact and principle, which, in all its metaphysical, ontological, and transcendental forms, has always functioned within the system of *what is*" (*OG*. p. 75). Although no difference can be thought without presupposing the arche-trace, its constituting function can no longer be cast within the frame-work of such concepts as origin or principle. It cannot be fully and appropriately accounted for with the traditional judiciary questions.

How, then, is the arche-trace, as an irreducibly originary synthesis, capable of constituting differences? The arche-trace has already been described as the minimal structure of all difference, and hence of all alterity between terms or entities. Given the solidarity between tracing and effacing, the infrastructure *arche-trace* can now be made more precise by determining it in terms of what Derrida calls a "structure de renvoi generalisée" (*M*, p. 24). The notion of *structure de renvoi* translates the German *Verweisungsstruktur* and has been rendered by its English translators as "referential structure," "structure of refer-ral," or "structure of reference." The arche-trace is a minimal struc-ture of generalized reference, whereby *reference* must be understood, in the broadest sense of referring, as alluding or pointing to something other. The arche-trace is a minimal structure of referral to the extent that it constitutes difference between terms or entities. Indeed, what it describes is that all reference to self takes place by way of a *detour* through an Other and thus presupposes an originary self-effacement. The arche-trace unites the double movement of reference (to self or Other) and of self-diversion. Derrida conceptualizes this structure of referral, a structure closely related to what Husserl calls "forward and backward references" *(Hin-und Rückweisungen)*, in *Speech and Phenomena,* as part of a discussion of Husserl's first investigation in *Logical Investigations.* Aided by the discrepancy between various strata of description within the work of Husserl, Derrida proceeds, against Husserl's express wish, to a deconstructive generalization of *indication,* which this philosopher had attempted to distinguish from *expression* as one sign-function from another. For Husserl, indication is a mode of association of ideas characterized by empirical motivation; consequently, it is void of any truth value. In indication, a thing does not count separately but only insofar as it helps to present and point to another thing. Husserl writes, "The single item itself, in these various forward and backward references, is no mere experienced content, but an apparent object (or part, property, etc., of the same) that appears only in so far as experience *(Erfahrung)* endows contents with a new phenomenological *character,* so that they no longer count separately, but help to present an object different from themselves."⁹

According to Husserl, expression and its meaning function are entirely different from indication. In solitary mental life, where it achieves total purity, expression is free of all indication and intimation. Derrida's argument in *Speech and Phenomena* demonstrates that this essential Husserlian distinction (essential because the privileging of expression over indication inaugurates the specific domain of phenomenological research—intentional consciousness and experience) cannot ultimately be upheld, since indication, in the form of self-intimation, must inhabit expression even in its pure form of mental soliloquy. Obviously enough, the ensuing generalization of indication implies the necessity for a complete rethinking of indication, which, in the essential Husserlian distinction, had been entirely determined from the perspective of expression—that is, as a deficient and derivative mode of expression. The arche-trace thus names a radical generalization of the indicative function.

As an originary nonpresence and alterity at the root of what Husserl conceptualized under the name *expression*—the ideal self-presence of meaning without the mediation of signs—the arche-trace is thought as the condition of the ideality of meaning and of self-presence in general, insofar as both must be infinitely repeatable in order to be what they are supposed to be. This necessary possibility of re-petition in its most general form—without which the ideality of meaning or self-presence, that is, of the domain proper of phenomenological investigation, could not come about—is the "trace in the most universal sense." The irreducible and unavoidable nonpresence and alterity within self-presence and meaning strikes, says Derrida, "at the very root of the argument for the uselessness of signs [of indication, intimation, and so on] in the self-relation." Indeed, for an ideal entity to repeat *itself*, it must be able to intimate *itself* in contrast to an Other from which it is different. The trace that makes possible such reference to self by way of an Other is "more 'primordial' than what is phenomenologically primordial," or pristine to expression—that is, meaning, self-presence, evidence, and so on. The originary trace is thus the constituting impurity or alterity, the constituting nonpresence, that allows the phenomenologically primordial to come into its own by providing the phenomenologically primordial with the mark of a minimal difference within which it can repeat itself infinitely as the same by referring to an Other and to (an Other of) itself within itself. In short, the arche-trace must be understood as the fold of an irreducible "bending-back," as a minimal (self-)difference within (self-)identity, which secures selfhood and self-presence through the detour of oneself (as Other) to oneself.

The arche-trace is both the minimal difference required by self-repetition, and thus by ideality, and the minimal relation to an Other (the relation of indication), without which a self could not be self. As the very condition of being a self, the arche-trace is the inscription within the *stigme* of self of "the *other* point toward which it continually drifts" (D, p. 241). Yet clearly enough, in this most universal sense, the trace is also that which forever prevents a self from being self, since the relation to Other is "older" than selfhood. The structure of generalized reference that is the arche-trace is also the limit of the self-identical referent. In its capacity as such a general structure of referral, the arche-trace constitutes the minimal synthesis of self-presence and self-identity through self-deportation. The arche-trace is this minimal unity of being at once oneself and an Other; it is the minimal and general structure of the constitution of an identity through relation to alterity; it is, consequently, a structure of the retention of the mark of the Other by the self, by which the self is what it is only insofar as the interval that constitutes it simultaneously divides it. This double movement is not that of an already constituted identity or personality, but is the minimal logical structure of relation to alterity that such a constitution must presuppose. The difference that such a constitution entails is the trace *of* the arche-trace, the trace as which the arche-trace appears; but the minimal referential structure that is the arche-trace does not appear *as such* in what it constitutes as the trace of its effacement. As we have seen, it rather *disappears* in what it makes possible, since effacement, from the start, constitutes the trace as a trace. Effacement belongs to the structure of the trace, since the minimal synthesis of the referential structure makes self-diverting and being marked by the Other a condition of self-identity. For the same reason, the irreducible duplicity of the synthesis of this structure of referral is the origin of repetition and thus idealization. Because "this trace is the opening of the first exteriority in general, the enigmatic relation of the living to its other and of an inside to an outside: spacing," it is also the origin of space (*OG*, p. 70). Moreover, because the doubling characteristic of the structure of referentiality is a process of temporalization as well, it functions equally as the origin of what is called time. These different implications of the infrastructure, or general structure of referral, will be analyzed in more detail. As arche-trace, the general structure of reference—that is to say, the minimal unity of self and Other before all relations between constituted personalities, entities, or identities—explains the necessary inscription of all of philosophy's axial concepts (and of what they designate) within differential structures or systems. Also calling the arche-trace arche-writing, Derrida notes: "To think the unique *within* the system, to inscribe it there, such is the gesture of the arche-writing: arche-violence, loss of the proper, of absolute proximity, of self-presence, in truth the loss of what has never taken place, of a self-presence which has never been given but only dreamed of and always already split, repeated, incapable of appearing to itself except in its own disappearance" (*OG*, p. 112).

In its capacity as arche-trace, the general structure of reference, whereby constitution of self can take place only through relation to Other, accounts for the fact and the necessity that all concepts appear in opposition to other concepts and are, in fact and of necessity, formed by the difference in which they appear. "Such would be the originary trace. Without a retention in the minimal unit of temporal experience, without a trace retaining the other as other in the same, no difference would do its work and no meaning would appear. It is not the question of a constituted difference here, but rather, before all determination of the content, of the *pure* movement which produces difference" (*OG*, p. 62). As the minimal unit of differential determination, as the unity of the double movement of self-effacement and relation to Other—that is, as arche-trace—the general structure of referentiality is, then, the fabric from which systems can be cut. It is itself the general system—that is, the condition of possibility and, in accordance with the logic of the infrastructures, of impossibility of the systematic exposition of concepts.

The Infrastructure as Differance

For the same reasons that the arche-trace could not be fixed into place once and for all, differance is a heterogeneity whose movement cannot be bounded within a definitive setting. Nonetheless, this impossibility does not preclude us from outlining the nuclear traits of differance. The arche-synthesis of the arche-trace is the minimal structure of a relation to alterity, which, as pure difference, produces differends as an effect *"The (pure) trace is differance,"* writes Derrida (OG, p. 62).

In *Speech and Phenomena,* for the first time Derrida is compelled to think of differance as both a pure and an impure difference, without decidable poles and without independent or irreversible polar terms. After showing how Husserl achieves sense and presence through a transcendental reduction of everything indicative, of all mediation and relation to Other in the sphere of solitary mental life, Derrida argues that this same transcendental reduction also yields differance, once Husserl admits that auto-affection is the condition of self-presence. Indeed, without such auto-affection, no present could reflect itself into itself; yet to grant that without self-affection no present could truly be self-present is to admit a minimal and pure difference (and hence, relation to Other) into presence as the very hinge upon which it turns into itself. Auto-affection, concludes Derrida, is therefore "not something that happens to a transcendental subject; it produces it. Auto-affection is not a modality of experience that characterizes a being that would already be itself *(autos).* It produces sameness as self-relation within self-difference; it produces sameness as the non-identical" (SP, p. 82). But the interval of this pure difference, which divides self-presence so that it may fold itself into itself, also harbors everything that Husserl hoped to exclude from self-presence as a threat to its purity. To say, then, as Husserl does, that self-affection makes self-presence possible is also to say that self-presence can never be pure, that the very difference that allows self-presence to turn into itself also makes it forever differ from itself. Differance, then, like the pure self-presence reached in transcendental reduction, is clearly a transcendental concept, but it is just as clearly the reason why "no pure transcendental reduction is possible," and hence why no pure transcendental *concepts* are possible either (*SP*, p. 82). The pure difference of self-affection, while it makes self-presence possible, at the same time "fissures and retards presence, submitting it simultaneously to primordial division and delay" (*SP*, p. 88). It accounts at once for ideality and nonideality, and for their difference. How, then, does differance become the possibility of the difference between the ideal and the nonideal?

In *Positions*, Derrida has given the most exhaustive account of the formal features of differance. Differance is not simply deferring, because an act of delay does not necessarily entail a movement of differance. In addition to deferring, differance necessarily implies difference. As an infrastructure, it "is to be conceived prior to the separation between deferring as delay and differing as the active work of difference" (*SP*, p. 88); thus, it is more primordial than deferring and difference taken separately. Like all other infrastructures, differance, in having to account for a variety of theoretical phenomena, is an economical, conceptual, formal structure to the extent that it draws together a configuration of signifying movements from a variety of heterogeneous resources; it is not a homogeneous unity of heterogeneous features, however, and is even "inconceivable as a mere *homogeneous* complication of a diagram or line of time" (*SP*, p. 88). As an infrastructure, differance is a nonunitary synthesis of heterogeneous features.

As we know, the word *differance* is formed by substantivizing the participle of the verb *différer*, "to defer," "to postpone," "to adjourn." In creating this unusual noun, in which the *a* substituted for the *e* remains purely graphic, since the difference between the two vowels cannot be heard (it is a difference that depends on the mute intervention of a written trace, and thus of a trace that ties differance in with the functioning of the arche-trace), Derrida opens the semantic field of this noun to a variety of meanings, not all of which stem from the original verb *différer*. Like so many other infrastructures, the -*ance* ending of *differance* already leaves undecidable whether this word is to be understood as active or passive, thus enabling it to occupy a place beyond what phenomenology would distinguish as active and passive constitution or synthesis. More strikingly, *differance* knots together the different meanings of the word *difference* with the entirely different significations of the verb *to defer* (*différer*), from whose participle the noun *differance* was derived; yet there is no etymological justification for doing so. Only by means of quasicatachrestic violence can the neologism *differance* be made to refer to the semantic field of the word *difference*. The sort of linguistic abuse at stake here is required by the necessity of good economic "formalization," which the infrastructure differance is intended to achieve. The lack of harmony between such different things as deferment and difference, instead of being a misfortune for the intended coherence, is precisely what the term *differance* serves to account for. Furthermore, differance ties together in one arche-synthesis much more than the movement of deferral and difference; it is composed of at least three additional, entirely heterogeneous concepts of difference. However heterogeneous the different concepts that enter the structural configuration named by the plural noun *differance* may be, they act in unison to form a systematic and irreducible ensemble of possibilities that economically accounts for a variety of distinct concepts of difference simultaneously at work in the discourse of philosophy. Differance ties together five concepts, which owe their incommensurability to their scope, sphere of origin, and level of argumentation, in one synthesis that accounts for them all. Let us, then, discuss these different concepts of difference to which *differance* refers, in order to determine what this strange linguistic formation is intended to achieve:

First, *differance* refers to the (active *and* passive) movement that consists in deferring by means of delay, delegation, reprieve, referral, detour, postponement, reserving. In this sense, *differance* is not preceded by the originary and indivisible unity of a present possibility that I could reserve, like an expenditure that I would put off calculatedly or for reasons of economy. What defers presence, on the contrary, is the very basis on which presence is announced or desired in what represents it, its sign, its trace.   (*P*, p. 8)

In this first determination of differance, Derrida makes use of one of the meanings of the Latin verb *differre* insofar as it refers to time,

namely, the action of postponing until later, of taking into account, the taking-account of time and forces in an operation that implies an economic reckoning, a detour, a respite, a delay, a reserve, a representation—all the concepts that I will sum up here in a word . . . *temporalizing* [*temporisation*]. "To differ" in this sense is to temporalize, to resort, consciously or unconsciously, to the temporal and temporalizing mediation of a detour that suspends the accomplishment or fulfillment of a "desire" or "will," or carries desire or will out in a way that annuls or tempers their effect.   (*SP*, p. 136)

With differance as deferment, "time opens itself as the delay of the origin in relation to itself" (*M*, p. 290).

Let us now see in more detail how this temporalizing aspect of differance is the condition of possibility of temporalization *(temporalisation)*, temporality, and time—their "primordial constitution," as it would be called within the conceptual system and according to the classical requirements of metaphysics and transcendental phenomenology.

The operation of deferring implicated by the *a* of differance does not refer to the delaying of any already constituted or anticipated moment of presence. "To defer [*différer*] . . . cannot mean to retard a present possibility, to postpone an act, to put off a perception already now possible. That possibility is possible only through a *differance* which must be conceived of in other terms than those of a calculus or mechanics of decision." If the act of deferring related only to such a moment, it would represent nothing but "the lapse which a consciousness, a self-presence of the present, accords itself" (*WD,* p. 203) and would derive from the presence; yet the retardation in question is originary and thus not a relation between two moments of presence. Instead, what Derrida is attempting here is to think the present based on time as differance. Difference as time, as the minimal activity of postponing, is to be understood as constitutive of presence, as well as of past and future, to the extent that they are only modifications of the now. Difference as time, or rather as temporalizing *(temporisation)* is not, then, a more simple and authentic time compared to the vulgar time programmatic of the philosophy of time from Aristotle to Hegel. Indeed, as Derrida argues in "Ousia and Gramme," the very question concerning the meaning of time suppresses time by linking it to appearing, truth, presence, to essence in general. To think differance as temporalizing, however, does not complicate time by looking for its origin in the inner-time experience of consciousness; such an attempt, which belongs to the project of a transcendental phenomenology, cannot avoid thinking the time of the inner-time consciousness according to the model of mundane time. In distinction from the vulgar concept of time (which, according to Heidegger, has informed the philosophy of time since Aristotle), from Husserl's concept of an inner consciousness of time, and from Heidegger's notion of authentic temporality, difference as time points at an "absolute past," a past that is no longer a modification of a present, no longer a present-past, but a past to which, according to the logic of the arche-trace, a present moment must refer in order to be what it is:

Differance is what makes the movement of signification possible only if each element that is said to be "present," appearing on the stage of presence, is related to something other than itself but retains the mark of a past element

and already lets itself be hollowed out by the mark of its relation to a future
element. This trace relates no less to what is called the future than to what
is called the past, and it constitutes what is called the present by this very
relation to what it is not, to what it absolutely is not; that is, not even to a
past or future considered as a modified present.   (*SP*, pp. 142–143)

As a result of this radical alterity, without which presence could
never come into existence, presence is always belated with regard to
itself and comes *ex post,* as an effect, to the absolute past to which
it must relate in order to be constituted. Differance as temporalizing
names the irreducible temporal movements that thus affect the idea
of presence itself. While time has always been thought from the present
now, this is a time anterior to time, a past *of* time, a past that has
never been present. So if differance is conceived of as the primordial
constitution of temporality and time as commonly understood, then
differance allows time to come to the fore only as limited by what
makes it possible. This is why Derrida can contend that "the inter-
mission or interim of the hymen does not establish time: neither time
as the existence of the concept (Hegel), nor lost time nor time regained,
and still less the moment or eternity. No present in truth presents
itself there, not even in the form of its self-concealment" (*D*, p. 230).
But since the reference to an absolute alterity required by the constitution of a present now is the insinuation of a space into the supposedly self-sufficient present, its spacing, this reference to alterity, is
also the becoming-time of space, to the extent that what is referred
to is an absolute past. Indeed, differance as temporalizing is inseparable from, though not identical to, differance as spacing, since the
becoming-time of space is the condition proper of spacing.

"*Second,* the movement of *differance,* as that which produces different things, that which differentiates, is the common root of all the
oppositional concepts that mark our language, such as, to take only
a few examples, sensible/intelligible, intuition/signification, nature/
culture, etc" (*P*, p. 9). In this second determination of differance,
Derrida refers to the second meaning of the Latin verb *differre,* the
etymological root of the French *différer,* which translates the Greek
diaphorein (to carry different ways, spread abroad, scatter, disperse,
separate, differ, be different). Differance is here understood as the
productive and primordial constituting causality, as one would say
in traditional philosophy, of differends and differences. But since this
production of differences takes place through the opening of an in-
between, of a *polemos* based either on dissimilarity or allergy between
poles, terms, or concepts whereby hierarchical relations are installed,

differance is here determined primarily as *spacing (espacement)*. "In 'differents,' whether referring to the alterity of dissimilarity or the alterity of allergy or of polemics, it is necessary that interval, distance, *spacing* occur among the different elements and occur actively, dynamically, and with a certain perseverance in repetition" (*SP,* pp. 136–137).

Let us try to understand how differance as spacing renders possible spatiality and space in the common sense. Spacing is neither time nor space. Recall that the relation to an Other constitutive of a self, whose minimal unit is the arche-trace, presupposes an interval which at once affects and makes possible the relation of self to Other and divides the self within itself. In the same way, differance as the production of a polemical space of differences both presupposes and produces the intervals between concepts, notions, terms, and so on. In that sense, arche-trace and differance, each in a different manner, are spacing. From the perspective of the arche-trace, spacing "is the opening of the first exteriority in general, the enigmatic relationship of the living to its other and of an inside to an outside" (*OG,* p. 70). Spacing is the *space in general,* or "that minimum of essential spacing" that any entity (real or conceptual) must contain or be inhabited by in order to fall into a space 'exterior' to it" (*WD,* p. 219). Since spatialization—being befallen by space—is a possibility to which any entity is subject, this possibility must be inscribed within that entity. As this necessary possibility—that is, a possibility that must always be possible—spacing ensures the spatialization of entities. Consequently, the falling into space of an entity is never accidental—it never happens by surprise—because its interiority is already inhabited by its outside as the possibility of an outside befalling it. Spacing, then, also names the difference that insinuates itself within the self-relation of a self-identical entity and that prevents this entity from ever relating only to itself. Spacing in this sense is exteriority in general, without which "the outside, 'spatial' and 'objective' exteriority which we believe we know as the most familiar thing in the world, as familiarity itself, would not appear" (*OG,* pp. 70–71).

From the perspective of differance, spacing is the force of rupture by which concepts are separated from one another, the staging of concepts in an "arche-scene" at the origin of sense and, therefore, the condition of possibility of conceptual signification. "This spacing," notes Derrida, "is the simultaneously active and passive . . . production of the intervals without which the 'full' terms would not signify, would not function" (*P,* p. 27). The intervals opened by spacing allow the different conceptual elements to enter into relation without, however, permitting them to coincide. Still, "spacing is not the simple negativity of a lack" (*M*, p. 317); it is the emergence of concepts as already marked by their relation to other concepts in the primal scene of signification.

Space in general, then, as the condition of possibility of the exit of any entity outside of itself and of signification, insofar as the constitution of concepts as hierarchical or differential terms grounds their iterability, is the dimension neither of a surface nor of a depth. It is, as Derrida points out in *Dissemination,* literally *nothing.* He writes in *Positions,* "*Spacing* designates *nothing,* nothing that is, no presence at a distance; it is the index of an irreducible exterior, and at the same time a *movement,* a displacement that indicates an irreducible alterity" (*P,* p. 81). Spacing is the synthesis without reconciliation of this passive and active aspect: "it is not only the interval, the space constituted between two things (which is the usual sense of spacing), but also spac*ing,* the operation, or in any event, the movement of setting aside [*à l'écart*]" (*P,* p. 106). Spacing, which blends in part, and each time differently, with arche-trace, differance, and other undecidables, is in every instance the discrete synthesis of (1) the movement by which the self-identity of an entity is interrupted and (2) the passive constitution by inscription as habitation. The very nature of spacing does not permit its own synthetic structure to be one of reconciling the two aspects it reunites. For this same reason, spacing cannot serve as *one* explicative principle for all differences and for all specific spaces; to elevate spacing into a theological function of total accounting is a contradiction in terms. "Spacing certainly operates in all fields, but precisely as different fields. And its operation is different each time, articulated otherwise" (*P,* p. 82). This is also true of all the other infrastructures, whose purification and idealization is impossible because the specific sort of synthesis that they achieve is context bound. Another result of this kind of synthesis is that the function represented by each infrastructure also applies to itself, so that it remains essentially dislocated from itself. (This aspect of the infrastructures whose name is that of another infrastructure or undecidable, the *re-mark,* is analyzed later in this chapter.)

I have construed spacing to mean the originary constitution of exteriority and space as it is known in a sensible or intelligible manner. Yet this is not to say that the "transcendental" question concerning space elaborated here falls within a transcendental aesthetics—whether Kantian, Husserlian, or of an entirely new kind. As should be obvious at this point, this cannot possibly be the case. Spacing is not a form of (pure) intuition that structures a subject's experience of the world. Nor does spacing follow from Husserl's radicalization of the Kantian question, which concerns the prehistoric and precultural level of spatio-temporal experience as a unitary and universal ground for all subjectivity and culture. The notion of spacing as the condition of possibility of sensible and intelligible, or ideal, space undercuts the very possibility of a self-present subject of intuition or of universal and absolute experience; spacing authorizes such subjects by limiting them. Since it questions the very possibility of the distinction between sensibility and pure sensibility, the "transcendental" question of spacing has to be situated beyond what Husserl calls the logos of the aesthetic world. Nor does spacing coincide with the *logical* concept of space developed by Hegel. In his *Encyclopedia*, where he discusses the existential ground of contingency as that which prevents nature from being reducible to logical coherence—the "impotence of nature"—Hegel develops an ontological substratum wherein all the phenomena that lack affinity and are totally indifferent to one another can be gathered together. This substratum, this ideal medium of juxtaposition, is space, in which the unthinkable absolute incoherence characteristic of the phenomena of nature is transformed into a structured totality.[10] The birth of the logical concept of space serves to make the existence of incoherence logically possible. Although spacing has this one feature in common with logical space, in that it represents a medium of cohabitation of what is logically incoherent and indifferent, spacing, unlike logical space, is not governed by the telos of logicality within the boundaries of which space is one moment. Spacing, then, is not the object of a philosophy of nature, whether Hegelian or of an entirely new kind.

But could spacing be tributary to a hermeneutic philosophy? Is it the hermeneutical concept of that openness that primarily provides the space in which space as we usually understand it can unfold? This hermeneutical concept of space, "the prespatial region which first gives any possible 'where,' " consists of the foreunderstanding of separateness and manifoldness in general.[11] According to Heidegger, this foreunderstanding, thematized or not, is imperative to any understanding of spatiality and space; without it, spatiality or space would never be given to us. The hermeneutical concept of space thus names the meaning or truth of space. Yet spacing is not of the order of unthematized preunderstanding, nor is it a truer meaning of the common meaning of spatiality. As that according to which any

entity is what it is only by being divided by the Other to which it
refers in order to constitute itself, spacing is also the presignifying
opening of concealed and unconcealed meaning. Spacing as a presignifying openness is the very possibility of "laying out," of bringing
to understanding, or of the translating that distinguishes any *hermeneuein*.

As the movement by which any possible entity is separated within
itself, spacing also affects the *now* constitutive of the metaphysical
concept of time. It divides the present moment of the now within
itself. Insinuating an interval in each present moment because dependent on a movement of retention and protention (since that moment is present only with regard to a past and a future), the spacing
diastema is also the becoming-space of time, the possibility proper of
temporalization, as well as the becoming-time of space.

Third, differance is also the production, if it can still be put this way, of
these differences, of the diacriticity that the linguistics generated by Saussure,
and all the structural sciences modeled upon it, have recalled is the condition
for any signification and any structure. These differences—and, for example,
the taxonomical science which they may occasion—are the effects of *differance;* they are neither inscribed in the heavens, nor in the brain, which does
not mean that they are produced by the activity of some speaking subject.   (*P*, p. 9)

By tying the "scientific" concept of difference—difference as diacriticity—into the predicative cluster of differance, Derrida makes differance also serve as the principle of semiotic and linguistic intelligibility.
The differences at the basis of intelligibility are not to be confounded
with those constitutive of concepts; the differends under consideration
here are the differential or diacritical characteristics of signs and sign
systems. These differential features, situated in a horizontal structure
of dissimilarities (in contrast to the hierarchical network of the concepts), are the elementary components of possible signification. Derrida notes, "One has to admit, before any dissociation of language
and speech, code and message, etc. (and everything that goes along
with such a dissociation), a systematic production of differences, the
production of a system of differences—a *differance*—within whose
effects one eventually, by abstraction and according to determined
motivations, will be able to demarcate a linguistics of language and
a linguistics of speech" (*P*, p. 28). In its capacity as a matrix for these
differences of intelligibility, differance is thus the condition of signification, serving, in a way, as its primordial constitution. Clearly, as

the principle of diacritical differentiality, differance also overlaps with its meaning as conceptual spacing, inasmuch as concepts are necessarily and essentially inscribed within systems and structures wherein they refer negatively to other concepts.

"*Differance—fourth* . . . would name provisionally this unfolding of difference, in particular, but not only, or first of all, of the ontico-ontological difference" (*P*, p. 10). Here, differance is made into the preopening, an opening by right anterior to the ontico-ontological difference. In this sense the concept of differance "is what not only precedes metaphysics but also extends beyond the thought of being" (*OG*, p. 143), which, for Derrida, is nothing other than metaphysics. After all, the difference between Being and what is, between Being and beings, the ontological and the ontic, which grounds in the transcendence of the being-there *(Dasein),* coincides with Being in an authentic way, as Being no longer conceived within the perspective of what is present. *Dif-ference,* then, *is* Being as the opening in which Being sets itself forth as absent in what is present. According to Heidegger, difference as Being is determined in terms of the differences between presencing and presence *(Anwesen* and *anwesend),* presence and absence, and Being and what is. Yet this implies that the ontico-ontological difference, or difference in short, is described in terms of intrinsically metaphysical determinations; difference is thought within the horizon of the question of the meaning of Being. "Perhaps difference is older than Being itself" (*M*, p. 67), since Being has never been thought otherwise than as presence, as concealing itself in what is. Thus, a difference anterior to the ontico-ontological difference or to the truth or meaning of Being, a difference which would be the trace of the trace that is the ontico-ontological difference, insinuates itself of necessity. "There may be a difference still more unthought than the difference between Being and beings" (*M*, p. 67). This more originary difference is not yet determined as the difference between Being and what is but precedes it as the possibility of difference as such. Considering the metaphysical concept of the name and what it is supposed to achieve, it is impossible to name this more originary difference. The name *differance,* by emphasizing the active movement of difference that is comprehended by this infrastructural construction but that does not exhaust it, economically accounts for the dissimilarity of the diverse functions that such an originary difference would have to carry out.

"Beyond Being and beings, this difference, ceaselessly differing from and deferring (itself), would trace (itself) (by itself)—this *differance* would be the first or last trace if one still could speak, here, of origin and end" (*M*, p. 67). Compared to the ontico-ontological difference, whose difficult and urgent clarification Heidegger took upon himself in his epoch-making work, differance is a difference or trace preceding all possible dissociation and within which the ontico-ontological difference eventually carves itself out. In distinction to differance, the ontico-ontological difference is not as absolutely originary as Heidegger believed, since its form as difference depends on the possibility of that form. Since this possibility is differance, differance must also be construed as the condition of possibility of Being.

These, then, are the different kinds of differences drawn synthetically together in the term *differance:* difference as temporalizing, difference as spacing, difference as the result of opening a polemical rift between conceptual poles, difference as diacritical differentiality, difference as ontico-ontological difference, and so on. The list of these incommensurable and heterogeneous kinds of differences is, for structural reasons, open; their synthesis as differance is not complete, for such a synthesis necessarily defers its own closure. Differance as a synthesis is precisely "an altering difference" (*M*, p. 290), in the sense of a temporalizing and spacing of itself, which thus cannot be a synthesis in the classical sense.

Because differance is a synthesis of incommensurable modes of difference, their unity cannot represent the sublation of the conflictuality that distinguishes each difference in itself or in relation to the other kinds of differences. By insisting on the irreducible difference among differences, Derrida refuses to reduce them to logical difference—that is, to contradiction—which would make it possible to resolve them in one unity. "Since it can no longer be subsumed by the generality of *logical* contradiction, *differance* (the process of differentiation) permits a differentiated accounting for heterogeneous modes of conflictuality, or, if you will, for contradictions" (*P*, p. 101). Hence, because it knots predicates of logical (Aristotelian and Hegelian) difference—of contradiction—into its synthesis, differance is, fifth, an archesynthesis that no longer privileges contradiction as the one outstanding and dominating mode of difference, destined to subjugate all other kinds of difference. Differance, in this sense, is more originary than difference modeled after the law of thought according to which the opposite of a true proposition is necessarily false, or after the dialectical law according to which the negativity of true contradiction makes it the speculative Other, and hence one moment in the becoming of truth.

As a synthesis of differences of incommensurable identity, differance promotes the plurality of difference, of a conflictuality that does not culminate in contradiction but remains a contradiction without contradiction, that is, without eventual dissolution within the immanence of the Concept capable of interiorizing its own exteriorization or negativity. With this, differance appears to be a concept at odds with the Hegelian notion of difference as well as with the process of *Aufhebung* made possible by the interpretation of difference exclusively in terms of negativity.

I have attempted to distinguish *differance* (whose *a* marks, among other things, its productive and conflictual characteristics) from Hegelian difference, and have done so precisely at the point at which Hegel, in the greater *Logic,* determines difference as contradiction only in order to resolve it, to interiorize it, to lift it up (according to the syllogistic process of speculative dialectics) into the self-presence of an onto-theological or onto-teleological synthesis. *Differance* (at a point of almost absolute proximity to Hegel . . .) must sign the point at which one breaks with the system of the *Aufhebung* and with speculative dialectics. (*P*, p. 44)

Although differance entertains deep relations of affinity with the Hegelian discourse insofar as it is a "synthesis" of differences, differance must also be defined as "precisely the limit, the interruption, the destruction of the Hegelian *relève wherever* it operates" (*P.* pp. 40–41) As the essay "Differance" notes, it is for this reason, among others, that the active movement of the production of differences is not simply called *differentiation.* Apart from the fact that such a denomination would eliminate the temporalizing aspect of differance, it would also suggest the existence prior to its division of an originary homogeneous and organic totality. The neologism *differance* was coined in order to undercut the possibility of such a unity as the origin and telos of differences. It is the nonunitary synthesis of all these very different types of difference and, as such, the matrix from which they draw their existence.

The Infrastructure as Supplementarity

Supplement, says Derrida in *Of Grammatology,* is "another name for differance" (*OG,* p. 150). "Supplementarity is in reality *differance,* the operation of differing which at one and the same time both fissures and retards presence, submitting it simultaneously to primordial division and delay," because the supplementing difference "vicariously stands in for presence due to its primordial self-deficiency" (*SP,* p.

88). But unlike differance, supplementarity stresses more explicitly the function of substitutive supplementation in general, which is rooted in the "primordial nonself-presence" of "full" terms (*SP*, p. 87). It places greater emphasis on the structural necessity of the addition of a difference to a "full" entity such as an origin by showing it to be a consequence of the fact that "full" terms compensate for their lack of another origin. In this sense, supplementarity could also be said to be a variation of the arche-trace, but again, instead of *referring* to Other, supplementarity attributes the structural need of *adding* an Other to the vicarious nature of presence itself.

I do not intend to develop the "logic of supplementarity" by following Derrida's rich and detailed analysis of Rousseau's work in *Of Grammatology*. Nor will I enrich the exposition of that logic through recourse to analogical structures such as the pharmakon and the par-ergon.[12] In order to understand this particular infrastructure, however, we must be aware that it represents an attempt to account for a certain contradictory logic characteristic of the philosophical discourse on origin—in the case of Rousseau, on nature as origin. The idea of supplementarity attempts to reunite in one structure a number of contradictory statements and propositions on origin, in such a manner that this contradiction is not obliterated but, on the contrary, explicitly accounted for. As Derrida has argued in *Of Grammatology,* these statements make the following assertions: (1) origins, nature, animality, primitivism, childhood, and so on are pure; (2) compared to these pure and fully present origins, everything else (speech, society, reason) is an exterior addition which leaves their purity unbreached; (3) the necessity of these additions is not rationally explicable; (4) these additions themselves function as secondary origins; (5) these secondary origins are dangerous to the primal origins to the extent that they pervert and undermine them; and so on. The logic of supplementarity developed from Rousseau's own use of that term to describe the relationship between origins and the additions to origins accounts for the coherent incoherence of these statements within Rousseau's discourse. In his use of the term *supplement*, Rousseau displaces and deforms "the unity of the signifier and the signified, as it is articulated among nouns (supplement, substitute [*supplément, suppléant*]), verbs (to supply, to be substituted [*suppléer, se substi-tuer*], etc.) and adjectives (supplementary, suppletory [*supplémentaire, supplétif*]) and makes the signifieds play on the register of plus and minus. But these displacements and deformations are regulated by the contradictory unity—itself supplementary—of a desire" (*OG*, p. 245).

Derrida's attempt to construct supplementarity as an infrastructure in order to account for that regulated unity draws upon all the resources of that word. But first, let us see how Rousseau limits the play of supplementarity. Rousseau, writes Derrida,

wishes on the one hand to *affirm,* by giving it a positive value, everything of which articulation is the principle or everything with which it constructs a system (passion, language, society, man, etc.). But he intends to affirm simultaneously all that is cancelled by articulation (accent, life, passion yet again, and so on). The supplement being the articulated structure of these two possibilities, Rousseau can only decompose them and dissociate them into two simple units, logically contradictory yet allowing an intact purity to both the negative and the positive.   (*OG,* pp. 245–246)

Having thus dissociated the two possibilities into two conflicting units, Rousseau proceeds to define the supplement (in this case, everything of which articulation is the principle) as a mere exterior addition, as the nothing of a simple exteriority. In this way the addition is annulled (it is insignificant), while the origin remains untouched. *"What is added is nothing because it is added to a full presence to which it is exterior"* (*OG,* p 167). Falling back on the value of a simple outside, Rousseau can simultaneously affirm, in total isolation, both the origin and the supplement. Yet, not only must he assert the danger that follows from the supplement; he must also describe the supposedly pure plenitude of the origins in terms of seduction and threat—in terms of the negative, death, absence. Now, the logic of supplementarity is the attempt to tie all these different propositions together into a structure that explains both their possibility and the limits of their scope. This structure is construed as a field of relations that inscribes within itself the function and value of the philosophical concept of origin; it shows how the myth of an unbreached origin is dependent on the effacement of the logic of that supplementarity. "The concept of origin or nature is nothing but the myth of addition, of supplementarity annulled by being purely additive. It is the myth of the effacement of the trace, that is to say of an originary differance that is neither absence nor presence, neither negative nor positive. Originary differance is supplementarity as *structure"* (*OG,* p. 167).

Let us try to draw the basic features of this infrastructure which, by making the value of origin possible, also imposes its limitations on it. The logic of supplementarity is rooted in a recourse to two conflicting meanings intertwined within the term, but it also makes use of the entire constellation of concepts dependent on its system.

What are these two heterogeneous meanings harbored by the term *supplement*, "whose cohabitation is as strange as it is necessary"? (OG, p. 144). According to the first meaning, a *supplement* is something that "adds itself, . . . a surplus, a plenitude enriching another plenitude, the *fullest measure* of presence. It cumulates and accumulates presence. It is thus that art, *techne*, image, representation, convention, etc., come as supplements to nature and are rich with this entire cumulating function. This kind of supplementarity determines in a certain way all the conceptual oppositions within which Rousseau inscribes the notion of Nature to the extent that it *should* be self-sufficient" (OG, pp. 144–145). In this sense, the operation of supplementation is not a break in presence and plenitude but rather a continuous and homogenous reparation and modification of both. According to its second meaning, however,

> the supplement supplements. It adds only to replace. It intervenes or insinuates itself *in-the-place-of;* if it fills, it is as if one fills a void. If it represents and makes an image, it is by the anterior default of a presence. Compensatory [*suppléant*] and vicarious, the supplement is an adjunct, a subaltern instance which *takes-(the)-place* [*tient-lieu*]. As substitute, it is not simply added to the positivity of a presence, it produces no relief, its place is assigned in the structure by the mark of an emptiness. Somewhere, something can be filled up *of itself,* can accomplish itself, only by allowing itself to be filled through sign and proxy.   (OG, p. 145)

Now, instead of playing alternately on these two meanings of *supplement* and juxtaposing them in a contradictory fashion, as does Rousseau—a possibility contingent on the fallacious determination of the relation of the supplement to that for which it compensates (a full plenitude or an absence) as one of exteriority—Derrida draws the two meanings of *supplement* together in a structural manner. It is not, however, because of semantic ambiguity that "supplementarity" qualifies as an infrastructure. The new and thoroughly unnatural synthesis of the two conflicting meanings of supplement qualifies as an infrastructure only if the "proxy" aspect of "supplement" is generalized. According to the logic of identity and the principle of ontology, the supplement "*adds itself from the outside as evil and lack to happy and innocent plenitude*" (OG, p. 215). Yet if one combines the two meanings of *supplement*, then the supplement, which seemingly adds itself like a plenitude to another plenitude, also fills an absence of plenitude, makes up for a deficiency of plenitude. The vicariousness of the supplement or the surrogate, however, is not a function of something that somehow preexists it; the deficiency in question is much more radical, since the supplement replaces or takes the place of an absent origin. Supplementarity, then, as the action of addition to and vicarious substitution of an absent origin, is the minimal structure required to explain the contradictories that result from assuming the simple exteriority of the supplement and, simultaneously, its dangerous threat to self-present origins. As this minimal organizational unit, it is not only absolutely first, but also accounts for the possibilities from which it draws its major predicates.

What follows from the law of supplementarity is that origins (plenitudes, presences) are always already additions or surrogates compensating for a more originary absence of plenitude. An origin, consequently, is an effect brought about *ex post* by an originary substitution of an origin that had fallen short of itself from the start. Only under this condition can one explain why an origin *can* have supplements and also why it *must* call upon them and repel them at once. Only as a supplement for another origin already impaired can an origin itself require a substitute. If, according to Rousseau, the danger of the supplement stems from its structural ability to replace and take the place of what it is added to, then this danger is a clear function of the latter's belatedness. Since that unity which comes to substitute vicariously and compensate for a lack of a full unity must be at once sufficiently the same and sufficiently different to replace that absence, the origin belatedly reconstituted as plenitude and presence in the absence of another origin is also affected in its interiority by the lack for which it compensates. "As always, the supplement is incomplete, unequal to the task, it lacks something in order for the lack to be filled, it participates in the evil that it should repair" (*OG,* p. 226). Although the supplement is a plus, to the extent that it substitutes for a lack on the part of the origin, it is also less than an origin, since it is itself in need of compensation. In short, then, this "logic of supplementarity, which would have it that the outside be inside, that the Other and the lack come to add themselves as a plus that replaces a minus, that what adds itself to something takes the place of a default in the thing, that the default, as the outside of the inside, should be already within the inside, etc." (*OG,* p. 215), describes, within a logic of belatedness, an infrastructure that accounts for the emergence of origin as an aftereffect. It accounts for the possibility that such a reconstituted and reconstructed origin can itself be supplemented by additions, for the possibility that such additions can endanger so-called origins, and for the possibility that the oper-

ation of supplementation and the function of vicarious substitution
are unlimited. The infrastructure of supplementarity, by knotting together into one structure the minus and the plus, the lack of origin
and the supplementation of that origin, does not choose between
either one of them but shows that both functions are dependent on
one another in *one* structure of replacements, within which "all presences will be supplements substituted for an absent origin, and all
differences, within the system of presence, will be the irreducible effect
of what remains *epekeina tes ousias*" (*D*, p. 167).

Compared to the play of absence and presence on which it rests,
but which it also makes possible insofar as it ties both together in the
production of origins as supplements and of the supplements of origins,
the infrastructure is absolutely first. It is a last instance; yet as an
instance *epekeina tes ousias* it is, like all other infrastructures, *nothing,*
or *almost* nothing. It is not something that is either absent or present,
although it could be said to be absent on the condition that absence
is not understood as a modification of presence, as an absent-presence.
"The supplement occupies the middle point between total absence
and total presence," writes Derrida (*OG*, p. 157). It is a nondialectical
middle, a structure of jointed predication, which cannot itself be comprehended by the predicates which it distributes: origin and supplement, origin and what is derived from it, inner and outer, presence
and absence. Therefore, this economic intermediary that is supplementarity is inconceivable to reason and to its own logic of identity.
Although the logic of the supplement "should allow us to say the
contrary at the same time without contradiction" (*OG*, p. 179), its
logic is not simply irrational. Instead of being simply an opacity within
the system of rationality, which would thus be comprehensible by it,
it is nonrational, "as the origin of reason must" be (*OG*, p. 259).
Reason is structurally incapable of comprehending its origin in the
possibility of supplementarity: "The possibility of reason . . . the *supplementary possibility, is inconceivable to reason*" (*OG*, p. 259). Not
that this inability of reason to understand its origin in what it is not—
in the nonrational play of the structure of supplementarity—shows
a lack of power; rather, this inability is constitutive of the very possibility of the logic of identity, and of what appears of necessity to
reason, as its irrational Other according to that very logic. Still, reason
cannot turn the structure of supplementarity into simple irrationality,
into the opposite of reason, which would conform with the logic of
identity and thus be less irritating and waylaying than a structure that
refuses determination in terms of what it makes possible. Reason is

blind to the supplement as one is blind to the source of seeing. Thus, supplementarity has no sense and is given to no intuition. "It is the strange essence of the supplement not to have essentiality: it may always not have taken place. Moreover, literally, it has never taken place: it is never present, here and now. If it were, it would not be what it is, a supplement, taking and keeping the place of the other" (*OG*, p. 314).

Let us sum up. The structure of supplementarity makes the constitution of an origin dependent on an originary substitution of an absent Other (origin). It both explains the possibility of origin (presence, plenitude, and so on) and restricts it to a function of secondariness. Supplementarity can assume this role of an origin more originary than any origin, because supplements to supposedly full origins (supplements which the discourse of philosophy is bound to recognize, and which it experiences as threatening to the origin to which de jure it should remain indifferent) are pluses that compensate for a minus in the origin. The supplementation is thus also a compensation *(suppléance)*. Since an origin can invite supplements, it is already inhabited by their negativity and is not simply an origin but a substitutive supplement for a lack. In its positivity, an origin compensates for the lack of another origin, but is inhabited *ab intra* by this lack, because of which it can supplement itself and can serve as a supplement. Three consequences follow: (1) a generalization of the structure of supplementarity, which thus appears more originary than the substitutes or supplements and what these substitutes replace, compensate for, or supplement, that is, the origin; (2) the possibility of a supplement to the supplement, that is to say, of the infinite and indefinite play of repetition and substitution ("As soon as the supplementary outside is opened, its structure implies that the supplement itself can be 'typed,' replaced by its double, and that a supplement to the supplement, a surrogate for the surrogate, is possible and necessary," *D*, p. 109); and (3) the impossibility of going "back *from the supplement to the source:* one must recognize that there is *a supplement at the source*" (*OG*, p. 304).

By denoting what structurally exceeds any totality or whole, supplementarity is the *essential nothing* from which this whole and its doubles can surge into appearance; but, as "the excess of a signifier which, in its own inside, makes up (for) space and repeats the fact of opening" (*D*, p. 235), supplementarity also limits this whole in its plenitude by restricting it to secondariness or belatedness.

Supplementarity as an infrastructure is also the possibility of a doubling repetition; this aspect of the infrastructure, however, is thematized as the minimal structure of *iterability,* a subject to which we now turn.

The Infrastructure as Iterability

The issue of iterability has to do with "original repetition"—that is, a repetition prior to common repetition, the latter being always the repetition of an already constituted entity, moment, instance, or the like. One must think of a repetition that "already divides the point of departure of the first time" (*WD,* p. 213), and that would be capable of accounting for the fact—the possibility and the necessity—that any singular and unique moment must be repeatable in order to exist.

This "original repetition" is not of the same order as repetition in the ordinary sense, which presupposes the uniqueness, singularity, and integrity of a "first time." It is not, like empirical repetition, a repetition that could possibly *take place.* The term refers, rather, to the "repetition of repetition," or *repetition in general,* repeatability. In order not to mistake this possibility for the always accidentally occurring *repetition* of common sense, Derrida calls it not iteration but iterability; but this name does more than just designate the possibility of iteration. Like most of the other infrastructures, the designation *iterability* draws upon a cluster of concepts, and thus it simultaneously accounts for a variety of philosophical problems. *Iterability* reunites two opposite, or rather incommensurable, meanings: the possibility of iteration or repetition, and also the possibility of alteration. *Iter* comes from *itara*—"other" in Sanskrit—as Derrida has pointed out on several occasions. Whether this etymology is correct is beside the point, since it is only a pretext for condensing a variety of concepts in one linguistic mark, in order to exhibit a set of necessary relations between them. Since the validity of etymology is of an exclusively empirical nature, it cannot positively or negatively affect the infrastructural relations, which are conceived as necessary relations between possibilities.

Before investigating the nuclear traits of the mark *iterability,* let us recall that *iterability* is another name for *supplementarity,* to the extent that the latter is already the space of duplication and thus of repetition. Iterability is also another name for *differance,* with which it shares the structural deferring of the possibility of a present instant or entity. *Iterability* also partially overlaps the idea of arche-trace, because it names the relation to Other as constitutive of the relation

to self. But despite these overlaps, iterability is an original infrastructure insofar as it links its various filiations, each of which ac-
tualizes a slightly different aspect from those stressed by the other
infrastructures, in a new and original synthesis, which serves to muster
a unique set of philosophical phenomena. We can distinguish five
different functions of iterability:

Iterability as the origin of iteration or repetition. As we saw with
supplementarity, a repetition becomes possible only if a unit that is
both sufficiently similar and sufficiently different to occupy the place
of another comes to fill in the lack created by its absence. At that
moment, the supplementing unit both repeats the absent unit and
becomes an alterity that takes its place. Repetition thus hinges on the
structural possibility of an absence of the repeated. If the unit to be
repeated were totally present and present to itself, if it were not
breached by a certain lack of plenitude, no repetition could ever occur.
This absence, however, is not to be understood as a continuous and
ontological modification of presence. It is not the absent presence of
a full plenitude, of a once or at one time self-present presence; it is
an absence owing not to an empirically effective and hence accidental
occurrence of absence but, on the contrary, to the *possibility* of being
absent. This possibility, as Derrida has argued in "Signature Event
Context," and even more powerfully in "Limited Inc.," is what breaches
and divides the plenitude or self-presence of even the most unique
and singular event. This structural possibility makes its factual repetition possible, even if it occurs only once. The mere possibility of
the absence of a unit corresponds to "the time and place of the *other
time* [*l'autre fois*] already at work, altering from the start the start
itself, the *first time,* the *at once*" (*LI*, p. 200). Therefore, what is in
question here is not iteration or repetition but only their possibility,
or iter*ability,* which *can* occur as a possibility to any unit and is,
consequently, a necessary possibility that must be inscribed within
the essence of that unit itself. A priori, then, the possibility of iteration
divides the identity of all units; iterability is the impurity of an absence
that, from the start, prohibits the full and rigorous attainment of the
plenitude of a unit, and that in principle subverts its self-identity. Such
an absence makes it possible for that unit to be repeated, iterated,
which is of course not to say that it must be repeated. But the possibility of iteration inhabits the unit from the start in such a manner
that if its repetition does occur, it will not be accidental and will not
affect it only *ab extra.*

Iterability is also the condition of possibility of re-production, representation, citation, and so on, and can be read as the generalization of representation, reproduction, citation. "Everything begins with reproduction," writes Derrida in *Writing and Difference* (*WD*, p. 211). "Everything, 'begins,' then, with citation," he writes in *Dissemination* (*D*, p. 316). And in *Of Grammatology* he concludes his essay on Rousseau by stating "that the very essence of presence, if it must always be repeated within another presence, opens originarily, within presence itself, the structure of representation" (*OG*, p. 311). Everything, hence, begins with representation; the possibility of reproduction, representation, and citation must be inscribed in any entity, sign, or act of speech in order for an entity, sign, or speech act to be possible in its singularity in the first place. If Derrida calls the inscription of these possibilities the death from which life with its limitations and finitude springs forth, then this is not merely a metaphorical manner of speaking. This is a meaning of death prior to the proper meaning of what we commonly understand by death and, *mutatis mutandis*, to a figural, metaphorical meaning of death. Death is understood here as the condition of iterability without which no unit could be exchanged, transmitted, represented, referred to, reproduced, remembered, and so on.

Iterability as the origin of idealization and identification. Since "iterability supposes a minimal remainder (as well as a minimum of idealization) in order that the identity of the *selfsame* be repeatable and identifiable *in, through,* and even *in view of* its alteration" (*LI*, p. 190), it can be construed as the origin of idealization and identification. The possibility of repetition depends on the recognition of self-identical marks; yet repetition constitutes these very marks in their identity. A repeatable identity is an ideal identity, however, independent from the context and the factual and multiple events of its occurrence, most ideally conceived in the form of the ideality of the *eidos*: "the truth of the *eidos* as that which is identical to itself, always the same as itself and therefore simple, incomposite *(asuntheton)*, undecomposable, invariable . . . The *eidos* is that which can always be repeated as *the same*. The ideality and invisibility of the *eidos* are its power-to-be-repeated" (*D*, p. 123). Without iterability, there would be no truth; yet the minimal identity presupposed by iterability and the minimal identity that it makes possible is necessarily a divided identity. Only an identity that already inscribes in itself the possibility of nonidentity would lend itself to iteration.

The ideality broached by iteration is a breached ideality, a limited ideality, since iterability "ruins (even ideally) the very identity it renders possible" (*LI*, p. 217). Although iterability as such is the *becoming* of intelligibility and ideality, the very possibility of repetition as the root of truth also prohibits truth from ever becoming *itself*. Iterability, without which the ideality on which truth is based could not be achieved, is at once the death of truth, its finitude.

It does not help to try to distinguish between good and bad repetition, as Platonism has done since its incipience, to differentiate between a good repetition that gives and presents the *eidos*, the ideal and unchanging self-identity of truth, and a bad repetition that repeats repetition, merely repeating itself instead of the living truth. One cannot choose between the living repetition of life and truth and the dead repetition of death and nontruth because, as the infrastructure iterability demonstrates, these two repetitions relate to one another, implicate one another, and cannot even be thought except together: "These two types of repetition relate to each other according to the graphics of supplementarity. Which means that one can no more 'separate' them from each other, think of either one apart from the other, 'label' them, than one can in *the pharmacy* distinguish the medicine from the poison, the good from the evil, the true from the false, the inside from the outside, the vital from the mortal, the first from the second, etc" (*D*, p. 169). The infrastructure iterability ties these two repetitions together in such a way that their separation seems a violent decision, which results in the coincidence of the beginning of philosophy with the forgetting of the condition of origin of its values.

Iterability as the origin of alteration. As a result of the difference inscribed in each ideal unit as the possibility of its iteration, that unit is always already something other than it purports to be. As I have mentioned, the time and the place of an *other time* must from the outset affect the *first time* if the latter is to be susceptible to repetition as a first and unique moment, whether or not such a repetition actually happens. Now, the possibility of a displacement by iteration implies that "iteration alters, something new takes place" (*LI*, p. 175). The infrastructure iterability—an Other which is entirely heterogeneous to what it grounds, identity and difference—affects the grounded by altering it; it alters it by repeating it.

Iterability as duplication. Since iterability constitutes the minimal identity of the repeated as something divided by the possibility of repetition, iterability is the possibility of self-duplication, of redoubling, of metaphoricity—that is, of an elementary translation or transference by which the thing is always already transported "within its double (that is to say already within an ideality)" (*OG*, p. 292). Iterability is a duplication or reduplication which redoubles the first time, or the ideal identity, through its repetition as an identical *and* at the same time different moment or entity. It is a reduplication in which the repeated is already separated from itself, double in itself. Since I investigate this originary duplication and doubling in greater detail in the following chapter, I have limited myself here to these few remarks about this particular nuclear trait of iterability.

Iterability as the possibility of the effacement of the trace. As I emphasized in my treatment of the arche-trace, the possibility of an originary effacement is an essential trait of the trace. It now appears that such an effacement, owing to the fact that repeatability, be it linguistic or not, as a necessary possibility of each instance, is also a decisive mark of iterability. This is one manner in which iterability marginally overlaps the arche-trace.

Let me add a few remarks concerning iterability in general. Like all other infrastructures, iterability is a universal and necessary structure, a "transcendental" law on which the effects listed depend. Although iterability is such a law, this "does not amount to saying that this law has the simplicity of a logical or transcendental principle. One cannot even speak of it being fundamental or radical in the traditional philosophical sense" (*LI*, p 234). Iterability is not a pure principle. Its simplicity is thoroughly crossed out; iterability "can only be what it is in the *impurity* of its self-identity (repetition altering and alteration identifying)" (*LI*, p. 203). This impurity stems from the fact that an infrastructure ties heterogeneous threads together into "one" law. If it is a principle at all, it is, in Derrida's words, a "two-fold root." Yet "two-fold roots cannot play the role of philosophical radicality" (*LI*, p. 234). "As soon as there is a double bottom, there is no bottom or ground at all in process of formation," writes Derrida (*D*, p. 308). Because of this nonsimplicity, iterability is neither a transcendental condition of possibility, in the strict sense, nor an essence or substance clearly distinguishable from phenomena, attributes, or accidents. Since it is what makes idealization (the production of the different forms of the *eidos*) possible and, by virtue of its twofold radicality, also impossible, iterability does not lend " *'itself'* to any pure, simple, and idealizable conceptualization. No process or project of idealization is possible without iterability, and yet iterability 'itself' cannot be idealized. For it comports an internal and impure limit that prevents it from being identified, synthesized, or reappropriated, just as it excludes the reappropriation of that whose iteration it nonetheless broaches and breaches" (*LI*, p. 210). Therefore the infrastructures, and iterability in particular, are at once the condition and the limit of theorizing; they make philosophical mastery possible, but they themselves escape mastery.

The Infrastructure as Re-Mark

The re-mark cuts across all the other undecidables that we have examined up to this point. It is a form of the general law of supplementarity which dislocates all presence, plenitude, or propriety. As the re-mark demonstrates, supplementation always consists of adding a mark to another mark. "According to the structure of supplementarity, what is added is thus always a blank or a fold: the fact of addition gives way to a kind of multiple division or subtraction that enriches itself with zeros as it races breathlessly toward the infinite. 'More' and 'less' are only separated/united by the infinitesimal inconsistency, the next-to-nothing of the hymen" (*D*, p. 262).

The re-mark is also a form of the minimal structure of referral that I have analyzed as arche-trace. As I shall attempt to demonstrate in discussing the re-mark, "every determinate fold unfolds the figure of another," thus disrupting all presence in the mark (*D*, p. 270). Derrida can, therefore, speak of the re-mark as a form of articulation of the "differential-supplementary structure, which constantly adds or withdraws a fold from the series," with the effect that no possible theme of the fold is able "to constitute the system of its meaning or present the unity of its multiplicity" (*D*, p. 270). But the re-mark is also a form of the general law of iterability. A mark has the form of repetition and duplication because the re-mark by which any mark is marked in advance is part of the mark itself. "That which is remarkable in the mark, passing between the *re-* of the repeated and the *re-* of the repeating," is the break that intervenes in the mark. "Condition or effect—take your pick—of iterability" (*LI*, p. 190).

Considering the multitude of its intersections, the re-mark, whether or not it re-covers all of them by merging with them, is necessarily a very complex structure. Before trying to give a detailed account of the different movements that enter into its composition, I want to offer a brief definition and a succinct circumscription of the major problems the re-mark addresses. The mark (or *margin*, or *march*—in the sense of "boundary"—all of which belong to the same series of words) as re-mark is that particular infrastructural feature that prohibits any diacritically constituted series of terms, concepts, traces, or marks from ever closing upon itself. This impossibility of totalization or of self-closure is not due to an infinite abundance of meaning, which a finite consciousness would be unable to master; on the contrary, it hinges on the existence of a certain nerve, fold, or angle on which, as we shall see, this impossibility is structurally based.

The re-mark is an infrastructure that accounts both for the necessary illusion of totalization and for its simultaneous displacements. The re-mark interrupts the totalizations of which it is itself the condition of possibility. Yet the economic scope of this infrastructure is not limited to the sole problem of totalization (and reflection). The re-mark is also that which opens up the possibility of referentiality within the play of application of one mark to another. Since, in such a play, the referent is set aside (*à l'écart*) in infinite reference, the remark renders the function of truth possible by limiting it. In general, the re-mark is the structure that accounts for the possibility of all transcendental or theological illusions, because the supplementary status of the re-mark (as a mark added to another mark) can always be isolated from the mark it doubles and can thus be rendered independent of that mark. Derrida notes in *Dissemination* that the structural place of the theological trap is prescribed by the re-mark: "The mark-supplement [*le supplément de marque*] produced by the text's workings, in falling outside of the text like an independent object with no origin other than itself, a trace that turns back into a presence (or a sign), is inseparable from desire (the desire for reappropriation or representation). Or rather, it gives birth to it and nourishes it in the very act of separating from it"(*D*, p. 258).

Let us, then, distinguish the basic traits of the re-mark. It combines at least four different senses of the term *mark* and two distinct movements. As in our previous analyses, I shall discuss this infrastructure in abstraction from the rich context in which it is produced within Derrida's work. Consequently, I shall not take advantage of the examples of the re-mark, such as the fan, the blank, or the fold in the work of Mallarmé, on which Derrida relies in formulating this general law. I shall also privilege the general implications of this infrastructure over the possibility of its particular consequences for literary criticism, which represents part of the context of "The Double Session," in which Derrida develops this notion of remarking. Part III of this book focuses on these specific problems.

The term *mark* refers, first, to the empirical object commonly known by that name: a sign, an indication, a trait, or token. Second, it refers, through a tropic (analogical, metaphorical, metonymic) twist, to the totality of objects that function *as* marks, to the semantic unities and the chains or series that they form. And third, the doubling of these series, in a supplementary tropological movement, allows the mark to serve as the "concept" of all empirical marks. In all three cases the mark is understood to refer to a referent as a function of truth. In the first and second instances, the mark is a distinguishing trait or quality of something or someone; in the third it is the "concept," or rather the totalizing *seme (sema),* of the series of possible tokens— in other words, that which confers the meaning of relating to a referent upon the different forms of marks. In this last case, at least, the mark functions as a double of the mark, as the mark of the mark, as the mark or series of marks *thought.* As such a double of the mark, it adds itself to each individual mark, as well as to the series of its analogical, metaphorical, or metonymical substitutes.

The fourth sense of the term is more complicated. According to the law of the arche-trace, a mark is embedded in a differential system of marks in which it acquires the minimal identity necessary to refer to something other than itself. This identity hinges on its relation to another mark, on its detour through another mark in the very act of self-reference. A mark must be re-marked by what it is not (another mark) in order to be repeatable as the identical sign of a signified. Therefore, the tropological movement by which the mark (or seme) refers to the polysemic series of marks, totalizing or embracing them as their concept, as the concept that refers to them in their totality, must contain *an additional* tropological movement by which the seme *mark* refers to what demarcates the marks, to the blanks between the marks that relate the different marks to each other. Indeed, in addition to designating the totality of all marks within a series, and to re-marking in this manner the singular mark, or the series as a whole by the semic mark or concept of the mark—a marking by which the singular marks become the visible (or invisible) incarnations of the "content" of the semic mark—the nature "proper" of the mark also demands that it refer to that which opens up the possibility of marks in general. Through the additional tropological movement, the seme *mark* is thus made to refer to its asemic space of inscription, that is, to the mark or march (both mean boundary) of the mark. Derrida calls this space the mark's spaced-out semiopening *(l'entr'ouverture espacée).*

Because a mark acquires the ideal identity necessary to its iteration as the mark of something other than itself only to the extent that it is constituted by what it is not, the totalizing semic mark must also inscribe or insert within itself the differential structure of the mark, that which makes the mark possible. The mark must thus be marked, or re-marked, by its own mark (march, margin). Since in its irreducible duplication it must include a reference to what it is not, inserting something heterogeneous to itself in itself—namely, what demarcates it as a mark—the mark also names the space of inscription of the marks, what holds them together and separates them, what makes them resemble and differ from one another. Irreducibly double, the mark re-marked by the heterogeneous order of what makes it possible—the re-mark—is thus the concept of the totality of the semic valences of the mark *plus* the spaced-out semiopening of the whole of these valences. The re-mark is thus *more* than the totality of the marks and more than the totalizing concept of the mark; in addition it is what makes that totality possible. At this point the re-mark seems to coincide with the speculative concept of *Aufhebung* as a way in which reflexivity reflects itself into itself, even including its own possibility. Indeed, Derrida has acknowledged that *Aufhebung*, and thus the operation proper of speculation, is most similar to the graphics of the re-mark (D, p. 248). The trait by which the mark becomes doubled, however, is an undecidable trait, one that constitutes a limit to the (conceptualizing or representing) reflection of the limits or margins of the mark, and with which *Aufhebung* cannot come to grips.

Let me emphasize that this re-marking of the mark does not come from the outside, nor does it accidentally affect the mark, or series of marks. Since no mark, whether an individual mark or the "concept" of the mark, can function without referring to that which makes it possible, the mark is in advance re-marked. The re-mark only makes the mark a mark. As we shall see, however, the necessity of such re-marking, without which the mark could not hope to refer to anything at all, also affects the destiny of referentiality. We may anticipate the following: if the re-mark were a self-reflexive doubling, it would make all referring to another Other than the self impossible. It must consequently entail the failure of self-reflection so that the mark can assume a function of reference. Yet by virtue of the irreducibly double nature of the mark, a doubling constitutive of its ideality, the mark's reference to another Other than itself, to a nonmark, is also constantly deferred. Moreover, since the other to which the mark refers in order to be itself can only be another mark and not the punctuality of a present instance or moment, it must always be a referring without referent. But the metaphysical illusion of a self-present referent is inscribed within the structure of the mark as re-mark; its place is prescribed in advance. By dissociating the marks' referring from what demarcates them, from their space of inscription, by reducing the re-mark constitutive of the mark to a mere semic function, the mark begins to function as a signifier for a signified. From the fact that each mark, as well as the concept of all the semantic marks, must take on the fold of the asemic space that unfolds between the terms of the series or system, we may draw a double consequence. The re-mark is indeed double.

As we have seen up to this point, each individual mark and each series of marks is re-marked (doubled, reflected, mirrored) by its concept, as well as by its asemic space of possibility. Precisely because the mark *as* a mark must, irretrievably, refer to that non-sense space that demarcates it from other marks, no fulfilling equation between marks (or, for that matter, between their concept) and their meaning can ever be achieved.

By referring to "the place where nothing takes place but the place" (*D*, p. 257), to the mark's spaced-out semiopening, to "the re-marked site of the mark" (*P*, p. 46), Derrida shows that, fifth, the totalizing semic concept of all the semes or marks of a series, a valence that is not just one among others is added to that series. Such a valence does not enrich that series; what is added, necessarily, "through a redu-plication that is always represented" (*D*, p. 252), is the meaningful and signifying delegate or representative of the semantic void between the marks of the series. Only by making it signify can the heteroge-neous space of inscription, in an extra turn, be referred to by the mark (*D*, p. 222). Clearly, one trope too many is thus added to the series, and, in the form of a proxy (of a metaphor or metonymy), it represents what does not really belong to the series of semes, the nonmeaning against which the full marks stand out. If that trope is subtracted from the series to be totalized by the concept (of the mark), however, this totalization leaves at least one mark unaccounted for. Thus re-marked by the space of inscription that demarcates all marks, no concept or theme of the mark could hope to coincide with what it aims to embrace. The re-mark is an essential limit to all coinciding reflection or mirroring, a doubling of the mark that makes all self-reflective adequation impossible. For structural reasons, there is al-ways more than totality; the extra valence added by the delegate of the asemic space of diacritical differentiation of the totality of semes always—infinitely—remains to be accounted for.

Not only the marks of a series must bend to the fold of their asemic space of inscription; not only the full terms of a series are affected by the re-mark. To the extent that that asemic space is represented by a proxy within, and in addition to, the series, it becomes metaphorically or metonymically transformed into a mark, that is, into precisely what it is supposed to make possible. Hence, sixth, the heterogeneous space between the marks becomes re-marked as well, but this homogenizing re-mark effaces that which makes signification possible at the very moment that it begins to signify. Under the re-mark, the demarcating space that itself re-marks the signifying marks recoils, withdraws, retreats, disappearing—infinitely—in its own forward movement. The re-marking of the mark (or of the totality of the marks in a series) is, therefore, not only to be understood as the represented inscription of the spaced-out semiopening in the mark but also as the withdrawal of what makes the marks possible from the marks themselves.[13]

By re-marking itself, the mark effaces itself, producing in this manner the illusion of the referent. It effaces itself, disappears in the appearing of what it is not—a proxy of itself. In affecting itself by the re-mark, designating its own space of engenderment, the mark inscribes itself within itself, reflects itself within itself under the form of what it is not. The mark is heterogeneous to the mark. In marking what de-marcates it, the margin of the mark is turned into a mark that is heterogeneous to the heterogeneous space of its inscription. Infinitely re-marking that space by another semic mark, the mark renders its margin invisible. Likewise, it can be said that all the marks of a series are in the position of semic substitutes for the spaced-out semiopening that makes them possible.

As a result of this constant retraction, the re-mark does not lend itself to phenomenologization; the re-mark does not present itself as such to any intuition of it as a phenomenon.

In the recoiling of the blank upon the blank, the blank colors itself, becomes— for itself, of itself, affecting itself ad infinitum—its own colorless, ever more invisible, ground. Not that it is out of reach, like the phenomenological horizon of perception, but that, in the act of inscribing itself on itself indefinitely, mark upon mark, it multiplies and complicates its text, a text within a text, a margin in a mark, the one indefinitely repeated within the other: an abyss.   (D, p. 265)

Because of the re-mark's nature as an angle or fold to which each mark must bend if it is to function as a mark, the very inscription of its condition of possibility into the mark itself can never be the inscription of this "almost nothing" as such. The mark's transcendental opening withdraws in its representation, making manifest the limits of speculative *Aufhebung,* which is incapable of accounting for the re-mark *as such,* not only because this infrastructure cannot be phenomenologized and experienced, but also because at least one representation of it—that is, at least one figure in which it disappears—is left unaccounted for. This last figure is ultimately the figure of *Aufhebung* itself.

By effacing itself, the infrastructural angle of the re-mark provides room for the possibility of truth as *adequatio* or *homoiosis,* as I have already mentioned. Moreover, the infrastructure of the re-mark is also the matrix for the conception of truth as *aletheia,* of truth as revealing and concealing, since the angle of the re-mark—the undecidable play between the *re-* of the doubling repetition of the mark, and of the *re-* of the repeated and thus altered double, and the *re-* of the retraction of the mark—also accounts for the movement of coming to the fore and withdrawing in that which presents itself in this manner. Consequently, the infrastructure of the re-mark, inscribing within itself the possibility of the difference between appearing and what appears, as well as the possibility of *adequatio* and *homoiosis,* accounts, in an economical structure, for the major theories of truth as they have been formulated in Western metaphysics.

In light of the foregoing review of the five systems of predicates, which Derrida calls infrastructures or *graphematic in general* (M, p. 322), some concluding remarks may be appropriate. A certain systematicity exists among these five infrastructures. Although the formalizing capacity of each infrastructure differs from the others, the variety in scope or range of the organizing power of the undecidables does not prevent our recognizing the ways in which they overlap. Let us first review the five infrastructures themselves: (1) The *arche-trace* is a structure of referral linking all relation to self to the self's effacement in its relation to an Other which is not the speculative other of the self. (2) *Differance* corresponds to a nonunitary yet originary synthesis of the movements of differing, deferring, differentiation, and so on that relegates the possibility of plenitude and self-presence to that of an aftereffect. (3) *Supplementarity* designates the law according to which the possibility of the unbreached plenitude of an entity is dependent on the absence of an Other which it comes to replace, and which, consequently, marks its proxy in depth. (4) *Iterability,* by linking together in one structure the possibilities of repetition and alteration, is the explication of idealization constitutive of both identity and its limits, to the extent that the duplication presupposed and made possible by repetition is also the constant alteration of identity. (5) The *re-mark,* which knots together in one cluster of predicates the movements of doubling, repetition, and retraction (or effacement), makes the possibility of reference hinge on the mark's or the trace's withdrawal in the doubling movement of the reflection of its heterogeneous space of inscription.

Each infrastructure draws together in a different manner a different set of concepts: hence the varying scope and reach of what can be derived from each. Since they represent the systematic exploration of what Derrida calls the space of inscription, they exhibit the density of a fanned-out volume, within which systematic overlappings, recoverings, and intersections between the different structures can easily be distinguished. This does not mean, however, that they can be derived from one another within the totality of what is traditionally called a system. For many reasons, the polysemic, or rather disseminating, structure of the necessarily open ensemble of the infrastructures cannot be governed "by the unity of a focus or of a horizon of meaning which promises it a totalization or a systematic adjoinment."[14] One such reason is the strategic, contextual, and historical nature of the economical infrastructures. Another reason is that the infrastructures are not *strictu sensu* transcendentals of conditions or possibilities; since the unity of these originary syntheses is not unitary, their explicatory power is not theologically absolute. Among the reasons I have not yet considered, one in particular needs to be mentioned here. It stems from the fact that each infrastructure as a relation to Other—as a structure of self-deferring, self-effacement, duplication, repetition, and alteration—can be substituted for another, and can ultimately come to represent the whole chain of infrastructures, or what Derrida calls text in an infrastructural sense (see Chapter 11). Although each singular infrastructure is one among others, each one also describes the chain itself, the being-chain of an infrastructural chain, that is, the structure of substitution in which they are caught and which they articulate. Owing to this possibility of each infrastructure to inscribe within itself the being-chain of the chain, each infrastructure becomes the nucleus of a system; but since each infrastructure can and must assume this role, no system is ultimately possible on the level of the infrastructures. What can be grasped, however, in the play of substitution of the infrastructures is the *general system.* Before discussing this decisive aspect of Derrida's thought, I want to concentrate on what in this philosophy corresponds to a general theory of doubling.

THE GENERAL THEORY OF DOUBLING

It may not seem appropriate to privilege the problem of duplicity and duplication in attempting to formulate the *general system*. Yet if one considers that iterability, for instance, as a necessary possibility constitutive of idealities, "produces" as much as it "presupposes" alterity; and that the necessary possibilities of supplementarity, differance, and arche-trace broach the identity of a full instant, entity, or moment by establishing an Other, a double opposite to them, then duplicity must appear to be a major feature of all infrastructures. The whole logic of the *re-* that I have tried, explicitly and implicitly, to prove decisive in understanding the infrastructures seems to presuppose an initial duplication. The Latin particle *re-*, which corresponds to the English "again" and "against," properly denotes a turning back (upon oneself or itself) or an opposition. Its figurative meaning denotes either a restoration of a thing to its original condition, a transition into an opposite state, or the repetition of an action. Insofar as some of the infrastructures make explicit use of the logic of *re-* by tying all or several of these meanings together, as is the case of the re-mark or the re-trait (but also re-presentation, re-production, *restance,* and so on), and others, such as the infrastructures of iterability and supplementarity, presuppose it, a general theory of duplication seems necessarily to underlie all the infrastructures. Yet duplication is not more original than, say, iteration, although one could show duplication to be a presupposition as easily as an effect of that infrastructure; rather, as I have suggested, they are equiprimordial. This becomes particularly obvious in those infrastructures, such as iterability, in which duplication and repetition are clearly tied together. Thus, although I am about to concentrate on doubling, I could just as easily focus on iterability, differance, or re-marking.

A general theory of doubling should help account for duplicity in general. In conformity with what infrastructures are supposed to achieve, such a theory will not explain duplicity by way of an undivided whole that would precede it. As all the infrastructures demonstrate, such a whole is only an aftereffect, a necessary illusion produced by the play of the undecidables. To explain duplicity and doubling presupposes an originary doubling, which would not be preceded by any unity, and which thus annuls the traditional restriction of doubling to a matter of accidentality and secondariness. Traditionally, the double comes *after* the simple, and *subsequently* multiplies it. In order, then, to account for the possibility of an opposition such as that between a simple and its double, a general theory of doubling must conceive of "a double that doubles no simple, a double that nothing anticipates, nothing at least that is not itself already double" (*D,* p. 206). Such a theory must conceive of an a priori, and from the start irreducible, double, of "a double rootedness," of a duplication that constitutes the simple, and only within which it can emerge as a simplicity. Indeed, if the simple could not be doubled, the simple would not be what it is. As a consequence of its identity, the simple must inscribe the possibility of being divided within itself; in order to be simple, the simple must already be double. A general theory of doubling will have to focus on this duplicity, which logically precedes the philosophical opposition of the simple and the derivative double.

How is this originary duplication or doubling to be understood? In *Of Grammatology,* Derrida notes on several occasions that the reflection, the image, the double splits what it doubles, by adding itself to it, and the reflected or doubled is also split *in itself.* Because the possibility of reflective duplication must be inscribed within it, the reflected is divided by its reflection in itself. An original division of the reflected must double the dual relation between the double and the original if the original is to lend itself to duplication at all. The originary duplication eliminates the possibility of establishing a last source, origin, and original, installing instead an infinite reference between originals and doubles. The dual relation of the simple and the secondary, of the original and the double, becomes derivative of this structure of dividing reference, or infinite duplicity.

According to the requirements of technical philosophy, one may want to understand this structure of duplicity, which doubles the relation between the simple *(eidos)* and its simulacra *(eidolon* or *eikon)* as a simulacrum itself. A *simulacrum,* as defined by Plato, is a copy of a copy, a double of a double, which itself signifies an original. Within philosophy, the simulacrum is indeed dependent on an ontology, since the nontruth of the copy of the copy is linked to the truth of the present referent of which the first copy is the true repetition. Therefore, the subtle excess of truth and ontology that the originary duplication designates cannot be qualified simply as a simulacrum. To call it by this name *within* philosophy is not only to call it by one of the names of that which is severely condemned by this discourse as spurious, if not bad duplication (and repetition), but also to strip it of its most unsettling implications. To name the originary duplication—that is, a doubling anterior to the metaphysical oppositions of truth and nontruth—a simulacrum is to continue to speak within these comforting oppositions. Yet what this asks us to conceive is a simulacrum *without an ultimate referent,* in other words, a non-Platonic simulacrum. Indeed, the original duplication, doubling the opposition between copy and original, is neither preceded nor followed by any referent, presence, or unbreached identity. The originary duplication, or non-Platonic simulacrum, initiates but also displaces the metaphysical opposition of original and copy, and of the copy of a copy, into a completely different field. Doubling, consequently, is no longer derivative of present *onta* or of their totality; it is no longer a phenomenon within the world, but that within which the *onta* and their images, phantasms, or simulacra carve themselves out. To cite Derrida: "Imagine that mirrors would not be *in* the world, simply, included in the totality of all *onta* and their images, but that things 'present,' on the contrary, would be in *them.* Imagine that mirrors (shadows, reflections, phantasms, etc.) would no longer be *comprehended* within the structure of the ontology . . . but would rather envelop it in its entirety, producing here or there a particular, extremely determinate effect" (*D,* p. 324). As such a non-Platonic simulacrum, the originary duplication escapes binary logic. As an unflaggingly dislocated and displaced identity, as an identity that incessantly refers to another (double), it is not governed by opposition and contradiction. The concept of the negative is unable to cover up its play; on the contrary, its status consists of doubling the play of the negative and inscribing it within itself as one of its many possibilities.

The function of such an originary doubling serves as a matrix for the simultaneous possibility and impossibility of any self-present entity. It accounts for the fact that any *on* can come into presence only by immediately producing the possibility of its duplication. Included in the *at once* of the originary duplication is the necessity of each appearing *on* to be able to appear *as such* only by reflecting, mirroring, or doubling itself in another. No *on* can come into presence without simultaneously referring to something it is not. *At once,* then, means that the movement of duplication to be accounted for is that of a simultaneous opening and closing of the possibility of self-reference.

"At once" means that the being-present *(on)* in its truth, in the presence of its identity and in the identity of its presence, is *doubled* as soon as it appears, as soon as it presents itself. *It appears, in its essence,* as the possibility of its own most proper non-truth, of its pseudo-truth reflected in the icon, the phantasm, or the simulacrum. What is is not what it is, identical and identical to itself, unique, unless it *adds to itself* the possibility of being *repeated* as such. And its identity is hollowed out by that addition, withdraws itself in the supplement that presents it. (*D,* p. 168)

To say that the originary duplication accounts *at once* for the classical
opposition of the double and what is doubled, by demonstrating that
the original can appear solely on the condition that it is (possibly)
doubled, is to maintain duplication as the explicatory "cause," instead
of dialectically deducing it from a presupposed anterior unity. To
account *at once* for the duplicity of the double and what is doubled
is to double the "cause" of duplication, and to think a primary "double rootedness."

The general theory of doubling attempts both to legitimize and to
undercut the possibility of dialectics and speculation. The possibility
of dialectically comprehending the opposition between what is doubled and its double as a relation of exteriorization and reappropriation
of the double as the negative of what is doubled is logically dependent
on the originary duplication according to which no *on* can refer in
its appearing to itself except by doubling itself in an Other. Since the
possibility of all identity is dependent on a referral to Other (and
therefore on a limited possibility), the unity between identity and
difference, between what is doubled and the double—or, as Hegel
would say, between reflection-into-self and reflection-into-other—is
derived from an originary duplication which is never sublated in the
process of speculative reappropriation of the Other. Although I shall
return to this in more detail later in this chapter, for the moment I
would like to emphasize another critical implication of this general
theory of doubling.

The general theory of duplication not only undercuts speculative
dialectics but reaches beyond phenomenology as well, in particular
in its Husserlian form. Derrida's critique of Husserlian phenomenology does not focus only on the privilege Husserl attributes to the
instance of the *living presence,* nor is it limited to Husserl's bending
of the form of all experience to this essentially metaphysical motif,
whether it concerns experience in general or, more particularly, transcendental experience. In addition to this criticism, and to his questioning of transcendental phenomenology's unadmitted complicity with
the mundane, Derrida asks the more fundamental question whether
"the phenomenological model [is] itself constituted, as a warp of
language, logic, evidence, fundamental security, upon a woof that is
not its own? And which—such is the most difficult problem—is no
longer at all mundane?" (*OG,* p. 67). As Derrida insists, such a
question is undoubtedly provoked by certain developments in Husserl's phenomenology itself. Yet phenomenology cannot entirely cer-
tify this question, which refers phenomenology "to a zone in which

its 'principle of principles' (as we see it, its *metaphysical* principle: the *original self-evidence* and *presence* of the thing itself in person) is radically put into question" (*WD*, p. 164). As a matter of fact, the theory of originary duplication dislocates and displaces this principle of principles. If it is true that the principle of principles of phenomenology hinges on the possibility of the self-presentation of the thing itself, originary duplication puts the very possibility of that which is called a *phenomenon* radically into question.

From the very beginning of Western philosophy, the notion of phenomenon has been linked to the movement of duplication. Thus, for instance in the philosophy of Plato, phenomena double the *ontos on* as the becoming perceptible to the senses, that is, as the nonideal. As derived from the self-presence of truth, phenomena for Plato are of the order of phantasms, icons, simulacra, and so on. At least since Kant, however, phenomena have no longer been understood as mere appearances *(Schein)*, but rather as that which appears to the senses *(Erscheinungen)*, in contrast to the noumena of which they are, so to speak, the doubles. This motif of duplication is tied up with Husserl's understanding of phenomena as much as it is with Kant's; indeed for Husserl, phenomena are appearances reflexively bent upon themselves, and thus capable of presenting themselves in themselves. As Husserl makes quite clear throughout *Philosophy as Rigorous Science,* only those appearances of which reflection is an intrinsic part can be called phenomena.[15] The phenomenality of phenomena—that is, their quality of appearing as themselves to themselves—distinguishes them, insofar as they constitute the realm of meaning, from all sheer, mundane existence. As pure appearing itself, phenomena are opposed to what is, to what appears, and of course to mere appearances as well.

Yet the general theory of duplication questions precisely the possibility of distinguishing, in a clear and distinct manner, between appearing and what appears, between phenomena as the nuclei of meaning and presence, on the one hand, and the mundane appearances, which lack all constituting immanent intuiting, on the other. Still, Husserl makes all other differences depend on this difference. For him, "the unheard [the remarkable, amazing, and so on] difference between the appearing and the appearance . . . (between the 'world' and 'lived experience') is the condition of all other differences" (*OG*, p. 65). Derrida argues, however, that this difference is preceded by the originary duplication of which it is but a trace, since the movement of the self-presentation of the phenomenon in pure appearing, in presenting itself *as such* to an intuitive consciousness, already presupposes a movement of doubling without which the appearing could not relate to itself. In other words, in order to present itself as such, the phenomenon must already have divided itself. Precisely this difference is what baffles appearing and limits to a secondary role the unheard-of and remarkable difference between appearing and appearance. With the thought of such an originary duplication, more originary than the difference between phenomena and the world, the possibility of clear-cut distinctions becomes altogether questionable: "What is lifted, then, is not difference but the different, the differends, the decidable exteriority of differing terms. Thanks to the confusion and continuity of the hymen, and not in spite of it, a (pure and impure) difference inscribes itself without any decidable poles, without any independent, irreversible terms. Such difference without presence appears, or rather baffles the process of appearing, by dislocating any orderly time at the center of the present" (D, p. 210). It is as impossible to bend the language of phenomenology, with its oppositions of absence and presence, so that it may name this irreducible doubling that reduplicates the unheard-of difference between appearing and appearance as it is to account for it within phenomenology, because this originary doubling does not present itself *as such*. This originary doubling is not a pure and infinite opening for the experience of phenomenal meaning; it is, in structural terms, in withdrawal, in disappearing as an opening; it is impossible to phenomenologize, since in attempting to do so, it always becomes more invisible.

The invisibility of the infrastructure, of originary duplication as the impure opening in retreat from the difference capitalized by phenomenology, seems to be linked to a powerful motif in classical philosophy according to which what makes visibility possible must itself remain invisible. If that source were seen, it would blind the beholder. "Visibility should—not be visible. According to an old, omnipotent logic that has reigned since Plato, that which enables us to see should remain invisible: black, blinding"[16] According to this logic, one cannot face the source of light, one cannot speak of that which makes speech possible, because one cannot withstand so powerful a plenitude. Yet the motif of this invisible source of light, this unheard source of speech, is only the negative image of what I have called the irreducible and originary doubling. If the absolute origin of vision or speech is marked by invisibility and inaudibility, it is because, as Derrida has demonstrated in "Plato's Pharmacy," what is *epekeina tes ousias* should not be perceived as an already divided (and hence impossible) plenitude. As we have seen, for structural reasons, that which, as the absolute ground, does not belong to the totality of what it makes possible cannot possibly offer itself to perception (invalidating in this manner the possibility of perception *in general*). Consequently, to speak of this ground as the blinding origin of visibility—that is, to subject it to the ethico-theoretical code of philosophy—is to continue to speak in the language of that which that origin makes possible. This coded blindness to the originary duplication that divides origins robs duplication of its most pristine features.

Now, how does this originary duplicity, which doubles the classical opposition of that which is doubled and its double, make reflexivity, specularity, and ultimately autoaffection possible and, in making them possible, trace their limits as well? To answer these questions, let us circle back to the attempt to situate Derrida's thought with respect to that tradition in philosophy that, in the aftermath of Hegel's speculative solution of the aporetics of reflection, seeks new ways to come to grips with this problem. In what follows, I shall also show how deconstruction is to be seen as a critique of reflexivity (and implicitly of all the other themes and motifs that are in complicity with this major philosophical theme).

What, then, is the general structure of auto-affection? Derrida has analyzed this structure in *Speech and Phenomenon* in particular, under the form of the "hearing-oneself-speak" constitutive of the metaphysical privilege of speech. In the system of the hearing-oneself-speak, the exteriority of the vocal signifier is experienced as effacing itself entirely in the very moment of its utterance, with the effect that the subject of uttering comes into an immediate relation with the full meaning of his speech. The structure of auto-affection consists of "giving-oneself-a-presence," of mastering all exteriority in pure interiority, by assimilating and idealizing it, by mourning its passing. Auto-affection is the suppression of difference or duplication. It is at the basis of a dream of immediacy, spontaneity, and undivided self-presence, the dream of a mode of being that would not have to borrow from outside itself anything foreign to its own spontaneity. Yet, although auto-affection in this sense is an enormous phantasm, it is irreplaceable because it is, in essence, the structure proper of experience, insofar as experience is always experience of presence. Derrida writes in *Of Grammatology*:

Auto-affection is a universal structure of experience. All living things are capable of auto-affection. And only a being capable of symbolizing, that is to say of auto-affecting, may let itself be affected by the other in general. Auto-affection is the condition of an experience in general. This possibility—another name for "life"—is a general structure articulated by the history of life, and leading to complex and hierarchical operations. Auto-affection, the as-for-itself or for-itself—subjectivity—gains in power and in its mastery of the other to the extent that its power of repetition *idealizes itself*. Here idealization is the movement by which sensory exteriority, that which affects me or serves me as signifier, submits itself to my power of repetition, to what thenceforward appears to me as my spontaneity and escapes me less and less.   (*OG*, pp. 165–166)

Despite the fact that auto-affection is a universal structure—the very condition of experience (of the Other)—and whether or not it explicitly gives rise to the "phantasms" Derrida alludes to, auto-affection has a border, an "absolute overboard."[17] "Auto-affection is a pure speculation" (*OG*, p. 154), writes Derrida. The border of the pure autarchy of auto-affection, or pure speculation and specularity, concerns both the possibility and necessity of what, in the context from which this last quotation has been drawn, is understood as a mere chimera.

Auto-affection has been characterized by its exclusion of difference. This exclusion is essential for auto-affection to be auto-affection, for it to achieve an immediate and spontaneous identity in self-presence. Yet paradoxically enough, "*auto*-affection constitutes the same *(auto)* as it divides the same" (*OG*, p. 166). Most generally, the structure of auto-affection requires a minimal division of the same in order for this same to constitute itself *as* itself. This minimal division takes on manifold shapes. It explains why auto-affection is possible only through an immediate exiting from interiority and why the same *as* the same, the retroflected same, must affect itself by Otherness. Thus the presence that is achieved in auto-affection is a supplement for a lack of self-presence, an absence that structurally haunts the self-affecting self. In short, "utterly irreducible hetero-affection inhabits—intrinsically—the most hermetic auto-affection" (*VP*, p. 56). As a result, and as Derrida has demonstrated in the case of Rousseau, who was vividly aware of this, in "affecting oneself by another presence, one *corrupts* oneself [makes oneself other] by oneself [*on s'altère soi-même*]" (*OG*, p. 153). Moreover, since the presence one gives oneself in auto-affection is possible only on condition of a prior privation of presence, and since each such presence is itself an idealized substitute for another absent presence, auto-affection leaves an impregnable worldly residue. Apart from the trace of absence that continues to cohabit the presence one gives oneself in auto-affection, apart from the "narrow gulf that separates doing from suffering" wherein one receives the Other, auto-affection "admits the world as a third party," whose space remains irreducible (*OG*, p. 165). All these residues, which prevent the general structure of auto-affection from closing upon itself and from achieving a faultless self-presence, are essential cracks, absences, *écarts,* without which there would be no such thing as auto-affection. As a result, the *auto* constituted in auto-affection is constituted as divided, as differing from itself.

Auto-affection, as this brief analysis clearly indicates, yields to the general infrastructural laws, to the law of supplementarity. For instance, as Derrida points out with respect to Husserl's concept of self-presence: "What we would ultimately like to draw attention to is that the for-itself of self-presence *(für-sich)*—traditionally determined in its dative dimension as phenomenological self-giving, whether reflexive or pre-reflexive—arises in the role of supplement as primordial substitution, in the form 'in the place of' *(für etwas),* that is, . . . in the very operation of significance in general. The *for-itself* would be *in-the-place-of-itself;* put *for-itself,* instead of itself" (*SP,* pp. 88–89). Furthermore, it also yields to a fundamental law of duplication—more precisely, of reduplication—as we shall see.

To give oneself a presence entails relating to oneself; this is the meaning of auto-affection. Still, if one can achieve self-presence exclusively by referring to oneself, auto-affection also implies a condition of self-division. The difference of self-division yields nothing less than that angle at which it is necessary to fold oneself upon oneself. This angle is, so to speak, the inexterminable evil that insinuates itself within the relation to oneself, because of which the full interiority aimed at in auto-affection remains deferred. Its possibility hinges on what will never allow it to close upon itself fully, namely, an instance of spacing. Therefore, the interiority, however successfully produced in auto-affection, appears to be dependent on structures of finitude; a certain outside inhabits this interiority, which is thus prevented from fully coinciding with itself. Yet without the impurity of this outside, a self could not even hope to aim at coinciding with itself.

This angle, which structurally constitutes auto-affection, is not an empirical exteriority, not any particular remainder left standing in the process of giving-oneself-a-presence. "Such a separation in effect remains ungraspable in linguistic, poetic, or phenomenological terms" (*M,* p. 288). As an example, Derrida, in discussing Valéry, formulates the problem of the "hearing-oneself-speak" in the following way:

Neither in the form nor the content of a statement could we assign an intrinsic difference between the sentence I am pronouncing here, now, in my so-called speaking voice, which soon will return to the silence from which it proceeds, very low in my voice or on my page, and the *same* sentence retained in an inner instance, mine or yours. The two events are as different as possible as events, but in the qualitative description of events, in the determination of predicative traits, form or content, the principle of discernibility, the concept of difference evades us. Like the separation that disjoints the circle, a certain tangency here appears to be both null and infinite. (*M*, p. 288)

The difference, the spacing, the angle at the heart of self-affection is not an exteriority of the order of either form or content. It is a difference caused not by "external prolation which accidentally would come to interrupt the circle," but by a disjunctive folding point that occurs in the circuit's return to itself. "The circle turns in order to annul the cut, and therefore, by the same token, unwittingly signifies it. The snake bites its tail, from which above all it does not follow that it finally rejoins itself without harm in this sucessful auto-fellatio" (*M*, p. 289).

At stake is thus the structural disjunction of an altering difference without which no auto-affection would be possible, but owing to which it is also, rigorously speaking, impossible. The difference in question accounts *at once* for the possibility and impossibility of auto-affection, without dialectically annulling the disjuncture. This difference or originary duplication, which does not belong to simple exteriority, which is of the order of neither content nor form, and which is not a leftover that the self or the same was incapable of assimilating, is a structural agency or instance whose nonthematization is precisely the condition under which auto-affection can work successfully. It is thus not a negativity or a contradiction within auto-affection. Successful auto-affection functions precisely as a sublation of contradictions. "The negative is its business and its work. What it excludes, what this very work excludes, is what does not allow itself to be digested, or represented, or stated—does not allow itself to be transformed into auto-affection by examplorality. It is an irreducible heterogeneity which cannot be eaten either sensibly or ideally and which—this is the tautology—by never letting itself be swallowed must therefore *cause itself to be vomited.*"[18]

It now becomes imperative to understand that the originary duplication, which parallels the difference auto-affection attempts to resolve by its speculative and specular enterprise, is not a mere doubling but is rather a duplication that has the structure of an angle, a fold, or rather of a re-fold or re-mark. Owing to this angling of duplication, originary duplication is originarily divided, or doubled. It is a principle of duality duplicated by itself in such a manner that its own "reflection" divides it in depth. For this reason, originary duplication is better characterized as reduplication. Only because of

its structurally abyssal condition can the minimal structure of reduplication assume the double function of constituting and deconsti-
tuting auto-affection on both a prereflective and a reflective level.
Were it not doubly double, it would function as a theological principle
of dualism, as an ultimate and infinite instance. The originary duplication's reduplication is precisely what infinitely prevents it from becoming a self-sufficient ground. Of this self-division in reduplication,
of this folding of duplicity upon itself, Derrida notes the lack of
coinciding: "The fold is not a form of reflexivity. If by reflexivity one
means the motion of consciousness or self-presence that plays such a
determining role in Hegel's speculative logic and dialectic, in the
movement of sublation *(Aufhebung)* and negativity (the essence is
reflection, says the greater *Logic*), then reflexivity is but an effect of
the fold as text" (*D*, p. 270).

As concerns auto-affection, Derrida's philosophy is aimed at "disclosing the remaining angles of round frames" (*VP*, p. 94). Since auto-
affection is not only a pure speculation, in the sense that it is the
dream of total autarchy, but also correlatively, in the sense of a total
reflection, Derrida's regrounding of auto-affection concerns speculation and reflection, specularity and reflexivity as well. Auto-affection
and what it promises, undivided self-proximity, is not only the much
longed-for fulfillment of metaphysical desire; it is also that which is
experienced, paradoxically, as identical to death. Rousseau's anxieties
concerning the state of plenitude he so desired are a good example
of the threat that total self-reflection represents. This insight into the
paradoxical nature of philosophy's relation to the absolute as something dreaded as well as desired leads Derrida, particularly in his
analysis of Rousseau, to the recognition that this apparent contradiction can be accounted for only if one assumes that difference already inhabits indifferent proximity. Yet if the illusion of indifference
or the dream of total self-reflection by auto-affection is dependent in
the first place on a difference (a doubly double fold) around which
the dream of the abolition of difference can be dreamt, then a contradiction such as the one I have just referred to acquires a status that
can no longer be addressed by traditional means of problem solving.
If difference must breach indifference, inasmuch as it reposes on the
possibility of auto-affection, then those aporias and contradictions
traditionally associated with reflexivity take on an entirely different
meaning from that which they possess in the discourse of philosophy,
since within it these riddles cannot hope to be solved. From the moment the possible domination of the source by what has flown from

the source is ruled out by a recognition of the source's originary structural duplicity, problems such as the spatial and temporal hiatuses between the source's constitutive function and the return to that source in the operation of self-reflection, the difference of levels between source and what has been made possible by the source, and so on gain a different meaning.

With this insight, the traditional philosophical paradoxes and contradictions become less symptomatic of the originary duplication than of the very instances of division constitutive of auto-affection and self-reflection. From the perspective of the knowledge based on autoscopy and autognosis—that is, of the knowledge made possible in self-reflection and speculation as absolute self-reflection—these aporias have the form of contradictions. Each of the conflicting arguments may be shown to contain the negation of the other, and thus to be susceptible of sublation in a dialectical logic. Yet for the philosophical perspective that I am elaborating here, the paradoxes of reflection are neither unresolvable problems nor manifestations of the negative, which would yield to a dialectical process whereby the conflicting arguments would be overcome, but rather the very "presence" of heterogeneity, of a certain exteriority at the heart of all self-relation. Whereas the heterogeneous, the exterior, begins only at the limits of the hoped-for totality that metaphysical philosophy believes it is able to think, for Derrida it starts in that interiority itself, at the very point at which it must fold upon itself to be itself, autonomous and autarchical. From this perspective the elements of the aporias of reflection evade all final solution, since their "contradiction" is the very condition (of possibility and impossibility) of what is aimed at. They are not, for that matter, witness to a pseudoproblem; although there is no intrinsic way of solving them, a law regulates their "contradiction" to the extent that they are constitutive difficulties. In order for any self or any speculative totality to relate to itself, either at one blow or through a process of mediation, immediately or as a result, there must be a supplementary trait. While referring to itself alone, such a self must at once refer to an Other, indefinitely. While referring to itself (only), it must repeat itself in duplication and duplicate itself in repetition. But according to the logic of duplication, this also implies that what is doubled becomes doubled. As a result, Derrida can state that "the origin of the speculation becomes a difference" (OG, p. 36). Speculation is based on the structural repeatability of a mark, as well as on the structural relation to Other. Most important, it is dependent on infrastructural re-marking or on the re-fold, which, as we have seen, is not itself a reflexivity. Because of this angle, which cannot be thematized from within reflexivity or speculation, the reflexive totality differs from itself in itself at the moment it relates to itself. Because of this angle of reflection, the ring of reflection does not close itself. It bars reflection forever from rejoining a unity, from achieving a unity or totality. Hence one can say "that the specular agency, far from constituting the I in its properness, immediately expropriates it in order not to halt its march." Instead of folding the self into itself, instead of embracing the totality of all the reflexive determinations, speculation or absolute reflection, the mirror of reflection, "manifests in this double loss the singular operation of a multiplying division which transforms the origin into effect, and the whole into a part" (*M*, p. 285).

Dissemination is the name by which the in-advance divided unity is *affirmed*. This in-advance divided unity of the infrastructures is not the polysemic dispersion of a once unitary meaning but is, as we have seen, an always open ensemble of structures, presupposed by the project of unity and totality and affirmed by reflection and speculation, without their knowledge, as the limit of their possibility. The general theory of duplication or reduplication outlines in this manner the limits of the philosophical presuppositions of the philosophy of reflexivity—presuppositions of an original spontaneity, of productive imagination, of intellectual intuition, and so on—as they have been made explicit by Hegel, who could then resolve the traditional aporias of reflexivity in the speculative manner we have witnessed. Derrida has made it quite clear that insofar as an originary intuition presupposes an originary synthesis, it is a myth, a "fiction" (see for instance *WD*, p. 226). No virgin substance or homogeneous and organic unity precedes or superintends the originary duplication and the "system" of the infrastructures. The myth of a unity is only an effect made possible and irrevocably undercut by reflection itself, insofar as it must rely, in order to take place in the first place, on what it cannot hope to reflect. What lies beyond the mirror, on the other side of the speculum, in the beyond of the presuppositions of the philosophy of reflection—that is to say, the "system" of the infrastructures—cannot be understood in terms of unity, synthesis, totality, and the like, or in terms of spontaneity, without engaging in a conceptual monstrosity. Derrida, addressing the problems of the more originary origin of the infrastructures, writes, "The spontaneous can emerge as the pure initiality of the event only on the condition that it does not itself *present itself,* on the condition of this inconceivable and *irrelevable* passivity in which nothing can present itself to itself" (*M*, pp. 296–297). In other words, spontaneity can be ascribed to originary duplication only on the condition that it withdraws (itself) in the very act in which it allows reflexivity to dream its dream of achieving homogeneity and unity. The "spontaneity" that "grounds" in this manner the spontaneity of synthetic reflection at the heart of all philosophies of identity evades all the characteristics of true spontaneity. It is scandalously passive and is in constant retreat from presentation and self-presentation. It is infinitely divided.

The generalization of reflexivity, which I claimed at one point to be the first step of its deconstruction, thus implies a breaking through of the tinfoils of the mirrors of reflection, demonstrating the uncertainty of the speculum. In this first step of the deconstruction of reflection and speculation, the mirroring is made excessive in order that it may look through the looking glass toward what makes the speculum possible. To look through the mirror is to look at its reverse side, at the dull side doubling the mirror's specular play, in short, at the *tain* of the mirror. It is on this reverse side—on the tinfoil—that dissemination writes itself, remarks Derrida (*D*, p. 33). On this lining of the outside surface of reflection, one can read the "system" of the infrastructures that commands the mirror's play and determines the angles of reflection. Yet since this foil is made of disseminated structural instances, the mirror's tinfoil necessarily becomes semitransparent and, as a correlate, only semireflective. Reflection, then, appears to be affected by the infrastructures that make it possible; it appears broached and breached as an inevitably imperfect and limited *Scheinen*. Total reflection is a limited play, not because of some defect owing to its finitude—as Hegel has shown, it is a *truly* infinite play—but because of the structurally limitless play of the undecidables that make it possible, which the mirror's play cannot accommodate without at the same time relinquishing the telos of its operation: the actualization of the unity of all that is reasonable. At first the mirror that Derrida's philosophy holds up seems to show us only its tain; yet this opaque tain is also transparent. Through it one can observe the play of reflection and speculation as it takes place in the mirror's mirroring itself. Seen from the inside this play gives an illusion of perfection, but observed through the tain, it appears limited by the infrastructural agencies written on its invisible side, without which it could not even begin to occur. In all its perfection, the specular play shows itself incapable of reflecting, of sublating its limits.

In short, unlike a certain criticism of reflexivity, Derrida's criticism does not reject reflection and speculation in favor of total immediacy, nor does it presuppose an originary unity by virtue of which the traditional problems of reflexivity can be dialectically overcome in absolute reflection or speculation. Derrida's debate with reflection and speculation is not dependent on the essentially philosophical problem of the aporias, contradictions, or negations of reflection, in terms of which it refuses to criticize or solve the problems of reflection. As we have seen, both operations are intrinsically speculative. Focusing on an analysis of those heterogeneous instances that are the "true" conditions of possibility of reflection and speculation without being susceptible to accommodation by the intended totality, Derrida's philosophy reinscribes, in the strict meaning of this word, reflection and speculation into what exceeds it: the play of the infrastructures. Instead of disposing of reflexivity in an empiricist or positivist manner (the surest way for it to reenter through the backdoor), the philosophy we have been considering takes reflection's exigencies seriously. It is the only way to trace the limits of reflection without falling prey to the fictions on which it is based.

THE GENERAL SYSTEM

In describing a number of particular infrastructures, I have shown that they are susceptible to a classification of sorts and that, by overlapping, replacing, and supplementing one another, they form a certain system. We also saw that several of the infrastructures represent conditions of the possibility and impossibility of systematicity in general, or of what I have called the *general system*. In what follows, I shall try to show more precisely what sort of system one can attribute to infrastructures and also in what sense they can be said to make systematicity in general possible (and impossible).

Let us first recall that systematicity is an essential philosophical requirement. In the system, knowledge lays itself out and thus comes to know itself. The system as a complete and in itself necessary order of foundation in which philosophical truths acquire their required internal coherence and unity is a function of the philosophical desire for self-conceptualization. As I have said, infrastructures are economically and strategically minimal distributions or constellations—archesyntheses—of essentially heterogeneous predicates. The principle articulated by each singular infrastructure applies to itself as well, and although each one of the by right infinite number of infrastructures can be replaced (or supplemented) by another, they are not synonymous with or even identical to one another. Thus one can see clearly how infrastructures contain the *possibility* of tying elements together into a totality of foundation, as well as of self-thematization and of element combination and transformation.

Since infrastructures combine heterogeneous predicates, however, and apply to themselves only the better to unground themselves, they also appear to be strangely ambiguous or ambivalent. Yet it is not the sort of ambiguity that would be witness to an absence of clarity in the process of their determination, to the negativity of a lack of precision, to vagueness or looseness of terms, in short to semantic confusion, nor is it an ambiguity concerning the meaning of the infrastructures, owing to some polysemic richness. Ambiguity in these senses is always a function of presence—that is, of an ultimately self-identical signification—as is demonstrated by the possibility of the dialectical sublation of ambiguous meanings, whereas the ambiguity of the infrastructures is not the positive sign of a dialectical or speculative state of affairs. Finally, this ambiguity does not signify the enigma of all truth as an unconcealing. Indeed, the ambiguity of the infrastructures is not univocal in a higher sense. It does not simply coincide with what Heidegger calls *zweideutige Zweideutigkeit,* an ambiguity grounded in a gathering *(Versammlung)* or unison *(Einklang),* whose unity itself remains unspeakable.[19] The specific ambiguity of the infrastructures cannot be sublated or made to sound in unison. If determinacy requires self-identity, then the ambiguity of the infrastructures has no boundaries.

For all these reasons, it is advisable to avoid the term *ambiguity* altogether in characterizing the infrastructures. By analogy to Gödel's discovery of undecidable propositions, Derrida suggests that they be qualified, provisionally, as undecidables. In an essay published in 1931, "On Formally Undecidable Propositions of Principia Mathematica and Related Systems," Gödel demonstrates that metalogical statements concerning the completeness and consistency of systems any more complex than logical systems of the first order cannot be demonstrated within these systems.[20] Derrida, in *Dissemination,* transcribes Gödel's theorem in the following terms: "An undecidable proposition, as Gödel demonstrated in 1931, is a proposition which, given a system of axioms governing a multiplicity, is neither an analytical nor deductive consequence of those axioms, nor in contradiction with them, neither true nor false with respect to these axioms. *Tertium datur,* without synthesis" (D, p. 219). To call the infrastructures undecidables is thus not merely to stress the essential incompleteness and inconsistency of their level of formalization. Without denying the philosophical ideal of exhaustive deductivity—in other words, of the possibility of determining every element of a multiplicity as either an analytic consequence or as a contradiction of a system of axioms said to govern that multiplicity—the undecidability of the infrastructures questions that ideal from a structural point of view. Finally, as Derrida remarks in *Positions,* to call infrastructures undecidables is to stress that they are "unities of simulacrum, [of] 'false' verbal properties (nominal or semantic) that can no longer be included within philosophical (binary) opposition, but which, however, inhabit philosophical opposition, resisting and disorganizing it, *without ever* constituting a third term, without ever leaving room for a solution in the form of speculative dialectics" (*P,* p. 43).

Before continuing this analysis, let us recall that Derrida emphasized that infrastructures were to be called undecidable only by analogy. The notion of the undecidable, he remarks in his *Introduction to the Origin of Geometry,* in its very negativity, "has such a sense by some irreducible reference to the ideal of decidability." Its revolutionary and disconcerting sense "remains essentially and intrinsically haunted in its sense of origin by the *telos* of decidability—whose disruption it marks" (*O,* p. 53). Yet what is being thought under the title of the infrastructures transcends the project of *definiteness* itself. Therefore, *undecidable* must be understood to refer not only to essential incompleteness and inconsistency, bearing in mind their distinction from ambiguity, but also to indicate a level vaster than that which is encompassed by the opposition between what is decidable and undecidable.

As "originary" syntheses, or economic arrangements of traits, the undecidables constitute both the medium or the element between the binary philosophical oppositions and between philosophy and its Other, as well as the medium that encompasses these coupled terms. They are undecidable because they suspend the decidable opposition between what is true and false and put all the concepts that belong to the philosophical system of decidability into brackets. By virtue of their constituting a space in between conceptual dyads and, at the same time, comprising them, the infrastructural undecidables are "the medium in which opposites are opposed, the movement and the play that links them among themselves, reverses them or makes one side cross over into the other" (*D,* p. 127). Their undecidability, their "floating indetermination," permits the substitution and the play of the conceptual binary oppositions, which, by turning into one another, become incapable of denominating and defining the medium from which they emerge (*D*, p. 93). Thus, if one calls infrastructures "ambivalent" or "ambiguous," it is in the sense that they do not offer themselves to mastery in terms of simple and clear-cut distinctions. Indeed, conceptual couples and their play essentially represent nothing other than the attempt to bring the play of the medium of the undecidables to a stop, to make rational what, according to their implicit and explicit ethos, can only be irrational, to appropriate it, to identify it by forcing a self-identity upon it. The restricted play of the philosophical conceptual couples proceeds to this task by trying to reconstitute the undecidables as dialectical contradictions susceptible of eventual dissolution; but, Derrida notes, undecidability "is not contradiction in the Hegelian form of contradiction" (*P*, p. 101). The undecidables, on the contrary, are what suspend decidability in all its forms, particularly in its dialectical form of a mediation of contraries *and* of that in which decidability and definiteness carve themselves out. Above all, the "ambiguity" of undecidables is rigorously irreducible and irresolvable because of its essentially *nonsemantic* character. Speaking of the "hymen," Derrida says:

"Undecidability" is not caused here by some enigmatic equivocality, some inexhaustible ambivalence of a word in a "natural" language, and still less by some *"Gegensinn der Urworte"* (Abel). In dealing here with *hymen*, it is not a matter of repeating what Hegel undertook to do with German words like *Aufhebung, Urteil, Meinen, Beispiel,* etc., marveling over that lucky accident that installs a natural language within the element of speculative dialectics. What counts here is not lexical richness, the semantic infiniteness of a word or concept, its depth or breadth, the sedimentation that has produced inside it two contradictory layers of signification . . . What counts here is the formal or syntactical *praxis* that composes and decomposes it.   (*D*, p. 220)

The undecidability of infrastructures results from the *syntactic arrangement* of their parts. But what does Derrida mean by syntax? As opposed to semantics (and pragmatics), as another major aspect of the grammatical construction of sentences (and of the general theory of signs), *syntax* refers traditionally to the formal arrangements of words and signs, to their connection and relation in phrases or sentences, as well as to the established usages of grammatical construction and the rules deduced therefrom. Derrida's use of the concept of syntax, however, is not simply a reference to the formal properties of language insofar as these are traditionally considered to refer to the articulation of the signifieds. Indeed form is just another name for presence, Derrida notes. His use of *syntax* does not imply the traditional subjection of syntax to semantics. In distinction from the grammatical opposition of the syntactic and the semantic, of form and content, and so on, Derrida's use of *syntax* is intended to undo these oppositions systematically. Syntax is conceived by Derrida as being irreducibly in excess of the semantic, and consequently as disequilibrating that traditional grammatical and philosophical distinction. How, then, are we to think such an "irreducible excess of the syntactic over the semantic?" (*D*, p. 221). Such an excess takes place where it can be shown that the formal properties of language are not simply a function of signifieds, of the content of the words, but that they are arranged in and intrinsically dependent on a syntax of their own. Yet if it can be demonstrated that formal syntactic properties can be syntactically composed and decomposed, a *syntax of syntax* comes into play, along with the problem of the simulacrum, which, as we have seen, is no longer subject to truth or, in the case of syntax, to the content of the words. In "The Double Session," Derrida has shown that the writing of Mallarmé is precisely such an attempt to explore the possibilities of syntactical excess. It is, therefore, a literature in which "the suspense is due only to the placement and not to the content of words" (*D*, p. 220).

Now, the syntactic excess responsible for the infrastructures' undecidability stems from the fact that their formal arrangements, dispositions, distributions, or constellations of predicates refer to a supplementary mark. The infrastructure of re-marking or of the double mark demonstrates this essential character of infrastructures in general, which consists of their being folded upon themselves in such a manner that they themselves become a paradigm of the law they represent. Infrastructures apply to themselves. The arrangement that they represent is always rearrangement by themselves. For this reason they are, as we have seen, in constant displacement, incapable of assuming any stable identity. By re-marking the syntactic disposition with a supplementary syntactic trait, the infrastructures can no longer be brought to a semantic halt. They seem to be purely syntactic; yet since these purely "formal" or syntactic structures or knots of intersections are their own paradigm, they also, unquestionably, signify and are thus not purely syntactic. "Through the re-marking of its semantic void, it in fact begins to signify. Its semantic void *signifies,* but it signifies spacing and articulation; it has as its meaning the possibility of syntax; it orders the play of meaning. *Neither purely syntactic nor purely semantic*, it marks the articulated opening of that opposition" (*D*, p. 222).

The infrastructures thus float indefinitely between the possibilities of the semantic and the syntactic, in short of meaning. Though not purely syntactic (or, for that matter, purely semantic), they are in a position of anteriority and possibility to both aspects of language, precisely because of the excess of the syntactic over meaning—that is, of the re-marked syntax—of a syntax that arranges (itself). It is in this sense that I shall continue to speak of the infrastructures as syntactically undecidable. After having demonstrated, in "The Double Session," that the infrastructure *hymen* is undecidable because of syntactic re-marking, Derrida writes:

What holds for "hymen" also holds, *mutatis mutandis,* for all other signs which, like *pharmakon, supplement, differance,* and others, have a double, contradictory, undecidable value that always derives from their syntax, whether the latter is in a sense "internal," articulating and combining under the same yoke, *huph'hen,* two incompatible meanings, or "external," dependent on the code in which the word is made to function. But the syntactical composition and decomposition of a sign renders this alternative between internal and external inoperative. One is simply dealing with greater or lesser syntactical units at work, and with economic differences in condensation. (*D,* p. 221)

Because of this undecidability, the infrastructures can serve as "originary" syntheses, without, at the same time, lending themselves to a movement of (teleological or archaeological) reappropriation: "these points of indefinite pivoting . . . mark the spots of what can never be mediated, mastered, sublated, or dialecticized through any *Erinnerung* or *Aufhebung*" (*D,* p. 221). If they mark dialectics as sterile by undercutting the possibility of a reduction of their undecidability through sublation, how much more do they evade nondialectical philosophy and its reflexive oppositions!

As undecidables, infrastructures *resemble* syncategoremata. Like those secondary parts of discourse, distinguished in grammar and logic from the medieval William of Shyreswood to Husserl's *Logical Investigations,* which, in contradistinction to categoremata, are unclosed expressions that have no determined and fixed meaning, undecidables also predicate jointly. They cannot function as terms and thus are not of the order of the *phone semantike.* Similar to syncategoremata such as *and, or, not, if, every, some, only, in between,* expressions that cannot be used by themselves but only in conjunction with other terms, infrastructures are essentially used together with predicates, categoremata, or concepts with respect to which they exercise a specific organizational function. Yet syncategoremata, which are considered logical constants determining the logical form (as in Buridan), never relate to themselves in the complex manner that we have seen to be true of infrastructures. If they never signify their own semantic quasivoid, it is because the ethical orientation of grammar, giving priority to categoremata, cannot afford to blur its hierarchical and clear-cut distinctions. As Mallarmé's texts reveal, however, syncategoremata such as *in between* or *or* lend themselves to an operation of re-marking. Speaking of *entre*, "in between," Derrida stresses that "it can be nominalized, turn into a quasi-categorem, receive a definitive article, or even be made plural" (*D*, p. 222). When I speak of the infrastructures as syncategoremata, it is in this sense of a nonreflexive doubling of their incomplete meanings.[21]

For the remainder of these reflections it is imperative to recall that Derrida's references to syncategoremata occur in the context of "The Double Session," that is, in an essay that sets out to prove the irreducible excess of syntax over semantics. This demonstration is framed by a critique of thematic criticism and its overevaluation of the role of the word, in both philosophy and literary criticism. As the totality of Derrida's work clearly indicates, in particular but not exclusively *Of Grammatology*, this critique of thematic criticism is aimed at the mainstream of Western philosophy, which until recently ignored and trivialized the difference between words and sentences, between semantics and syntax, by confining the latter to a lateral role at best. All of Derrida's work is engaged in a systematic critique of the status accorded to the word, the noun, in order to uphold the secondariness of the syntactical; it is perhaps the most radical attempt ever made at allowing syntax an independent form. To conclude this part of the present study, let us restate what has already been sufficiently developed, namely, that Derrida's criticism of the word, of semantics, in favor of the forms of syntactic construction is also aimed at what he perceives as phenomenology's (particularly Husserlian phenomenology's) continuation of metaphysics. What still needs to be developed is that this critique is linked to Derrida's *complex* continuation of Husserl's project in *Logical Investigations* of a universal and a priori, in short, "pure logical grammar." Derrida continues this idea, which Husserl never developed, in a complex manner, because his critique of phenomenology, of the values of presence that it shares with metaphysics in general, of form as another name for presence, of semantics, thematism, and so on radically displaces what he calls in *Positions* the "remarkable project of a 'purely logical grammar' that is more important and more rigorous than all the projects of a 'general rea-

soned grammar' of seventeenth- and eighteenth-century France, projects that certain modern linguists refer to, however" (*P*, p. 32).

Before elaborating on this project, I should add a brief note on
Derrida's indebtedness to Husserlian phenomenology. Not infre-
quently one hears the opinion that Husserlian phenomenology is a
dead end and that, consequently, any attempt to continue the questioning of that philosophy is doomed to failure from the start. Certainly what is true of other philosophers is true of Husserl as well:
by evading what is worthy of questioning in their texts, they all lead
us to dead ends. As far as Derrida is concerned, his relation to Husserl
is at least threefold. First, it is a relation, to use Granel's words, to
"simply the greatest philosopher who appeared since the Greeks."[22]
To put it differently, it is a relation to the philosophical as a battle
of gods and giants about being *(gigantomachia peri tes ousias)*, as
Plato calls it in *Sophist,* as well as to the philosophical in all its
technical and thematic richness. Second, Derrida's relation to Husserlian thought is radically critical of the metaphysical implications
of the project of phenomenology itself, as has been amply docu-
mented. Third, it is a continuation and radicalization of a number of
motifs in Husserl's own works that are capable of unhinging the major
metaphysical themes at the center of his philosophy, such as the idea
of a primordial axiomatical grounding, the ideal of deductivity in
general, the idea of evidence, and the idea of the idea itself. Yet to
contend, as I do here, that Derrida continues Husserl (and this is true
of his relation to Heidegger as well) precisely on those issues that
foreground the classical ethico-theoretical decisions constitutive of
philosophy as philosophy is also to say that such a continuation is at
the same time a decisive break with the idea of tradition, continuity,
Oedipality, and so on. Indeed, since the motifs in question are of such
a nature that they themselves are radically more fundamental than
the possibility of continuity, and since, moreover, they cannot be
developed *within* the philosophical discourse as such, their continuation is possible only from a perspective that is marginal with respect
to the history of philosophical development. From this standpoint,
the fact that Derrida may have discovered these motifs in Husserl's
works is, in a certain way, radically contingent.

Now, let us recall, in as succinct a manner as possible, what the
project of a pure logical grammar corresponds to. *Logical Investigations,* in which this idea is set forth, are preliminary investigations
required by Husserl's anticipated project of a pure logic or theory of
theory, a logic thoroughly different from what one commonly calls

epistemology or theory of science, which would govern the implications of the very *possibility* of an idea such as knowing. In these preliminary examinations, Husserl is soon led to the insight that such a pure logic would have to include, as at least one of its parts if not its foundation, a purely logical grammar, a logic that would be a purely formal mapping out of the *primitive* essential concepts or the ideal singulars contained a priori in the very content or meaning of certain *genera,* such as knowing. Indeed, if such a pure logic investigation of what constitutes the idea of knowing anterior to its objective validation and "intentional fulfilment" must also, necessarily, investigate the laws related to these primitive concepts, laws that organize the ideal singulars constitutive of the genera, then the task of fixing these a priori laws would be incumbent on a discipline such as a pure logical grammar. This grammar must not be mistaken for a "universal science comprehending all particular grammars as contingent specifications," Husserl warns us in *Logical Investigations.*[23] Unlike such a science, which would still be empirical, the pure logical grammar is exclusively concerned with that field of laws relative to the pure semantic forms contained a priori in the idea of knowing. Such laws affect these forms insofar as they regulate their compoundings and modifications and watch over their meaningfulness, even before these forms and their possible combinations enter the truth relations that are the object proper of logic in a cogent sense. The sense or non-sense of these forms is based on these laws, independent of the objectivity and validity of these forms, which themselves depend on their prior semantic fullness. The purely logical grammar is thus a form-theory of meaning or intentionality prior to all possible objective validation of meaning or intentional fulfilment. The task of this metaempirical logic is to provide traditional logic with "the abstractly possible forms of meaning, whose objective value it then becomes its first task to determine" (p. 522). It is important here to mention that on more than one occasion, Husserl conceived of these forms of meaning, of the laws of essence that regulate the primitive elements and structures of meaning, as *trivia,* as obvious commonplaces. Yet these trivia, which are "intrinsically prior in the sense of Aristotle," behind whose obviousness "the hardest problems lie hidden," and which have never been thematized by the logicians, become the true object of the project of a pure logic, if not, for Husserl, of philosophy in general, especially since philosophy could be called "paradoxically, but not unprofoundly, . . . the science of the trivial" (p. 528). Now, what are these trivia, these forms of meaning, which, although they make no knowledge possible, are still full of meaning because they obey certain rules? What are these trivia that are the a priori conditions of the intelligibility of discourse?

The primitive forms of meaning that constitute the whole semantic realm are the formal laws that govern "the formation of unitary meanings out of syntactical materials falling under definite categories having an *a priori* place in the realm of meanings, a formation according to syntactical laws which are likewise fixed *a priori,* and which can be readily seen to constitute a fixed system of forms" (p. 513). Thus, the pure logical grammar or form-theory of meaning faces the task of fixing in a system the categorical and syntactical primitive laws built a priori into the general idea of meaning. As Husserl points out, this system of categorical and syntactical laws following from the generic essence of meaning as such, which is constitutive of the articulation of its elements, is an ideal framework and, as the essence of all speech as such, holds a position of primacy over all actual languages and their empirical grammar. For that reason, it is to be called a "pure logical grammar" (p. 526).

At this point it should not be difficult to see, by analogy with the trivia in Husserl (and with what Heidegger has thematized under the name of the most obvious or most simple), that the infrastructures to some extent continue Husserl's (and Heidegger's) research into the a prioris of meaning (including that of Being). In discussing Husserl's project of a purely logical grammar in *Speech and Phenomena,* however, Derrida also points out that its formalizing power does not cover the whole field of possibility for language in general, to the extent that it "concerns only the *logical a priori* of language," and that "it is *pure logical grammar*" (*SP,* p. 8). In spite of its interest in the system of rules that make a discourse, properly speaking, a discourse, and not non-sense, before any objective fulfilment of the meaning-intention, pure logical grammar remains "governed more or less immediately by the possibility of a relationship with objects" (*SP,* p. 71). Indeed, "the purification of the formal is [itself] guided by a concept of *sense* which is itself determined on the basis of a *relation with an object*" (*SP,* p. 98). Derrida, apart from insisting that there are modes of sense that do not point to any possible objects, also sets out to demonstrate that the rigorous distinction in Husserl between meaning-intention and its possible fulfillment by an intuition of an object is itself possible only because all meaning-intention is structurally testamentary. In other words, it functions only because it is always already supplementing a lack of actuality. The discovery of the infrastructures extends Husserl's project of a purely logical grammar. The expansion of its formalizing power implies a reinscription of the logical as merely one of a plurality of linguistic functions. Whereas in Husserl the primitive laws of essence of all meaning prior to its validation are all laws concerning the unity of meaning, thus giving priority to the categorical over the syncategorical and the syntactical, the infrastructures question the very *differences* between the a priori and the world they open, as well as the difference between the categorical and syncategorical, between the semantic and the syntactic. In this sense the infrastructures and their system are anterior, in an unheard-of way, to a phenomenology of meaning, that is, in short, to phenomenology. Reflecting on those unthematized differences, the system of the infrastructures precedes "by right" the discourse of phenomenology.

Having established that much, let us now circle back to the *general system*. It now becomes possible to determine it as a system of undecidables, of syntactically re-marked syncategoremata articulating prelogical and lateral possibilities of logic. To put it differently, the system can be viewed as a syntax of an infinity of "last" syntactically overdetermined syntactical objectivities. To characterize the *general system* in these terms not only serves to conclude all that has been laid out up to this point but also, and above all, indicates a decisive point at which this system leaves the philosophical realm of phenomenology. This point is that of a radicalized, no longer phenomenologizable notion of syntax. Derrida's concept of a re-marked syntax undercuts, in fact deconstructs, Husserl's distinction, made toward the beginning of *Ideas,* in paragraph 11, of formal ontological syntactical categories and formal ontological substrative categories. This distinction becomes important to the whole project of *Ideas,* since it allows Husserl to make the syntactical forms and their categories depend on what he terms the "*ultimate content-laden substrata* as the nucleus of all syntactical constructions."[24] As a result, "syntactical objectivities appear in the formal region of objectivities in general, as *derivatives* of these ultimate substrata, that is, of objects *which are no longer constructions of a syntactico-categorical kind,* [and] which contain in themselves no further vestige of those ontological forms which are mere correlates of the functions of thought" (p. 70). As *ultimate terms,* which no longer contain in themselves any residue of syntactical formation, they are "pure and syntactically formless individual units," and/or "ultimate substantive [*Sachhaltiges*] essences" (p. 74). In one of the most classical gestures, Husserl, after having

opened the radical formal province of pure objectivities, makes syntactical categories secondary to those terms, which as *eide* or *tode ti*
(as essences or individualities) link substance *(ousia)*, in the fullest
and most primary sense, to presence. The re-marked and undecidable
infrastructures are the outcome of a deconstruction of these hierarchical distinctions in the purely formal region of the logical, distinctions by which form is subjected to content, syntax to semantics,
purely formal forms to nonformal forms, that is, to singularities or
identical subject matters *(Sachverhalte)*. The system of these infrastructures as one of syntactically re-marked syncategoremata is a system that escapes all phenomenologization as such; it constantly
disappears and withdraws from all possible presentation. In privileging the syntactical in the sense in which I have been developing it—
that is, in the sense of re-marked, doubled sytactic structures no longer
suspended from semantic subject matters of whatever sort—the *general system* spells out the prelogical conditions of logic, thus reinscribing logic, together with its implications of presence and evident
meaning, into a series of linguistic functions of which the logical is
only one among others. Derrida remarks in "Limited Inc.":

The matter we are discussing here concerns the value, possibility, and system
of what is called logic in general. The law and the effects with which we
have been dealing . . . govern the possibility of every logical proposition . . .
No constituted logic nor any rule of a logical order can, therefore, provide
a decision or impose its norms upon these prelogical possibilities of logic.
Such possibilities are not "logically" primary or secondary with regard to
other possibilities, nor logically primary or secondary with regard to logic
itself. They are (topologically?) alien to it, but not as its principle, condition
of possibility, or "radical" foundation.   *(LI,* p. 235)

    As the system of these impure and nonideal grounds, grounds so
different from what they ground as to be thoroughly alien to it, the
system of the infrastructures is also the exposition of what I have
termed heterology. The *general system,* then, is the system of what is
Other to the *logos*—Other, however, not in the sense of absolute,
that is, abstract opposition, or in the sense of the Other of the same,
but rather in terms of what is alien to its own self-thematization. It
is the system of what, in spite of its thorough alterity to the self-
understanding of thought, is presupposed by such thought, precisely
insofar as its handed-down goal is to secure its own foundation in
itself and by itself.
    By taking the classical exigencies of philosophy to their logical end,

without, however, giving in to its ethico-theoretical, ethico-onto-logical, ethico-teleological, or ethico-political decisions, Derrida brings philosophy to a certain close. This, however, is an accomplishment in an unheard-of sense. Opening the discourse of philosophy to an Other that is no longer simply *its* Other, an Other in which philosophy becomes inscribed, and which limits its ultimate pretension to self-foundation (a pretension independent of philosophical orientation), is an accomplishment that marks not the end but the structural limits of philosophy's autonomy and autarchy. Philosophy comes to a close, paradoxically, because its heterological presuppositions constitute it as, necessarily, always incomplete.

PART THREE

Literature or
Philosophy?

10

Literature in Parentheses

❧

In a recent text, or more precisely in the text of his thesis defense in 1980, Derrida reminded his committee that his most constant interest, even more constant than his philosophical interest—if this were possible—was in literature, that writing that is called literary. In fact his first thesis, in 1957, was to have been entitled "The Ideality of the Literary Object." As originally planned, this thesis was to have put the Husserlian techniques of transcendental phenomenology in the service of "a new theory of literature, of that very peculiar type of ideal object that is the literary object."[1] My contention is that Derrida's marked interest in literature, an interest that began with his questioning the particular ideality of literature, has in his thinking never led to anything remotely resembling literary criticism or to a valorization of what literary critics agree to call literature. Paradoxically, Derrida's initial inquiry into the ideality of the literary object had the effect of situating his work at the margins not only of philosophy but of literature as well.

Such an observation does not mean, however, that Derrida's philosophy is without any relevance to literary criticism. Rather it implies that the importance of Derrida's thinking for the discipline of literary criticism is not immediately evident, and that any statement of its relevance to that discipline requires certain mediating steps beforehand. So-called deconstructive criticism, which, however important, is but an offspring of New Criticism, has not, to my knowledge, undertaken these preparatory steps and has done little more than apply what it takes to be a method for reading literary texts to the unproblematized horizon of its discipline. As a result, the genuine impact that Derrida's philosophy could have on literary criticism has not been, or at best has hardly been, noticed. The following remarks are not intended to offer a "true" version of deconstructive criticism but only to clarify some of the preliminaries which any deconstructive criticism would have to observe.

If it were possible to draw one major proposition from Derrida's statements on literature, it would certainly not be that everything is literature, but on the contrary that "there is no—or hardly any, ever so little—literature" (D, p. 223). How are we to understand this seemingly provocative claim? What this statement first of all suggests is that Aristotle's production of *the concept* of literature in the *Poetics* (in the aftermath of Plato's determination of poetry as *mimesis*) inaugurates the history of literature as a history in which the certification of literature's birth, the declaration of its name, coincides with its disappearance. Literature, says Derrida, was born of that history, which lasted until the nineteenth century, and died of that history (D, pp. 138–139, 183).

The interpretation of mimesis as subject to truth, as a mimetologism that proclaims the priority and precedence of the imitated over imitation, subjects literature to a status of metaphoric secondariness. Accordingly, literature possesses no specificity of its own and is reducible to its signified, its message, the truth it expresses. Yielding from the outset to the constraints of its philosophical conceptualization, literature, like philosophy, includes "the project of effacing itself in the face of the signified content which it transports and in general teaches." The specificity of philosophy and literature alike rests on this systematic curtailment of the signifier. Consequently, reading is in essence always a transcendental reading in search of the signified. Derrida writes of "the entire history of texts, and within it the history of literary forms in the West," that it "has almost always and almost everywhere, according to some fashions and across very diverse ages, lent itself to this *transcendental* reading, in that search for the signified" (OG, p. 160).

What is more, this philosophical inauguration has not only governed the reading of literature but has determined the mode of its writing as well. With the exception of certain rare examples, literary writing has subjugated itself to the constraints of the concept and to the ethos of philosophy. Literature, then, speaks the voice of philosophy. It is a mere proxy, stillborn. There has hardly ever been any literature, if literature is supposed to mean something other than philosophy. The contemporary trend—a trend that begins with early Romanticism—of minimizing the difference between literature and philosophy is at least to some extent an involuntary recognition of this state of affairs. It remains within the tradition of literary secondariness.

When Derrida asserts that today, or more specifically from Mallarmé on, a certain determined form of "literary" practice announces the subversion of logocentrism (*P*, p. 10), that certain texts seem "to mark and to organize a structure of resistance to the philosophical conceptuality that allegedly dominated or comprehended them, whether directly, or whether through categories derived from this philosophical fund" (*P*, p. 69), certainly this is not simply in order to assert that literature has finally found its specificity or come into its own. Indeed, if that specificity is understood to be constituted by "literariness," a second reading of Derrida's statement concerning the scarcity of literature becomes possible.

It is well known that the question of literariness was first formulated by the Russian Formalists in order to determine what, in literature, remains irreducible to the message, to metaphor, to the voice, and so on. Yet as Derrida has argued, this interest in "pure literature," in the *"literary* element," "in what in literature passes through an irreducibly graphic text" does not free literature from its philosophical or logocentric subjugation, for it ties "the *play of form* to a determined substance of expression" (*OG*, p. 59). Undoubtedly the emergence of the question of literarity has permitted the avoidance of a certain number of thematic reductions, of misconstructions owing to a *transcendental* reading; yet such a focus on the irreducible literariness of the graphic (as opposed to the phonic) substance leads to a symmetric limitation and restriction of the play of form. This respect for the literariness of a work of art consists, indeed, in the mere isolation, "in order to shelter it, [of] a formal specificity of the literary which would have its own proper essence and truth which no longer have to be articulated with other theoretical or practical fields" (*P*, p. 70).

Literariness or literarity, therefore, denotes the essence, the truth, the literary-being and the being-literary of literature. By making all literature exemplify this one essence of literature, however, literature is, once again, condemned to nonexistence. If we thus determine the essence of literature (as that which confers being upon it), literature once more loses its specificity, at the very moment when it seemed most firmly established. Hence Derrida's wariness of the concept of literarity, and likewise of its opposition to the stubborn authority of mimetologism. Mimetologism and literarity are the birth and death of literature through philosophy. What has been represented and determined under the name of literature throughout the history of literature, from Plato to Mallarmé, has almost always yielded to either mimetologism or literariness, says Derrida. Ultimately, neither the one nor the other has put the authority of philosophy into question. Therefore, the attempt to play out the fact that philosophy is always written, that it is marked by literariness, and that philosophy's desire to control and eliminate the opacity of its signifier must necessarily fail is at best an empiricist argument against the domination of literature by philosophy. In exchanging one essence for another, this Platonic inversion of sorts only confirms the superiority of philosophy.

Given the insufficiency of these two interpretations of the proposition that "there is no—or hardly any, ever so little—literature," we must examine a third possibility. If, as Derrida asserts, with Mallarmé literary writing became a thrust or a point of resistance against the dominant concept of literature; if, as he goes so far as to state, it was normal that the breakthrough in philosophy "was more secure and more penetrating on the side of literature and poetic writing" (OG, p. 92), the question arises as to what, in the end, endows literature with such power. As we have seen, under no circumstances can this power flow from its mimetological or literary (formal) quality. Literature, or what was called literature up to the nineteenth century, does not undermine philosophy through its content or through an empirical excess of writing on the page. Rather, if the first break in the most entrenched Western tradition of both literature and philosophy stems from literary or poetic writing's destruction of "the transcendental authority and dominant category of the *episteme:* being" (OG, p. 92), then this vacillation could have been achieved only through its "generalized putting-in-quotation marks of literature, of the so-called literary text" (D, p. 291). In other words, it is by suspending its *being* as literature that literature becomes capable of challenging philosophy's dominant categorization. Literature puts itself between quotation marks by opening itself to the absolute loss of its meaning, whether of content or of form. Literature becomes a radical interrogation of philosophy, and of most past literature as well, not only by refusing its foundation in a preceding and prior being of meaning but also by disclaiming any formal essence as concerns its substance of expression. Therefore, Derrida must regard the use of the term *literature* for that sort of literary writing with suspicion, since it "subjects the concept to belles-lettres, to the arts, to poetry, to rhetoric, and to philosophy" (P, p. 69). He must write "literature" or "literary" between quotation marks precisely because the new practice of this sort of writing "supposes a break with what has tied the history of the literary arts to the history of metaphysics" (*P*, p. 11). "Literature" thus acquires a subversive function with regard to philosophy and the literature under its dominion, not by restoring its specificity at any cost but, precisely, by recognizing that it can effect such a subversion only by hardly being literature. "Literature" (is) almost no literature. It appears, then, that the disruptive and subversive effects of "literature" are directed not against logocentric philosophy alone but against literature as well, to the extent that the latter submits to philosophy's demands. Hence, what subverts philosophy is not in fact literature, for it also solicits the very foundations of literature, depriving it of its external foundation in philosophy, or in other words of its being. Indeed "literature" has a greater power of formalization than literature and philosophy alike. In a recent interview Derrida stated, "My 'first' desire certainly did not lead me toward philosophy but rather toward literature, no, toward something which literature accommodates more easily than philosophy."[2]

In the light of this third interpretation of Derrida's statement on the scarcity of literature, let us briefly reflect on the nature of the argumentation that I have laid out. After arguing that there is hardly any literature because all literature is either mimetological or formalist, Derrida makes the suspension of being a major characteristic of "literature." In a movement that resembles, to the point of confusion, a phenomenological transcendental reduction in which literature is subjected to a sort of *epoche*, bracketing its mimetological and formalist determinations, Derrida, rather than producing the to-be-expected essence of literature, yields a radically nonphenomenologizable structure. Indeed, Derrida's parenthesizing of literature reveals what I would call the *epochal* character of "literature" itself. "Literature," instead of having a true essence of its own, a standing in being, appears to be characterizable only by its structure of bracketing, which puts the transcendental authority and dominant category of being into question. Thereby, however, "literature's" epochal nature is not only no longer in the service of being but also radically displaces phenomenological reduction. In short, Derrida's interest in the "ideality" of the literary object permits the production of a structure of bracketing that escapes phenomenologization, that cannot be beheld *in person,* and which is thus what allows for the phenomenological *Wesenschau* while at the same time drawing its irreducible limits. The nonessence of what Derrida has called "literature" is an "ideal" structure of parenthesizing which has no foundation in being;

it is basically a function of the debate concerning the status of phenomenological idealities and the method by which they become apprehensible. "Literature," then, is scarcely of the order of being. It
has as little being as, say, a between, a corner, an angle. "Literature's"
subversion of both philosophy and literature, of both truth and the
simulacrum, as Derrida remarks at the beginning of "The Double
Session," proceeds from its status as a between, forming a certain
corner, a certain angle, with respect to both literature and philosophy.
This angle, which resists the history of philosophy and literature, is
further determined by Derrida as the "general text." From what has
already been established, *text* in this sense is not restricted to writing
on the page, nor does it imply that both literature and philosophy
are de facto always written.

Before elaborating in some detail on Derrida's concept of the general text as a structure of nonreflexive *re-marking* and *retrait,* I should
like to note that "literature," or the general text, as that which forms
an angle with both philosophy and literature, is what limits both
discourses, whose authority is *marked* by this margin and thus dependent on it. From this it also becomes obvious what the subversive
function of the general texts consists of. The general text does not
annihilate literature and philosophy; rather, by putting their authority
"back into the position of a *mark* in a chain that this authority
intrinsically and illusorily believes it wishes to, and does in fact, govern" (*P,* pp. 59–60), it assigns them their respective places. In other
words, by reinscribing the discourses of philosophy and literature into
their margin, the general text unsettles their pretensions to authority
and autonomy, and "grounds" them in what they do not control. The
deconstruction effected by the general text is both a destruction and
a "regrounding," or reinscription. In short, then, in terms of the
classical language of philosophy, "literature," or the general text, is
a grounding agency for philosophy and literature in their difference.
Yet since "literature" is a nonphenomenologizable structure, it also
ungrounds what it makes possible.

Consequently, if Derrida puts the transcendental authority of the
categories of philosophy, in particular that of being, into question,
or if he questions whether the literary operation yields to the philosophical demand of evaporating the signifier on behalf of the signified,
it is not in order to annul them but rather to understand them within
a system to which they are blind. Without the general text as that
which inscribes literature and philosophy within that angle that marks
them from a certain outside, no philosophy, no logocentrism, no

authority of being would be possible. Without the general text, there would be no literature, or what has been called literature in the history of literature. Also, it is owing to the "constituting" marginality of the general text with respect to literature and philosophy that, despite their own ideology, neither philosophy nor literature is ever simply and entirely governed by a message, a form, or their dialectical interplay. Thus, although it is only in the modern practice of writing that the dominant representation of literature is practically deconstructed, it is "well understood that long before these 'modern' texts a certain 'literary' practice was able to operate against this model, against this representation. But it is on the basis of these last texts, on the basis of the general configuration to be remarked in them, that one can best reread, without retrospective teleology, the law of the previous figures" (*P*, p. 69). Only on the basis of marginality, which modernity represents with regard to the entire tradition, has modernity, as that which already breaches that tradition from within, been able to become manifest in the first place. Yet it must not be forgotten that although the philosophical and literary text may always fail to evacuate or minimize the encompassing power of language at the benefit of the signified, such is indeed the project of philosophy and literature; consequently, they must be studied from this point of view. Literature and philosophy are constituted by the attempt to efface themselves before their content or aesthetic message.

Therefore, it should be apparent that literary criticism, in all its traditional forms, is not simply to be dismissed. Literature, or what has been called by that name, is a province within the general text; and since within these (however unsettling) boundaries it is characterized by the project of achieving transparency for its message, literary criticism as the discipline that presupposes the decidability of meaning prior to the literary text is a legitimate offspring of the very project constitutive of literature. Thus, the principles organizing different critical readings are not simply to be refuted or criticized. "They are legitimate, fruitful, true," says Derrida, especially if "they are informed by a critical vigilance" (*WD*, p. 174). These readings are perfectly valid, at least insofar as literature prior to the nineteenth century is concerned. Yet it is obvious that the delimitations of that criticism required by literary writing since Mallarmé are not without certain retroactive effects on traditional criticism. For the time being, let us consider only the case of traditional literary criticism. To begin with, let us recall that the self-effacing and deferential doubling of literature in the form of critical commentary is rooted in the history of philosophy, determined as the history of "the reflection of poetic inauguration" (*WD,* p. 28). Knowingly or not, voluntarily or not, literary criticism has been determined as the philosophy of literature. This essential link to philosophy also explains "the security with which the commentary considers the self-identity of the text, the confidence with which it carves out its contour, [and which] goes hand in hand with the tranquil assurance that leaps over the text toward its presumed content, in the direction of the pure signified" (*OG,* p. 159). Yet that which authorizes the commentary—the metaphysics of the commentary—does minimal violence to the works of literature because this metaphysics already governs the works commented upon. The critical commentary seems to be commensurate with traditional literary works. Literary criticism, then, is a philosophy of a literature which has from the outset yielded to the categories of philosophy, or in other words to literature as such. The critical enterprise is, as its name reveals, a philosophical enterprise. It is linked to the possibility of the *krinein*—that is, to the possibility of decision—of a mastery of the meaning or signified of the literary text. Since the critically assured and secured identity and prior existence of the meaning or the signified of literature is what literature exemplifies, literary criticism as such is part of what Derrida has called the *ontological* interpretation of mimesis, or metaphysical mimetologism.

One of the more specific names for such a critical approach to literature is *thematic* criticism. Although in Derrida's work it seems to be linked closely with the names of Jean-Pierre Richard and Gaston Bachelard, it is indeed a variety of phenomenological criticism representative of all criticism oriented toward content, meaning, or the signified. This becomes obvious when, in "The Double Session," Derrida circumscribes thematic criticism. It is, he writes, "at work wherever one tries to determine a meaning through a text, to pronounce a decision upon it, to decide that this or that *is* a meaning and that it is meaningful, to say that this meaning is posed, posable, or transposable as such: a theme" (*D,* p. 245). Generally speaking, a theme is a correlate of attentiveness, the result of an attentional act in which the mind is applied to an object or to that which regulates such an act. More broadly defined, it is meaning or the signified. A theme is a more fundamental notion than meaning or the signified, however, because it denotes the minimal unit of meaning or signification. It is "a nuclear unit of meaning posed there before the eye, present outside of its signifier and referring only to itself, in the last analysis, even though its identity as a signified is carved out of the horizon of an infinite perspective" (*D*, p. 250). Manifest or invisible, empty or full, the theme is an originary—that is, a constituted—unity or substance. As such a constituted unity, the theme exercises a *totalizing* function with regard to all the signifiers of a literary work. The theme secures a work's unitary meaning, its inner continuity. It is in the logic of thematism to be monistic, monological: therefore, the totalization to be achieved by a theme can succeed only if there is no other competing theme.

And yet a structural semantics that proclaims polysemy or a plurivocality in meaning—a polythematism in short—does not in principle differ from the monothematic position. By opposing the plurality of meaning to the linearity of the monothematic which always anchors itself to the "tutelary meaning, [to] the *principal* signified of a text, that is, its major referent," structural semantics undoubtedly represents an advance over what preceded it; nevertheless polythematism remains "organized within the implicit horizon of a unitary resumption of meaning" (*P*, p. 45). In *Dissemination*, Derrida writes: "Polysemy always puts out its multiplicities and variations within the *horizon*, at least, of some integral reading which contains no absolute rift, no senseless deviation—the horizon of the final parousia of a meaning at last deciphered, revealed, made present in the rich collection of its determinations" (*D*, p. 350). However belated such a final retotalization might be, however far off its realization remains, it secures by right the multiplicities' reassemblage into a unitary totality of the meaning of a text and thus secures the totality of the text as well.

All content-oriented literary criticism occupies the in-between field staked out by these two critical approaches, mono- and polythematism. Whether philosophical, sociological, or psychoanalytical, content-oriented criticism presupposes that a more or less complex simple meaning (theme) can be construed as the unifying agency of a literary work. Whatever its specific nature, the theme is a unity of meaning that serves to constitute the literary work as a totality. To the extent that this teleology of factual and instantaneous or delayed and ideal retotalization also represents the very guideline of the operation of almost all literary writing—the horizon of its *vouloir-dire*—thematic criticism of all shades is undoubtedly a very legitimate approach to such writing.

Before elaborating, however, on the essential limits of thematic criticism with respect to both modern literature and writing composed in a thematic perspective, I should emphasize that Derrida's criticism of thematism, as well the relative importance he gives to the treatment of thematic criticism, must be understood as a function of his debate with phenomenology in general. His critique must be placed in the context of the phenomenological problematics of thematization and of the unthematized.

Husserl conceives of thematization, as he defines it in *Ideas,* as the articulate formulation of what was somehow already implicit in an unthematic, unthought, and unpredicated manner in the primary natural standpoint, an attitude toward the world that is also characteristic of the natural sciences. Thematization *objectifies* the unthematized of the natural standpoint in an articulate judgment. What is the unthematized in question? It is the natural standpoint's implicit assumption of the factual existence of what it encounters in the real world around it. As Husserl has shown, this thetical positioning—as the being out there of what natural consciousness encounters—is grounded in the originary general thesis *(Generalthesis)* of the natural standpoint, according to which consciousness has as its correlate a present reality, an existing world, and only such a world.[3] Thematization, then, is a predicative taking in of the originary universal thesis, which in this manner can become, together with the natural standpoint which grounds itself in it, the object of a phenomenological *epoche.* The antinatural standpoint that is philosophical reflection puts the unthought of the natural attitude into phenomenological parenthesis in order to unearth a truly radical unthematized upon which the very possibility of the general thesis of thetic natural consciousness depends. This phenomenologically unthematized is the phenomenon of the intentionality of consciousness, a relation of consciousness to its correlate that is prethetic in that it does not posit the existence of the *intentum.* Phenomenology thus appears as a superior thematization, as the *objectification* of transcendental and ideal structures of consciousness.

Whereas, in its Husserlian form, phenomenology is an attempt to "thematize" the unthematized transcendental structures of consciousness, phenomenology in Heidegger's early philosophy determines the unthematizable as essentially in withdrawal from the "thematizations" to which it lends itself. With this, the unthematizable *escapes all possible objectification* and predication, but becomes its very condition of possibility.

When Derrida points to an irreducible phenomenological nonthematization of the operative and nonthematic concept of Idea in Husserl's work, it becomes obvious that he is continuing the phenomenological problematics of thematization, yet with the decisive difference that instead of philosophizing in the perspective of a possible and eventual recuperation of the unthematized, Derrida shows the irreducibility of phenomenological nonthematization to be the very condition of possibility of phenomenology's thematic approach (see O, p. 141). If at first Derrida's debate with such a necessary unthematizable seems to prolong its Heideggerian interpretation, it must, however, be remarked that by tying the irreducibly unthematizable to the problematics of the *difference* between the unthematized and the thematized, Derrida also removes it from the sphere of jurisdiction of *aletheia* in that the latter unfolds only as and in that difference. Derrida's critique of thematic criticism, literary or philosophical, is a challenge to phenomenology insofar as it questions the ultimate possibility of an *Endstiftung* through thematization. Its scope reaches far beyond the problematics of literary criticism and finds its meaning in his debate with phenomenology.

A first insufficiency of the literary variety of thematic criticism is that it does not take the formal and syntactical aspect of literature into account. Thematic criticism, in principle, is not interested in the code, in the formal crafting, the pure play of signifiers, the way a text is assembled, the technical manipulations of the text object, and so on. If it deigns to consider these aspects of literature at all, it is only to subjugate them to the semantic. In general one could say, with Derrida, that thematic criticism excludes from its field everything that is not of the order of the word, of the "calm unity of the verbal sign" (D, p. 255). Hence the importance of *formalist* or *structuralist* criticism as opposed to content-oriented thematic criticism. But as Derrida has argued on several occasions, formalist or structuralist criticism is as insufficient as thematic criticism, and can no more than the latter measure itself against literature, because in focusing exclusively on the formal aspect of a text, it overlooks "the genetic effects or the ('historical,' if you will) inscription of the text read *and* of the new text this criticism itself writes" (P, p. 47). Moreover, formal and structuralist criticism is oblivious to the text in its uniqueness insofar as the discovery of the formal or structural arrangement of the text is dependent on an eidetic reduction that lays that arrangement bare as the text's essential truth. The "structure whose essential permanence becomes the prime preoccupation" of the structuralist commentary neutralizes the specificity of the text and raises it to the status of a mere example of the transcendental structure or universal essence of thought (WD, p. 170).

It thus appears that both forms of criticism are rigorously com-

plementary and complicitous. Once again, it must be emphasized that
these two brands of criticism—which together with dialectical criticism exhaust in principle all the possibilities of literary criticism—are
not simply to be rejected, to the extent that, within the history of
literature, literature has indeed conformed to philosophy. Yet one
cannot avoid recognizing that if certain literary texts, a certain literary
writing, as Derrida points out, put philosophy into question, then this
subversion will also cause the various forms of literary criticism to
vacillate. If philosophy is subverted by certain literary texts, then all
forms of literary criticism established in the shadow of the multiple
philosophies are similarly threatened. One could go so far as to say
that the very reasons why Derrida is interested in literature are reasons
that subvert the very possibility of the institution of literary criticism
as such. This subversion takes place through the tracing of the limits
of literary criticism. It is thus a subversion that is not absolute, that
is by no means an annihilation of literary criticism, but that is a
decapitation, so to speak, of its pretensions, and thus an assignment
of its locus. Therefore it is equally right to say that the very future
of the institution of literary criticism hinges on its deconstruction.

Since Mallarmé, say, modern literary texts offer that writing that
delimits both forms of criticism (and particularly the thematic); it
delimits them to a degree that not only makes apparent criticism's
inability to account for such writing, but suggests that the appropri-
ateness of criticism to what has hitherto been called literature is itself
questionable. Throughout his work, Derrida has tried to demonstrate
that this sort of text will always defy and baffle criticism, not because
criticism will not yet have sufficiently sharpened its analytical tools,
but for more essential reasons that preclude the decidability all criticism presupposes. Indeed, such texts rigorously sweep away the possibility of decision, of mastering their meaning as unity, that is, of
mastering their meaning at all. But the fact that these texts cannot be
thematically exhausted in terms of content or form does not at all
imply, as Derrida points out in *Spurs,* that one ought to abandon the
search for their meaning. Such a conclusion would amount to an
aestheticizing and obscurantist reaction by the *hermeneuein,* that is,
by understanding. This search for meaning should not be abandoned
but rather intensified, and in such a manner as to account for the
ultimate possibility of these texts' meaninglessness. The gesture of
thought required to deal with the structural possibility of meaninglessness, however, is thoroughly alien to the critical gesture, which
presupposes the decidability of its attentional object, its theme. But

since the textual structure of the possibility of the meaninglessness of certain texts owes its structural status to the impossibility of its own thematization, the gesture of thought that takes this structural possibility into account must *affirm* its unthematizability. It must, in other words, affirm an ultimate impossibility of knowing this nonthematic condition of possibility, an impossibility that is the result neither of its unfathomable depth nor of the finitude of its human beholder but rather of the structural nature of this condition. Indeed, such a structure must withdraw itself from being mastered in totality, from being decidable, from being itself a theme if it is to account for the possibility of the meaninglessness of a text. If it could be fully determined, in fact, it would be the text's ultimate meaning and would no longer account for its essential undecidability. If, *in the last resort,* the unthematizable because undecidable agencies of modern literary texts—agencies that are not of the order of image or concept, content or form, but that are textual structures—radically subvert the possibility of literary hermeneutics, it is because they represent the limits from which understanding and knowing become possible. Therefore, understanding its gesture of unifying deciphering must be pushed to exasperation in order to account as rigorously as possible for its structural limits. Consequently, far from being a sort of empiricist agnosticism or skepticism, deconstruction is, so to speak, a hypercognition of a truth beyond truth, "a supplement of truthless truth," to the extent that it also inscribes the structural limits of cognition—thus, however, radically altering the concept of cognition as such.[4]

At this point the question of the relation between deconstruction and literary criticism may lend itself to a more decisive clarification. Undoubtedly Derrida's opinion is that literary criticism fails to account for the specificity of the literary work of art, especially insofar as it proceeds thematically. This specificity is lost at the moment we bring to it, as Heidegger says, "only this or that dull sense of unambiguous meaning."[5] What is wrong with literary criticism, to refer to Heidegger once again, is that it experiences too little in the neighborhood of the work and that it expresses its already diminished experience too crudely and too literally.[6] Yet this critique of criticism is not rooted in a moral or aesthetic indignation over criticism's inability to catch the subjective existence, the originality and force of the work, or the singularity of the beautiful. It is just as little an invitation to take hold of that uniqueness by further and further decomposition. This critique of criticism acknowledges, first of all, that the flaws of literary criticism owing to the uniqueness of works of literature are intrinsically linked to literary criticism's status as commentary. As commentary, certainly the discourse of criticism presupposes the works' uniqueness. But as commentary it can only turn that work into an example of a universal truth. Literary criticism can overcome these fatal deficiencies only under the condition that "it destroy itself as commentary by exhuming the [originary] unity in which is embedded the differences" between work and commentary, force and signification, literature and philosophy, and so on. (*WD*, p. 174). Such a liberation from its status as mere commentary would coincide with its liberation from philosophy. If literary criticism were to open itself to an exchange with literary writing, if it were to become attentive to what takes place in texts, particularly in modern texts, it—in essence a philosophy of literature, and thus dependent on the master discourse of philosophy—would have to do so all by itself. In one of his first essays Derrida writes: "Criticism, if it is called upon to enter into explication and exchange with literary writing, some day will not have to wait for this resistance first to be organized into a 'philosophy' which would govern some methodology of aesthetics whose principles criticism would receive" (*WD*, 28).

Yet this independence cannot imply a rejection of all analytical approaches to the text. Once again, this would represent a mere aesthetic response, programed by philosophy. Literary criticism must manage a place for the redoubling commentary, for its epistemological project, lest it become entirely subjective, illusory, and limited. Without the recognition of and respect for all the classical exigencies, critical production runs the risk of becoming idiosyncratic and of authorizing itself to advance almost anything. What is necessary, then, if literary criticism is to address literary writing is a connection of deconstruction and scholarship, of deconstruction and tradition. The program that Derrida developed for a "science" of grammatology is also valid for a literary criticism liberated from philosophy: "Now a reflection must clearly be undertaken, within which the 'positive' discovery and the 'deconstruction' of the history of metaphysics, in all its concepts, are controlled reciprocally, minutely, laboriously" (*OG*, p. 83). If such a "critical" discourse, liberated from philosophy but extremely aware of the latter's exigencies, were to achieve an exchange with literary writing, this exchange would not take place by poeticizing the critical discourse, as the Romantics intended, but through reflecting on the originary unity in which is embedded the differences that organize the literary and critical discourses. Whereas a poeticization of the critical discourse would lead to a mutual overcoming of both in a higher, fuller synthetic unity, and would thus yield to the most elementary telos of philosophical thinking, a reflection on the originary unity in which literature and criticism are embedded maintains their difference and respective uniqueness, while at the same time accounting for this difference. The originary unity by which criticism and literature come into an exchange precisely insofar as they are unique does not, therefore, represent a more primitive or higher synthetic unity preceding or following the process of differentiation. It must be a unity of the order of that which Derrida has called "infrastructures." In other words, a "critical" discourse in full respect of the uniqueness of literature would have to be a discourse productive of such infrastructures, also called "signifying structures."

The contact between literary writing and criticism is established when the latter exhibits the phenomenologically unthematizable unities, that is, the nonsynthetic unities that organize and limit the conceptual differences that make up the critical discourse. It is here that one can glimpse what deconstructive literary criticism could be about. Without confounding itself with the deconstruction of philosophy, the specificity of a deconstructive literary criticism would proceed from the signifying structures that reinscribe, and thus account for, the differences constitutive of the literary work and the critical discourse. Except marginally, Derrida has not systematically undertaken to establish the particular infrastructures of the critical discourse. More than once he has shown a variety of forms of literary criticism to be absolutely insensible to the most insistent operations of literary writing. Yet while questioning the originary nonsynthetic unity of literature and philosophy, Derrida has, by reading literary writing itself, exhibited precisely those structures of textuality and "literature" with which literary criticism is to enter into exchange. Still, the kind of infrastructures that underlie this exchange have not yet been developed as such.

The phenomenologically unthematizable unities—that is, supplementarity, *mise-en-abyme,* and re-mark—that Derrida has exhibited in his reading of literary texts are numerous, as are those (writing, text, quasimetaphoricity, and so on) that resulted at first from a deconstruction of the philosophical discourse. A certain brand of literary criticism has avidly appropriated these notions in a thematic manner, losing sight of what these notions were initially meant to achieve. In addition, only on rare occasions have the critical discourses in which they have been accommodated opened themselves to these notions via a deconstruction of themselves as critical discourses. Such a deconstruction, however, is the condition under which they would have been able to establish contact not only with literary writing but with the deconstruction of philosophy as well.

Just as any possible extrapolation of Derrida's philosophy for literary criticism can be fruitful only if even his developments concerning literature and literary criticism are understood within the boundaries of his debate with the philosophy of phenomenology, all the so-called infrastructures can be put to use in literary criticism only on the condition that their status is fully recognized, as well as their purpose, or what, precisely, they are to achieve in Derrida's controversy with phenomenology. Of the many infrastructures that catch the literary critic's eye, of the many issues of interest to the critic and upon which Derrida has elaborated, such as genre, mimesis, plot, event, fiction, and so on, I shall examine only three notions, which have been appropriated by a certain criticism: writing, text, and metaphor.

11

The Inscription
of Universality

❧

WRITING

Rather than discussing in detail the numerous analyses in which Derrida has developed the notion of writing, I shall attempt only to define in general the system of essential predicates which he calls writing. Before I venture a definition, however, it is imperative to outline the context in which the problematics of writing becomes a subject of meditation for Derrida. Since this context is manifold, I shall restrict the discussion to certain instances in which "writing" becomes problematized.

In the first instance, the notion of writing becomes a crucial issue in Derrida's work as early as *Edmund Husserl's Origin of Geometry: An Introduction.* As Derrida points out, it is at least striking that Husserl, in "The Origin of Geometry," resorts to the very possibility of writing—in flagrant disregard of the contempt in which writing is held throughout the history of philosophy—in order to secure the absolute ideal objectivity, and thus the traditionalization of meaning. Husserl argues that without such scriptural spatio-temporality and the ultimate objectification that it permits, all meaning would "as yet remain captive of the *de facto* and actual intentionality of a speaking subject or community of speaking subjects" (O, pp. 87–88). The ultimate liberation of ideality, its highest possibility of *constitution,* that which inaugurates its iterability and its relation to a universal transcendental subjectivity guaranteeing its intelligibility in the absence of all actually present subjective intentionality, is thus the possibility of being written. Note that it is not the factual spatio-temporalization by writing that ensures meaning's ideality but, more primordially, only its possibility. Considering the context, writing "is no longer only the worldly and mnemotechnical aid to a truth whose own being-sense would dispense with all writing down. The possibility or necessity of being incarnated in a graphic sign is no longer simply extrinsic and factual in comparison with ideal Objectivity: it is the *sine qua non* condition of Objectivity's internal completion" (*O*, pp. 88–89). Hence, the effect and the value of transcendentality become linked in an essential manner to the possibility of writing.

In the second instance, as Derrida has shown in *Of Grammatology*, the attempt to account for the principle of difference, differentiality or diacriticity, as conditions of signification, forces Saussure, in spite of his initial condemnation of writing, to fall back on scriptural metaphors. Here, it appears that meaning is dependent on a determination through alterity, on an irreducible relation to otherness. Since Saussure is concerned with linguistic meaning, and since the Other par excellence of speech is writing, the recourse to scriptural metaphors to expose the principle of differentiality cannot be fortuitous.

In the third instance, in "Plato's Pharmacy," Derrida demonstrates how Plato, in *Phaedrus*, after having severely rejected Thot's invention of writing as a mnemotechnical tool because of its detrimental effects on living memory, cannot avoid turning to a "metaphor" borrowed from the order of the very thing he is trying to exclude—the order of the simulacrum—at the precise moment when he tries to define the specificity of the living discourse that he wants to oppose to writing. By determining the living discourse as an *inscription* of truth in the soul, the self-presence of speech, or the intelligible, is made to hinge structurally, as far as its possibility is concerned, on the empty repetition of writing, or the copy, previously excluded.

And in the fourth instance, on several occasions Derrida has pointed out the "contradiction" that exists between the philosopher's condemnation of writing and the necessity of effectuating this condemnation in writing. Thus, for instance in *Marges*, "the philosopher writes against writing, writes in order to make good the loss of writing, and by this very gesture forgets and denies what occurs by his hand." If it is true that this "contradiction" is in no way contingent, then philosophical ideality, its logocentric ethos, is constituted "from its first breath as a system of differential traces, that is as writing before the letter" (*M*, p. 291). The discursive valorization of the *phone*—logocentrism in short—appears to be irreducibly linked to the exteriority, alterity, discontinuity, and delaying effect of writing.

However succinct, these four contextual examples should suffice to indicate that the problem addressed under the title of "writing" concerns the paradoxical economy of the philosophical condemnation and (metaphorical) rehabilitation of writing. It is, therefore, of great importance that we realize that the analysis of the constitutive function of writing for ideality, transcendentality, signification, speech, philosophical discourse, and so on does not imply a rehabilitation of writing as it has been determined by philosophy. Nor do these analyses entail any reevaluation of literary writing with respect to philosophical discourse. Derrida, from *Of Grammatology* on, has repeatedly suggested that the question cannot simply be one of reversing the traditional hierarchy in order to make writing innocent (*OG*, p. 37). Nor can it be a question "of returning to writing its rights, its superiority or its dignity" (*D*, p. 182). "Nothing would be more ridiculously mystifying than such an ethical or axiological reversal, returning a prerogative or some elder's right to writing" (*P*, p. 13). Indeed, such a restoration of writing to a prelapsarian state, beyond the debased and degraded field of history, would still yield to the category of *abasement,* which "is precisely the *representation* of writing, of its situation *in* the philosophical hierarchy" (*P*, p. 53). Therefore, all substitution of a graphocentrism for logocentrism is thoroughly excluded. The order of dependence between speech and writing cannot be argued. As long as one thinks of speech and writing in conceptual terms, writing *must* efface itself before speech as its truth. As I have suggested, Derrida's analyses pursue a different goal, aiming to establish the law that governs the "contradictions" of philosophical discourse, the law that explains why and how what is supposedly pure, ideal, transcendental, and so on is unavoidably contaminated by its opposite, and why speech in its purity cannot be thought except by referring to writing. To deconstruct the ethico-theoretical hierarchy of speech and writing—a deconstruction that includes an account of the factual return of debased writing in the form of metaphors (for instance) in the very attempt to describe the purity and self-presence of the logos— is to construct the signifying structure or system of referral that accounts for both exclusion and contamination.

The name that Derrida gives to this infrastructure, or rather, as we shall see, cluster of infrastructures, is that of the arche-synthesis of "writing," or more properly, general writing or *arche-writing.* As such a synthesis, arche- or proto-writing is necessarily "transcendental" in the sense that I have established. Since, as a law, it is able to account for the economy that organizes the various relations of speech and what is commonly called writing, it exceeds the conceptual symmetry of speech and writing. Derrida writes, "The concepts of general writing can be *read* only on the condition that they be deported, shifted outside the symmetrical alternatives from which, however, they seem to be taken, and in which, after a fashion, they must also remain" (*WD*, p. 272). The concepts of writing and speech, as they are commonly used, cannot serve to explain arche-writing. Writing, in its colloquial sense, as the visible and coded script in the world, is only the metaphor of general writing (*WD*, p. 209). Major writing, as Derrida calls the arche-synthesis of writing in the context of his essay on Bataille, and which is opposed to minor writing, is not reducible to the sensible or visible presence of the graphic or the "literal" (*P*, p. 65). General writing, having nothing mundane about it, is beyond being, *epekeina tes ousias* (*D*, p. 168). In short, writing, in the sense of arche-writing, a concept that has been so easily accommodated by so-called deconstructionist criticism, has little or nothing to do with the (anthropological, subjective, and so on) act of writing, with the psychological pleasures and displeasures to which it gives rise, with an instrument of notation or communication, or with an aesthetic and merely self-referential signifying practice. Not only have the so-called deconstructionists misconstrued the signification, and consequently the status, of arche-writing; philosophers have as well. Taking "writing" in Derrida to mean the scriptive and worldly practice of writing, a practice that would differ from its usual philosophical interpretation to the extent that the object it is about is no longer the world but texts, Rorty, for instance, in "Philosophy as a Kind of Writing," is bound to misunderstand it as literary writing.[1] Writing in Derrida's sense is not determined by what it is about, nor has it anything essentially in common with the signs present on the page, or with the (literary or philosophical) production of these signs. Neither is it the essence of the literal sign or of the act of its engendering. Despite its quasitranscendental status, or precisely because of it, arche-writing is not essence. It has no proper value of its own, positive or negative (*D*, p. 105). Arche-writing is *only*, if one may say so, the quasitranscendental synthesis that accounts for the necessary corruption of the idealities, or transcendentals of all sorts, by what they are defined against, and at the very moment of their constitution. Arche-writing is a construct aimed at resolving the philosophical problem of the very possibility (not primarily the empirical fact, which always suffers exceptions) of the usurpation, parasitism, and contamination of an ideality, a generality, a universal by what is considered its other, its exterior, its incarnation, its appearance, and so on. It is nothing but the "originary" structural unity that accounts for the philosophical "contradiction," or instance, that the ethos of philosophy, the value of the proximity in the "hearing-oneself-speak," can establish itself only through a reference to what it is not—writing—as well as to what it resents as the practice of writing. It is not writing itself that is at issue here but the system of relations that link it to speech. It is this system that Derrida names general writing. If Derrida persists in calling this system writing, although writing in the vulgar sense is its dissimulation in the form of a metaphor, it is because, he admits, arche-writing essentially communicates with the vulgar concept of writing, insofar as, historically speaking, writing has signified by its situation "the most formidable difference" from speech (OG, p. 56). Writing or its Other, arche-writing, is, *within* the boundaries of philosophy, a most likely name for the originary structural unity in question.

Rather than being the exterior double of speech, proto-writing is that synthetic structure of referral that accounts for the fact that in the play of differences between, say, speech and writing, ideality and writing, meaning and writing, philosophical discourse and writing, to name only those to which I have already alluded, the pole allegedly present in and of itself, which allegedly refers to itself alone, must in fact constitute itself through the element that it abases. Because this synthetic structure demands the detour of all self-referential, self-reflexive, and self-present elements through the Other, arche-writing can be said to be the unity of difference that opens and comprehends language as the common root of both speech and writing. Obviously enough, this detour is also what fundamentally limits all self-appropriating acts. Thus writing, in Derrida's sense, links together in one structure the possibility of self-reflexive ideality and its irreducible limits, both owing to the same referral to otherness, without which no ideality could ever hope to found itself.

As the originary difference within which an element can begin to refer to itself on the sole condition that it refer to the element it abases as exterior to it, and which seems to be entirely derivative, arche-writing is a synthetic concept of sorts. One might wish to call such an originary synthesis ideal, in the sense that Kantian transcendental functions are ideal. Yet how could a structure that accounts for both the possibility and impossibility of idealities still deserve to be called "ideal," particularly since the originary synthesis in question, unlike Kantian originary syntheses, is not a structure of unification and totalization? Although synthetic, because it links together in one structure of possibility self-reference and reference to Other, the unity of arche-writing cannot be a totality precisely because it is a structure of referral to Other, and hence of self-deferral. In the same way that this structure allows nothing to be a mere self-present element in a system of differences, it cannot present itself as a mere self-contained structural totality either. Thus, despite its seemingly ideal status, it is an idea not in the Kantian but rather in a Husserlian sense, provided, of course, that one takes into consideration Derrida's analyses of that notion in *Edmund Husserl's Origin of Geometry.* Arche-writing, while not being reducible to any ordinary intraworldliness, is not, for that matter, simply transcendental or ideal. It is in fact a synthesis which, by respecting both orders, erases their distinction. Arche-writing foregrounds this distinction by opening the difference between the origin of the world and intraworldly being. In a strange way, arche-writing is at once both more and less transcendental than the Kantian transcendental originary syntheses.

As I have suggested, arche-writing, instead of being one synthesis, is a cluster of syntheses. In *Of Grammatology,* Derrida holds that arche-writing opens "in one and the same possibility, temporalization, as well as relationship with the other and language" (*OG,* p. 60). In other words, arche-writing is a cluster of infrastructures. It is made up of the infrastructures differance (spacing/temporization), archetrace, iterability, and so on, which Derrida analyzed separately and in great detail following his discovery of the problematics of arche-writing. If the infrastructures are minimal syntheses, then general writing is a synthesis of syntheses. Writing in the sense of arche-writing is thus a possible name for what I have called the system of the infrastructures. It names the "unity" of *inscription in general.* But it is equally correct to say that writing is only a representative of the infrastructures in question. Because the infrastructures *do not exist,* because they are not entities, not beings-present, writing cannot be said to be the arche-trace, differance, or iterability *itself.* Derrida's assertion in *Of Grammatology* that "writing is one of the representatives of the trace in general, it is not the trace itself" holds true for all other infrastructures as well (*OG,* p. 167). Therefore, the task of thinking the infrastructural chain *in general* remains, even if, in order to think this generality, we must settle for the structural limits of generality itself.

Let us linger for a moment on the nature of the unity of the complex, because clustered, syntheses of writing. The individual and singular infrastructural syntheses are syntheses in a new sense. These syntheses, which "originarily" ground the classical distinctions of the One and the manifold, the Self and the Other, essence and its appearances, and so on, and thus replace and reinterpret the classical unity of meaning, are not dialectical syntheses. They do not reground the distinctions of the One and the manifold, the Self and the Other, as would a more essential totality, with respect to which the elements would be the bipolar and separated representations. The unity that characterizes the infrastructures is not that of the One as opposed to the manifold, not that of the dialectical One encompassing both the One and the manifold. The infrastructures have the unity of the difference between the One and the manifold *and* their dialectical synthesis in the One that dialectically encompasses both. Since within the unity of this difference both the opposition and the sublation of opposition takes place, this unity is more originary than either. Thus its unity grounds the One while at the same time representing its limit. Although a unity, it is not *one* unity, not an essence, origin, or totality. It is plural by nature. General writing as a cluster of infrastructures, however, is plural not only because it links a variety of self-deporting structures but also because it is operative on a variety of levels. All these different levels of writing do not form one totality. "There is more than one kind of writing: the different forms and genres are irreducible" (*D*, p. 242). By nature there can be no such thing as a mono-writing; writing is plural by essence. To suspect "writing" of monism is sheer absurdity; the different forms and genres of writing call for rigorous distinction. The pluralism of writing, however, is not a liberal—that is, ultimately totalizable (and hence monistic)—pluralism but is witness to a savage pluralism, embracing heterogenous forms of writing. What these irreducible forms of writing have in common is the generality of writing as the production of generality and its limitation. "The heterogeneity of different writings is writing itself, the graft. It is numerous from the first or it *is not*" (*D*, p. 356). The generality of writing consists in the operation of referring to irreducible Otherness, of grafting one form of writing onto another. In short, it represents the generality of inscription.[2]

Inscription in general is therefore to be considered as the specificity, so to speak, of the clustered synthesis of arche-writing. *Inscription in general*—that is to say, *the generality of the inscription or institution of the general*—is the feature common to a variety of infrastructures linked together in what is called general writing. Writing as arche-writing is thus not reducible to the production of durable signs. It affirms the originarity of the trace *as* trace over the general and universal in what most properly defines them—their self-sufficient one-ness. Needless to say, any attempts by literary criticism to seek self-authorization in the Derridean notion of writing would have to con-front the full philosophical impact of its delimiting thrust. At stake is not only the universality of the discourse of literary criticism but also its escapist alternative tendency of particularization and private self-discovery. Nor is the latter free of the claim to generality; if it were, it would not be heard.

TEXT

Toward an Entirely Different Text

On several occasions, Derrida has clearly emphasized that the gen-eralization of the concept of the text in no way implies a "theology of the Text" (D, p. 258). In *Positions* he plainly acknowledges that the "necessary generalization of the concept of text, its extension with no simple exterior limit (which also supposes the passage through metaphysical opposition)," must not wind up "(under the influence of very precise interests, reactive forces determined to lead work astray into confusion) . . . as the definition of a new self-interiority, a new 'idealism' if you will, of the text" (P, p. 66). The literary critics, as well as those philosophers who have been speaking of textualism, pantextualism, text-fetishism, and things of that sort with respect to Derrida's philosophy, therefore share a similar if not symmetrical confusion.

Before attempting to define precisely what Derrida means by the "general text," I should like to enumerate the traditional ways of understanding *text*. Paradoxically, these traditional meanings of *text*, from which Derrida's concept of text must be clearly set off, also happen to be those attributed to Derrida by literary critics and a number of philosophers. We can distinguish three kinds of concepts of text:

1. A text can be determined as the sensibly palpable, empirically encounterable transcription of an oral discourse, as a material opacity that must efface itself before its oral reactivation and the meaning it represents. In the same way, however, as writing in the sense of arche-writing has little or nothing in common with the scriptural figures on the page, "text" in Derrida's understanding is not reducible "*either* to the sensible or visible presence of the graphic or the 'literal' " (P, p. 65).

2. A text can be determined as an intelligible object. According to this conception, which is indeed the prevailing one, a text is thought to correspond to the signifying organization of diacritically or differentially determined signifiers and signifieds. In order to prove that this definition of *text* cannot coincide with Derrida's "general text," let me merely quote the following passage from *Dissemination:* "a text is never truly made up of 'signs' or 'signifiers' " (*D*, p. 261).

3. Another, and perhaps final, concept conceives of *text* as the dialectical sublation, either as "form" or "content," of both its sensible and ideal determinations. Unlike the previous definitions of *text*, which, by virtue of their opposition and isolation, could be termed intellectual *(verstandesmässige)* concepts, the dialectical determination of text is its reasonable or rational concept. All those analyses that link a text's sensible and intelligible constituents, as well as the etymologies, allusions, implications, and *sous-entendues* of all sorts, within one totality of either form or content, understand *text* within the limits of speculative philosophy (Idealist or Romantic). By exhibiting the text as the totality of a positioning and reciprocal annihilation of oppositions, as the play of a mutual limitation of self and Otherness, the text is determined as the milieu, the element of *Aufhebung*, or, which is the same, of the dialectical exposition of that which is implied in its very concept *(was im Begriffe liegt)*. Instead of recalling Derrida's sustained critique of such a concept of text, it is enough here to recall his lapidary remark, "The text excludes dialectics" (*D*, p. 122).

The generalized concept of text overrides all three definitions, "all those boundaries that form the running border of what used to be called a text."[3] Yet does this delimitation and consecutive generalization of the concept of the text imply that there is nothing outside the text, that everything is text, and that all that is is only text? One knows the indignation excited by Derrida's proposition, taken out of context and transformed into a slogan, "*Il n'y a pas de hors-texte (There is nothing outside the text)*" (*OG*, p. 158). As recently as 1983 a critic could still write that "the most distinctive element in Derrida," and "of course the element that has appealed to some of the experts about texts—literary critics," is his "reduction of thought and experience to 'textuality.' "[4] Before establishing that the statement that there is no "extra-text" does not allow the inference that all is, therefore, text—and this even less if one understands "text" in any of the traditional manners—and before venturing an interpretation of the proposition in question, one ought to recall that according to Derrida the generalized concept of text is precisely that which exceeds the

traditional determination of text as a totality. In whatever terms—
empirical, idealist, or dialectical—*text* is defined, it always implies a
closure upon itself with a clear inside and outside, whether it is the
empirical closure of the unity of a corpus, the intelligible unity of a
work, or the dialectical totality of its formal or thematic meanings.
Yet if the general text delimits the traditional totalizing concepts of
what has been called text, it also implies that the entirely different
text, because it is no longer a totality, has no inside or outside. The
generalized text is not something that is closed upon itself in such a
manner that its limits would demarcate an inside from an outside. As
"Living On" argues, the general text is rather that border itself, from
which the assignment of insides and outsides takes place, as well as
where this distinction ultimately collapses.

Before I take up this definition of the general text, let us remember
that the idea of an outside makes sense only with regard to the common notions of text. The generalization of the text, however, is not
an extension or application of the traditional concept of the text to
its traditional outside. Derrida writes in "Living On": "It was never
our wish to extend the reassuring notion of the text to a whole extratextual realm and to transform the world into a library by doing away
with all boundaries, all framework, all sharp edges . . . , but that we
sought rather to work out the theoretical and practical system of these
margins, these borders, once more, from the ground up."[5] In *Positions*,
after cautioning against an idealism of the text, Derrida remarks that
"we must avoid having the indispensable critique of a certain naive
relationship to the signified or the referent, to sense or meaning,
remain fixed in a suspension, that is, a pure and simple suppression,
of meaning or reference" (*P*, p. 66). In other words, the rejection of
the text as a totality dependent on a unifying last reason or transcendental signified does not simply mean the suppression of the text's
referentiality.

Indeed, Derrida has never contested that texts, or for that matter
"literature," are mimetic or referential. "The Double Session" is ample
proof of this. What Derrida calls the general text is characterized, if
not constituted, by reference, but that does not imply that the term
refers to a referent that would come to stop and thus exhaust its
reference. The general text is mimetic, but its mimesis is not suspended
upon an ultimate imitated and is thus not subject to truth as *adequatio*,
or even, as Derrida argues in "The Double Session," to truth as
aletheia. But, as he remarks in this essay, although the referent is
lifted, "reference remains" (*D*, p. 211). Though truth is set side from

the general text, relation to truth, projected coinciding, remains. In short, then, the general text *is about,* yet without a decidable referent that could saturate, in the last instance, its referral to Otherness. "There is no extra-text" means just this: nothing outside the text can, like a last reason, assume a *fulfilling function (Erfüllungsfunktion)* of the textual referrals. It certainly does not permit the conclusion that there is nothing else but texts, or for that matter, that all is language.

At this point it should also become clear what philosophical problem is met by the general text. If the text is characterized by reference, and if no extra-text (the existence of which is not being put into question) can ever hope to saturate the text's referring function, then it represents, phenomenologically speaking, an intentionality without an intentum. Such a decapitated or beheaded intentionality, because it lacks a decidable intentum, cannot be *fulfilled* by a corresponding extraintentional referent. The text, as defined by Derrida, does not do away with the phenomenological idea of intentionality. On the contrary, it inscribes and displaces the intentionality of consciousness with its corresponding intentum and its possibly fulfilling object. From a grounding perspective, the text as an intentionality without intentum is of a greater power of formalization than phenomenological inten-tionality, since the unsaturatable relation to Otherness that charac-terizes it can serve as the matrix to account for the possibility of phenomenological intentionality, and thus of the principle of all prin-ciples, evidence, as a necessary effect. As such it can serve to account also for the structural impossibility of a final coincidence of intention and its intentum.

Besides interpreting Derrida's statement "there is no extra-text" to mean that all is text, critics pro and con have also inferred from this statement that the text is about itself. But if the text is characterized by structures of referral without a referent, then it can be as little about itself as it is about something extratextual. Derrida could just as well have stated *there is no inside of the text.* As the textual structure of the re-mark demonstrates, for structural reasons the text has no identity or self with which to coincide. Though the text necessarily refers to itself, this movement never comes to completion. In addition, all self-referral, as shown in "The Double Session," is grafted on a structurally endless referral to other determinate texts, thus making all textual self-reflexivity *ultimately* impossible.

To sum up, then, what does Derrida mean when he claims in *Of Grammatology* that there is no extra-text, or when in *Dissemination* he writes, "There is nothing before the text; there is no pretext that is not already a text" (*D*, p. 328)? Rather than negating the existence of everything besides the text, these statements simply indicate that the general text ("literature" which is not literature) has no extratextual signified or referent, no last reason, whether empirical or intelligible, at which its referring function could come to a final halt. It also means that the generalized text does not refer to something outside the system of referentiality that could do without being referred to, but that its referentiality is such that it extends abysmally out of sight without, however, entailing the text's self-reflexivity. The absence of all extra-text, about which one could decide independently of the textual system of referral, implies that there is no one final meaning to the text. Again, it must be repeated that this is so not because of the general text's semantic wealth or unfathomable depth, nor because of the finitude of its human decipherer, but for structural reasons.

Let me add that although there is no extra-text with respect to the general text, it does not follow from this that the novel, the poem, the short story, or more generally the literary work of art, has no extra-text. First, the absence of an extra-text is affirmed in the case of the general text only and not of the traditional, reassuring because totalizing, concepts of text. The novel, the poem, the short story, and so forth may depend on the preexistence of a totalizing referent or signified outside the text, especially if they are conceived within the perspective of mimetologism. But it may also be that their meaning cannot be exhausted in such a manner. If that possibility exists at all, however, it must be accounted for. The notion of the general text is nothing other than a philosophical "construct" which gives that essential possibility its full importance.

Since all literary criticism hinges on the possibility of decidability with respect to an extra- or intra-text, the notion of the general text ruins the very project of that discipline. But at the same time, the notion of the general text opens a horizon of new possibilities in literary studies. The concept of text that we are thus invited to think has to be understood in an infrastructural sense. What this means is that the concept of the *general* text is to be thought, beyond the distinction between empirical and merely universal concepts, as a "truly" or *general ideal* concept. Nothing empirical or abstractly universal—abstracted, that is, from empirical representations—may enter the determination of the law of the text. To interpret the general text in an infrastructural sense is not, however, to make the text *one* infrastructure. As we shall see, it is on the contrary like writing a cluster of infrastructures. To render this infrastructural sense of the text more precise, we must next determine its ontological status.

Of Textual Ontology

Like Sartre's inquiry "What is literature?" the more recent question "What is a text?"—the title of an essay by Paul Ricoeur published in a festschrift for H. G. Gadamer—is a hermeneutical question whose modalities and form anticipate the answer.[6] The question "What is a text?" asks for the whatness, the essence, the being of the text. It consequently presupposes, by its very nature as a question concerning the *ti esti* of the text, the existence, the being (or absence as a negative mode of presence) of the essence of the textuality of the text. Textuality, in this sense, grounds the being of the text, causes the text to come into presence, into existence. Of course, textuality as the ontological ground of the text can accept a variety of determinations, corresponding respectively to the three definitions of text outlined above. Whether determined by empirical or ideal criteria or as a synthesis of both, textuality is an essence or substance, that is, a more authentic and more fundamental mode of being than that of the texts which, in their empirical variety, depend on it as to their last reason. Yet if textuality in this sense is to account for the being or presence of texts, of the empirically given texts, it must unquestionably fail, since it is itself a mode of being (however authentic or originary). Thus it is incapable in the last instance of explaining the being of the text. As Heidegger would have said, it is as if one wanted to derive the source from the river. The ontological horizon which inevitably comprises the question "What is a text?" limits the explicatory power of textuality as an answer to the "nature" of texts.

It is my contention that, with the notion of the general text, Derrida transcends the opposition of text and textuality, of appearance and essence, by paradoxically denying all ontological status to the general text. "There is no present text in general, and there is not even a past present text, a text which is past as having been present" (*WD*, p. 211). If, according to Aristotle's definition, essence is what has been *(to ti en einai)*, then the general text certainly is no essence. Indeed, the general text's "preontological" and "preessential" status enables it to account for the fundamental difficulties that all theories of textuality must face: to have to presuppose in their explanation precisely what they are supposed to account for—the being or presence of their object.

In what follows I shall attempt to clarify further the notion of the general text by commenting on a seemingly contradictory statement by Derrida in "The Double Session": "If the text does not, to the letter, exist, then *there is [il y a]* perhaps a text" (D, p. 270). What this statement claims is that *there may be* a text only on condition that, to the letter, or literally, it does *not exist.* The proposition contends that in order for a text to be there, it must be deprived of all property, ownness, essence, and so on. It is a statement that makes the being there of a text dependent on its independence from what one usually associates with the text, the existence of the letter (or signifier), as either a material or ideal substratum. The being there of a text is thus made to hinge on the nonexistence of the text as either an empirical substratum or an intelligible essence. In short, the text is said to *be there* only if it *is not,* if it is not endowed with being, if it lacks presence. Obviously this cannot mean that there would be text solely *in absentia,* as one could hastily conclude; absence is another mode of presence and being. One must, consequently, qualify Derrida's statement as follows: there is perhaps a text if it does not, to the letter, exist, which is not, however, to say that it would therefore be a nonpresence, a nonexistence, an absence, or a mere *nihil negativum.*

What the statement enunciates, that for a text to be there it must not exist, is not reversible. The nonexistence of the text is not a sufficient condition for there to be a text. This is marked by the adverb *perhaps,* although this meaning does not, as we shall see, exhaust that word's function in the proposition. These few remarks may clarify in part the meaning of Derrida's statement, but they do not do away with the obscure and seemingly contradictory nature of a statement that affirms that the being-there of a text depends on its nonexistence. Yet there is nothing contradictory about this statement, for *to be there* and *to exist* do not mean the same thing. Instead of being synonyms, they represent two entirely heterogeneous levels of description. *To exist* means to be present, to be endowed with being and meaning, and applies to the order of both the sensible and the intelligible. *To exist* is a qualification of phenomena in the Husserlian sense. *To be there,* or more precisely *there is,* which translates the German *es gibt,* has, first of all, the ideal meaning this expression has in mathematics. Second, *there is* serves to express the pure idea of the pure possibility of a meaning *in specie: there is* is thus to be said of truly general or ideal concepts. Third, *there is* characterizes the mode of giveness of phenomena in general, and of Being in particular, as the phenomenon par excellence. According to Heidegger, Being as the radical ground of all beings cannot itself be; it only has the mode of *being there*. If Being were to exist, if it were to be endowed with being, it would be a ground unable to account for that which it has been summoned to explain: the Being of beings. Derrida, who through a meditation on the general text aims at regrounding or rather reinscribing the difference between text and textuality, between the empirical manifold of texts and the text's ever-present essence, at first uses this Heideggerian qualification to characterize the general text. *There is,* perhaps, a general text.

The general text accounts for the difference between texts and textuality, both of which are endowed with modes of being, or presence, only on the condition that it (the general text) does not exist. Yet it does not partake in any ontology, however fundamental. The question *what is* the general text is an illegitimate question. To ask the hermeneutical question of the essence of the general text is to confuse issues and to mix levels of thought.

Indeed, if the general text is in a position to account for the ontological status, or rather ontological illusion, of texts and their textuality, it is because it is not a phenomenon. Therefore there is, *perhaps,* a general text. It never appears *(as such),* it never becomes present *as such* in either a sensible or intelligible mode. It cannot, therefore, become the object of a perception, whether such a perception is an apperception or an intuitive act of ideation. Derrida writes at the beginning of "Plato's Pharmacy": "A text is not a text unless it hides from the first comer, from the first glance, the law of its composition and the rules of its game. A text remains, however, forever imperceptible. Its law and its rules are not, however, harbored in the inaccessibility of a secret; it is simply that they can never be booked, in the *present*, into anything that could rigorously be called a perception" (*D,* p. 63). The general text escapes all possible phenomenologization. Instead of appearing as such, it *disappears.* "What disappears," Derrida explains in *Edmund Husserl's Origin of Geometry,* "is what is annihilated, but also what ceases, intermittently or definitely, to appear *in fact* yet without affecting its being or being-sense" (*O,* p. 93). This possibility of disappearance without dissolving into sheer nothingness characterizes the status of the general text with respect to what is phenomenologizable—the phenomenon of Being in particular.[7]

As we have seen, the general text accounts for the *textual difference* (or the difference between the texts and textuality) to the extent that it disappears, that is, to the extent that it is not a phenomenon endowed with existence, presence (and meaning). It is evident, then, that the relation between the general text and what it accounts for can no longer be thought in traditional terms. It can certainly not be a relation of emanation, engenderment, or creation, nor can it be a relation of derivation, of constitution, or even of possibility. Both series of relations between ground and what is grounded presuppose the existence, presence, phenomenality of the ground. When Derrida states that "if the text does not, to the letter, exist, then *there is* perhaps a text," he at first suggests the possibility of thinking the relation between a ground such as the general text and what it accounts for, texts and their textual essence, within the scope of the Heideggerian problematics of the gift *(Gabe)*. *Es gibt* is indeed to be translated as "it gives" and not simply as "there is." Heidegger's attempt to think the gift of Being is an attempt to think, in a more fundamental manner, the relation between what as ground must be entirely heterogeneous to what it grounds and what is grounded. Although Derrida borrows the expresson *es gibt* from Heidegger and addresses a problem similar to the one concerning the ontico-ontological difference, it is not put to work in the same way. As we shall see, Derrida's transference of the problematics of donation to the question of the general text results in an even more radical regrounding or unsettling, if you will, of ontology than does Heidegger's investigation into the question of Being.

Indeed, Derrida notes in *Dissemination* that the general text, which is never present but in constant withdrawal, "has no proper, literal meaning; it no longer originates in meaning as such, that is, as the meaning of being" (D, p. 229). "No present in truth presents itself there, not even in the form of self-concealment" (D, p. 230). The question of the text clearly demarks itself from the question of Being. As he shows in "The Double Session," the general text whose structure of re-marking folds the text upon it(self) in a nonsymmetrical and nonreflexive manner defers, discards, or sets Being aside (*à l'écart*). The general text marginalizes Being, being itself the margin of Being. As the margin of Being, the general text has no ontological status; with regard to Being it is neither absent nor present, since both modes of temporality and of being are particular to Being alone. In "The Double Session" one reads with respect to the figure of the hymen, which is just one figure of the general text: "At the edge of Being, the medium of the hymen never becomes a mere mediation of work of the negative; it outwits and undoes all ontologies, all philosophemes, all manner of dialectics. It outwits them and—as a cloth, a tissue, a medium again—it envelops them, turns them over, and inscribes them" (D, p. 215).

Now, the *being there (es gibt)* of the text indicates precisely this marginal status of the general text with regard to Being. Although "nothing says the present better, it seems, than *there is,*" it, rather, points at a "scission" (D, p. 307), at the cut-off of Being, of the present, of presence. This "there is . . . is in the present only through the 'illusions' of statement or utterance" (D, p. 311). The *being there* of the text sets the existence, the presence and the signification of the text aside; it suspends it on its margin. The *being there,* in Derrida, thus characterizes that which makes the margin, which takes place as the margin of Being (and of what is), in short, the nonphenomenologizable. In *La Vérité en peinture* we read, "*There is* frame, but the frame does not exist" (VP, p. 93).

We must, consequently, recognize that the relation of *being there* (or donation) to what is, to what exists, to what is present in either a sensible or intelligible manner, is one of framing, of marginality. Applied to the general text, this would mean that it frames or marginalizes that which it accounts for, texts and textuality. In short, the general text, in its relation to the phenomenologizable, to the texts, to their essence, to Being in general, no longer preserves "*the order of all appearance,* the very process of appearing in general," the order of truth (D, p. 192). The general text questions what this order presupposes—the possibility of distinguishing between essences and appearances, between phenomena and what they allow to come into appearance. Indeed the possibility of decision hinges on that of the perception *(Anschauung)* of the thing itself *(die Sache selbst) in person,* or as Merleau-Ponty would have said, in flesh and blood. In its relation to the texts and to textuality as their essence, the general text is a nonphenomenologizable "ground" which by virtue of the mode of its givenness—its *being there*—broaches and breaches the difference within which the distinction characteristic of the order of appearance takes shape. Yet by opening the possibility of such a distinction, the general text also circumscribes the decidability of what is thus set free into opposition.

Here, in particular, it becomes clear that Derrida's investigation of the general text and its particular status with regard to Being is part of his systematic debate with Heidegger. Whether or not the notion of text has been borrowed from literary criticism, Derrida's use of it implies a radical rethinking of this notion in the direction of what one may call the unthought of Being, its yielding to the process of appearing. When Derrida states that there is no extra-text but the general text (only), then this also means that Being itself, in order to be the gift of Being, must already be within the text. Without its "textual" margin, Being could not fulfill its fundamental role as the ontico-ontological difference, which in Heidegger preserves the order of appearance. But at the same time this margin severely limits the grounding function of Being. This relation of reinscription to Being and to Heidegger's meditation on "Dif-ference" characterizes the Derridean concept of text. Although the notion of the general text is not limited to this debate with Heidegger—and to representing a solution for a specific philosophical problem—it receives its essential determinations from this debate.

Unlike Heidegger's concept of Being, which accounts in a fundamental way for the ontico-ontological difference, there is nothing "fundamental," "profound," or "deep" about the general text. It does not function as what one used to call an essence with regard to what it makes possible through reinscription. On the contrary, the general text functions as the margin of the opposition of texts and textuality, as the frame of the *textual difference*. Without this margin no texts could be, no essence could ever hope to set texts free. Yet one cannot legitimately claim of a margin, of the general text, that it engenders or constitutes that which it is the margin of, texts and textuality. One cannot even contend rigorously that it is a relation of conditions of possibility. Yet what exists, the text and textuality, is possible only because there is a text. What exists, the determinable and decidable text, is possible only because it is inscribed into the margin of an indeterminable: text. To cite again:

There is such a general text everywhere that (that is, everywhere) this discourse and its order (essence, sense, truth, meaning, consciousness, ideality, etc.) are *overflowed*, that is, everywhere that their authority is put back into the position of a *mark* in a chain that this authority intrinsically and illusorily believes it wishes to, and does in fact, govern. This general text is not limited, of course, as will (or would) be quickly understood, to writings on the page. The writing of this text, moreover, has the exterior limit only of a certain *re-mark*. Writing on the page, and then "literature," are determined types of this re-mark.   (*P*, pp. 59–60)

The general text functions as that which delimits and renders possible the limits of the empiricity and immediacy of the writing on the page on the one hand and of "literature" on the other, as well as of the empirical plurality of the sensible and palpable texts and of the essence or textuality shared by them. Roland Barthes, making use of Lacanian terminology in his essay "From Work to Text," formulates this relation very succinctly by saying that the work is the text's imaginary tail.[8] As what broaches and breaches the opposition of text and textuality, the general text accounts for the possibility of an essence of texts by limiting, marginalizing, or framing it. The general text, although it makes textuality possible, also makes it impossible, since textuality as the essence of existing texts is structurally incapable of essentializing the plus or minus, the more or less of its margins. If one decided, however, to call *textuality* the general text, one would have to make this concept express the lack of an essence of texts. To speak of textuality, then, would imply that discourses and "literature" have no final and last essence, that there is nothing proper to discourses and literature, no discursivity, and no such thing as literarity or literariness *as such*.

A System of Traces

As I have mentioned, the text in the infrastructural sense is not one infrastructure but a composite of these fundamental subunits. The text is never constituted by what one calls signs or signifiers—that is to say, by units signifying a signified outside the text—but by traces. A text in the infrastructural sense is a fabric of traces, a system of linking of traces, in other words a network of textual referrals *(renvois textuels)*. Because of this differential network, this tissue of traces endlessly referring to something other than itself yet never to an extratext that would bring its referring function to a clear stop, the general text is by nature heterogeneous. It ties in with Otherness in an irreducible manner; the threads it combines are not of the same order, and its interlacing of these filaments is not subjected to an ultimate unity. Thus the text in an infrastructural sense leads back to Derrida's critique of the Platonic concept of *symploke* discussed at the end of Part I. Although a "system," against which the present, living, and conscious representation of the text stands out in relief, the text is constituted by a mode of linkage that is not oriented by oneness and totality. This also explains why Derrida expressed reservations as to the representation of the text as a fabric. Not only is the weaving metaphor an all too artisanal, aesthetic, and empirical representation of the general text, which impinges upon the rather abstract and quasitranscendental status that it has in Derrida, but the philosophical past of this image governed by the category of unity also makes it an inappropriate description of the general text. If the general text is a fabric or interlacing at all, it is not because it interconnects homogeneous threads into one totality but precisely because, in an almost nonsensible, nonaesthetic manner, it links heterogeneous forces, which constantly tend to annul the texts' precarious unity, a unity constituted by an essential incompletion. As a system of textual referrals, of differences and differences of differences, a text, therefore, cannot be a totality. Yet if the text is impossible to totalize, this is due not to the excess of an infinite richness of content, meaning, or intention but to structural reasons. As Derrida has noted, it is the very structure of the textual agency as a system of referrals that turns "the 'whole' into the *too much* or the *too little* of the text" (*D*, p. 246). The ideal of totality is thoroughly foreign to the text; it is the text's imaginary. What this means is that the text cannot be totalized by a theme constituted independently of the play of the text, a theme that would supervise its own inscription as well as the signs through which it is expressed. Nor can the text be a formal totality. All formal self-reflection of the text faces structural limits similar to those owing to totalization by content. The fate of these totalizations, based on a preexisting signified or a formal self-representation, is *decided* upon by what Derrida calls the *reserve* of textual operations which takes place deep in back, in the shadow of the pharmacy, so to speak.

Yet one may perhaps want to object at this point that in *Of Grammatology*, Derrida contends that Rousseau, for instance, "inscribes textuality in the text," that he "tells us in the text what a text is," that Rousseau's text "tells us in writing what writing is" (*OG*, p. 163). Is not this "self-consciousness" of the text, the discursive representation by which a text represents its own roots, a clear sign of the text's self-reflexivity? First, two things need to be rigorously distinguished: the self-reflexive strata of texts on the one hand, and on the other the textual operations in the background that both permit such reflection and prevent it from finally coinciding with itself. After attributing the text's self-reflection to the discursive actual, living, and conscious representation of a text, Derrida writes: "If a text always gives itself a certain representation of its own roots, those roots live only by that representation, by never touching the soil, so to speak. Which undoubtedly destroys their *radical essence,* but not the necessity of their *racinating function*" (*OG*, p. 101). The circumscribed discourse in which a text presents itself is a representation that is constantly overrun by the entire system of the text's own resources and laws. At the same time, since this representation plays an organizing role in the structure of the text, it must be accounted for, and it must be accounted for by the very resources and laws of the text.

If Derrida can say in *Of Grammatology* that a theme such as "supplementarity" is not only one theme among others in a chain but also that it describes the chain itself, "the being-chain of a textual chain," this does not imply that the whole chain would be governed by this one theme. This theme does not reflect the whole chain, if reflection means what it has always meant, a mirroring representation through which a self reappropriates itself. Instead of reflecting the chain of the text into itself, "supplementarity" *re-marks* that chain in the same way as it is itself re-marked, that is, put back into the position of a mark within the textual chain. Reflexivity is only an effect of what Derrida has called *re-mark,* and which I have analyzed in some detail in Part II. The illusion of a reflexive totalization by a theme or a concept is grounded in the representational effacement of their position as marks within the chain that they tend to govern. Because of the re-mark, self-representation and self-reflection never quite take place. A theme or concept can only designate the text *en abyme;* that is, its representation is the representation of a representation. Yet instead of producing a saturation of difference, the representation of representation keeps the difference endlessly open and thus prevents any ultimate self-representation or self-presence of the text.

The illusion of self-reflection of a text is witness only to the representational function of a text, not to its representation of something outside the text or its self-representation. It is an effect of the text's nature as a system of referral. The general text is generalized representation, or as Derrida also calls it in "The Double Session," generalized reference. Within such a system, no self-reflection or self-representation can coincide with itself to constitute itself as presence, because as representation it is already inscribed in the space of repetition and splitting or doubling of the self. Thus, the structure that best characterizes the text, and at the same time accounts for the necessity and essential limits of a text's self-reflection, is the structure of the *re-mark,* in which all textual traces are not only elements of referral but are also overmarked by the space of their engenderment and inscription. The re-mark, by which the text is folded upon itself, is not, then, to be mistaken for a reflection. The angle of the re-mark by which the text as text is folded back upon itself excludes "any possibility of its fitting back over or into itself" (*D,* p. 251). "The fold is not a form of reflexivity," Derrida concludes (*D*, p. 271). Instead, like the *arête* in "Living On," it keeps all "reflecting representation from folding back upon itself or reproducing itself within itself in perfect self-correspondence, from dominating or including itself, tautologically, from translating itself into its own totality."[9]

At this point, where the structure of the general text has revealed itself as one of reference and re-marking—as a system of re-marked traces—it becomes clear that the text can set Being aside precisely because of its structure of generalized reference. Yet since the structure of re-marking is, as I have tried to show, an extension and radicalization of the logic of the trait, with which the later Heidegger continued his elaboration of the question of Being, the text as constituted by the re-mark can also set its own being aside. Indeed, in the same way as the trait of Being is at once the retreat *(retrait)* of Being, the mark that is folded upon itself, the re-marked trace, also retreats in its being. It is the constant casting aside of its own being. This, then, is one more reason to understand Derrida's notion of text as an attempt to come to grips with the Heideggerian question of Being, for Derrida inscribes this casting aside of Being into the text of the logic of the trait, which, for Heidegger, may have remained subservient to the question of the meaning of Being. What Derrida thus calls the text, instead of being governed by Being, makes Being a function of the general text. The text, rather than being primarily the body or the ideal form of a literary written work, as are the objects of literary criticism, is, if taken in an infrastructural sense as the general text, the nonunitary fabric of laws that allow for the possibility of Being. These laws, which at once inhibit Being from articulating itself without difference, thus making it ultimately impossible, are those of the cluster of infrastructures linked together in the macrosynthesis of the text. Consequently, text as understood by Derrida is the nonphenomenologizable structure of referral and re-marking whose nonunitary fabric is the quasitranscendental frame "constitutive" of phenomena in the Husserlian sense—more broadly, of essences, last reasons, grounds, as opposed to what they allow to appear—and of Being, as the phenomenon par excellence in all its radical difference from beings.

As an irreducible background, the general text undercuts the order of all appearance. While lending itself to the philosophical operation of the *krinein* and its effects of decidability, the general text remains in retreat and reserve from everything that comes into its own within its frame, either by an interruption of the unlimited process of reference or by a self-reflection owing to the illusory effect of the re-mark. Hence, although the general text is a condition of possibility for phenomena (and all they entail: ideality, presence, purity, and so on), it is also their condition of impossibility. Needless to say, if the notion of the general text is to become an operative concept of literary criticism at all, its function in Derrida's debate with Husserlian phenomenology and Heidegger's philosophy cannot simply be overlooked. The context of this debate alone makes the general text a significant term, and determines its specific features and implications. No mere invocation or magical conjuration of this term can make up for the indispensable reconstruction of its actual context.

METAPHOR

Derrida's insistence upon the fact that philosophy, from its beginnings, has conceived of itself as a discourse entirely transparent to Being and free of all figurative use of language has fostered the mistaken opinion that Derrida's aim would be to challenge or "deconstruct" the *regina scientiarum* by playing literature and its metaphoric use of language off against this discipline that pretends to dominate all other disciplines. Nothing, however, could be more inaccurate than to confound the deconstruction of philosophy with a nonargumentative, literary, and metaphoric play. This belief is incorrect not only because of its reductive understanding of literature but, as we shall see, for other, more essential reasons.

Derrida has never left the slightest doubt that metaphor is by nature a metaphysical concept. In spite, or rather because of its negativity, it belongs to the very order and movement of meaning: the provisory loss of meaning that metaphor implies is subordinated to the teleology of meaning as one moment in the process of the self-manifestation of meaning in all its propriety. The philosophical concept of metaphor (and there is no other) makes metaphor depend on the absolute *parousia* of meaning.

Metaphor denotes a reality derivative of proper meaning whether the metaphoric displacement is seen as a moment of loss anticipating a future recuperation or only as an ornamental and exterior supplement to proper meaning. Instead of uncritically revalorizing metaphor, instead of simply playing it off against philosophy, Derrida's repetition of the question of metaphor is an interrogation of the philosophical concept of metaphor, of its limits, and, as is to be seen in "White Mythology," of philosophy's attempt to question systematically the metaphorical origins of its concepts. In other words, Derrida's reformulation of the question of metaphor is concerned with the fundamental complicity between the philosophical determination of the concept of metaphor and the apparently subversive attempt to challenge philosophy on the grounds that its concepts are hidden tropes. Rather than participating in this double enterprise, Derrida's efforts involve an analysis of the presuppositions of this problematic, and an attempt to delimit the metaphysical and rhetorical schemes that constitute it. This analysis implies a profound suspicion of the concept of metaphor as a metaphysical concept; consequently, one never finds Derrida flirting with this concept of metaphor as if it possessed within its limits and all by itself any decisive proprieties that would be potentially subversive of logocentrism.

Yet there is of course no such thing as a purely metaphysical concept. If concepts could be purely metaphysical, they would resist all questions concerning them. As a result, Derrida can nonetheless point to a certain irreducibility of metaphor with respect to its possibility, and short of its rhetorical repetition and philosophical conceptualization. Focusing on this specific irreducibility, Derrida shows metaphor to be the metaphysical name for something "older" than the philosophical distinction between the proper and the metaphoric (*SP*, p. 103), and which might thus be in a position to upset the conceptual columbarium of philosophy. Consequently, rather than simply attempting to reverse the classical hierarchical opposition of the proper and the figural, the philosophical and the metaphoric, Derrida aims at something that is only very improperly called metaphoric without being proper in itself. Being no longer either metaphoric or literal, an allegorical illustration without a concept or a pure concept without a metaphoric scheme, the irreducible in question can no longer be referred to by the *name* of metaphor; indeed it is properly unnamable. As Derrida has argued in "The *Retrait* of Metaphor," the sort of metaphor in question is in withdrawal; it retires.[10] Being of the order neither of the concept nor of the metaphor, the irreducible in question escapes the order of the noun in general, within which, as Derrida has shown in his analysis of Aristotle's *Poetics* and *Rhetoric*, the philosophical elaboration of metaphor takes place, an elaboration that links metaphor, via a theory of mimesis, to the doctrine of being or ontology. It is unnamable not because of some Romantic nostalgia for the ineffable, nor because the limited faculties of man as a finite being would be too narrow to express what overpowers them, but because of this irreducible's exorbitant position with regard to the opposition of the proper and the figural, Being and beings, God and men, a position that escapes the logic that ties logos and Being together. Derrida refers to it as *quasimetaphoricity,* or simply metaphoricity.

Metaphoricity, then, is not a quality that presupposes an already constituted and philosophically determined metaphor. Nor is metaphoricity the savage production, unmediated by concepts, of metaphors as a quality attributed to, say, literary language. As that which opens the play between the proper and the metaphoric, and which metaphysics can only name as that which it makes possible, metaphoricity is not endowed with those qualities traditionally attributed to metaphor but rather with attributes which in traditional philosophy would be called constituting or transcendental. Metaphoricity is a transcendental concept of sorts. Yet it does not follow that Derrida would simply do away with the so-called ornamental and poetic functions of metaphor, reducing them, as does philosophy, to a literary border phenomenon of philosophy. The absence of such a derogative gesture, however, does not mean, as is often assumed, that Derrida would turn the literary qualities of metaphoricity against the conceptual language of philosophy, with its desire for univocality, exactitude, and clarity. In truth, the notion of metaphoricity as advanced by Derrida is neither opposed to the philosophical concept of metaphor (and there can be no other), nor simply identical with what philosophy calls the ornamental poetic function of metaphor; nor does it view metaphor as a moment in the process of meaning. Metaphoricity, in Derrida's sense, refers to something *structurally* phenomenal, to something of the order of the conceptual, the transcendental, but which in spite of its heterogeneity to the so-called real world also combines with the supplementary and ornamental mode of the rhetorical figure of poetics. As the result of a destruction of metaphor, and *eo ipso* of the proper and the literal, metaphoricity yields a structure that accounts for the difference between the figural and the proper, and which comprises properties that are by right "older" than those traditionally attributed to the transcendental and the empirical. Since, as an "originary" synthesis, metaphoricity is more originary than what I have formerly referred to as transcendentality, and since it also combines with the most exterior qualities of metaphor, with metaphor's exteriority to the concept, I shall try to define it as a nonphenomenologizable *quasitranscendental.*

The following analysis of "White Mythology" is an attempt to characterize a bit more fully the status of metaphoricity by examining the different ways in which Derrida is led to elaborate this notion. I have already stated that metaphoricity is something structurally phenomenal that serves to account for the philosophical difference between the proper and the figural. It is evident that this notion is altogether different from what either the literary critic or the philosopher designates, or would designate, by such a notion. This gap widens even further as soon as we explore the problem that this notion of metaphoricity ultimately serves to address in Derrida's work. Such a demonstration, however, requires a detour of sorts.

The Multiple Senses of Being

As Heidegger himself points out, his interest in philosophy was awakened by his reading in 1907 of Franz Brentano's dissertation "On the Several Senses of Being in Aristotle" (1862).[11] Studying Brentano's analysis of the multiple ways in which being is expressed (pollakos legomenon), Heidegger began to reflect on the primary and fundamental meaning of Being presupposed by these multiple senses. It is important to recall here that within the problematical horizon of classical philosophy, the question concerning the unity and the manifold of the senses of Being is none other than that of analogy. Indeed, a tradition that starts with scholastic philosophy has Aristotle determining the relation between being and its multiple senses in terms of this figure of thought. It is precisely within this same tradition that Brentano situates his own investigation of the problem. Although Heidegger's fundamental philosophical concern is not subsumed under the explicit title of "analogy," it is clear that his investigation into the question of the meaning of Being, or into that of the difference as difference, is essentially an attempt to come to grips with the traditional problem of analogy, whether or not he mentions that notion. In what follows, I shall try to substantiate this point with a brief analysis of some paragraphs of Being and Time.[12]

Whether or not certain philosophies explicitly reflect on the problem of analogy, all metaphysics, insofar as it is concerned with the unity in difference, must understand itself primarily as a philosophy of analogy, as Puntel has most forcefully argued. Although "analogy" acquires the explicit status of a philosophical issue only with Plato, analogy, as the problem of the identity that lets differences (as well as the various linguistic articulations of being), come to the fore was already a, if not the, major figure of thought in philosophical thinking from its very inception.[13] Up through Aristotle, analogy had the meaning of mathematical proportion, relation, ratio, correspondence, thus reflecting its origin as a mathematical concept formulated by the Pythagoreans. It did not signify a simple relation or a simple proportion but a system of relations or proportions. Puntel writes, "Analogy is a relation of relations, a proportion of proportions, in short, a correspondence of relations."[14] According to this originary meaning of analogy, the unity or the identity that difference presupposes, and which mediates between what is different, becomes manifest in the similitude of opposing but back-stretched relations. As a matter of fact, the whole problematic of analogy is one of determining these relations. As I have mentioned, scholastic philosophy extended the problem of analogy to the question of being and made Aristotle the first thinker to have determined being in such a manner. Indeed, the Scholastics contended that Aristotle conceived of the relation between the different senses of being and being itself as one of similarity by analogy. Ever since Ockham's view that there is no analogy of being, this question has been an issue in philosophy. I cannot attempt here to develop in full this most difficult problem, nor can I discuss Aubenque's thesis, in *Le Probleme de l'être chez Aristote,* that the Scholastic position does not correspond to Aristotle's thought, but that the doctrine of the analogy of being represents, on the contrary, a Platonization of Aristotle.[15] Nor shall I linger on Ricoeur's contention in *The Rule of Metaphor* that the entire theory of analogy is no more than a pseudoscience, the result of theological pressure on a specifically philosophical discourse.[16] Suffice it to say that the fundamental reason why these and other authors reject the idea of an analogy of being is that they contend that Aristotle knew only the mathematical notion of analogy as a quantitative proportion which, strictly speaking, could not be applied to the relation between the meanings of being and being itself, for being itself can no longer be posited in relation to an Other.

This argument would seem to be substantiated by the fact that Aristotle never applies the concept of analogy—a concept which he uses on several other occasions in the strict sense of a relation of proportion—when speaking of the multiple meanings of being. When, for instance, at the beginning of Book 4 of *Metaphysics* he writes that " 'being' has several meanings but that they all have a central reference to some *one* nature [*pros hen kai mian tina physo*] and are not entirely different things that happen to have the same name [*homonymos*]," he does not use the word *analogy.*[17] Moreover, the *pros hen* in the proposition, instead of signifying a correspondence of relations, indicates only the simple relation of a manifold to an originary oneness, with respect to which everything else is derivative and dependent. In the aftermath of Trendelenburg's attempt to save the analogy of being by elaborating a qualitative proportionality, and hence a concept of analogy more general than its first and original sense as quantitative proportionality, Brentano, following in this Scholastic tradition, also assumed a second type of analogy in order to explain the relation in Aristotle between the nongeneric concept of being and its different senses.[18] This second type of analogy is not, however, one of proportionality (quantitative or qualitative) but, as the Scholastics called it, one of attribution, or, to use Brentano's words, one with respect to one and the same *terminus*. Being, according to Brentano, has the unity of analogy, a unity that grounds the manifold and categorial senses of being, because its different meanings relate to it in an *ad unum* relation. Being's equivocal meanings are connected to the unity of a *nonaccidental* name *(homonymos)*. Although of different meanings, the categories relate to a common name as to a common origin by virtue of an analogy of attribution. They are indeed not entirely different things that happen *(accidentally)* to have the same name, but refer to one necessary name as the source of their plurality. The unity of this *homonymon* is the nongeneric unity of analogy. For Brentano, therefore, being is doubly analogical: its different meanings relate to it according to the analogy with respect to the same terminus, and, as Trendelenburg has shown, they also form an equality of relations. Indeed, although Aristotle in Book 4 does not use the term *analogy* with regard to the question of the multiple senses of being, he nevertheless says in Book 5 that whatever is related as a certain thing to another, and "bears to each other the same ratio or relation that another pair has" *(osa ekei os allo pros allo),* is analogical.[19] Yet it is such an equality that Aristotle claimed for his categories, and which, along with *on* and *ousia,* are, according to Brentano, the major senses in which being is said.

For what follows, it is important to note that the theory of the analogy of being implies that being is in itself relational. Yet as Puntel has intimated, this self-relationality of being presupposes that "being is in itself and as itself *difference,* i.e., a self-relation that repeats itself in and through itself."[20] Only to the extent that being is difference can it be said to be analogical. Although this conclusion may not have been thematized in the tradition that stretches from Aquinas to Brentano, the critics' objections to the doctrine of the analogy of being may well in essence pivot around this issue of difference. In any case, it is as a doctrine of the difference of being that the theory of the analogy of being is of interest to us here. It is only in this perspective that this doctrine is taken up again by both Heidegger and Derrida, as I shall now attempt to show.

As an inquiry into the manifold senses of Being from the perspective of *Dasein,* Heidegger's investigation in *Being and Time* at first continues the classical problematics of analogy, for it displays a nongeneric conception of Being. As *"the* transcendens *pure and simple,"* to quote *Being and Time,* Being lies beyond what is, beyond all imaginable ontic determinations. Heidegger conceives of his fundamental theme in a genuinely Aristotelian sense as "no sort of genus of beings."[21] But the true reason for seeing Heidegger's philosophy as a continuation, even as a radicalization, of this tradition is that his investigation of the different modes of *saying* Being is an investigation of Being as the difference that, within Being as a *terminus,* makes it possible for one mode of uttering Being to relate—analogously—to that terminus, in the two senses of analogy I have distinguished. The difference of Being as a difference of the same is the title under which Heidegger engages his debate with the traditional philosophical problem of analogy.

In *Being and Time* this problem takes shape as the *as-structure* of the understanding of Being. After having established that understanding and states-of-mind *(Verstehen* and *Befindlichkeit)* are fundamental *existentialia* of the being of the *Da—existentialia* which secure the primordial disclosedness of *Dasein* as Being-in-the-world—Heidegger completes the structures of *Dasein* by adding to it not language but the *possibility* of language. In section 32 of *Being and Time,* Heidegger starts out by demonstrating that understanding is made explicit *(ausdrücklich)* through interpretation *(Auslegung).* The analysis of interpretation in the sense of *Auslegung (hermeneuein)* is an intermediary step in the discovery of the third fundamental structure of the *Dasein,* which is discourse *(Rede).* Discourse is indeed the *possibility* of speech.

It is imperative to understand in what way interpretation is said to make explicit what is implicitly understood or sensed by the *Dasein.* We must realize that interpretation of what is understood must take place, according to the *structural* status of *Dasein* (which, one must repeat, is therefore not just another name for subject or for *anthropos),* in an essentially prelinguistic, nonpropositional, prepredicative, and nonthematic manner. The *Dasein* encounters the things that surround it primarily as things that serve this or that purpose, and not as pure things or objects upon which it subsequently bestows determining attributes. Hence, the interpretation of what is understood circumspectively is characterized by the structure of *something as something*. Heidegger writes: "That which is disclosed in understanding—that which is understood—is already accessible in such a way that its 'as which' can be made to stand out explicitly. The 'as' makes up the structure of the explicitness of something that is understood. It constitutes the interpretation" (p. 189). In other words, interpretation is the laying out *(Auslegen)* of the primary articulation of what is understood according to the as-structure, which is an a priori articulation *(Gliederung, Artikulation)*. Interpretation makes explicit that all understanding is primarily articulated according to the structure of "something as something," or in other words "with regard to something" *(auf etwas hin)*. Heidegger calls this primary articulation of understanding and interpretation *Rede*, which one may translate as "discourse," if one keeps in mind that it marks a structural level of articulation anterior by right to all possible linguistic utterance. As "the articulation of intelligibility," discourse is coeval with states-of-mind and understanding and precedes all predicative and thematic expression and vocalization of understanding and states-of-mind (pp. 104–105). As the third fundamental *existentiale* of the *Dasein* it represents the very *possibility* of vocalization, of speech, of speech acts, of language as the mundane or worldly mode of the being of the logos. Discourse in the sense of *Rede* is merely a translation of *logos*. It signifies the "logical" articulation of *Dasein*'s preunderstanding of Being and thus corresponds to the ontologically fundamental structure of the meaning of Being. The meaning of Being hinges on its articulation in terms of the as-structure.

The "existential-*hermeneutical* 'as' " is the name Heidegger gives to the primordial *as* of all interpretation that understands circumspectively, in other words "with regard to something" (p. 201). This *as* is the fundamental structure of the logos as discourse, as the primary articulation of understanding and interpretation, and achieves the originary dis-covering and dis-closure, which Heidegger later calls the primary opening, within which propositional predication may (or may not) come forth. I shall not deal here with the leveling modifications that are required to transform the existential-hermeneutical *as* into the apophantic *as* which is itself the structure of possibility of assertion (pp. 196–210).[22] Let me say only that as little as vocalization is an attribute of the logos as *Rede*, it is just as little an integral part of assertion. Yet just as logos as *Rede* contains the *possibility* of language in the form of the structural determination of expressedness *(Hinausgesprochenheit)*, it also contains the possibility of assertion in the structural form of what is called *Ausgesprochenheit,* and which ensures that stating *can* become communicative revealing. These structural determinations are structurally phenomenal and belong to an order altogether heterogeneous to that of factual realization and vocalization. I am concerned here only with these originary structures of the logos, apart from its factual and contingent vocalization. These structures are not discovered at the expense of the logos's vocalization but inscribe it as a possibility.

Having characterized, with Heidegger, logos as discourse—that is, as constituted by the articulation of intelligibility according to the as-structure—I must point out that the primary disclosure achieved by the as-structure is at the same time a primary covering-up. Indeed, since the as-structure uncovers "with regard to," it veils *and* reveals in the same gesture. Thus, Heidegger has inscribed an originary falsehood into the very articulation of the logos, which will allow him, with one structure, to explain why propositions *can* be wrong. The as-structure as the primary articulation of the understanding of Being, made explicit in interpretation by the logos as discourse, is thus a structure that makes all understanding of Being by *Dasein* structurally dependent on circumspective inference. Everything, as it were, is understood primarily not by focusing on the thing as such but with regard to something else, say, to the *what-for* of the thing. As far as the meaning of Being is concerned, it can be known only *as* its different senses. Since the originary articulation of the understanding of Being— its interpretation—precedes any particular determination of Being, and since each such particular sense of Being is structurally covered-up Being, Being itself is always only in its own deferral. Being is difference; it is analogical in the sense that it is articulated within itself as the unity of its selfsame senses. Being is nothing *in itself,* but it is the very "logical" articulation of its own understanding within which it appears in a multitude of irreducible senses.

Ricoeur, in *The Rule of Metaphor,* shows a certain awareness of the continuity between the traditional problematic of analogy and the philosophies of Heidegger and Derrida, when, in Chapter 8, after a discussion of the problem of the analogy of being in Aristotle and of the *analogia entis* in Thomas Aquinas, he discusses Heidegger's and Derrida's treatment of metaphor. Yet because Ricoeur is primarily concerned with warding off any intrusion of poetics into philosophy, he remains blind to the fact that Heidegger's and Derrida's investigations into metaphor and metaphoricity are not simply poetical inquiries but are based on a *philosophical* concept of metaphor, and are thus a debate with that *philosophical* concept. Moreover, he fails to see that this debate is engaged with the classical problem of the analogy of being. One can perceive the real continuity of all these problematics only by recognizing that the concept of metaphor in Heidegger and Derrida is not simply one of poetic resemblance but one that receives a transcendental qualification from the field it is applied to, to use Ricoeur's words—a qualification similar to the one that Ricoeur powerfully demonstrates in the case of the analogy of being, and with regard to the concept of the *analogia entis,* both of which are said to be nonmetaphorical theories of analogy (supposing that metaphor is one with poetic resemblance).

I should now like to argue that Derrida's treatment of metaphor is a resumption not of what Heidegger explicitly developed about metaphor but of the more fundamental structure of the logos and of the much older problem of the analogy of being. Consequently, I shall attempt to show that Derrida's critique of the philosophy of language or of linguistics opens itself, not unlike Heidegger's critique, to an exploration of ground structures which account for the phenomenon of language. Yet, as we shall see, the status of these ground structures in Derrida is, for essential reasons, very different from what I shall call the immanent or finite transcendental structures in Heidegger.

Since analogy is, according to Aristotle, not only one genre of metaphor but the metaphor par excellence insofar as it is based on an equality of relations, the doctrine of the analogy of being—whatever the meaning of analogy may be—indicates that a certain metaphoricity is constitutive of the very unity of being. The as-structure of understanding unearthed by Heidegger characterizes understanding and the saying of Being as hinging on a movement of transfer. The relation "with regard to" in the primary mode of circumspective understanding makes all understanding of something understanding of *something as something.* A movement of *epiphora,* the movement constitutive of metaphor, is present in all understanding of the *as what.* With this, we face a clear continuity between the traditional problem of the analogy of being, Heidegger's investigations into the fundamental structures of the logos, and, as we shall see next, Derrida's treatment of the problem of metaphor.

The Generalization of Analogy

Before embarking on an analysis of "White Mythology," I should first establish that my linkage of Derrida's treatment of the concept of metaphor to the question of the analogy of being is not an artificial imposition but is supported by the texts. Indeed, Derrida explicitly recognizes that his analysis of metaphor cuts into the problems delineated by the analogy of being. What remains implicit perhaps is that these analyses of metaphor are intrinsically connected with the problem of the analogy of being. After having reminded Benveniste, in "The Supplement of Copula," that the very possibility of a science of language hinges on a knowledge about the essence of what is called "category," Derrida writes:

> The categories are the figures *(skhemata)* according to which the "simple term" being is said in that it is said in several ways, through several tropes. The system of the categories is the system of being's turns of phrase. It brings the problematic of the analogy of Being, its equivocalness or unequivocalness, into communication with the problematic of the metaphor in general. Aristotle explicitly links these problematics in affirming that the best metaphor coordinates itself to the analogy of proportionality. Which would suffice to prove that the question of metaphor is no more to be asked in the margins of metaphysics than metaphorical style and the use of figures is an accessory embellishment or secondary auxiliary of philosophical discourse. (*M,* pp. 183–184)

The problem of metaphor, then, is clearly seen to encroach upon both the problems of analogy and being. Any inquiry into metaphor is thus per se an investigation into the possibility of the univocality of being. Yet Derrida does not explicitly address the problem of the relation of his analysis of metaphor in general to the problem of the analogy of being. Although he claims in "White Mythology" that all the features that distinguish metaphors in the theory of metaphor seem to "belong to the great immobile chain of Aristotelian ontology, with its theory of the analogy of Being" (*M,* p. 236), and that the privilege that Aristotle attributes to the metaphor by analogy shows that "this privilege articulates Aristotle's entire metaphorology with his general theory of the analogy of Being" (*M,* p. 242), he refrains from clarifying this relation. "We cannot undertake this problem here," he writes, referring the reader to the studies of Aubenque and Vuillemin (*M,* p. 244). Still, throughout his work Derrida has repeatedly linked the problem of analogy and metaphor, and has systematically questioned the relation of these two figures with respect to the problem of being.

Although in the *Poetics,* Aristotle conceived of analogy as only one species of metaphor—metaphor by analogy—in his *Rhetoric* it becomes *the* paradigm of metaphor. "Analogy is metaphor par excellence. Aristotle emphasizes this point often in the *Rhetoric,*" notes Derrida in "White Mythology" (*M,* p. 242). Such a privilege makes the whole of Aristotle's metaphorology dependent on his general theory concerning the analogy of being. "Metaphor in general, the passage from one existent to another, or from one signified meaning to another, [is] authorized by the initial *submission* of Being to the existent, the *analogical* displacement of Being" (*WD,* p. 27). Elsewhere he writes, "Metaphor, thus, as an effect of *mimesis* and *homoiosis,* [is] the manifestation of analogy" (*M,* p. 238). In other words, analogy is a phenomenally more fundamental mode of transport than the *epiphora* constitutive of metaphor. Metaphor and the movement of *epiphora* are to be thought against the background of and with respect to the more general problematic of analogy.

It is in particular in his analyses of Condillac and Kant that Derrida has pointed out that this "fundamental analogism" (*AF,* p. 83) from which metaphor is derived is not only a principle of methodical and universal linkage for philosophy but a general principle par excellence insofar as it concerns the proper name of being. Indeed, within metaphysics, analogy ensures both the continuity of all derivation and the homogenization of opposite orders (*M,* pp. 311–312). Thus, for instance in Kant, "the recourse to analogy, the concept and the effect of analogy, are or make the *bridge* itself," as and through which the *Third Critique* bridges the abyss between the two absolutely heterogeneous worlds of Nature and the Ethical (*VP,* p. 43). The analogy "brings together without-concept and concept, the universality *without* concept and the universality *with* concept, the *without* and the *with*" (*VP,* p. 88). It serves to seal up *(cicatriser)* the gap and to think the difference (*VP,* p. 43).

But the function of analogy is not exhausted by establishing such continuity and homogeneity through a relation of proportionality or of attribution between homologous elements. "The analogical process is also a refluence towards the *logos.* The origin is the *logos.* The origin of analogy, that from which analogy proceeds and towards which it returns, is the *logos,* reason and word." In metaphysics, analogy is suspended upon the nonanalogical *logos* as its origin. In "Economimesis" we read that what "regulates all analogy and which itself is not analogical, since it forms the ground of analogy, [is] the *logos* of analogy towards which everything flows back but which itself remains without system, outside of the system that it orients as its end and its origin, its embouchure and its source."[23] As Derrida has demonstrated in "Plato's Pharmacy," a certain dominating and decisive hierarchization takes place between the terms of the relations that enter into correspondence in a relation of analogy. This hierarchizing authority of logocentric analogy comes from the fact that one term within the relation of relations comes to name the relation itself. Consequently, all the elements that make up the relations find themselves comprised by the structure that names the relation of analogy as a whole. That name, ultimately, is that of the logos (see *D*, p. 117).

Suspended at the nonanalogical ground of the logos, analogy is dominated by the proper name of the logos outside and beyond language, which, according to Derrida, is "analogy through and through" (*SP*, p. 13). Dependent on the proper saying of Being by the logos, the initial submission of Being to what is in the analogical displacement becomes sublated in the nonanalogical ground. And yet what Derrida's analyses consistently show is that the attempt to name analogy properly, and consequently to ground it in that name, takes place only through analogies of analogies. As a result, the "analogy makes itself endlessly abysmal" (*VP*, p. 43). It continues to belong to language and to the laws of difference, relation, and proportionality which characterize it. Thus, although the analogy serves to connect the heterogeneous and to homogenize the differences at the benefit of its allegedly external ground (the logos), analogy also engenders, as Condillac knew, a negative product, "the analogue of the analogue, the useless and vain simulacrum of discourse, prattle, nonsense," in short, the frivolous (*AF*, p. 83). The message of this double of analogy is that the proper or literal meaning of analogy is analogical. Hence analogy is the rule, not logos.

In light of what I have tried to develop up to this point, the generalized analogism that I have pointed out must serve to account for at least two things: The first is the fundamental analogism in metaphysics which, under the form of the analogy of being, secures the univocality and the proper name of Being through an idealization and a simultaneous destruction of analogy by casting metaphor against metaphor in a war of language against itself, in short through the metaphysical *Aufhebung* of analogy, metaphor, and all other rhetorical figures. Even in Heidegger, where it is clear that "Being is nothing outside the existent" and that "it is impossible to avoid the ontic metaphor in order to articulate Being in language," Being itself is still said to be "*alone* in its absolute resistance to *every metaphor*" (*WD*, p. 138). And the second is the ineradicably analogical nature of the proper name of Being and the irreducible plurality—Nothingness— that separates the different senses of Being and haunts Being's proper name precisely insofar as it is a proper name.

One may argue, as Ricoeur does in *The Rule of Metaphor*, that the introduction of the problematics of analogy into the transcendental discourse on being is the result of an exterior pressure of the discourse of theology upon the discourse of philosophy. One may also argue, as he does, that philosophical discourse maintains its sovereignty by stripping the mathematical notion of analogy of its conceptual rigor, a loss through which it acquires the necessary transcendental qualities of the field to which it is applied. One may, in addition, recognize in this reduction of the notion of analogy a movement similar to Hegelian *Aufhebung* through which a notion foreign to the philosophical discourse is turned into a truth of being. Yet however one attempts to explain away the impact of the question of analogy on that of being, the simple fact that the notion of analogy *can* and *must* be brought to bear upon the question of being shows that this notion profoundly affects the very concept of being. It can be surmised that this affection cannot necessarily be entirely controlled by *Aufhebung*. If the concept of being—the concept of that which is supposed to be the most original, unique, and irreplaceable—can be affected at all by analogy, then this possibility has to be accounted for and must be inscribed into the concept of being itself. If being *can* be said in different senses, it is because the name of being is *not* a proper name. In that case, however, analogy or metaphor does not surprise being from the outside. The possibility of being affected by analogy must, then, come to being from the inside. Indeed, it is the very idea of a unity of being, the idea of a being *as such,* of being as thought *(als Gedachtes),* that requires the inner doubling of being in order to appear *as such*. The space of this inner doubling within being is the original space of analogy or metaphor in general. The analogy of being reveals what Derrida, in *Of Grammatology,* calls "a metaphoricity, and elementary transference" (OG, p. 292). This irreducible metaphoricity of the *as such* cannot be sublated in a gesture of idealization, because the space of doubling and repetition that it opens, within which being can be related to itself, is the very condition of idealization. Ideation, or the beholding of the general, of the universal, is the intuition of the *as what* of species and singularities. Yet the generality of the *as what,* that which corresponds to the proper, literal meaning of singularities, is the accomplice of analogy or metaphoricity in general. Indeed, it is "from the trope that we learn about the status of literal, proper meaning, the status of that which *gives itself as* proper meaning" (*M,* p. 280). Hence, generality, universality—that is, the "origin in general"—is clearly derivative of derivation, of the generality of analogy or metaphoricity. I shall discuss in more detail this complicity between the general as the proper, the origin, Being, and so on, and a general analogism which at the same time constantly disappropriates and particularizes the general, as I engage in an analysis of "White Mythology."

Quasimetaphoricity

One would be severely misguided if one took "White Mythology," as Ricoeur does in *The Rule of Metaphor,* as an essay developing some thesis or truth about the concept or reality of metaphor. To do so would be to miss Derrida's whole argument, and to attribute to Derrida one or several of the traditional philosophical or rhetorical positions on metaphor that are dealt with critically in that essay. "White Mythology" is not primarily concerned with metaphor. From the outset, Derrida makes it clear that metaphor is a philosophical concept through and through, and that it fosters a continuist (diachronic and symbolic) conception at the expense of the systematic, the syntactic, and the arbitrary. The subordination of the syntactic is inscribed in the most invariable traits of the concept of metaphor to such an extent that a valorization of metaphor, say over concept—a philosophical thesis par excellence—is radically excluded by the premises of Derrida's philosophy. "White Mythology" is a text concerned with the *difference* (and its economy) between metaphor and concept. If we assume that both are irreducible to one another, Derrida examines here the more general analogy that allows metaphor and concept to relate to one another and organizes the exchanges that take place between them. Focusing on the regulated play within which these exchanges take place implies the (relative) autonomy of both metaphor and concept, and precludes any final resumption of the concept by metaphor.

From this perspective, the philosophical positions on metaphor displayed in the essay—that philosophy is a white mythology on the one hand and on the other that philosophy is free of all metaphors—are not positions on which to capitalize, but whose implicit logic is rather to be exhibited. This logic belongs neither to a rhetoric of philosophy nor to a metaphilosophy; it represents the larger vista of a discourse on figure no longer restricted to a regional or specific science, linguistics, or philology. As soon as one reflects on the conditions of possibility of a general metaphorology according to which all philosophical concepts would be hidden, worn out, or dead metaphors, the need for a more embracing discourse on figure becomes evident. Following the presupposition of such a (philosophical) position to its logical end—the belief that one can demystify the discourse of philosophy by forcing it to deliver the metaphorical credentials of its concepts—Derrida demonstrates that the conditions of possibility of a general philosophical metaphorology are by right its conditions of impossibility. Indeed, if a general metaphorology that systematically investigates the metaphorical credentials of philosophy's conceptuality must presuppose the concept of metaphor, then at least one concept, the concept of metaphor, necessarily escapes the enterprise of accounting for the metaphoricity of all philosophical concepts. At least one metaphor, the metaphor of the concept of metaphor required to make a philosophical metaphorology possible, escapes the enterprise of classification as well. Thus the metaphor that escapes a general metaphorology, the metaphor of metaphor, the metaphor of the philosophical concept of metaphor which one presumes in order to reduce all other concepts to the metaphors they conceal, can, of course, no longer be a simple metaphor. It cannot merely be identical with the improper figure of a proper concept, which, however, is not to say that it would be a more fundamental proper concept. The metaphor of metaphor, since it is no longer derivative of a concept, or an ultimate signified, signifies a *mise en abyme* of the philosophical concept of metaphor. As a relation of figure to figure, of the improper to the improper, it is indicative of a different articulation between metaphor and concept, which Derrida substitutes for the classical opposition.

The larger vista of a discourse on figure to which Derrida refers is primarily concerned with this *other* articulation. It is imperative to see that this articulation is not some common essence of both concept and metaphor, not a truer definition or proposition that would embrace both in a more global concept. As the conditions of impossibility of a general philosophical metaphorology have shown, this different articulation is that of a *general metaphoricity* on which metaphorology's claim to universality is based. This general metaphoricity enables metaphor and concept to enter into a relation in the first place, and thence to indulge in a mutual exchange. It is an articulation that allows a concept to be an idealized counterpart of a sensible image, without, however, lending itself to any final reduction to its sensible substrate. The general metaphoricity organizes these exchanges, their generality and universality, without ever having been thematized in traditional philosophy.

I shall now try to characterize in more detail the irreducible meta phoricity in question. The following lengthy passage helps sum up the conditions of impossibility of a philosophical metaphorology:

Metaphor remains, in all its essential characteristics, a classical philosopheme, a metaphysical concept. It is therefore enveloped in the field that a general metaphorology of philosophy would seek to dominate. Metaphor has been issued from a network of philosophemes which themselves correspond to tropes or to figures, and these philosophemes are contemporaneous to or in a systematic solidarity with these tropes or figures. This stratum of "tutelary" tropes [tropes "instituteurs"], the layer of "primary" philosophemes (assuming that the quotation marks will serve as a sufficient precaution here), cannot be dominated. It cannot dominate itself, cannot be dominated by what it itself has engendered, has made to grow on its own soil, supported on its own base. Therefore, it gets "carried away" each time that one of its products— here, the concept of metaphor—attempts in vain to include under its own law the totality of the field to which the product belongs. If one wished to conceive and to class all the metaphorical possibilities of philosophy, one metaphor, at least, always would remain excluded, outside the system: the metaphor, at the very least, without which the concept of metaphor could not be constructed, or, to syncopate an entire chain of reasoning, the metaphor of metaphor. This extra metaphor, remaining outside the field that it allows to be circumscribed, extracts or abstracts itself from this field, thus subtracting itself as a metaphor less. By virtue of what we might entitle, for economical reasons, tropic supplementarity, since the extra turn of speech becomes the missing turn of speech, the taxonomy or history of philosophical metaphors will never make a profit. The state or status of the complement will always be denied to the interminable *dehiscence* of the supplement . . . The field is never saturated. (M, pp. 219–220)

Let us recall that both metaphor and concept are philosophical concepts. If a general metaphorology claims that all concepts are worn-out metaphors, then the same must be true of the philosophical concept of metaphor. Yet this metaphor of metaphor must remain unthematized if a general metaphorology is to succeed at all (and thus to fail). The metaphor of metaphor is therefore the "founding" trope of the project of a metaphorology. As a tutelary or instituting trope, as a "first" philosopheme, as a "defining trope" (M, p. 255), as Derrida also calls it, the metaphor of metaphor forms a system with a chain of other such "archaic" tropes, giving the character of a "natural" language to the so-called "founding" concepts of philosophy (*theoria, eidos, logos,* and so on). But, asks Derrida, "can these defining tropes that are prior to all philosophical rhetoric and that produce philosophemes still be called metaphors?" (M, p. 255).

A concern with the founding concepts of the entire history of philosophy does not coincide with the work of the philologist, etymologist, or classical historian of philosophy, nor with that of the rhetorician of philosophy. In other words, setting out the defining tropes of the founding concepts of philosophy, such as the metaphor of metaphor, neither proclaims the literary or poetic nature of philosophy nor generalizes metaphor as a figure. The Nietzschean "generalization of metaphoricity by putting into *abyme* one determined metaphor," Derrida notes, "is possible only if one takes the risk of a continuity between the metaphor and the concept" (*M*, p. 262). Indeed, such a generalization of metaphor may well signify the *parousia* of the proper and the concept. Insofar as the investigation into the tropological movements at the basis of the grounding concepts of philosophy lends itself to a generalization, it is one that deconstitutes the borders of the propriety of philosophemes.

Of this generalization Derrida remarks in *Dissemination* that "since everything becomes metaphorical, there is no longer any literal meaning and, hence, no longer any metaphor either" (*D*, p. 258). What is being generalized here is neither the proper nor the improper, neither metaphor nor concept. On the contrary, it is something that explodes "the reassuring opposition of the metaphoric and the proper, the opposition in which the one and the other have never done anything but reflect and refer to each other in their radiance" (*M*, pp. 270–271). The generalization hinted at by the metaphor of metaphor— general metaphoricity—is that of the logic of contamination and of the contamination of the logical distinction between concept and figure. Therefore, what is thus generalized can no longer be designated by the philosophical names of metaphor, trope, or figure, much less by the philosophical name of concept. In short, the metaphor of metaphor, or more generally the founding tropes of the founding concepts, are not, strictly speaking, tropes. As Derrida asks in "Plato's Pharmacy," how could the heart of all metaphoricity be a simple metaphor? Hence, Derrida has recourse to Fontanier's notion of catachresis in order to characterize the instituting tropes or the primary (*de "premier degré"*) metaphors as the "nontrue metaphors that opened philosophy" (*M*, p. 259). Indeed, these "forced metaphors" or catachreses are none other than violently creative tropological movements which, within language, found the values of propriety. For the same reason for which the metaphor of metaphor is a *mise en abyme* of the concept of metaphor—the absence of any ultimate concept of which this metaphor would be the metaphor—the metaphor of metaphor is also a catachrestic production of concepts (and subsequently of metaphors of these concepts). Consequently, the metaphor of meta-phor is a nontrue metaphor, a "philosophical phantom" of metaphor (M, p. 258), at the basis of the philosophical values of propriety, conceptuality, Being, and so on and their derivatives, such as impro-priety, figurality (metaphor), nothingness.

In the essay "The *Retrait* of Metaphor," Derrida advances his elaboration of the structure of metaphoricity, or quasimetaphoricity as he calls it here, by analyzing a tropic movement which is comple-mentary to the violent catachrestic production I have outlined. In this essay, the articulation that is said to be more originary than the distinction of metaphor and concept, that splits, intersects, and recuts it, is analyzed in terms of the Heideggerian notion of trait *(Zug)*. The trait, writes Derrida, "is their common origin and the seal of their alliance, remaining in this singular and different from them, if a trait could be something, could be properly and fully originary."[24] Yet the quasimetaphoricity of the trait through which a relation or reference in general is traced, by which something *can* come to the fore in the first place, also implies an originary withdrawal, a *retrait* or retreat of the trait. Consequently, within the catachrestic production of the instituting nontrue tropes, metaphoricity does not reveal itself as such. On the contrary, because the trait is by essence *retrait,* the act of instituting, grounding, and defining, inaugurated by the "first" tropes, is self-effacing. It is by the *retrait* of the trait that the originary tropic movements of metaphoricity permit the likes of the proper, the con-cept, Being, and so on to come forth as the very obliteration of their relation to the trait.

At this point let us reflect on what Derrida's inquiries into the question of metaphor aim at. As is well known, the problematic of the trait, for Heidegger, is linked to the question of Being. The trait of Being reveals itself in its very withdrawal. Now, we have seen that the question of metaphoricity is that of the generalization of some-thing anterior to what is traditionally considered to be general and universal. It concerns the general conditions (and limits) of general-ization. By tying the problem of this more "originary" generality to the problematic of the trait as *retrait,* Derrida makes it clear that this more "primary" generality—beyond and at the root of the distinction of the proper and the improper, the concept and metaphor, the literal and the figural—cannot be a more proper general. It cannot be ex-hibited as such. Moreover, by linking the problematic of this gener-ality anterior to the general to the Heideggerian notion of the *Zug* as *Entzug,* Derrida shows that his exploration of metaphoricity is also an attempt to come to grips with the question of Being. More precisely, it is an undertaking that inquires into the generality of the most general and proper—the generality of Being. It is an attempt to link, in one nonphenomenologizable synthesis, the general or universal and Being.

From everything that has been said thus far, it should be clear that the linking of Being to the no longer metaphysical concept of quasi-metaphoricity does not promulgate, in a Nietzschean or Renanian fashion, a metaphorical origin of Being. Such an enterprise is grounded in etymological empiricism. What we are dealing with here is, on the contrary, a *sort of* transcendental undertaking. Let me comment briefly on the following passage from *Writing and Difference:*

Every philology which allegedly reduces the *meaning* of Being to the meta-phorical origin of the *word* "Being," whatever the historical (scientific) value of its hypothesis, misses the history of the meaning of Being. This history is to such an extent the history of a liberation of being as concerns the deter-mined existent, that one may come to think of the eponymous existent of Being, for example, *respiration,* as one existent among others. Renan and Nietzsche, for example, refer to respiration as the etymological origin of the word *Being* when they wish to reduce the meaning of what they take to be a concept—the indeterminate generality of Being—to its modest metaphor-ical origin . . . Thus is explained all of empirical history, except precisely for the essential, that is, the thought that respiration and *non-respiration are,* for example. And are in a determined way, among other ontic determinations. Etymological empiricism, the hidden root of all empiricism, explains every-thing except that at a given moment the metaphor has been thought *as* metaphor, that is, has been ripped apart as the veil of Being. This moment is the emergence of the thought of Being itself, the very movement of me-taphoricity. For this emergence still, and always, occurs beneath an *other* metaphor. As Hegel says somewhere, empiricism always forgets, at the very least, that it employs the words to be. Empiricism is thinking *by* metaphor without thinking the metaphor *as such.*   (WD, pp. 138–139, translation slightly modified)

The fallacy of empiricism as outlined here affects both the general project of a philosophical metaphorology and the attempt to explain philosophy (and the question of Being) by its linguistic, literary, or metaphorical origins. The enterprise of reducing philosophical con-cepts to figures of speech, tropes, and particular rhetorical operations amounts to a facto-genetic description, with the help of available empirical tools, of what by right absolutely resists these empirical linguistic roots. Without denying the utility and legitimacy of such reductions, "such attempts, however, would have their full value only insofar as they would be conducted with the certainty that everything is spoken of then *except* the reduction *itself, except* the origin of philosophy and history *themselves* and as such" (O, p. 132). Indeed, what the empirical etymologism and/or tropologism cannot account for is the rift in the finite linguistic and tropological figure through which it designates nothing less than Being. In *Writing and Difference* we read: "Supposing that the word 'Being' is derived from a word meaning 'respiration' (or any other determined thing), no etymology or philology—as such, and as determined sciences—will be able to account for the thought for which 'respiration' (or any other determined thing) becomes a determination of Being among others" (*WD*, p. 139). What all these empirical approaches cannot hope to account for is the interruption of metaphor by the thought of metaphor as such, by which rift metaphor *as such*, or metaphoricity, becomes thinkable as the movement of Being itself. Without the thinking of metaphor *as* metaphor, one particular metaphor could not be raised to the status of naming Being as that which renders metaphors mere existents. Being, then, is absolutely resistant to metaphor, as Heidegger claimed, because (as the ontico-ontological difference) it corresponds to the very movement of metaphoricity itself. Consequently, to investigate metaphoricity as Derrida does is to continue, in a certain way, the Heideggerian question of Being. As I have explained, both Heidegger's exploration of the fundamental structure of the logos, the as-structure, and Derrida's exploration of the irreducible metaphoricity of the founding tropes represent debates with the much older problem of the analogy of being, and are thus related to the question of Being as such, and particularly insofar as this question pertains to the being of language. For Heidegger, the being of language resides in the as-structure characteristic of the logos; for Derrida, it coincides, within the context of this given problematic, with metaphoricity as previously outlined.

But to the extent that Heidegger's notion of Being, according to Derrida, is also a proper name, a proper unified meaning outside the system of differences and metaphors that it makes possible—in other words, a metaphysical concept—Derrida's inquiry into quasimetaphoricity is also an attempt to displace more radically the question of Being. Derrida achieves this displacement first by demonstrating that Being, the proper, and so on do not escape the chain and system of differences *(Il n'y a pas de hors-texte)* and second by "deepening" the question of Being through a systematic exploration of the movements of quasimetaphoricity that it designates. Schematically, the first demonstration takes place in "White Mythology," whereas "The *Retrait* of Metaphor" addresses the second aspect of the displacement. In "White Mythology" everything developed with respect to the proper name of the sun as implicated within the general law of metaphorical value also applies to Being. If the proper name of the sun *can* give rise to heliotropic metaphors, if the sun, this "nonmetaphorical prime mover of metaphor, the father of all figures" (M, p. 243), can be said to " 'sow,' then its name is inscribed in a system of relations that constitute it. This name is no longer the proper name of a unique thing which metaphor would *overtake;* it already has begun to say the multiple, divided origin of all seed." (M, p. 244) Similarly, the proper and the essence of Being can be said analogously. Being is not One or unique: "the determination of the truth of Being in presence passes through the detour of . . . [a]tropic system" (M, p. 254). Although the concept in its universality is irreducible to metaphor, figure, or trope, its status *as* concept (its intelligibility and universality) hinges on its possibility of lending itself to metaphorization. General metaphoricity, or quasimetaphoricity, is the name for that possibility that inaugurates the concept's universality. At the same time it limits this universality by virtue of its generality, a generality that cannot be subsumed under universality inasmuch as the latter has grown on its soil.

The displacement of the question of Being is thus twofold. On the one hand, it appears to be inscribed in a system of differences; on the other, it appears to be a function of quasimetaphoricity. In withdrawing, the forthcoming trait makes it possible for something such as Being to come forth as the proper name *hors-texte* for a nonmetaphorical origin of metaphors. Metaphoricity names the "origin" of an unavoidable illusion, the illusion of an origin. Obviously enough, the "origin" of what has always been construed as origin can no longer be understood in terms of origin. The concept of origin *(arkhe)* is a founding concept of philosophy. The instituting tropes which, in a catachrestic movement, give birth to that concept cannot be original, first, and elementary in the sense of origin, or derivative of the founding trope's act of founding. To cite again, "Supposing that we might reach it (touch it, see it, comprehend it?) this tropic and prephilosophical resource could not have the archeological simplicity of a proper origin, the virginity of a history of beginnings" (M, p. 229).

Yet there is still one more reason why the instituting tropes cannot have the simplicity of an origin, a reason that may be coeval with the founding trope's production of the concept of origin. This reason

concerns the plurality of the tutelary tropes: "Metaphors. The word
is written only in the plural. If there were only one possible metaphor,
the dream at the heart of philosophy, if one could reduce their play
to the circle of a family or a group of metaphors, that is, to one
'central,' 'fundamental,' 'principal' metaphor, there would be no more
true metaphor, but only, through the one true metaphor, the assured
legibility of the proper" (*M*, p. 268). This plurality of the defining
tropes, of the irreducible metaphoricity, contributes toward characterizing in depth the sort of transcendental status of this prephilosophical resource. The irreducible metaphoricity of the instituting
tropes—tropes that are not preceded by any proper sense or meaning
but are the "origin" of sense or meaning—is essentially of the order
of syntax. The last chapter of "White Mythology," which demonstrates that an exploration of the founding tropes of philosophy cannot be a metaphilosophical enterprise comparable to Bachelard's
metapoetics, opposes this value of syntax to the primarily *thematic*
and semantic understanding of metaphor in traditional philosophy
and poetics: "Now, it is because the metaphoric is plural from the
outset that it does not escape syntax" (*M*, p. 268). The inextricable
plurality and residuary syntax of the metaphoricity of the founding
tropes leads to a dissemination of the metaphorical in the prelogical,
within which metaphor destroys itself. It is a destruction that "passes
through a supplement of syntactic resistance, through everything (for
example in modern linguistics) that disrupts the opposition of the
semantic and the syntactic, and especially the philosophical hierarchy
that submits the latter to the former" (*M*, p. 270). How, then, are
we to characterize the irreducible metaphoricity to which a deconstruction of the philosophical discourses on metaphor gives rise, that
is, an operation that follows a certain logic of these discourses to its
necessary conclusion, and that recognizes the necessity of marking
off that result from its homonym within the discourse of philosophy?
The irreducible metaphoricity of the instituting tropes of philosophy
is to be characterized as a *structure* of instituting, of grounding, of
defining, which *qua* structure, and by virtue of its plural and residuary
syntax, eliminates itself as origin. This self-destruction of metaphor,
although similar in so many ways to the Hegelian *Aufhebung* of
metaphor in the *parousia* of meaning, is totally different from it, if
for no reason other than the absence of all teleology. This self-destruction of metaphor allows Derrida to write, "Metaphor, then, always carries its death within itself" (*M*, p. 271). This death within
metaphor reaches beyond the traditional opposition of dead or living

metaphors, that is to say, beyond the grid within which Ricoeur attempted to corner Derrida.

Metaphoricity, because of its structure and the problems it accounts for, is thus not to be confused with its empirical (philosophic or literary) homologue. In Derrida's sense, metaphoricity is a structure of referral that accounts for the possibility and impossibility of the philosophical discourse, yet not insofar as this discourse may be construed as literary (sensible, fictional, and so on) because of its inevitable recourse to metaphor and poetic devices, but insofar as it is a *general discourse on the universal.* The literary dimension of the philosophical text is by nature incapable of pointing to, let alone accounting for, this constituting nonorigin of philosophy. Seen in this perspective, metaphoricity is a transcendental concept *of sorts.* Although it is likely that the term I propose will meet with a good bit of disapproval, I shall call metaphoricity a *quasitranscendental.* With *quasi-* I wish to indicate that metaphoricity has a structure and a function similar to transcendentals without actually being one.

In conclusion, let me elaborate briefly on what I understand by such a notion. It certainly makes sense here to define the quasitranscendental by demarcating it from that to which it seems to correspond in Heidegger's philosophy, from what I should like to call *finite* or *immanent transcendentals.* Awaiting further systematic and technical clarification of the notion of a finite transcendental, and its difference from and continuity with Kant's a priori forms of objective knowledge—forms that characterize the finite subjectivity and reason of the human subject of cognition—I shall call finite those structures in Heidegger's fundamental ontology that characterize *Dasein.* Since *Dasein* is, according to the Heidegger of *Being and Time,* the exemplary locus of the understanding of the meaning of Being—that is, of the *transcendens* pure and simple—the finite transcendentals are those existential structures that constitute Being as Being understood and interpreted. It is clear that such a determination of the transcendental in Heidegger's thought hinges upon Heidegger's concept of finitude, insofar as it pertains to *Dasein* or man *(Mensch)* and in particular, after the so-called *Kehre,* to Being itself, although the term of finitude is, as Birault has shown in his excellent study of Heidegger, no longer mentioned after Heidegger's *Kant and the Problem of Metaphysics.* [25] It is a concept that has little or no relation to the Judaeo-Christian idea of finitude. As Birault has demonstrated, Heidegger's concept of finitude does not coincide with the ontico-ontological idea of a *summum ne-ens* in its difference from a *summum ens.* Nor can it be conceived of in terms of the classical or modern forms of the *ouk on* or the *me on*. Rather, Heidegger's finite concept of the transcendental is a function of his investigation into the structures of the logos *of* Being, whether this investigation is pursued in the perspective of an analytic of the *Dasein* or, as after the *Kehre,* in the perspective of Being itself.

Whereas Heidegger's discovery of the finite transcendentals is the result of his philosophizing logic, the logos of Being, Derrida's quasi-transcendentals are a function of his inquiry into the conditions of possibility and impossibility of the logic of philosophy as a discursive enterprise. (*Discursive* is meant here to include the conceptual, rhetorical, argumentative, and textual order of philosophy as the thought of unity.) The quasitranscendentals—metaphoricity, for instance—upon which philosophy's universality is grounded are no longer simply transcendentals, for they represent neither a priori structures of the subjective cognition of objects nor the structures of understanding of Being by the *Dasein.* The quasitranscendentals are, on the contrary, conditions of possibility and impossibility concerning the very conceptual difference between subject and object and even between *Dasein* and Being. Nor are quasitranscendentals finite, as one could prove by pointing to Derrida's persistent critique of the notion of finitude. Instead of being situated within the traditional conceptual space that stretches from the pole of the finite to that of infinity, quasitranscendentals, more important, are at the border of the space of organized contamination which they open up. Unlike the finite transcendental structures that preserve the difference between the a priori and the empirical order (though for Heidegger, Being is clearly not exterior to the existent) because they represent answers to *fundamental* questions, onto-phenomenological or not, concerning the *essence* of Being, the quasitranscendentals are situated at the margin of the distinction between the transcendental and the empirical. They reinscribe "the opposition of fact and principle, which, in all its metaphysical, ontological, and transcendental forms, has always functioned within the system of the question *what is*" (*OG,* p. 75). Therefore, the quasitranscendentals cannot be said to account by means of more *radically* fundamental concepts—say, by a more radical concept of presence *(Anwesen)*—for the presence *(Präsenz)* of metaphysics. By dislocating the opposition of fact and principle—that is, by accounting for this conceptual difference *as* difference—the quasitranscendentals, instead of being more radical, seem to be characterized by a certain irreducible erratic contingency. This contingency of the Derridean transcendentals, their aleatory heterogeneity, is, however, nothing less than that of the structural constraints that simultaneously open up and close philosophy's argumentative discursivity. The question of the quasi-transcendental, of quasimetaphoricity in this case, is a judiciary question in a new sense. Instead of inquiring into the a priori and logical credentials of the philosophical discourse, Derrida's heterology is the setting out of a law that is written on the tinfoil of the mirrors between which thought can either maintain the separation of fact and principle in an endless reflection of one another, or sublate them in an infinite synthesis.

Again, it must be emphasized that Derrida's developments concerning metaphor cannot simply, without mediation, be integrated into literary criticism. First of all, metaphor as a figure and trope—and that is the only way in which it affects the discipline of criticism—is overcome in Derrida's work by the more general notion of metaphoricity. Second, owing to the particular status of this quasitranscendental, determined by the very specific philosophical problems to which it responds, Derrida's theory of metaphoricity cannot be of any *immediate* concern to literary theory. Finally, the problematic of metaphoricity is also a radical challenge to the generality and universality of a discipline such as literary criticism. Only when these difficulties have been acknowledged by a discipline that at the same time would have to free itself from its status as a regional discourse without being tempted to elevate itself into a new *regina scientiarum* could literary criticism acquire the independent means to open itself to such issues as those I have discussed. This, however, would also imply that literary criticism had opened itself to a new kind of "rationality" and a new practice of "knowledge."

Notes

Bibliography

Index

Notes

Introduction

1. See my " 'Setzung' and 'Übersetzung': Notes on Paul de Man," *Diacritics*, 11, no. 4 (Winter 1981), 36–57, and especially "In-Difference to Philosophy: De Man on Kant, Hegel, and Nietzsche," in *Reading de Man Reading*, ed. Wlad Godzich and Lindsay Waters (Minneapolis: University of Minnesota Press, 1987). Above all, see Stefano Rosso, "An Interview with Paul de Man," *Nuova Corrente*, 31 (1984), 303–314, where De Man himself speaks of this difference between his own work and Derrida's.

2. Barbara Johnson, "Taking Fidelity Philosophically," in *Difference in Translation*, ed. J. F. Graham (Ithaca: Cornell University Press, 1985), p. 143.

3. Jacques Derrida, "The Time of a Thesis: Punctuations," in *Philosophy in France Today*, ed. A. Montefiori (Cambridge: Cambridge University Press, 1982), p. 39.

4. Edgar Allan Poe, "The Purloined Letter," in *Poetry and Tales* (New York: Library of America, 1984), p. 694.

1. Defining Reflection

1. Dieter Henrich, *Identität und Objektivität: Eine Untersuchung über Kants transzendentale Deduktion* (Heidelberg: Carl Winter, 1976), p. 83. Here and elsewhere throughout this book, where no translator is named, the translation is my own.

2. Edmund Husserl, *Ideas,* trans. W. R. Boyce Gibson (New York: Humanities Press, 1969), p. 191; Johann Gottlieb Fichte, *Werke,* ed. I. H. Fichte (Berlin: de Gruyter, 1971), I, 67.

3. Hans Blumenberg, "Licht als Metapher der Wahrheit," *Studium Generale,* 10, no. 7 (1957).

4. Herbert Schnädelbach, *Reflexion und Diskurs: Fragen einer Logik der Philosophie* (Frankfurt: Suhrkamp, 1977), pp. 65ff. For the following brief characterization of the history of reflection, I am greatly indebted to Schnädelbach's study.

5. Immanuel Kant, *Critique of Pure Reason,* trans. N. K. Smith (New York: MacMillan, 1968), p. 267.

6. Ibid., p. 287.

7. Husserl, *Ideas,* pp. 215, 219; see also Martin Heidegger, *Prolegomena zur Geschichte des Zeitbegriffs, Gesamtausgabe,* XX (Frankfurt: Klostermann, 1979), p. 132.

8. Apart from the more narrowly psychological or introspective sense of *reflection,* the "naturalistic" concept of reflection, there are obviously more types of reflection than those I have distinguished here. For a more exhaustive review, see the entry "Reflexion," by Hans Wagner, in *Handbuch Philosophischer Grundbegriffe,* ed. H. Krings et al. (Munich: Kösel Verlag, 1973), pp. 1203–1211. See also Hans Wagner, *Philosophie und Reflexion* (Munich: Reinhardt, 1980).

9. Hans Heinz Holz, "Die Selbstinterpretation des Seins," in *Hegel-Jahrbuch* (Munich: Dobbeck, 1961), II, 83.

2. The Philosophy of Reflection

1. Georg Wilhelm Friedrich Hegel, *Faith and Knowledge,* trans. W. Cerf and H. S. Harris (Albany: State University of New York Press, 1977), p. 189.

2. Georg Wilhelm Friedrich Hegel, *Phenomenology of Spirit,* trans. A. V. Miller (Oxford: Oxford University Press, 1979), p. 18.

3. As to the determination of reflection as freedom, Hegel shows that this remains an abstract determination whose relation to the objective world is one of an endless process of approximation, of a *Streben* or *Sollen.*

4. Hegel, *Faith and Knowledge,* p. 77.

5. Eugène Fleischmann, *La Science universelle ou la logique de Hegel* (Paris: Plon, 1968), p. 138.

6. Jean Hyppolite, *Figures de la pensée philosophique* (Paris: Presses Universitaires de France, 1971), I, 195.

7. Fleischmann, *La Science universelle,* p. 183. Fleischmann continues: "In all cases does Kantian mediation have this reflexive character . . . : there are two separate things defined as in opposition, and one is in search of a third to link them together. This third element is not a 'thing' properly speaking, but a 'relation' *(Verhältnis),* i.e., an entirely pejorative term for Hegel . . . It is impossible to tie the separated and bipolarly opposed elements together by means of an exterior link situated *between* both" (pp. 183–184).

8. Hegel, *Faith and Knowledge,* p. 72. Subsequent references to this work will be cited parenthetically in the text.

9. Georg Wilhelm Friedrich Hegel, *Science of Logic*, trans. A. V. Miller (New York: Humanities Press, 1969), p. 589.

10. Friedrich Wilhelm Joseph Schelling, *System of Transcendental Idealism*, trans. P. Heath (Charlottesville: University Press of Virginia, 1978), pp. 24–31.

11. Hegel, *Phenomenology of Spirit*, p. 10.

12. Jean Hyppolite, *Logique et existence* (Paris: Presses Universitaires de France, 1953), p. 106.

13. Hegel's critique of reflection can thus also be viewed as the radical departure of a philosophy of integral immanence from the idea of a beyond. Hyppolite describes this aspect of Hegel's criticism of Kant's philosophy of reflection in the following terms: "Hegelian philosophy rejects all transcendence. It is the attempt at a rigorous philosophy that could claim to remain within the immanent, and not to leave it. There is no other world, no thing in itself, no transcendence, and yet finite human thought is not condemned to remain a prisoner of its finitude. It surmounts itself, and what it reveals or manifests is being itself" (*Figures*, I, 159).

3. The Self-Destruction of Reflection

1. See also Dominique Dubarle, "La Logique de la réflexion et la transition de la logique de l'être à celle de l'essence," in *Die Wissenschaft der Logik und die Logik der Reflexion*, ed. D. Henrich, *Hegel-Studien*, supplement 18 (Bonn: Bouvier, 1978), p. 174.

2. Georg Wilhelm Friedrich Hegel, *The Difference between Fichte's and Schelling's System of Philosophy*, trans. H. S. Harris and W. Cerf (Albany: State University of New York Press, 1977), p. 94. Further references to this work will be cited parenthetically in the text.

3. Georg Wilhelm Friedrich Hegel, *Science of Logic*, trans. A. V. Miller (New York: Humanities Press, 1969), p. 611.

4. For the difference in the use of *speculative* in the early Schelling and Hegel, see Klaus Düsing, "Spekulation und Reflexion," in *Hegel-Studien* (1969), V, 95–128.

5. See Werner Becker, "Spekulation," in *Handbuch philosophischer Grundbegriffe*, ed. H. Krings et al. (Munich: Kösel Verlag, 1974), V, 1368.

6. Ibid., p. 1370.

7. Paul Ricoeur, *The Rule of Metaphor*, trans. R. Czerny (Toronto: University of Toronto Press, 1977), p. 300.

8. Hans-Georg Gadamer, *Truth and Method* (New York: Seabury Press, 1975), p. 423.

9. Hegel, *Science of Logic*, pp. 440–441.

10. Georg Wilhelm Friedrich Hegel, *Werke in zwanzig Bänden* (Frankfurt: Suhrkamp, 1970), XI, 271.

11. Georg Wilhelm Friedrich Hegel, *Phenomenology of Spirit,* trans. A. V. Miller (Oxford: Oxford University Press, 1979), p. 38.

12. The categorial distinction between subject and predicate on which habitual (material or formal) thought is based presupposes, as Josef Simon has demonstrated, an implicitly static conception of language. See Josef Simon, "The Categories in the 'Habitual' and in the 'Speculative' Proposition: Observations on Hegel's Concept of Science," trans. G. Heilbrunn, *Contemporary German Philosophy,* ed. D. E. Christensen et al. (University Park: Pennsylvania State University Press, 1983), II, 122-123.

13. Georg Wilhelm Friedrich Hegel, *Faith and Knowledge,* trans. W. Cerf and H. S. Harris (Albany: State University of New York Press, 1977), p. 80.

14. Jean Beaufret, "Hegel et la proposition spéculative," in *Dialogue avec Heidegger* (Paris: Minuit, 1973), II, 115.

15. Werner Marx, *Absolute Reflexion und Sprache* (Frankfurt: Klostermann, 1967), p. 16.

16. Hegel, *Phenomenology of Spirit,* pp. 38-39.

17. Martin Heidegger, "Seminar on Hegel's *Differenzschrift,*" *The Southwestern Journal of Philosophy,* 11, no. 3 (1980), 38.

18. This solution of the reflective differences on the level of judgment precedes, in *Science of Logic,* the birth of the Concept, which alone is the true synthesis of these reflective difficulties insofar as, in it, syllogism and self-consciousness become identical.

19. Hegel, *Phenomenology of Spirit,* pp. 39-40.

20. Marx, *Absolute Reflexion,* p. 22.

21. See ibid., pp. 31-32, and Gadamer, *Truth and Method,* p. 423.

22. Ricoeur, *The Rule of Metaphor,* p. 304.

23. Jean Hyppolite, *Logique et existence* (Paris: Presses Universitaires de France, 1953), pp. 94-95.

24. Ibid., p. 95.

4. Identity, Totality, and Mystic Rapture

1. Georg Wilhelm Friedrich Hegel, *The Difference between Fichte's and Schelling's System of Philosophy,* trans. H. S. Harris and W. Cerf (Albany: State University of New York Press, 1977), pp. 181, 162. Further references to this work will be cited parenthetically in the text.

2. Georg Wilhelm Friedrich Hegel, *Faith and Knowledge,* trans. W. Cerf and H. S. Harris (Albany: State University of New York Press, 1977), p. 132.

3. Georg Wilhelm Friedrich Hegel, *Science of Logic,* trans. A. V. Miller (New York: Humanities Press, 1969), p. 414.

4. Before distinguishing this concept of totality from its Romantic counterpart, let us linger one moment longer on how it results from a dialectical

overcoming of the aporias of reflection. I have argued that Hegel's speculative critique of the metaphysics of reflection brings to the fore the idea of totality as the ground presupposed by all reflective separation. But in order to grasp what distinguishes Hegel's concept of totality, and thus his critique of the philosophy of reflection, from that of Fichte, Jacobi, Schelling, and Friedrich Schlegel, one must understand the way in which the progressive evolution or self-construction of the Absolute or all-encompassing totality takes place.

As we have seen, the totality is rooted in a systematic mediation of the opposed poles created by the separating action of understanding. This mediation can best be grasped in Hegel's discussion of the reflective determinations. For Kant, the reflective determinations are the most universal laws normative of thinking. They are the categories of understanding by which an entity perceived as singular be necessarily related to another such entity. The reflective determinations fix the different ways in which understanding links one entity to another. Yet for Kant, particularly in *Critique of Judgment*—and for Fichte as well—these reflective determinations are determinations of understanding and form rigid antinomies. As Fichte's system clearly demonstrates, reflective determinations remain suspended in antinomial syntheses, which are not truly dialectical because they open up to an infinite or rather endless process of mediation. As Georg Lukács has observed, one of Hegel's most important methodological discoveries is that these reflective determinations are not static but are dynamically linked to the passage from understanding to Reason. Hegel recognized that they are essential to the overcoming of the difference, which is abyssal to understanding, between appearance and essence, the singular and the universal. See Georg Lukács, *Zur Ontologie des Gesellschaftlichen Seins* (Neuwied: Luchterhand, 1971), p. 84.

Although the reflective determinations appear to be *essential* determinations *(Wesenheiten)* compared to the singular entities of perception, and thus seem resistant to any possible inversion into their opposite, Hegel demonstrates, in the greater *Logic* in particular, that the reflective determinations are not essences entirely indifferent to and independent from one another but are, on the contrary, entirely dominated by Positedness, that is, by their relation to Other. But if the categories' seemingly self-sufficient and isolated nature hinges on their relation to other categories, they can no longer be rigidly opposed to what they serve to explain: the objects of perception. Nor can they any longer be juxtaposed to each other. Thus the categories, or reflective determinations, appear as parts of a whole, of the Absolute, or more precisely, they are shown to acquire their concreteness only in the passage they bring about from their abstract isolation as determinations of understanding to determinations of the thinking of the Absolute. Hegel emphasizes their relative necessity, if not indispensability, with respect to the passage from philosophical reflection to speculation. This passage appears to be the result of an inner dialectic of the reflective determinations rooted in their Positedness, by which the negativity resulting from their relation to one another causes them to evolve progressively into the developed totality of thought, which they could not but presuppose as their, and their object's, common ground.

It is thus important to realize that for Hegel, the absolute totality is not a vague idea but a ground that truly assumes its grounding function when expounded in all its logical ramifications.

5. Post-Hegelian Criticism of Reflexivity

1. I shall not examine here the ways in which speculative reflection coincides with or differs from the Romantic notion of reflexivity, but shall mention only that Hegel severely criticized the Romantics for their religious mysticism and for prolonging the Kantian dichotomies rather than coming to grips with them. I intend to examine this particular problem in a different study.

2. Georg Wilhelm Friedrich Hegel, *Phenomenology of Spirit,* trans. A. V. Miller (Oxford: Oxford University Press, 1979), p. 12.

3. Hans-Georg Gadamer, *Truth and Method* (New York: Seabury Press, 1975), p. 308.

4. Dieter Henrich, "Hegels Logik der Reflexion: Neue Fassung," in *Hegel-Studien,* Supplement 18 (Bonn: Bouvier, 1978), p. 305.

5. For a more detailed definition of the procedure of reconstruction, see Dieter Henrich, *Identität und Objektivität* (Heidelberg: Carl Winter, 1976), p. 10.

6. The word *sophrosyne* is untranslatable in English. It refers, however, to something at the intersection of self-knowledge and temperance, with temperance understood to consist in an easy and natural self-restraint grounded not in graceless and difficult self-discipline, but in the pleasure of knowing oneself to be temperate.

7. Plato, *Collected Dialogues,* ed. E. Hamilton an H. Cairns (Princeton: Princeton University Press, 1969), p. 113, see 167c–e.

8. Hans-Georg Gadamer, "Vorgestalten der Reflexion," in *Subjektivität und Metaphysik: Festschrift für Wolfgang Cramer,* ed. D. Henrich and H. Wagner (Frankfurt: Klostermann, 1969), pp. 138ff. See also Herbert Schnädelbach, *Reflexion und Diskurs* (Frankfurt: Suhrkamp, 1977), p. 201.

9. Characterized by the property of self-movement, the Platonic soul, not *sophrosyne,* suggests an antecedent to absolute reflection. Absolute reflection is defined as self-movement of the Concept or Notion, as a movement that in the very act of its forward drive turns around and upon itself within itself.

10. Sextus Empiricus, *Against the Logicians,* trans. R. G. Bury (Cambridge, Mass.: Harvard University Press, 1957), pp. 163–164.

11. Dieter Henrich, "Fichte's Original Insight," trans. D. R. Lachter-

man, in *Contemporary German Philosophy,* ed. D. E. Christensen et al. (University Park: Pennsylvania State University Press, 1982), I, 20.

12. Ibid., p. 21.

13. Ibid., p. 22; see also Dieter Henrich, "Selbstbewusstsein: Kritische Einleitung in eine Theorie," in *Hermeneutik und Dialektik,* ed. R. Bubner et al., (Tübingen: Mohr, 1971), I, 265–266.

14. Henrich, "Fichte's Original Insight," p. 21.

15. Henrich, "Selbstbewusstsein," p. 267.

16. Henrich, "Fichte's Original Insight," p. 22.

17. Henrich, "Selbstbewusstsein," p. 280.

18. Henrich seems to link his theory of a selfless consciousness to Husserl's theory of consciousness in *Logical Investigations* (especially in its first version). Husserl had tried to establish by this theory (which he later abandoned) that to assume a "subject" or "self" as a constitutive principle or as an irreducible moment of consciousness is only to posit a *ratio remota,* which explains nothing. See Konrad Cramer, "Erlebnis: Thesen zu Hegel's Theorie des Selbstbewusstseins mit Rücksicht auf die Aporien eines Grundbegriffs Nachhegelscher Philosophie," in *Hegel-Studien,* Supplement 11, ed. H.-G. Gadamer (Bonn: Bouvier, 1974), p. 547.

19. Ulrich Pothast, *Über einige Fragen der Selbstbeziehung* (Frankfort on the Main: Klostermann, 1971), pp. 76–77.

20. Ibid., pp. 104–105.

21. Walter Schulz, *Das Problem der Absoluten Reflexion* (Frankfurt: Klostermann, 1963), p. 17.

22. Ibid., pp. 16–17.

23. Ibid., p. 31.

24. Georg Wilhelm Friedrich Hegel, *Science of Logic,* trans. A. V. Miller (New York: Humanities Press, 1969), p. 405.

25. Cramer, "Erlebnis," p. 594.

26. Ibid., p. 603.

27. Ernst Tugendhat, *Selbstbewusstsein und Selbstbestimmung* (Frankfurt: Suhrkamp, 1979), pp. 33–34.

28. Ibid., p. 57.

29. Schnädelbach, *Reflexion und Diskurs,* p. 136.

30. Ibid., p. 9.

6. Beyond Reflection

1. Aristotle, *Metaphysics,* trans. R. Hope (Ann Arbor: University of Michigan Press, 1975), 1041a15.

2. Friedrich Nietzsche, *On the Genealogy of Morals* and *Ecce Homo,* ed. W. Kaufmann (New York: Vintage, 1969), p. 15.

3. Ibid., p. 254.

4. Wilhelm Dilthey, *Selected Writings,* trans. H. P. Rickman (Cambridge: Cambridge University Press, 1976), p. 242.

5. Martin Heidegger, *Being and Time,* trans. J. Macquarrie and E. Robinson (London: SCM, 1962), p. 175. Further references to this work will be cited parenthetically in the text.

6. Martin Heidegger, *The Basic Problems of Phenomenology,* trans. A. Hofstadter (Bloomington: Indiana University Press, 1982), p. 175. Further references to this work will be cited parenthetically in the text.

7. Dieter Henrich, "Hegels Logik der Reflexion: Neue Fassung," in *Hegel-Studien,* Supplement 18 (Bonn: Bouvier, 1978), p. 307.

8. Martin Heidegger, *Hegel's Concept of Experience,* trans. K. R. Dove (New York: Harper and Row, 1970), p. 147.

9. Werner Flach, *Negation und Andersheit: Ein Beitrag zur Problematik der Letztimplikation* (Würzburg: Ernst Reinhardt Verlag, 1959), p. 45. Further references to this work will be cited parenthetically in the text.

10. Such a distinction between two concepts of heterogeneity is reminiscent of a similar distinction in the work of Georges Bataille. See my essay "L'Almanach hétérologique," *Nuovo Corrente,* 66 (1975), 3–60.

11. Plato, *The Collected Dialogues,* ed. E. Hamilton and H. Cairns (Princeton: Princeton University Press, 1980), pp. 1018ff. References to this work will be cited parenthetically in the text.

12. Flach thus seems to share with Plato the theme of complementarity. Although Flach's complementarity of the one and the Other seems to be quite different from Plato's complementary virtues, whose complementarity is a function of their negatively determined content within one whole, the question remains whether Flach's heterology is not already programmed by Plato.

13. In response to an essay by R. D. Cumming, "The Odd Couple: Heidegger and Derrida," *The Review of Metaphysics,* 34, no. 3 (1981), 487–521, let us note that instead of illustrating in an exemplary fashion a certain limitation of Derrida's reading of a famous Van Gogh painting in "Restitutions," in *La Vérité en peinture,* as Cumming suggests, Derrida's choice of the shoelaces as a guiding thread, constantly untied and reknotted in his analyses, opens up rather than closes his reading not only to a reinscription of Heidegger's and Shapiro's interpretation within his own but in particular to the decisive question of *symploke.* Instead of a limitation, the choice of the laces proves to be a *fil conducteur* toward a deconstruction of the traditional concept of *symploke* and its rearrangement, so as to make it capable of including that kind of heterogeneity that is disruptive of totality.

14. Hegel, *The Difference between Fichte's and Schelling's System of Philosophy,* trans. H. S. Harris and W. Cerf (Albany: State University of New York Press, 1977), p. 158.

15. Aristotle, *Metaphysics,* 1006b10.

7. Abbau, Destruktion, *Deconstruction*

1. I have written elsewhere of the relation of deconstruction to *hyper-reflection* in Merleau-Ponty. See "Deconstruction as Criticism," in *Glyph* 6 (Baltimore: Johns Hopkins University Press, 1979), pp. 177–215.

2. Edmund Husserl, *Experience and Judgement,* trans. J. S. Churchill and K. Ameriks (Evanston, Ill.: Northwestern University Press, 1973), pp. 47–48.

3. David Carr, *Phenomenology and the Problem of History* (Evanston, Ill.: Northwestern University Press, 1974), p. 231; see also pp. 200–231 and pp. 261–265 for a more detailed development of the previous argument.

4. For the manner in which this whole problem is linked to the question of finitude in Husserl's later work, see O, p. 105.

5. Edmund Husserl, *Ideas,* trans. W. R. Boyce Gibson (New York: Humanities Press, 1969), p. 147.

6. Martin Heidegger, *The Basic Problems of Phenomenology,* trans. A. Hofstadter (Bloomington: Indiana University Press, 1982), pp. 22–23.

7. Ibid., p. 21.

8. Martin Heidegger, *Being and Time,* trans. J. Macquarrie and E. Robinson (London: SCM, 1962), p. 63.

9. Ibid., p. 44.

10. Heidegger, *Basic Problems of Phenomenology,* p. 21.

11. Ibid., p. 22.

12. Ibid., pp. 22–23.

13. Ernst Cassirer and Martin Heidegger, *Débat sur le Kantisme et la philosophie (Davos, March 1929) et autres textes de 1929–1931,* ed. P. Aubenque (Paris: Beauchesne, 1972), p. 24.

14. Martin Heidegger, *On the Way to Language,* trans. P. D. Hertz (New York: Harper and Row, 1971), p. 96.

15. Heidegger, *Being and Time,* p. 44.

16. Martin Heidegger, "On the Being and Conception of *Physis* in Aristotle's *Physics* B, 1," trans. T. J. Sheehan, *Man and World,* 9, no. 3 (August 1976), 241.

17. Ibid., pp. 225–226.

18. Ibid., p. 226.

19. Martin Heidegger, *Identity and Difference,* trans. J. Stambaugh (New York: Harper and Row, 1969), p. 52.

20. Ibid., p. 49.

21. Martin Heidegger, *The Question of Being,* trans. W. Kluback and J. T. Wilde (New York: Twayne, 1958), p. 103.

22. Heidegger, *Identity and Difference,* p. 64.

23. Martin Heidegger, *Basic Writings,* ed. D. F. Krell (New York: Harper and Row, 1977), p. 236.

24. Martin Heidegger, *The Question Concerning Technology and Other Essays,* trans. W. Lovitt (New York: Harper and Row, 1977), p. 180.

25. Ibid.

26. *L'Oreille de l'autre: Textes et débats avec Jacques Derrida,* ed. C. Levesque and C. V. McDonald (Montreal: Vlb Editeur, 1982), pp. 116–119.

27. Jacques Derrida, "The Time of a Thesis: Punctuations," in *Philosophy in France Today,* ed. A Montefiori (Cambridge: Cambridge University Press, 1982), p. 44.

28. *L'Oreille de l'autre,* p. 118.

8. Deconstructive Methodology

1. Georg Wilhelm Friedrich Hegel, *Phenomenology of Spirit,* trans. A. V. Miller (Oxford: Oxford University Press, 1979), p. 29.

2. Georg Wilhelm Friedrich Hegel, *The Science of Logic,* trans. A. V. Miller (New York: Humanities Press, 1969), p. 826.

3. Jacques Derrida, "La Langue et le discours de la méthode," in *Recherches sur la philosophie et le langage,* no. 3 (Grenoble: Université des Sciences Sociales de Grenoble, 1983), pp. 44–48.

4. See also *WD,* p. 263, where Derrida refers to Hegel as one "who is always right, as soon as one opens one's mouth in order to articulate meaning."

5. See Vincent Descombes, *Modern French Philosophy,* trans. L. Scott-Fox and J. M. Harding (Cambridge: Cambridge University Press, 1980), p. 139.

6. See also Jacques Derrida, "Economimesis," trans. R. Klein, *Diacritics,* 11, no. 2 (Summer 1981), 22.

7. Paul Ricoeur, *The Rule of Metaphor,* trans. R. Czerny (Toronto: University of Toronto Press, 1977), p. 287.

8. Louis Althusser, *For Marx,* trans. B. Brewster (London: NLB, 1977), p. 194.

9. See Sigmund Freud, *The Interpretation of Dreams,* trans. J. Strachey (New York: Avon Books, 1965), pp. 152–153, and *Jokes and Their Relation to the Unconscious,* trans. J. Strachey (New York: Norton, 1963), pp. 62, 205.

10. See, for instance, Jacques Derrida, "The *Retrait* of Metaphor," trans. F. Gasdner et al., *Enclitic,* 2, no. 2 (Fall 1978), 19.

11. "Outwork, Prefacing" is the introduction to *Dissemination.* "Titre à préciser," *Nuova corrente,* 28 (1981), 7–32.

12. *Friedrich Schlegel's Lucinde and the Fragments,* trans. P. Firchow (Minneapolis: University of Minnesota Press, 1971), p. 247.

13. Derrida's criticism of neutrality aims not only at a certain neutralizing aspect of Hegelian dialectics but also at Husserl's concept of "neutrality-modification," which is entirely different from that of negation; see

Edmund Husserl, *Ideas,* trans. W. R. Boyce Gibson (New York: Humanities Press, 1969), pp. 306ff. For reasons of brevity, however, I shall not further investigate this line of thought.

14. It is interesting to note in passing that this Romantic conception of poetry and literary criticism was the first to earn the epithet *nihilistic,* which now serves traditionalist critics to designate deconstructive criticism.

15. "Inasmuch as *one* of them [Fichte refers here to opposite percepts] is further determined, the *other* is likewise, simply because they stand in a relation of interdetermination. But for the same reason, one of the two must be determined *by itself,* and not by the other, since otherwise there is no exit from the circle of interdetermination." Johann Gottlieb Fichte, *The Science of Knowledge,* trans. P. Heath and J. Lachs (Cambridge: Cambridge University Press, 1982), p. 210.

16. Hegel, *Science of Logic,* p. 433. Further references to this work will be cited parenthetically in the text.

17. Immanuel Kant, *Critique of Pure Reason,* trans. N. K. Smith (New York: MacMillan, 1968), p. 9.

18. In this context, Derrida's interest in autobiography must be partly explained by his ongoing debate with the classical problem of philosophical accounting. Indeed, one of the bases of autobiography is the classical form of the *encomium,* by which the autobiographical and biographical self-consciousness of an individual is shaped in the public square. See, for instance, M. M. Bakhtin, *The Dialogic Imagination,* trans. C. Emerson and M. Holquist (Austin: University of Texas Press, 1981), pp. 130–135.

19. As a point of interest it should be mentioned that the problem of the infrastructure implicitly informs Derrida's introduction to Husserl's *Origin of Geometry.* It is important to note that what this introduction attempts is nothing less than to show the *possibility* of history. Indeed, it is in this context that the idea of infrastructure is first put to work.

20. Jacques Derrida, "The Time of a Thesis: Punctuations," in *Philosophy in France Today,* ed. A. Montefiori (Cambridge: Cambridge University Press, 1982), p. 45.

21. Martin Heidegger, *Poetry, Language, Thought,* trans. A. Hofstadter (New York: Harper and Row, 1971), p. 25.

22. See also Derrida, "Economimesis," p. 4, for a discussion of the relation of restricted and general economy. Derrida writes, "Their relation must be one neither of identity nor of contradiction but must be other."

23. Plato, *Timaeus* 52b-c, in *The Collected Dialogues,* trans. E. Hamilton and H. Cairns (Princeton: Princeton University Press, 1980), p. 1179.

24. Derrida, "Economimesis," pp. 22–24.

25. Martin Heidegger, *Nietzsche,* I, *The Will to Power as Art,* trans. D. F. Krell (New York: Harper and Row, 1979), p. 209.

26. For further discussion of the two steps of deconstruction, see my essay "Deconstruction as Criticism," *Glyph* 6 (Baltimore: Johns Hopkins

University Press, 1979), pp. 177–215. Considering that the term that is privileged by the reversal of hierarchical bipolar conceptual oppositions is only the first step of deconstruction, a step by which the phantoms of the beyond of philosophy become singled out, it is improper to believe that this reversal would imply a valorization of these phantoms. How indeed could an image or concept that serves to hold the Other of philosophy in check be valorized? Writing, for instance, is nothing but a negative way in which philosophy has dealt with the beyond of its own discourse. For this reason, it is absurd to accuse Derrida of a sort of graphocentrism without even remarking that such a notion is a contradiction in terms. The second step of deconstruction, in which the negative image is bestowed with traits repressed within the metaphysical determination of the concept of writing—traits that become liberated to their full force of generality—radically displaces the negative image of the beyond of philosophy that is writing. The infrastructure called arche-writing is an "outside" of the discourse of philosophy and no longer has anything in common with its negative image, except for the name. The accusation of graphoçentrism is thus erroneous for these two reasons at least.

27. Hegel, *Phenomenology of Spirit,* p. 40.

9. A System beyond Being

1. Plato, *The Collected Dialogues,* ed. E. Hamilton and H. Cairns (Princeton: Princeton University Press, 1980), p. 744.

2. Martin Heidegger, *The Essence of Reason,* trans. T. Malick (Evanston, Ill.: Northwestern University Press, 1969), p. 93ff.

3. Yet as Dieter Henrich has remarked, it was Fichte who first used this concept, in the context of an elucidation of the structure of the self *(Ich).* See Dieter Henrich, "Fichte's Original Insight," trans. D. R. Lachterman, *Contemporary German Philosophy* (University Park: Pennsylvania State University Press, 1982), I, 30.

4. Martin Heidegger, *Being and Time,* trans. J. Macquarrie and E. Robinson (London: SCM, 1962), p. 170.

5. Martin Heidegger, *Logik: Die Frage nach der Wahrheit, Gesamtausgabe,* XXI (Frankfort: Klostermann, 1976), p. 226.

6. Werner Flach, *Negation und Andersheit: Ein Beitrag zur Problematik der Letztimplikation* (Munich: Ernst Reinhardt Verlag, 1959), p. 18.

7. Ibid., p. 44.

8. Rodolphe Gasché, "Nontotalization without Spuriousness: Hegel and Derrida on the Infinite," *The Journal of the British Society for Phenomenology* (Fall 1986).

9. Edmund Husserl, *Logical Investigations,* trans. J. N. Findlay (New York: Humanities Press, 1970), I, 274.

10. Georg Wilhelm Friedrich Hegel, *Enzyklopädie der Philosophischen*

Wissenschaften, II, *Werke in zwanzig Bänden* (Frankfort: Suhrkamp, 1970), IX, 35ff.

11. Martin Heidegger, *On Time and Being,* trans. J. Stambough (New York: Harper and Row, 1977), p. 16.

12. For the similarity between the supplement and the *pharmakon,* see *D,* p. 109; between the supplement and the *parergon,* see *VP,* pp. 65, 69, 74.

13. Derrida has analyzed this aspect of the re-mark under the name *retrait* in his article "The *Retrait* of Metaphor," trans. F. Gasdner et al., *Enclitic,* 2, no. 2 (Fall 1978), 5–33.

14. Ibid., p. 18.

15. Edmund Husserl, *Phenomenology and the Crisis of Philosophy,* trans. Quentin Lauer (New York: Harper and Row, 1965), pp. 106ff.

16. Jacques Derrida, "Living On: Border Lines," in *Deconstruction and Criticism,* ed. H. Bloom et al. (New York: Seabury, 1979), pp. 90–91.

17. Jacques Derrida, "Economimesis," trans. R. Klein, *Diacritics,* 11, no. 2, (Summer 1981), 20.

18. Ibid., p. 21.

19. Martin Heidegger, *On the Way to Language,* trans. P. D. Hertz (New York: Harper and Row, 1971), p. 192.

20. Kurt Gödel, *On Formally Undecidable Propositions of Principia Mathematica and Related Systems,* trans. B. Meltzer (New York: Basic Books, 1962).

21. See also in this context the reference in "The Double Session" to the rhetorical figure of the syllepsis (*D,* p. 220).

22. Gérard Granel, *Traditionis Traditio* (Paris: Gallimard, 1972), p. 71.

23. Edmund Husserl, *Logical Investigations,* II (1977), p. 527. Further references to this work will be cited parenthetically in the text.

24. Edmund Husserl, *Ideas,* trans, W. R. Boyce Gibson (New York: Humanities Press, 1969), p. 74. Further references to this work will be cited parenthetically in the text.

10. Literature in Parentheses

1. Jacques Derrida, "The Time of a Thesis: Punctuations," in *Philosophy in France Today,* ed. A. Montefiori (Cambridge: Cambridge University Press, 1982), pp. 36–37.

2. "Derrida l'insoumis," *Le Nouvel observateur,* September 9, 1983, p. 85.

3. Edmund Husserl, *Ideas,* trans. B. Gibson (New York: Humanities Press, 1969), pp. 105–110.

4. Jacques Derrida, "Living On: Border Lines," trans. J. Hulbert, in *De-*

construction and Criticism, ed. H. Bloom et al. (New York: Seabury Press, 1969), p. 139.

5. Martin Heidegger, *On the Way to Language,* trans. P. D. Hertz (New York: Harper and Row, 1971), p. 192.

6. Martin Heidegger, *Poetry, Language, Thought,* trans. A. Hofstadter (New York: Harper and Row, 1971), p. 36.

11. The Inscription of Universality

1. Richard Rorty, *Consequences of Pragmatism* (Minneapolis: University of Minnesota Press, 1982), pp. 90–109.

2. Let us recall that everything that I have developed so far about writing is valid for "literature" as well. "Literature" too is necessarily plural, and thus calls for the clear distinction of its different genres. Instead of dreaming of a romantic mixture of all genres—the dream of the literary absolute or transcendental poetry—"literature" is a grafting according to well-defined laws of what in essence remains distinct. See, for instance, *D,* pp. 243 and 244, as well as "The Law of the Genre," *Glyph 7* (Baltimore: Johns Hopkins University Press, 1980), pp. 202–232.

3. Derrida, "Living On: Border Lines," trans. J. Hulbert, in *Deconstruction and Criticism,* ed. H. Bloom et al. (New York: Seabury Press, 1979), p. 83.

4. E. D. Hirsch, Jr., "Derrida's Axioms," *London Review of Books,* July 21–August 3, 1983, p. 17.

5. Derrida, "Living On," p. 84.

6. Paul Ricoeur, "Qu'est-ce qu'un texte?" in *Hermeneutik und Dialektik: Festschrift für Hans-Georg Gadamer,* II (Tübingen: Mohr, 1971), pp. 181–200.

7. Because of this impossibility of phenomenologizing the text in general, the text cannot be *saved,* as Geoffrey Hartman claims it must be in his recent book *Saving the Text* (Baltimore: Johns Hopkins University Press, 1981). In the preface to this study, Hartman explains: "By calling this book *Saving the Text* I do not imply a religious effort in the ordinary sense: the allusion is to the well-known concept of 'saving the appearances' *(sozein ta phainomena),* and my title suggests that we are still endeavoring to convert thinking to the fact that texts exist" (p. xv). The expression "to save the phenomena" means to reconcile observed and admitted facts with some theory or doctrine with which they appear to disagree. But in the present context it also implies that Hartman is setting out, although not in an ordinary religious effort, to save the text as an existing phenomenon against a philosophy such as Derrida's in which the text's phenomenality is being put into question. To save the text is indeed an operation that restores the qualities of essence, presence, and, *eo ipso,* meaning to the text. Yet in so doing, it renders null and void the explicatory power of a notion such as the general

text. Instead of facing the problem that the difference between texts and textuality represents, the operation of saving the text reinstalls itself in an unquestioned textual ontology.

8. Roland Barthes, "From Work to Text," in *Textual Strategies,* ed. J. Harari (Ithaca: Cornell University Press, 1979), p. 75.

9. Derrida, "Living On," p. 105.

10. Jacques Derrida, "The *Retrait* of Metaphor," trans. F. Gasdner et al., *Enclitic,* 2, no. 2 (1978), 8.

11. Martin Heidegger, "My Way to Phenomenology" in *On Time and Being,* trans. J. Stambaugh (New York: Harper, 1972), p. 74.

12. See L. Bruno Puntel, *Analogie und Geschichtlichkeit: Philosophie-geschichtlich-kritischer Versuch über das Grundproblem der Metaphysik* (Freiburg: Herder, 1969). For the later Heidegger and the problem of analogy, see pp. 455–531 of Puntel's study.

13. See Eberhard Jüngel, *Zum Ursprung der Analogie bei Parmenides und Heraklit* (Berlin: De Gruyter, 1964).

14. Puntel, *Analogie und Geschichtlichkeit,* p. 16.

15. Pierre Aubenque, *Le Problème de l'être chez Aristote,* 2d ed. (Paris: Presses Universitaires de France, 1966), pp. 199–205.

16. Paul Ricoeur, *The Rule of Metaphor,* trans. R. Czerny (Toronto: University of Toronto Press, 1977), pp. 259–280.

17. Aristotle, *Metaphysics,* trans. R. Hope (Ann Arbor: University of Michigan Press, 1975), 1003a33–34.

18. Franz Brentano, *On the Several Senses of Being in Aristotle,* trans. R. George (Berkeley: University of California Press, 1975), pp. 58–66.

19. Aristotle, *Metaphysics,* 1016b34.

20. Puntel, *Analogie und Geschichtlichkeit,* p. 26.

21. Martin Heidegger, *Being and Time,* trans. J. Macquarrie and E. Robinson (London: SCM, 1962), p. 63. Further references to this work will be cited parenthetically in the text.

22. For more detail, see also Martin Heidegger, *Logik: Die Frage nach der Wahrheit, Gesamtausgabe,* XXI (Frankfurt: Klostermann, 1976), pp. 153ff.

23. Jacques Derrida, "Economimesis," trans. R. Klein, *Diacritics,* 11, no. 2 (Summer 1981), 13, 19.

24. Derrida, "The *Retrait* of Metaphor," p. 28.

25. Henri Birault, "Heidegger et la pensée de la finitude," *Revue Internationale de Philosophie,* 62 (1960), 135–162.

Bibliography

Althusser, Louis. *For Marx,* trans. B. Brewster. London: NLB, 1977.

Aristotle. *Metaphysics,* trans. R. Hope. Ann Arbor: University of Michigan Press, 1975.

Aubenque, Pierre. *Le Problème de l'être chez Aristote,* 2d ed. Paris: Presses Universitaires de France, 1966.

Bakhtin, M. M. *The Dialogic Imagination,* trans. C. Emerson and M. Holquist. Austin: University of Texas Press, 1981.

Barthes, Roland. "From Work to Text." In *Textual Strategies,* ed. J. Harari, pp. 73–81. Ithaca: Cornell University Press, 1979.

Beaufret, Jean. "Hegel et la proposition spéculative." In *Dialogue avec Heidegger,* vol. 2, pp. 110–142. Paris: Minuit, 1973.

Becker, Werner. "Spekulation." In *Handbuch Philosophischer Grundbegriffe,* ed. H. Krings et al., vol. 5, pp. 1368–1375. Munich: Kösel, 1974.

Birault, Henri. "Heidegger et la pensée de la finitude," *Revue Internationale de Philosophie,* 62 (1980), 135–161.

Blumenberg, Hans. "Licht als Metapher der Wahrheit," *Studium Generale,* 10, no. 7 (1957), 432–477.

Brentano, Franz. *On the Several Senses of Being in Aristotle,* trans. R. George. Berkeley: University of California Press, 1975.

Carr, David. *Phenomenology and the Problem of History.* Evanston: Northwestern University Press, 1974.

Cramer, Konrad. "Erlebnis: Thesen zu Hegels Theorie des Selbstbewusstseins mit Rücksicht auf die Aporien eines Grundbegriffs Nachhegelscher Philosophie." In *Hegel-Studien,* supplement 11, ed. H.-G. Gadamer, pp. 537–603. Bonn: Bouvier, 1974.

Cumming, R. D. "The Odd Couple: Heidegger and Derrida," *The Review of Metaphysics,* 34, no. 3 (1978), 487–521.

Derrida, Jacques. *The Archeology of the Frivolous,* trans. J. P. Leavy. Pittsburgh: Duquesne, 1980.

―――. "Derrida l'insoumis," *Le Nouvel observateur* (September 9, 1983), 84–89.

―――. *Dissemination,* trans. B. Johnson. Chicago: University of Chicago Press, 1981.

―――. "Economimesis," trans. R. Klein, *Diacritics,* 11, no. 2 (Summer 1981), 3–25.

―――. *Edmund Husserl's Origin of Geometry: An Introduction,* trans. J. P. Leavy. Stony Brook: Nicolas Hays, 1978.

―――. "La Langue et le discours de la méthode," *Recherches sur la philosophie et le langage.* 1983, no. 3, 35–51.

―――. "The Law of Genre," trans. A. Ronell. In *Glyph 7,* pp. 202–229. Baltimore: Johns Hopkins University Press, 1980.

―――. "Limited Inc.," trans. S. Weber. In *Glyph 2,* pp. 162–254. Baltimore: Johns Hopkins University Press, 1977.

―――. "Living On: Border Lines," trans. J. Hulbert. In *Deconstruction and Criticism,* ed. H. Bloom et al., pp. 75–176. New York: Seabury Press, 1979.

―――. *Margins of Philosophy,* trans. A. Bass. Chicago: University of Chicago Press, 1982.

―――. *Of Grammatology,* trans. G. C. Spivak. Baltimore: Johns Hopkins University Press, 1976.

―――. *L'Oreille de l'autre: Textes et débats avec Jacques Derrida,* ed. C. Lévesque and C. V. McDonald. Montreal: Vlb, 1982.

―――. *Positions,* trans. A. Bass. Chicago: University of Chicago Press, 1971.

―――. "The *Retrait* of Metaphor," trans. F. Gasdner et al., *Enclitic,* 2, no. 2 (Fall 1978), 5–33.

―――. *Speech and Phenomena,* trans. D. Allison. Evanston: Northwestern University Press, 1973.

―――. *Spurs: Nietzsche's Styles,* trans. B. Harlow. Chicago: University of Chicago Press, 1979.

―――. "The Time of a Thesis: Punctuations." In *Philosophy in France Today,* ed. A. Montefiori, pp. 34–50. Cambridge: Cambridge University Press, 1982.

―――. *La Vérité en peinture.* Paris: Flammarion, 1978.

―――. *Writing and Difference,* trans. A. Bass. Chicago: University of Chicago Press, 1978.

Descombes, Vincent. *Modern French Philosophy,* trans. L. Scott-Fox and J. M. Harding. Cambridge: Cambridge University Press, 1980.

Dilthey, Wilhelm. *Selected Writings,* trans. H. P. Rickman. Cambridge: Cambridge University Press, 1976.

Dubarle, Dominique. "La Logique de la réflexion et la transition de la logique de l'être à celle de l'essence." In *Hegel-Studien,* supplement 18, *Die Wissenschaft der Logik und die Logik der Reflexion,* ed. D. Henrich, pp. 173–202. Bonn: Bouvier, 1978.

Düsing, Klaus. "Spekulation und Reflexion." In *Hegel-Studien*, vol. 5, pp. 95–128. Bonn: Bouvier, 1969.

Fichte, Johann Gottlieb. *The Science of Knowledge*, trans. P. Heath and J. Lachs. Cambridge: Cambridge University Press, 1982.

———. *Werke*, vol. 1, ed. I. H. Fichte. Berlin: de Gruyter, 1971.

Flach, Werner. *Negation und Andersheit: Ein Beitrag zur Problematik der Letztimplikation*. Munich: Ernst Reinhardt, 1959.

Fleischmann, Eugène. "Hegels Umgestaltung der Kantischen Logik." In *Hegel-Studien*, vol. 3, pp. 181–207. Bonn: Bouvier, 1956.

———. *La Science universelle ou la logique de Hegel*. Paris: Plon, 1968.

Freud, Sigmund. *The Interpretation of Dreams*, trans. J. Strachey. New York: Avon Books, 1965.

———. *Jokes and Their Relation to the Unconscious*, trans. J. Strachey. New York: Norton, 1963.

Gadamer, Hans-Georg. *Truth and Method*. New York: Seabury Press, 1975.

———. "Vorgestalten der Reflexion." In *Subjektivität und Metaphysik: Festschrift für Wolfgang Cramer*, ed. D. Henrich and H. Wagner, pp. 128–143. Frankfurt: Klostermann, 1966.

Gasché, Rodolphe. "L'Almanach hétérologique," *Nuovo Corrente*, no. 66 (Milan, 1975), 3–60.

———. "Deconstruction as Criticism." In *Glyph 6*, pp. 177–215. Baltimore: Johns Hopkins University Press, 1979.

Gödel, Kurt. *On Formally Undecidable Propositions of Principia Mathematica and Related Systems*, trans. B. Meltzer. New York: Basic Books, 1962.

Granel, Gérard. *Traditionis Traditio*. Paris: Gallimard, 1972.

Greisch, Jean. *Herméneutique et grammatologie*. Paris: Editions du CNRS, 1977.

Hartman, Geoffrey. *Saving the Text*. Baltimore: Johns Hopkins University Press, 1981.

Hegel, Georg Wilhelm Friedrich. *The Difference between Fichte's and Schelling's System of Philosophy*, trans. W. Cerf and H. S. Harris. Albany: State University of New York Press, 1977.

———. *Faith and Knowledge*, trans. W. Cerf and H. S. Harris. Albany: State University of New York Press, 1977.

———. *Phenomenology of Spirit*, trans. A. V. Miller. Oxford: Oxford University Press, 1979.

———. *Science of Logic*, trans. A. V. Miller. New York: Humanities, 1969.

———. *Werke in Zwanzig Bänden*. Frankfurt: Suhrkamp, 1970.

Heidegger, Martin. *The Basic Problems of Phenomenology*, trans. A. Hofstadter. Bloomington: Indiana University Press, 1982.

———. *Basic Writings*, ed. D. F. Krell. New York: Harper and Row, 1977.

———. *Being and Time*, trans. J. Macquarrie and E. Robinson. London: SCM, 1962.

———. *The Essence of Reason*, trans. T. Malick. Evanston: Northwestern University Press, 1969.

———. *Hegel's Concept of Experience*, trans. K. R. Dove. New York: Harper and Row, 1970.

———. *Identity and Difference*, trans. J. Stambaugh. New York: Harper and Row, 1969.

———. *Logik: Die Frage nach der Wahrheit, Gesamtausgabe*, vol. 21. Frankfurt: Klostermann, 1976.

———. *Nietzsche*, vol. 1, *The Will to Power as Art*, trans. D. F. Krell. New York: Harper and Row, 1979.

———. "On the Being and Conception of *Physis* in Aristotle's *Physics* B, I," trans. T. J. Sheehan, *"Man and World,"* 9, no. 3 (August 1976), 219–270.

———. *On the Way to Language*, trans. P. D. Hertz. New York, Harper and Row, 1971.

———. *On Time and Being*, trans. J. Stambaugh. New York: Harper and Row, 1977.

———. *Poetry, Language, Thought*, trans. A. Hofstadter. New York: Harper and Row, 1971.

———. *Prolegomena zur Geschichte des Zeitbegriffs, Gesamtausgabe*, vol. 20. Frankfurt: Klostermann, 1979.

———. *The Question Concerning Technology and Other Essays*, trans. W. Lovitt. New York: Harper and Row, 1977.

———. *The Question of Being*, trans. W. Kluback and J. T. Wilde. New York: Twayne, 1958.

———. "A Seminar on Hegel's *Differenzschrift*," *The Southwestern Journal of Philosophy*, 11, no. 3 (1980), 9–45.

———, and Cassirer, Ernst. *Débat sur le Kantisme et la philosophie (Davos, March 1929), et d'autres textes de 1929–1931*, ed. P. Aubenque. Paris: Beauchesne, 1972.

Henrich, Dieter. *Identität und Objektivität: Eine Untersuchung über Kants transzendentale Deduktion*. Heidelberg: Carl Winter, 1976.

———. "Fichte's Original Insight," trans. D. R. Lachterman. In *Contemporary German Philosophy*, vol. 1 (1982), ed. D. E. Christensen et al., pp. 15–53. University Park: Pennsylvania State University Press, 1982.

———. "Hegels Logik der Reflexion: Neue Fassung." In *Hegel-Studien*, vol. 18, pp. 203–324. Bonn: Bouvier, 1978.

———. "Selbstbewusstsein: Kritische Einleitung in eine Theorie." In *Hermeneutik und Dialektik*, vol. I, ed. R. Bubner et al., pp. 257–284. Tübingen: Mohr, 1971.

Hirsch, E. D. "Derrida's Axioms," *London Review of Books* (July 21–August 3, 1983), 17–18.

Holz, Hans Heinz. "Die Selbstinterpretation des Seins." In *Hegel-Jahrbuch*, vol. 2, pp. 61–124. Munich: Dobbeck, 1961.

Husserl, Edmund. *Experience and Judgement,* trans. J. S. Churchill and K. Ameriks. Evanston: Northwestern University Press, 1973.

———. *Ideas,* trans. W. R. Boyce Gibson. New York: Humanities, 1969.

———. *Logical Investigations,* trans. J. N. Findlay, 2 vols. New York: Humanities, 1977.

———. *Phenomenology and the Crisis of Philosophy,* trans. Quentin Lauer. New York: Harper and Row, 1965.

Hyppolite, Jean. *Figures de la pensée philosophique,* 2 vols. Paris: Presses Universitaires de France, 1971.

———. *Logique et existence.* Paris: Presses Universitaires de France, 1953.

Jüngel, Eberhard. *Zum Ursprung der Analogie bei Parmenides und Heraklit.* Berlin: De Gruyter, 1964.

Kant, Immanuel. *Critique of Judgement,* trans. J. H. Bernard. New York: Hafner, 1951.

———. *Critique of Pure Reason,* trans. N. K. Smith. New York: Macmillan, 1968.

Lukács, Georg. *Der Junge Hegel.* Zurich: Europa Verlag, 1948.

———. *Zur Ontologie des Gesellschaftlichen Seins.* Neuwied: Luchterhand, 1971.

Marx, Werner. *Absolute Reflexion und Sprache.* Frankfurt: Klostermann, 1967.

Nietzsche, Friedrich. *On the Genealogy of Morals* and *Ecce Homo,* ed. W. Kaufmann. New York: Vintage, 1969.

Plato, *The Collected Dialogues,* ed. E. Hamilton and H. Cairns. Princeton: Princeton University Press, 1980.

Pothast, Ulrich. *Über einige Fragen der Selbstbeziehung.* Frankfurt: Klostermann, 1971.

Puntel, L. Bruno. *Analogie und Geschichtlichkeit: Philosophiegeschichtlich-kritischer Versuch über das Grundproblem der Metaphysik.* Freiburg: Herder, 1969.

Ricoeur, Paul. "Qu'est-ce qu'un texte?" In *Hermeneutik und Dialektik: Festschrift für H.-G. Gadamer,* vol. 2, pp. 181–200. Tübingen: Mohr, 1971.

———. *The Rule of Metaphor,* trans. R. Czerny. Toronto: University of Toronto Press, 1977.

Ritter, Joachim, ed. *Historisches Wörterbuch der Philosophie,* vols. 1–6. Darmstadt: Wissenschaftliche Buchgesellschaft, 1971–1984.

Rorty, Richard. *Consequences of Pragmatism.* Minneapolis: University of Minnesota Press, 1982.

Schelling, Friedrich Wilhelm Joseph. *System of Transcendental Idealism,* trans. P. Heath. Charlottesville: University Press of Virginia, 1978.

Schlegel, Friedrich. *Lucinde and the Fragments,* trans. P. Firchow. Minneapolis: University of Minnesota Press, 1971.

Schnädelbach, Herbert. *Reflexion und Diskurs: Fragen einer Logik der Philosophie.* Frankfurt: Suhrkamp, 1977.

Schulz, Walter. *Das Problem der Absoluten Reflexion.* Frankfurt: Kloster-
    mann, 1963.
Sextus Empiricus. *Against the Logicians,* trans. R. G. Bury. Cambridge, Mass.:
    Harvard University Press, 1957.
Simon, Josef. "The Categories in the 'Habitual' and in the 'Speculative'
    Proposition: Observations on Hegel's Concept of Science," trans.
    G. Heilbrunn. In *Contemporary German Philosophy,* vol. 2 (1983), ed.
    D. E. Christensen et al., pp. 112–137. University Park: Pennsylvania
    State University Press, 1983.
Tugendhat, Ernst. *Selbstbewusstsein und Selbstbestimmung.* Frankfurt:
    Suhrkamp, 1979.
Wagner, Hans. *Philosophie und Reflexion.* Munich: Reinhardt, 1980.
———. "Reflexion." In *Handbuch philosophischer Grundbegriffe,* ed.
    H. Krings et al., pp. 1203–1211. Munich: Kösel, 1973.

Index